21 世纪高等院校教材

英美文化博览

An Introduction to American and British Culture

王淑花　李海英
贾　颖　张　娜　主编

科 学 出 版 社
北　京

内容简介

本书以介绍英美国家的社会与文化概貌、地理、历史、政治、经济、教育体制、节日习俗、社会生活、文化传统、英美主流价值观念等方面的基本知识和现象为主，兼顾大学生感兴趣和关注的热点话题，引导学生将语言学习与文化知识紧密结合起来，为培养大学生的跨文化交际能力打下基础。本书在文后附有英语思维训练题，涵盖了理解、概括、分析、批判、创造等多个高级英语思维能力发展层次，有利于培养大学生的批判性思维能力和创新思维能力。

全书知识覆盖面广，反映时代发展的最新动态，较为系统地介绍英美文化的典型特色，并通过丰富的图片、影视素材的介绍使英美文化特征具体化、形象化、生动化。本书所选文章皆出自以英语为母语者之手，语言优美，信息量大，内容新颖，与时俱进。本书词汇注释准确、详细，为读者阅读扫清障碍，每章配有专题词汇库，不仅有利于读者增强语感、扩大词汇量，还有利于学习者针对话题拓展听说读写能力。

图书在版编目(CIP)数据

英美文化博览/王淑花等主编. —北京：科学出版社，2013
21世纪高等院校教材
ISBN 978-7-03-037833-0

Ⅰ. ①英… Ⅱ. ①王… Ⅲ. ①英语-高等院校-教材 ②英语-概况 ③美国-概况 Ⅳ. ①H31

中国版本图书馆CIP数据核字(2013)第126956号

责任编辑：张　宁 / 责任校对：桂伟利
责任印制：徐晓晨 /封面设计：蓝正设计

科学出版社出版
北京东黄城根北街16号
邮政编码：100717
http://www.sciencep.com
北京凌奇印刷有限责任公司印刷
科学出版社发行　各地新华书店经销
*
2013年6月第 一 版　开本：787×1092 1/16
2019年7月第三次印刷　印张：17
字数：403 000
定价：68.00元
（如有印装质量问题，我社负责调换）

前　言

英语学习在我国是外语学习，阅读成为学习者掌握英语知识、获取信息的主要渠道。学习英语不仅需要掌握与语言本体相关的知识，更需要了解语言所承载的文化，了解英语国家的历史、政治、经济等方面的基本信息。只有在阅读中了解了国外的文化和习俗，培养起分析批判的能力、独立思考的习惯，才能够吸收西方文化的精华、提高人文素养，才会在用英语交流时言之有物、言之有理。

英语是语言学科也是思维学科，在学习英语的过程中，学习者不仅需要发展英语能力，同时要发展思维能力，激发想象力和创造力，掌握科学的思维方法。我们将英语阅读视为对书面信息进行理解的复杂过程，也视为训练、发展思维的过程。英美文化历史悠久、林林总总、五光十色。学习者面对这林林总总的浩繁内容，需要主动建构意义，获取新知识，而不是被动地接受、记忆事实。英语阅读中学习者需要发展基本的认读能力、归纳总结能力、分析能力、批判鉴赏能力，以及应用和创造能力。

基于上述指导思想，我们撷取英国和美国的地理、历史、教育、经济、外交、休闲生活等方面的内容作为非英语专业大学生素质拓展阶段的阅读内容，使他们能够博览英美文化。同时，我们将高级思维能力的训练作为本书的重点和特色，在每章的主要课文之后提出问题供学习者思考，思考题包含字面理解、归纳总结、分析推断、评判与鉴赏、创造应用五个层次，有意引导学习者突破机械认读和浅层理解的局限，引导他们分析文本字里行间的意思，学会理性、客观、全面地看问题，养成分析、思辨的习惯，培养发散思维及寻求真理的本领。

除此之外，本书还有如下特点:

1. 选材内容有代表性，满足学习者的兴趣和需求。我们对非英语专业的学生进行了多年的分级教学，给已经通过了大学英语四级考试的学生开设了英美文化选修课，对学生未知的内容和感兴趣的话题有较为全面的了解。本书内容的选择考虑了学习者的需求和兴趣。

2. 选材新颖，语言地道。英美文化包罗万象，我们在内容上不求面面俱到，但力求包含近年来的热点话题、新现象和新问题。选材均来自英美两国的官方网站、报刊、杂志、科研机构论文以及外交部门的官方网站等，兼顾了语言文字的水平及内容的时效性、信息性和趣味性。

3. 建立专题词汇库，培养英语学习者敏捷的英语理解力和表达力。除在每篇文章之后附上单词和术语的解释外，围绕每一个文化专题，我们都拓展了相关的词汇和术语，建立专题词汇库，供学习者学习，以便在英语交际时理解更顺畅，英语表达言辞更丰富。

4. 文章详略有序，用途广泛。全书共 14 个单元，每个单元分为四个部分。Section A 和 Section B 的文章长度在 1200 词左右，皆配有思维训练题和拓展训练题，通过此部分的精讲细练，学习者既能掌握这两部分提供的文化知识，同时也通过拓展练习，打开更多的窗口，思考和掌握更多的知识和技能。Section C 为补充阅读材料，长度在 2000 词左右，有利于业余训练阅读速度、拓展词汇和文化知识。Section D 为本单元的专题词汇库，有利于读者提高英语理解能力和表达能力，做到事半功倍。

5. 图文并茂，易学易懂。图片和图表有助于学习者理解文字内容，并且在真实的阅读环境下，阅读材料通常是图文并茂的，这种形式有助于加强读者对异域风情和异域文化的感性认识。

本书可供高等院校已通过大学英语四六级考试的学生以及英语自学者进行阅读训练使用，还可供广大英美文化爱好者、研究者、出国人员及英语教师参考使用，也可作为大学英语素质拓展课程的专门教材，具有较高的实用价值。

本书的疏漏之处，请广大读者不吝赐教。

编　者

2013 年 3 月

Contents

Contents

Chapter 1

Traveling in Britain and America

英国，全称大不列颠及北爱尔兰联合王国，包括英格兰、威尔士、苏格兰（三者在大不列颠岛上）和北爱尔兰四个部分，首都为伦敦。英国历史悠久，风景优美，有多处旅游胜地，如大本钟、伦敦塔、大英博物馆、威斯敏斯特大教堂、马克思墓地、格林尼治天文台、莎士比亚故居、巨石阵遗址等。

幅员辽阔的美国，拥有丰富多元的气候与地质景观，二百多年的兼容并蓄，则让此地成为民族的大熔炉。美国也是旅行的理想去处。在美国，不可不看的景点有黄石公园、科罗拉多大峡谷、自由女神像、帝国大厦、好莱坞、尼亚加拉大瀑布、金门大桥等。

读万卷书，行万里路。阅读本章，我们足不出户，却可以领略英美的异国风情，漫游名山大川，在泰晤士河边漫步，在伦敦街头徜徉，畅游在美利坚的著名景点，浏览河山。

Section A Intensive Reading

The United Kingdom of Great Britain and Northern Ireland

➢ **Introduction**

The United Kingdom is very small compared with many other countries in the world. The total area of Great Britain is 244,820 square kilometres. However, there are only nine other countries with more people, and London is the world's seventh biggest city. The population of Great Britain is 60,776,238 (2007 estimate).

The flag of The United Kingdom of Great Britain is called **the Union Jack**. The main areas of high land are in Scotland, Wales and Cumbria. In the centre of England is a range of hills called the **Pennines,** which are also known as the "backbone of England". The highest mountains are in Scotland and Wales: **Ben Nevis** is 4,406 feet (1,343 m) and **Snowdon** is 3,560 feet (1,085 m). Of course, these are very small compared with other mountains in the world—**Everest**, the highest mountain in the world, is 29,000 feet (8,839 m). In fact, everything in the United Kingdom is rather small—the longest rivers are the **Severn,** 220 miles (354 km) and **the River Thames**, 215 miles (346 km). Compare these with the River Amazon in South America which is 4,195 miles (6,751 km) long!

Despite its size, there is a great deal of variety within the islands of the United Kingdom.

➢ **Geography**

The River Thames lies off the north-western coast of **Continental Europe**. Great Britain is the largest island consisting of **England**, **Scotland**, and **Wales**. **The United Kingdom of Great Britain and Northern Ireland**, often abbreviated to the UK, is the **political name** of the country which is made up of England, Scotland, Wales, and Northern Ireland (also known as Ulster):

Some small islands off the coast of Great Britain are part of the UK (e.g. **the Isle of Wight, the Orkneys, Shetlands, Hebrides**), whereas others are not even part of **the Commonwealth** although they have very close political, economic, and cultural relations with Britain, and recognize the Queen as the Head of State (e.g. the Channel Islands of Jersey and Guernsey, and the Isle of Man). The latter ones have their own legislatures and administration. The number of islands and islets of the British Archipelago amounts to 750.

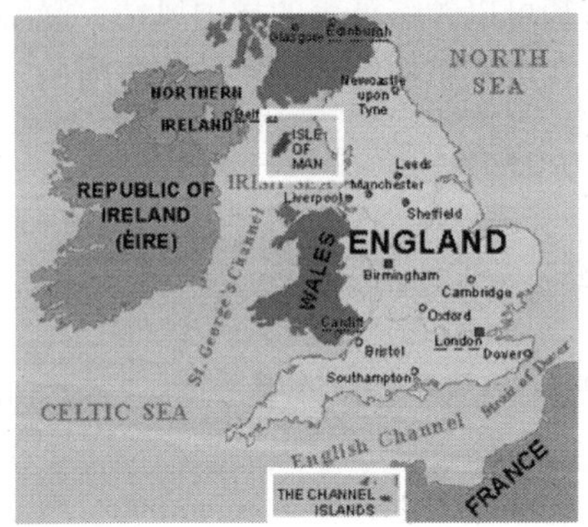

The total area of the UK is 241,752 square kilometres. The area of England is 130,423 sq km; that of Scotland is 78,080 sq km; Wales is 20,766 sq km; Northern Ireland is 13,483 sq km. The UK **coastline** is 4057-kilometre long. In Britain the highest mountains are found in the north and west (**the Scottish Highlands** and the Welsh mountains). The part of Britain which lies in the south-east of a line drawn from Devon to Durham is mainly a **plain** broken by **low hills**. **Highland** Britain has **poor soils** and is **sparsely populated**, whereas **Lowland** Britain has **fertile soils** and is **densely populated**.

The chief rivers are the Severn and the Thames. Scotland's largest river is **the Clyde** (169 km). The largest lake in the UK is **Lough Neagh** in Northern Ireland (396 sq km). The highest mountains are Ben Nevis in Scotland and Snowdon in Wales. **Glaciation** has been responsible for most of Britain's **mountain scenery**, especially in Snowdonia (Wales), the **Lake District** (North England), and the Scottish Highlands.

In prehistoric times most of Britain was covered by oak, ash, birch and beech trees. As the population began to grow, forests were cut down to clear the land for farming, for use as fuel, and for the building of homes and building of ships. By the time of the **Industrial Revolution** in the 18th century vast areas of forests had been cleared. In recent decades a programme of **afforestation** has been carried out on a large scale. Modern agricultural methods have caused serious transformation of the natural environment in Britain. **Moorland** and **heaths** have been ploughed up in many regions, land has been **drained**, and many **hedgerows** have been removed by farmers in order to increase the size of fields.

The UK is warmed by the **North Atlantic Drift**. The climate is **temperate**, generally **mild**, and frequently wet. The temperature seldom reaches extremes of heat or cold. An average temperature in winter is 40°F (5°C) and in summer 60°F (15°C). Britain is famous for its unpredictable and changeable weather. The UK used to receive a plentiful supply of rain, but **rainfall** is not evenly distributed, and the eastern side of the country gets less rain than the west, due to the **prevailing wind**. **Drought** is now a serious threat to British rivers and **reservoirs**. Contrary to popular legend, fog is not a common occurrence. The old London "**smog**", a combination of fog and smoke from chimneys, is now a thing of the past, as a result of the *Clean Air Act* (1968) which banned the burning of **untreated** coal in city areas.

Britain lies in the **Greenwich Mean Time** zone. Greenwich, in south-east London, is the place, at **longitude** 0°0', from which all the other **time zones** are calculated. Zones west of Greenwich have earlier time, and zones to the east have later time. The time in **Poland**, for example, is one hour later than in Britain. When it is midnight in Britain, it is 1 a.m. in Poland.

➢ **Climate**

The climate of Britain is more or less the same as that of the north-western part of the European mainland. The popular belief that it rains all the time in Britain is simply not true. The image of a wet, **foggy** land was created two thousand years ago by the invading Romans and has been perpetuated in modern times by Hollywood. In fact, London gets no more rain in a year than most other major European cities, and less than some.

The amount of rain that falls on a town in Britain depends on where it is. Generally speaking, the further west you go, the more rain you get. The mild winters mean that snow is a regular feature of the higher areas only. Occasionally, a whole winter goes by in **low-lying** parts without any snow at all. The winters are in general a bit colder in the east of the country than they are in the west, while in summer, the south is slightly warmer and sunnier than the north.

Why has Britain's climate got such a bad reputation? Perhaps it is for the same reason why British people always seem to be talking about the weather. This is because of its **changeability.** There is a saying that Britain doesn't have a climate, it only has weather. It may not rain very much altogether, but you can never be sure of a dry day; there can be cool (even cold) days in July and some quite warm days in January.

The lack of extremes is the reason why, on a few occasions when it gets genuinely hot or **freezing cold**, the country seems to be totally **unprepared** for it. A bit of snow and a few days of **frost,** and the trains stop working and the roads are blocked; if the **thermometer** goes above 27°C (80°F), people behave as if they were in the Sahara and the temperature makes **front-page headlines**. These things happen so rarely that it is not worth organizing life to be ready for them.

(length: 1,207 words)

Vocabulary

afforestation	n. 造林	low-lying	adj. 低洼的
changeability	n. 可变性；易变性	low hills	phr. 丘陵
climate	n. 气候	mild	a. 温和的；轻微的
coastline	n. 海岸线	moorland	n. 荒野
densely populated	phr. 人口稠密	mountain scenery	phr. 山景
drain	v. 耗尽；使流出；排水；流干	plain	n. 平原
drought	n. 干旱	political name	phr. 行政区划名称
European mainland	phr. 欧洲大陆	poor soil	phr. 贫瘠土壤
farming	n. 农业；耕作	population	n. 人口
fertile soil	phr. 肥沃的土壤	prevailing wind	phr. 盛行风；主风向
foggy	a. 有雾的	rainfall	n. 降雨；降雨量
freezing cold	phr. 非常冷	reservoir	n. 水库
front-page headline	phr. 头条	sparsely populated	phr. 人口稀疏
frost	n. 霜；严寒；冷冻	square kilometres	phr. 平方公里
glaciation	n. [地质] 冰川作用；冻结成冰	smog	n. 烟雾
heat	n. 热度；高温	temperate	adj. 温和的；有节制的
heath	n. 荒野	thermometer	n. 温度计
hedgerow	n. 灌木篱墙	time zone	phr. 时区
highland	n. 高地；丘陵地带	unprepared	a. 无准备的；尚未准备好的
longitude	n. 经度；经线	untreated	a. 未经过处理的
lowland	n. 低地	wet	a. 潮湿的；有雨的

Proper Names

Ben Nevis	本尼维斯山（位于英国苏格兰中西部）	Scotland	苏格兰
Continental Europe	欧洲大陆	Severn	塞文河(英国西南部地方的河名）
Cumbria	坎布里亚郡（英国英格兰西北部郡）	Shetlands	设得兰群岛（位于苏格兰东部的一群岛）
Everest	珠穆朗玛峰（世界最高峰）	Snowdon	斯诺登峰（英国威尔士西北部）
Great Britain	大不列颠	the Clyde	克莱德河（英国苏格兰河流，注入克莱德湾）
Greenwich Mean Time	格林尼治标准时间	the Commonwealth	英联邦
Industrial Revolution	phr. 工业革命	the Isle of Wight	怀特岛（英国）
Hebrides	赫布里底群岛（位于英国苏格兰西部）	the Orkneys	奥克尼群岛(苏格兰东北方群岛）
Lake District	湖区	the River Thames	泰晤士河
Lough Neagh	内伊湖（英国最大的淡水湖）	the Scottish Highlands	苏格兰高地
North Atlantic Drift	北大西洋洋流	the Union Jack	英国国旗
Northern Ireland	北爱尔兰（在爱尔兰岛东北部）	The United Kingdom of Great Britain and Northern Ireland	（简称 UK）大不列颠及北爱尔兰联合王国
Pennines	奔宁山脉		
Poland	波兰	Wales	威尔士

Exercises

I. Comprehension

1. Recall

1) What is the flag of the United Kingdom of Great Britain called?

2) What is the United Kingdom of Great Britain and Northern Ireland made up of?

2. Summarize

What is the passage mainly about?

3. Make Inferences

What do British people always talk about?

4. Analyze

1) On what occasions do the trains stop working and the roads are blocked in the UK?

2) Why is it said that "Britain doesn't have a climate, it only has weather" ?

5. Evaluate

What do you think of the *Clean Air Act*? Can British people benefit from it? Cite evidence to support your answer.

II. Further study

Choose one map of the UK and identify the places mentioned in the passage. Then choose one question you are interested in concerning the climate and weather to ask your classmates.

Section B Extensive Reading

➢ **Who are the British?**

Why British not English?

Many foreigners say "England" and "English" when they mean "Britain", or the "UK", and "British". This is very annoying for the 5 million people who live in Scotland, the 2.8 million in Wales and the 1.6 million in Northern Ireland who are certainly not English (46 million people live in England). However, the people from Scotland, Wales, Northern Ireland and England are all British. So what is the difference between the names "Great Britain" and "the United Kingdom" and what about "the British Isles"?

➢ **The United Kingdom**

This is an abbreviation of "the United Kingdom of Great Britain and Northern Ireland". It is often further abbreviated to "the UK", and is the political name of the country which is made up of England, Scotland, Wales and Northern Ireland (sometimes known as Ulster). Several islands off the British coast are also part of the United Kingdom (for example, the Isle of Wight, the Orkneys, Hebrides and Shetlands, and the Isles of Scilly), although the Channel Islands and the Isle of Man are not. However, all these islands do recognize the Queen.

> **Great Britain**

This is the name of the island which is made up of England, Scotland and Wales, and so, strictly speaking, it does not include Northern Ireland. The origin of the word "Great" is a reference to size, because in many European languages the words for Britain and the **"Brittany"** in France are the same. In fact, it was the French who first talked about Grande Bretagne! In everyday speech "Britain" is used to mean the United Kingdom.

> **The British Isles**

This is the geographical name that refers to all the islands off the north-western coast of the European continent: Great Britain, the whole of Ireland (Northern and Southern), the Channel Islands and the Isle of Man. But it is important to remember that Southern Ireland—that is the Republic of Ireland (also called "**Eire**") —is completely independent. So you can see that "the United Kingdom" is the correct name to use if you are referring to the country in a political, rather than in a geographical way. " The British" refers to the people from the UK, Great Britain or the British Isles in general.

> **How Was the United Kingdom Formed?**

This took centuries, and a lot of armed struggles were involved. In the 15th century, a Welsh prince, Henry Tudor, became King Henry Ⅶ of England. Then his son, King Henry Ⅷ, united England and Wales under one parliament in 1536. In Scotland a similar thing happened. The King of Scotland inherited the crown of England and Wales in 1603, he became King James Ⅰ of England and Wales and King James Ⅵ of Scotland. The Parliaments of England, Wales and Scotland were united a century later in 1707. The Scottish and Welsh are proud and independent people. In recent years there have been attempts at **devolution** in the two countries, particularly in Scotland where the Scottish Nationalist Party was very strong for a while. However, in a **referendum** in 1979 the Welsh rejected devolution and in the same year the Scots did the same. So it seems that most Welsh and Scottish people are happy to form part of the UK even though they sometimes complain that they are dominated by England, and particularly by London.

The whole of Ireland was united with Great Britain from 1801 to 1922. In 1922 the independent Republic of Ireland was formed in the South, while Northern Ireland became part of the United Kingdom of Great Britain and Northern Ireland. The flag of the United Kingdom, known as the Union Jack, is made up of three crosses. The **upright** red cross is the cross of St George, the **patron saint** of England. The white **diagonal** cross (with the arms going into the corners) is the cross of **St Andrew**, the patron saint of Scotland. The red diagonal cross is the cross of **St Patrick**, the patron saint of Ireland. **St David** is the patron saint of Wales. The national anthem of the United Kingdom is "God Save the Queen".

> **Invasion**

What makes the Scottish, Welsh, English and Northern Irish different from each other? About 2,000 years ago the British Isles were inhabited by the Celts who originally came from the continental Europe. During the next 1,000 years there were many invasions. The Romans came from Italy in 43 AD and, in calling the country "Britannia", gave Britain its name. The Angles and Saxons came from Germany, Denmark and the Netherlands in the 5th century, and England got its name from this invasion (Angle-land). The **Vikings** arrived from Denmark and Norway throughout the 9th century, and in 1066 (It is the year in history that every British school-child knows) the Normans invaded from France. These invasions drove the Celts into where is now Wales and Scotland, and they remained, of course, in Ireland. The English are the descendants of all the invaders, but are more **Anglo-Saxon** than anything else. These various origins explain many of the differences to be found between England, Wales, Scotland and Ireland—differences in education, religion and the legal systems, but the most obviously, in language.

➢ **Language**

The **Celts** spoke **Celtic** which survives today in the form of Welsh, Scottish **Gaelic** and Irish Gaelic. Less than a quarter of all the Welsh people (600,000, out of 2,800,000) speak Welsh. Scottish Gaelic and Irish Gaelic are still spoken, although they have suffered more than Welsh from the spread of English. However, all three languages are now officially encouraged and taught in the schools.

English developed from Anglo-Saxon and is a Germanic language. However, all the invading peoples, particularly the Norman French, influenced the English language and you can find many words in English which are French in origin. Nowadays, all the Welsh, Scottish and Irish people speak English (even if they speak their own languages as well), but all the countries have their own special accents and dialects, and their people are easily recognizable as soon as they speak. Occasionally, people from the four countries in the UK have difficulty in understanding one another because of these different accents. A southern English accent is generally accepted to be the most easily understood, and is the accent usually taught to foreigners.

➢ **Multiracial Britain**

Recently, there have been many waves of immigration into Britain and movement within the UK. For example, many people from Wales, Scotland and Ireland have settled in England; and Jews, Russians, Germans, and **Poles** have come to Britain (particularly London) during the political changes in the rest of Europe.

British culture is being enriched through its contact with other cultures. For example, the British are becoming more adventurous in their cooking and eating habits, and Chinese, Indian and **Pakistani** restaurants are very popular. Another example can be found in the pop music scene where West Indian reggae music has become very influential.

(length: 1,151 words)

Vocabulary

devolution	n. 权力下放	patron saint	phr.守护神；保护圣徒
diagonal	adj. 对角线的	referendum	n. 公民投票；全民公决
	n. 对角线	upright	adj. 垂直的；直立的
multiracial	adj. 多民族的		n. 垂直的；直立的

Proper Names

Anglo-Saxon	n. 盎格鲁-撒克逊	Pakistani	n. 巴基斯坦人
Brittany	布列塔尼（法国西北部一地区）		adj. 巴基斯坦的
Celt	n. 凯尔特人	Pole	n. 波兰人
Celtic	n. 凯尔特语	St Andrew	圣安德鲁（苏格兰的守护神）
	adj. 凯尔特人的	St David	威尔士守护神圣大卫
Eire	爱尔兰	St Patrick	爱尔兰守护神圣帕特里克
Gaelic	n. 盖尔语	Viking	n. 维京人；北欧海盗
	adj. 盖尔人的	Union Jack	英国国旗

Exercises

I. Comprehension

1. Recall

What is the national anthem of the United Kingdom?

2. Summarize

Can you compare British with English?

3. Make Inferences

Are people on the British Isles British?

4. Analyze

1) How was the United Kingdom formed?

2) What makes the Scottish, Welsh, English and Northern Irish different from each other?

5. Evaluate

What do you think of different accents spoken in Britain? Is it good or bad for people to communicate with each other?

II. Further study

Choose one patron saint and find the story of him. Then tell the story you have searched to your classmates.

Section C Supplementary Reading

□ Passage 1 London

London is the capital of the United Kingdom and one of the world's oldest and largest cities. It is Great Britain's economic, cultural and political centre. Its sights attract millions of tourists every year.

➢ **Geography**

London lies on the River Thames, about 50 km from **the North Sea**. The river has influenced London for many centuries. Rising tides have flooded the city more than once. In the 1970s and 1980s a large barrier was built in the eastern part of the city to stop **incoming** water from flooding the nation's capital.

London is divided into three main sections.

The City is London's financial district and the oldest part of the capital. It is very small, with a size of only one square mile. Although only a few thousand people live here, hundreds of thousands pour into the City every day to work in the big office buildings of large banks and other institutions.

The West End includes London's government district Westminster as well as the famous shopping streets around **Piccadilly Circus** and **Trafalgar Square**. The city's famous cinemas, theatres and bars are located in the **West End**. Most of London's tourist attractions are concentrated here.

The South Bank is the area south of the River Thames. It is a cultural district with many concert halls, museums, theatres and **galleries**.

➢ **Population**

London became one of the first megacities in the world. Since the end of World War II, however, the population of the city has begun to decrease because many people have been moving to the suburbs and new towns outside of London.

London is a multicultural city. In the 19th century thousands of people began pouring into London as a result of the Industrial Revolution. At the beginning of the 20th century immigrants from other European countries came.

In the 1950s and 60s people from Britain's colonies came to London. Indians, Pakistanis and West Indians are a common sight in the city today. About 25% of London's population are immigrants or the children of immigrants.

➢ **History**

London has a 2000-year-old history. In the first century AD the Romans came to Great Britain and founded a settlement near the mouth of the River Thames. They called it **Londinium**. After they left London about four hundred years later the Saxons, a Germanic tribe, settled in the area. In the centuries that followed Vikings repeatedly attacked the city.

When William the Conqueror invaded Britain in 1066, London was already the biggest town on the island. William made the city its capital and crowned himself king in Westminster Abbey on Christmas Day. He also built the Tower of London to protect the city from invaders.

During the Middle Ages London grew steadily. It became one of Europe's trading centers and its population grew to about 200,000 by the beginning of the 17th century. Then disaster struck the city twice. The Great Plague of 1665 killed about a fourth of the city's population. A year later the Great Fire burned down most of the older part of the city. After this tragedy the city was rebuilt with houses made of stone and brick instead of wood.

At the beginning of the Industrial Revolution almost a million people lived in London. It was the largest city in the world and the centre of the British Empire, which at that time was growing at a rapid pace .

As more and more people moved to the city from the countryside, London needed more and better transportation systems. In 863 it became the first city in the world to start an underground railway system.

During the Second World War Nazi Germany bombed London heavily. 30,000 people were killed. The rebuilding of the city after World War II caused many problems. City planners did not want London to grow endlessly in all directions. A green belt was created around the city to stop its expansion. Outside of this green area, new towns emerged. They became small cities which many people moved to later on.

In the second half of the 20th century London faced many problems that other megacities also have: air pollution, traffic jams and unemployment.

In the 1970s and 80s the Docklands in the eastern part of London were rebuilt. They were once part of the world's largest harbour. The Docklands lost their importance as the British Empire lost its colonies. In the past decades new office buildings, shopping centers and a new airport have been created in an attempt to revitalize this region.

➢ **Economy and Tourism**

London is the UK's main economic and financial centre. It is the centre of trade and **banking**. Factories around the city produce all kinds of consumer goods—from clothes and electronic products to food and chemicals.

Trading companies were founded along the Thames at a time when Great Britain was still the biggest **colonial power** in the world. **Docks** and **wharfs** in eastern London became the centre of world trade. New **container terminals** were built in the 1960s, in order to handle the larger **cargo ships** that come to London.

London is Europe's most important banking and financial centre. Almost all of the world's large banks have regional headquarters in London. The Bank of England, located in the City of London, controls the country's money supply and is responsible for the value of the British pound sterling.

Tourism is an important economic factor for the city. Every year millions of people from all over the world come to London to see the city's well-known sights. Pupils and students from all over the world come here to learn English or to take language courses. Over 200,000 Londoners work in tourist-related industries.

➢ **Transportation**

As Europe's **gateway** overseas, London has two big international airports. **Heathrow**, in the western part of the city, is the main airport for international flights. **Gatwick**, halfway between London and the southern coast, was opened in 1958 in an attempt to get some of Heathrow's traffic away from the city. **Stansted**, in the north of London, handles regional flights and flights of budget airlines. London's new City Airport is only 15 minutes from the city centre and is used especially by the business travelers.

There is probably no other city in the world that has such a dense public transport system than London. **The Tube**, London's underground railway, is the oldest in the world. The red **double-decker buses** are well-known around the globe and a symbol of inner city transportation. All together, about 5 million people use London's public transport every day.

London has 6 railway stations that handle over 1.5 million commuters who travel in and out of the city every day. Fast trains from Paris and Brussels arrive in London daily through **the Channel Tunnel**.

- **Culture**

London is well known for its museums, art galleries and concert halls.

The British Museum is one of the oldest and largest museums in the world. It contains over seven million artifacts from all continents, cultures and civilizations.

The National Gallery, situated on Trafalgar Square, is home to a great deal of selections of European paintings. Tate Gallery has works of British modern art.

London's theatres perform works of Shakespeare and other great dramatists. The Royal Opera House at Covent Garden is host to performances of London's big **orchestras**.

(length: 1,239 words)

Vocabulary

banking	n. 银行业；金融	gallery	n. 美术馆；画廊
cargo ship	phr. 货船	gateway	n. 通道；途径
colonial power	phr. 殖民国家	geography	n. 地理；地形
container terminal	phr. 集装箱码头	incoming	a. 引入的
dock	n. 码头；船坞	orchestra	n. 管弦乐队；乐队演奏处
double-decker bus	phr. 双层的公共汽车	wharf	n. 码头

Proper Names

Gatwick	盖特威克（伦敦第二大机场）
Heathrow	希思罗机场（位于英国伦敦）
Londinium	伦底纽姆。罗马人是从公元 43 年开始攻入大不列颠岛的，站稳脚跟之后，他们在泰晤士河畔修建了一个聚居点，名字叫“伦底纽姆”（Londinium），也就是今天的伦敦
Piccadilly Circus	皮卡迪利广场(戏院及娱乐中心)
Stansted	斯坦斯特德(英国伦敦一机场名)

the British Museum	大英博物馆	the Tube	伦敦地铁
the Channel Tunnel	英法海底隧道	Trafalgar Square	特拉法加广场
the North Sea	北海	West End	伦敦西区

□ Passage 2 United States Travel Guides: Top Things to See

➢ Cities

The USA has some fabulous cities, the most famous being **the Big Apple** of New York on the east coast and the Golden Gate of San Francisco on the west. Yet there are plenty of other cities worth visiting such as the non-stop fun in **Las Vegas**, **the Hollywood** glamour and **Disneyland** magic in **Los Angeles**, the excitement in **Miami**, the history in **Boston**, the **patriotism** in **Washington D.C.**, the cowboys of **Dallas**, and the **tropical** escape in **Honolulu, Hawaii**. From coast to coast, America offers a taste of everything.

➢ National Parks

Nature lovers will be in heaven with over 300 national parks to choose from. Perhaps the most famous is the breathtaking **Grand Canyon**, "Nature's own capital city". Located 400km outside **Phoenix, Arizona,** this enormous stone canyon is a spectacular spectacle of nature. Have a **dizzying** look over the rim, take a donkey down the **switchback trail**, embark on a wild **rafting** ride in the **Colorado River** below or go for the flight of your life in a helicopter or plane above!

Yosemite National Park "is a paradise that makes even the loss of **Eden** seem **insignificant**. It is by far the grandest of all the special temples of Nature I was ever permitted to enter". These are the words of John Muir, the famous explorer and naturalist who was the first outsider to venture into the magnificent Yosemite Valley. Located 300km east of San Francisco, don't miss spending a few days here among towering waterfalls, majestic meadows and crystal streams. Accommodation is in **campgrounds**, cabins, hotels and **luxurious lodges**.

Yellowstone National Park is a vast wilderness of many colours in the **summit** of the Rocky Mountains. The park **bestows** an abundance of **geysers**, waterfalls and **multi-coloured** hot springs, along with an impressive **array** of wildlife such as **buffalo, bald eagles, moose**, wolves and bears. The nearby town of **Jackson Hole**, **Wyoming** offers fine lodging and a range of year-round outdoor activities.

The **volcanoes** of the past and present

have created some exceptional national parks on the tropical Hawaiian Islands. Ancient **Haleakala Crater** on the island of **Maui** is a **surreal** landscape, home to rare and **endangered** species. Hiking, camping, cycling, **horseback riding** and even swimming are some of the activities available in this unique **ecosystem**. Volcanoes National Park on the Big Island of Hawaii is home to two of the world's most active and friendly volcanoes. Visitors can inspect rivers and waterfalls of hot lava, cinder cones, gaping chasms and barren lava wrought into fantastic shapes.

There are literally thousands of monuments scattered across the country. The most famous are the Statue of Liberty in New York City harbour, the White House and the elegant US Capitol Building both in Washington D.C., the Empire State Building in New York City, Alcatraz Island Prison in San Francisco Bay and Mount Rushmore in the Black Hills of South Dakota—a 6,000-foot mountain peak carved into the faces of four famous US Presidents.

The Muir Woods National Monument is a peaceful park located on the other side of the Golden Gate Bridge from San Francisco. Here you can see the tallest trees in the world, the mighty Redwoods. The park occupies one of the verdant valleys of Mount Tamalpais and is home to many giant Redwood trees that are over 1000 years old. After a walk in the forest, visit the Mountain Home Inn on the mountain's ridge where you can enjoy a drink or delicious meal and a fabulous view!

- **Top Things To Do Be a Part of It in New York**

The pulse and excitement of New York City is like no other place on earth. An international centre of culture, commerce and cosmopolitan lifestyle, the Big Apple is a must-see on any travel itinerary. Check out the abundance of art galleries and some of the best museums in the world such as the Metropolitan Museum of Art, the Museum of Modern Art (MOMA) and the Guggenheim Museum. Don't miss a walk through in Central Park, the impressive art and architecture of Rockefeller Centre, Greenwich Village with its hip cafés and restaurants, and Times Square with its glittering lights and theatres. Take the ferry from Battery Park to the Statue of Liberty. Catch a Broadway show, a symphony, ballet or blues…Or simply be a part of the buzz of the City That Never Sleeps. The opportunities are endless!

- **Feel the Voodoo Magic of New Orleans**

This vibrant city is full of contrasts, cuisine, history and mystery. Situated on the mighty Mississippi River, New Orleans is an exciting hub of music, magic, and parties. Don't miss the famous French Quarter with its elegant buildings, Cajun restaurants, street musicians, jazz clubs and non-stop partying. The folks here on Bourbon Street can't wait for Mardi Gras to celebrate. Also adding colour to the city are the parks, museums (including a voodoo museum and the New

Orleans Museum of Art), beautiful gardens and the **Six Flags New Orleans** Theme Park. Outside the city in the marshlands known as the Bayou, you can take a boat tour with experienced guides who call on alligators to jump out of the water. New Orleans is a thrilling place to be!

➢ **Go Island Hopping in Hawaii**

The Hawaiian Islands are some of the most beautiful islands on earth. Here you can bask on pristine beaches in glorious sunshine, come face to face with an active volcano, learn to surf at Waikiki Beach, hike through breathtaking valleys, and enjoy a beach luau complete with fire dancing and roasted wild boar. Catch the magnificent Taurids Meteor Shower in October/November and the impressive surf competitions outside Honolulu on Oahu's North Shore from November to the next February. Go whale watching from November to the next April, or simply seek those daily rainbows in the sky while sipping a Mai Tai.

➢ **Live It Up in Las Vegas**

America's capital of fun, Las Vegas, will impress and entertain even the most jaded traveller. This dazzling desert oasis of non-stop action has become a family destination, offering a whole lot more than just gambling. Amusement parks, tropical beaches, water slides, celebrity entertainment, great shopping and of course the best casinos, provide hours of fun for the entire family.

➢ **Soak Up San Francisco**

Walk across the famous **Golden Gate Bridge**, experiment with science in the Exploratorium, stroll through Golden Gate Park, taking in the de Young Museum of Fine Art, Japanese Tea Garden, Steinhart Aquarium, Morrison Planetarium and the Conservatory of Flowers. Ride a cable car, cruise across the bay in a ferry to Sausalito or visit Alcatraz Island where **Al Capone** was imprisoned. Rent a paddle-boat at the beautiful Stow Lake. Indulge in homemade chocolate at Ghirardelli Square or fresh seafood and fun at Pier 39 at Fisherman's Wharf. Dine on Italian cuisine in the colourful North Beach district and walk across the street into China Town for a different flavour. Check out the surfers and sea-lions at Ocean Beach and grab a bite to eat at the nearby Cliff House. There are countless things to do in this city on the sea!

➢ **See a Rodeo**

Besides its fabulous cities, America is also known for cowboys and cowgirls. See these tough wranglers in action at an exciting rodeo! Rodeos are almost daily events in Wyoming, Oklahoma and Texas; you can catch the National Finals Rodeo in Las Vegas each December. This event brings cowboys and cowgirls from around the world for the ultimate showdown championship.

➢ **Sizzle in Miami**

Some would say Miami is a constant carnival, a flamboyant blend of cultures and lifestyles basking in sunshine. Explore the city or venture beyond its borders into the Everglades, a subtropical marshland where local wildlife can be seen such as alligators and crocodiles. Join the wild party during the annual Miami Carnival, one of the largest street festivals in the country held in September/October.

➢ **Spend Some Time in a National Park**

America boasts 388 national parks ranging from lunar landscapes and spectacular canyons to magnificent mountains and lush forests teeming with wildlife.

➢ **Take a Tour of Washington D.C.**

The nation's capital and seat of American government, Washington D.C. provides a grand insight into the birth, history and workings of America. Visit the historical monuments and memorials such as the U.S. Capitol Building, the Washington Monument, World War II Memorial, the Lincoln Memorial, Freedom Park and the White House. A convenient way to see the monuments and museums (which are pretty spread out) is to take the hop-on, hop-off "Tourmobile Sightseeing Trams". Or meet the "D.C. Party Shuttle" at the Old Post Office on Pennsylvania Avenue at 9:45 am for a great tour of many main sites.

➢ **Visit a Zoo**

The San Diego Zoo in San Diego and the National Zoo in Washington D.C. are among the best in the world. These are not just regular zoos where animals sit still in cages; these animals run in vast open spaces, swim in rivers and behave as they would in their natural habitats. The zoos are leaders in animal care, science, education, and sustainability. It is a real treat for the whole family.

(length: 1,525 words)

Vocabulary

array	n. 排列
bald eagle	phr. 秃鹰（美国的国鸟）
bestow	v. 授予；使用
buffalo	n. 野牛
campground	n. 野营地
dizzying	a. 令人昏乱的；极快的
ecosystem	n. 生态系统
endangered	a. 濒临灭绝的
geyser	n. 间歇泉
Golden Gate Bridge	金门大桥（美国加利福尼亚州）
horseback riding	phr. 骑马
insignificant	a. 无关紧要的；微不足道的
luxurious lodges	phr. 豪华住处
moose	n. 驼鹿；麋
multi-coloured	a. 多色的
patriotism	n. 爱国主义；爱国心
rafting	n. 筏运
summit	n. 最高点；顶点
surreal	a. 超现实主义的；不真实的
switchback	a. 使用“之”字爬坡路线的

trail	n. 小径，小路	volcano	n. 火山
tropical	a. 热带的	voodoo	n. 巫毒，巫术

Proper Names

Al Capone	阿尔·卡彭（美国纽约著名黑帮老大）	Las Vegas	拉斯韦加斯（美国内华达州的城市）
Arizona	美国亚利桑那州	Los Angeles	洛杉矶
Boston	波士顿（美国城市）	Maui	毛伊岛（在太平洋中北部）
Colorado River	科罗拉多河	Miami	迈阿密（美国佛罗里达州东南部港市）
Dallas	达拉斯（美国城市）		
Disneyland	迪士尼乐园	Phoenix	凤凰城（美国亚利桑那州首府）
Eden	伊甸园(《圣经》中亚当和夏娃最初居住的地方）	Six Flags New Orleans	六旗（世界上最大的主题公园连锁品牌）
Grand Canyon	（美）科罗拉多大峡谷	the Big Apple	大苹果城（美国纽约市的别名）
Haleakala Crater	哈雷阿卡拉火山口(世界最大的死火山)	the Hollywood	好莱坞
		Washington D.C.	华盛顿（哥伦比亚特区）
Hawaii	夏威夷	Wyoming	美国怀俄明州
Honolulu	火奴鲁鲁（美国夏威夷州的首府和港口城市）	Yellowstone National Park	黄石国家公园（美国第一个国家公园）
Jackson Hole	杰克逊·霍尔（地名）	Yosemite National Park	约塞米蒂国家公园

Section D Word Bank for This Unit

50 States of USA

亚拉巴马	Alabama	马里兰	Maryland
阿拉斯加	Alaska	马萨诸塞	Massachusetts
亚利桑那	Arizona	密歇根	Michigan
阿肯色	Arkansas	明尼苏达	Minnesota
加利福尼亚	California	密西西比	Mississippi
科罗拉多	Colorado	密苏里	Missouri
康涅狄格	Connecticut	蒙大拿	Montana
特拉华	Delaware	内布拉斯加	Nebraska
佛罗里达	Florida	内华达	Nevada
佐治亚	Georgia	新罕布什尔	New Hampshire
夏威夷	Hawaii	新泽西	New Jersey
爱达荷	Idaho	新墨西哥	New Mexico
伊利诺伊	Illinois	纽约	New York
印第安纳	Indiana	北卡罗来纳	North Carolina
艾奥瓦（又译“爱荷华”）	Iowa	北达科他	North Dakota
堪萨斯	Kansas	俄亥俄	Ohio
肯塔基	Kentucky	俄克拉何马	Oklahoma
路易斯安那	Louisiana	俄勒冈	Oregon
缅因	Maine	宾夕法尼亚	Pennsylvania

罗得岛	Rhode Island	弗吉尼亚	Virginia
南卡罗来纳	South Carolina	华盛顿	Washington
南达科他	South Dakota	西弗吉尼亚	West Virginia
田纳西	Tennessee	威斯康星	Wisconsin
得克萨斯	Texas	怀俄明	Wyoming
犹他	Utah	哥伦比亚特区	District. Of Columbia
佛蒙特	Vermont		

Famous Sites

英国伦敦大本钟	Big Ben in London, the UK	美国华盛顿白宫	The White House, Washington D.C., USA
白金汉宫	Buckingham Palace, the UK	美国纽约市世界贸易中心	World Trade Center, New York City, USA
英国海德公园	Hyde Park, the UK	美国纽约市中央公园	Central Park, New York City, USA
伦敦塔桥	London Tower Bridge, the UK	美国约塞米蒂国家公园	Yosemite National Park, USA
威斯敏斯特大教堂	Westminster Abbey, the UK	美国亚利桑那州大峡谷	Grand Canyon, Arizona, USA
美国纽约州尼亚加拉大瀑布	Niagara Falls, New York State, USA	美国加利福尼亚州好莱坞	Hollywood, California, USA
百慕大	Bermuda	加利福尼亚州迪士尼乐园	Disneyland, California, USA
美国夏威夷火奴鲁鲁	Honolulu, Hawaii, USA	美国内华达州拉斯韦加斯	Las Vegas, Nevada, USA
美国黄石国家公园	Yellowstone National Park, USA	美国佛罗里达州迈阿密	Miami, Florida, USA
美国纽约市自由女神像	Statue of Liberty, New York City, USA	纽约市大都会艺术博物馆	Metropolitan Museum of Art, New York City, USA
美国纽约市时代广场	Times Square, New York City, USA		

Chapter 2
History

英国历史是一部征服与吞并的历史。英国全称为大不列颠及北爱尔兰联合王国，由英格兰、威尔士、苏格兰和北爱尔兰组成，而整个英国的历史也就是由这四个区域的历史交织组成。美国全称美利坚合众国，原为英国殖民地，后逐渐兴起而成为一个强大的国家。

本章主要介绍了第二次世界大战期间著名的不列颠之战，历史原因造成的伦敦东区人特有的有趣而难以理解的口音，神秘的骑士及骑士精神，美国内战，以及英国最早的居民和社会等与历史有关的话题。

Section A Intensive Reading

The Battle of Britain

The Battle of Britain was the German air force's **attempt** to gain air superiority over the RAF (Royal Air Force) from July to September 1940. Their **ultimate** failure was one of the turning points of World War Two and prevented Germany from invading Britain.

➢ **Hitler Plans the Invasion of Britain**

On 18 June 1940, Churchill gave a rousing speech to the British people, announcing: "The Battle of France is over. The Battle of Britain is about to begin." Four days later, France surrendered to Germany and Hitler turned his attention to Britain.

German air **superiority** in the south of England was essential before Hitler could contemplate an invasion so Hermann Goering, the head of the Luftwaffe, was instructed that the RAF must be "beaten down to such an extent that it can no longer muster any power of attack worth mentioning against the German crossing".

➢ **British and German Aeroplanes**

The Luftwaffe's principal fighter planes were the Messerschmitt Bf109 and the Messerschmitt Bf110. It had a number of favoured bombers: the Dornier 17, the Junkers Ju88, the Heinkel 111, and the Junkers Ju87 (also known as the "Stuka" from Sturzkampfflugzeug, the German word for dive bomber). The RAF had the high-performance Hawker Hurricane and Super-marine Spitfire fighters.

Although on paper the Luftwaffe appeared to have the advantage in numbers of planes, pilots and experience, the two air forces were, in fact, evenly matched. The short range of the German planes and the fact they were fighting over enemy territory were both serious disadvantages for the Luftwaffe. The RAF also had **radar,** a priceless tool for detecting enemy raids.

➢ **The Battle Begins**

The battle began in mid-July and, initially, the Luftwaffe concentrated on attacking shipping in the English Channel and attacking coastal towns and defences. From 12 August, Goering shifted his focus to the destruction of the RAF, attacking airfields and radar bases. Convinced that Fighter Command was now close to **defeat**, he also tried to force air battles between fighter planes to definitively break British strength.

However, Goering grew **frustrated** by the large number of British planes that were still fighting off his attacks. On 4 September, the Luftwaffe switched tactics again and, on Hitler's orders, set about destroying London and other major cities.

Eleven days later, on what became known as "Battle of Britain Day", the RAF savaged the huge incoming Luftwaffe formations in the skies above London and the south coast.

➢ **The invasion is postponed**

It was now clear to Hitler that his air force had failed to gain air superiority so, on 17 September, he postponed his plans to invade Britain. His attention was now focused on the **invasion** of the Soviet Union, although the Luftwaffe continued to bomb Britain until the end of the war.

It's difficult to establish an exact figure of how many aircraft were shot down in the Battle of Britain, partly because both sides tended to exaggerate their successes and downplay their losses. However, it's **estimated** that between 10 July and the end of October 1940, the RAF lost around 1,023 aircraft **whilst** the Luftwaffe lost 1,887.

(length: 667 words)

Vocabulary

attempt	n. 进攻；（尤指）企图杀害	superiority	n. 优越性
defeat	v./n. 击败，战胜	ultimate	a. 最后的；极限的；首要的；最大的 n. 终极；顶点
estimate	v./n. 估计，估算	whilst	conj. 同时
frustrated	a. 挫败的		
invasion	n. 入侵，侵犯		
radar	n. 雷达		

Exercises

I. Comprehension

1. Recall

When did Churchill give a rousing speech to the British people?

2. Summarize

What does the Battle of Britain mean?

3. Make Inferences

What does the author mean by saying "It's difficult to establish an exact figure of how many aircraft were shot down in the Battle of Britain"?

4. Evaluate

In your opinion, what's the meaning of the Battle of Britain in World War II?

II. Further Study

Choose one important war in World War I or II and prepare a presentation in class.

Section B Extensive Reading

London's Cockneys Bask in Limelight

by Jill Lawless, London Associated Press

It's a safe bet that most of the 200 or so countries competing in the London Olympics are already **represented** in the British capital, one of the world's most **multicultural** cities.

Yet one of London's oldest communities is trying not to get lost in the clamor.

Cockneys have been proud residents of London's East End for centuries—and they want to make sure the world knows it.

"I'm a Cockney and I'm proud to be one," said Lutfur Rahman, mayor of Tower Hamlets, an inner-city **borough** that stretches from the Tower of London, across the East End to the edge of the city's new Olympic Park.

Bangladesh-born and East End-bred, Rahman may not fit the traditional image of a Cockney, but he is calling for the Cockney **dialect** to be recognized as an official language of the borough, whose residents already speak 126 different tongues.

➢ **What Is a Cockney?**

Traditionally, a Cockney is anyone "born within the sound of Bow bells"—the bells of St Mary-le-Bow Church in the heart of medieval London. It's usually taken to mean a working-class native Londoner, or more specifically an east Londoner.

University of London linguist Sue Fox says the name comes from the Middle English for "cock's egg" — "a small, misshapen thing...a misfit in society". A certain underdog combativeness has always been part of the Cockney character.

Cockneys speak in a **distinctive** accent, marked by elongated vowels and glottal stops—imagine the characters from the UK soap opera East Enders—and use a distinctive form of rhyming slang, in which "Would you believe it?" becomes " Would you Adam and Eve it?"

Cockney traditions **flourished** in the **tightknit** communities of the East End, but the area has been transformed since World War II, when thousands of homes were destroyed and thousands of people died in German bombings.

After the war, many East Enders moved further afield. The area, long a magnet for newcomers because of its proximity to the city's docks, now draws incomers from across Britain and around the world. Today's East End is a classic cultural mosaic, where traditional pubs sit alongside halal restaurants, art **galleries** and fruit and vegetable stalls. It's also a **magnet** for young people who come for jobs in London's traditional financial center, the city, and the new Canary Wharf business district nearby.

➢ **Pearly Kings**

Tower Hamlets officials decided to do a bit of Cockney awareness-raising ahead of the Olympics, offering journalists traditional grub such as **jellied eels** and meat pies in an East End pub, in the company of so-called Cockney royalty, Pearly Kings and Queens.

These flamboyantly dressed figures, their black costumes covered in thousands of pearl buttons, are among the most recognizable Cockney symbols—Rahman called them "London's other royal family".

The "pearlies" have their origins a century ago in a street sweeper named Henry Croft, who adapted the button-festooned clothes worn by London costermongers—apple-sellers—to help draw attention to his charity fund-raising. Today, pearlies across London elaborately decorated hand-sewn outfits to raise money for charity.

Many pass their honorary Cockney titles on from parent to child. But they worry their traditions may soon be lost.

"We are dying out a bit," said Jimmy Jukes, the Pearly King of Bermondsey and Camber-well in south London. " Now London's a multicultural city, and people are bringing their own culture and their own way of life.

"We do try to bring new blood in, but a lot of people think we're just about fancy dress".

➢ **Changing Times**

Some believe the distinctive Cockney brand of English is also in danger of dying out. In today's East End, the children of Somali and Bangladeshi **immigrants** speak with Cockney accents, but their slang is as likely to come from American jargon and Jamaican patois as Cockney argot.

Yet most Londoners recognize that "apples and pears" is rhyming slang for stairs or that "trouble and strife" means wife, even if they wouldn't use the expressions themselves.

Fox says trying to preserve the language is like trying to nail down water—it is always evolving.

"It has never been this pure linguistic variety," she said. "It is constantly in flux."

The area has changed, too, with long-term residents voicing the common big city complaints about atomization and anonymity.

"I can walk down this road—I've lived here 60 years—and I wouldn't know anyone," said John Proud, a lifelong East Ender. "It's the way of the world".

➢ Blitz Spirit

But don't count the Cockneys out just yet. This is a community that's proud of its **resilience**. East Enders, after all, withstood the **bulk** of wartime bombing and personify Britain's "Blitz Spirit".

"We're pretty **robust**," said Vicky Groves, the 32-year-old Pearly Queen of Bow, an east London neighborhood. "Keep your chin up, keep on, muddle through."

And the **ever-evolving** Cockney language endures. A curry used to be widely known as a "ruby", short for Ruby Murray, a 1950s singer. The dish now has started to be known as an "Andy", after the tennis player.

A TV ad for potato chips bills it as the perfect snack "for when you're Hank Marvin"—or starvin.

"I'm very proud to be a Cockney," said Groves, who has married into a family that boasts four generations of Pearly Kings and Queens. "It's where I'm from. It's who I am".

She hopes to share that culture with the world during the Games.

"All eyes are on London," she said. "I think it's great to be able to say we've got traditions that go back hundreds of years.

(length: 935 words)

Vocabulary

borough	n. 区，自治的市镇	jellied eel	n. 鳝鱼冻
cockney	n. 伦敦东区特有的方言；伦敦东区人	magnet	n. 磁铁
dialect	n. 方言	multicultural	a. 多种文化的
distinctive	a. 有特色的	represent	v. 代表，表现
ever-evolving	a. 不断发展的	resilience	n. 恢复力，弹力
flourish	n./v. 兴盛，繁荣	robust	a. 强健的，健康的
gallery	n. 画廊，走廊	tightknit	a. 构造结实的
immigrant	n. 移民，侨民		

Exercises

I. Comprehension

1. Recall

1) What is Cockney according to this passage?

2) What does "trouble and strife" mean in cockney?

2. Summarize

What is the main idea that the author tries to convey?

3. Analyze

What theme is the author conveying through this passage?

4. Evaluate

If you are one of the Cockneys, will you be proud of your language and culture?

II. Further Study

Try to collect information and find more interesting expressions in Cockneys.

Section C Supplementary Reading

□ Passage 1 American Civil War

The American Civil War, also known as the War between the States, or simply the Civil War, was a civil war fought from 1861 to 1865 between the United States (the "Union" or the "North") and several Southern slave states that had declared their secession and formed the Confederate States of America (the "Confederacy" or the "South"). The war had its origin in the fractious issue of **slavery**, and, after four years of bloody combat (mostly in the South), the Confederacy was defeated, slavery was **abolished**, and the difficult **Reconstruction** process of restoring unity and guaranteeing rights to the freed slaves began.

In the presidential election of 1860, Republicans led by Abraham Lincoln opposed expanding slavery into the territories. Lincoln won but before his inauguration on March 4, 1861, seven cotton-based slave states formed the Confederacy. Outgoing Democrat James Buchanan and the incoming Republicans rejected the legality of secession. Lincoln's inaugural address insisted his **administration** would not **initiate** civil war, leading eight remaining slave states to reject immediate calls for secession. A Peace Conference failed to find a compromise. Both sides prepared for war. The **Confederates** assumed that Europe was so dependent on "King Cotton" for its industry that they would intervene; none did and none recognized the new Confederate States of America.

Hostilities began on April 12, 1861, when Confederate forces fired upon Fort Sumter, a key fort held by Union troops in South Carolina. Lincoln called for the creation of an army to retake it; meanwhile, four border slave states joined the Confederacy, bringing their total to eleven. The Union soon controlled the border states and established a naval blockade that crippled the southern economy. The Eastern Theater was inconclusive in 1861-1862. The Fall 1862 Confederate campaign into Maryland ended at the Battle of Antietam, dissuading British intervention. Lincoln issued the Emancipation Proclamation, which made ending slavery a war goal. To the west, by summer 1862 the Union destroyed the Confederate river navy, then much of their western armies, and the Union at Vicksburg split the Confederacy in two at the Mississippi River. In 1863, Robert E. Lee's Confederate incursion north ended at the Battle of Gettysburg. Western successes led to Ulysses S. Grant command of all Union armies in 1864. In the Western Theater William T . Sherman drove east to capture Atlanta and marched to the sea, destroying Confederate infrastructure along the way. The Union marshaled the resources and manpower to attack the Confederacy from all directions, and could afford to fight battles of attrition through the Overland Campaign towards Richmond. The defending Confederate army failed leading to Lee's surrender to Grant at Appomattox Court House on April 9, 1865.

The American Civil War was one of the earliest true industrial wars. Railroads, the telegraph, steamships, and mass-produced weapons were employed extensively. The **mobilization** of civilian factories, mines, shipyards, banks, transportation and food supplies all foreshadowed World War I. It remains the deadliest war in American history, resulting in the deaths of an estimated 750,000 soldiers and an undetermined number of civilian casualties. Historian John Huddleston estimates the death toll at ten percent of all Northern males 20-45 years old, and 30 percent of all Southern white males aged 18-40.

➢ Causes of Secession

The causes of the Civil War were complex, and have been controversial since the war began. The issue has been further complicated by historical revisionists, who have tried to improve the image of the South by lessening the role of slavery. Slavery was the central source of escalating political tension in the 1850s. The Republican Party was determined to prevent any spread of slavery, and many Southern leaders had threatened **secession** if the Republican candidate, Lincoln, won the 1860 election. Following Lincoln's victory, many Southern whites felt that disunion had become their only option.

While not all Southerners saw themselves as fighting to preserve slavery, most of the officers and over a third of the rank and file in Lee's army had close family ties to slavery. To Northerners, in contrast, the motivation was primarily to preserve the Union, not to abolish slavery. Abraham Lincoln consistently made preserving the Union the central goal of the war, though he increasingly saw slavery as a crucial issue and made ending it an additional goal. Lincoln's decision to issue the *Emancipation Proclamation* angered both Peace Democrats ("Copperheads") and War Democrats, but energized most Republicans. By warning that free blacks would flood the North, Democrats made gains in the 1862 elections, but they did not gain control of Congress. The Republicans' **counterargument** that slavery was the mainstay of the enemy steadily gained support, with the Democrats losing decisively in the 1863 elections in Ohio when they tried to resurrect anti-black **sentiment**.

➢ Sectionalism

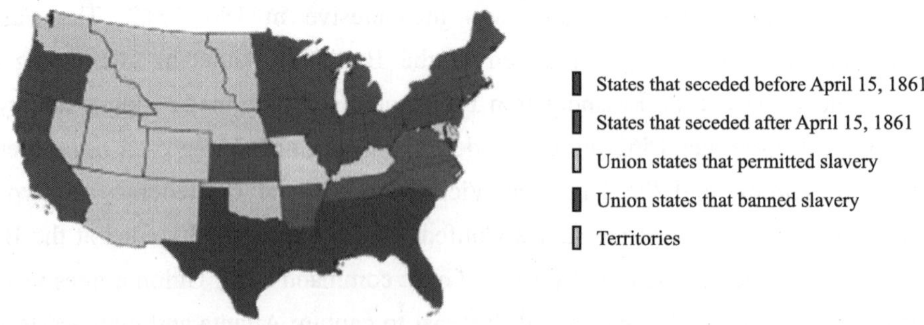

Status of the states, 1861

Sectionalism refers to the different economies, social structure, customs and political values of the North and South. It increased steadily between 1800 and 1860 as the North, which phased slavery out of existence, industrialized, urbanized and built prosperous farms, while the deep South concentrated on plantation agriculture based on slave labor, together with subsistence farming for the poor whites. The South expanded into rich new lands in the Southwest (from Alabama to Texas).

However, slavery declined in the border states and could barely survive in cities and industrial areas (it was fading out in cities such as Baltimore, Louisville and St. Louis), so a South based on slavery was rural and non-industrial. On the other hand, as the demand for cotton grew, the price of slaves soared. Historians have debated whether economic differences between the industrial Northeast and the agricultural South helped cause the war. Most historians now disagree with the economic determinism of historian Charles Beard in the 1920s and emphasize that Northern and Southern economies were largely **complementary**.

Fears of slave **revolts** and **abolitionist propaganda** made the South militantly hostile to abolitionism. Southerners complained that it was the North that was changing, and was prone to new "isms", while the South remained true to historic republican values of the Founding Fathers (many of whom owned slaves, including Washington, Jefferson and Madison). Lincoln said that Republicans were following the tradition of the framers of the *Constitution* (including the *Northwest Ordinance* and the *Missouri Compromise*) by preventing expansion of slavery.

The issue of accepting slavery (in the guise of rejecting slave-owning bishops and missionaries) split the largest religious denominations (the Methodist, Baptist and Presbyterian churches) into separate Northern and Southern denominations. Industrialization meant that seven European immigrants out of eight settled in the North. The movement of twice as many whites leaving the South for the North as vice versa contributed to the South's defensive-aggressive political behavior.

➢ **Protectionism**

New Orleans the largest cotton exporting port for New England and Great Britain textile mills, shipping Mississippi River Valley goods from North, South and Border states.

Historically, southern slave-holding states, because of their low cost manual labor, had little perceived need for mechanization, and supported having the right to sell cotton and purchase manufactured goods from any nation. Northern states, which had heavily invested in their still-nascent manufacturing, could not compete with the full-fledged industries of Europe in offering high prices for cotton imported from the south and low prices for manufactured exports in return. For this reason, northern manufacturing interests supported tariffs and protectionism while southern planters demanded free trade.

The Democrats in Congress, controlled by Southerners, wrote the tariff laws in the 1830s,

1840s, and 1850s, and kept reducing rates so that the 1857 rates were the lowest since 1816. The South had no complaints but the low rates angered Northern industrialists and factory workers, especially in Pennsylvania, who demanded protection for their growing iron industry. The Whigs and Republicans complained because they favored high tariffs to stimulate industrial growth, and Republicans called for an increase in tariffs in the 1860 election. The increases were finally enacted in 1861 after Southerners resigned their seats in Congress.

Historians in the 1920s emphasized the tariff issue but since the 1950s they have minimized it, noting that few Southerners in 1860-1861 said it was of central importance to them. Some secessionist documents do mention the tariff issue, though not nearly as often as the preservation of slavery.

➢ **Slave Power and Free Soil**

Anti-slavery forces in the North identified the "Slave Power" as a direct threat to republican values. They argued that rich slave owners were using political power to take control of the Presidency, Congress and the Supreme Court, thus threatening the rights of the citizens of the North.

"Free soil" was a Northern demand that the new lands opening up in the west be available to independent yeoman farmers and not be bought out by rich slave owners who would buy up the best land and work it with slaves, forcing the white farmers onto marginal lands. This was the basis of the Free Soil Party of 1848, and a main theme of the Republican Party. Free Solders and Republicans demanded a homestead law that would give government land to settlers; it was defeated by Southerners who feared it would attract to the west European immigrants and poor Southern whites.

➢ **National Elections**

Beginning in the American Revolution and accelerating after the War of 1812, the people of the United States grew in their sense of country as an important example to the world of a national republic of political liberty and personal rights. Previous regional independence movements such as the Greek revolt in the Ottoman Empire, division and redivision in the Latin American political map, and the British-French Crimean triumph leading to an interest in redrawing Europe along cultural differences, all conspired to make for a time of upheaval and uncertainty about the basis of the nation-state. In the world of 19th century self-made Americans, growing in prosperity, population and expanding west, "freedom" could mean personal liberty or property rights. The unresolved difference would cause failure—first in their political institutions, then in their civil life together.

➢ **Nationalism and Honor**

Nationalism was a powerul force in the early 19th century, with famous spokesmen like Andrew Jackson and Daniel Webster. While practically all Northerners supported the Union, Southerners were split between those loyal to the entire United States (called "unionists") and those loyal primarily to the southern region and then the Confederacy. C. Vann Woodward said of the latter group, "A great slave society...had grown up and miraculously flourished in the heart of a thoroughly bourgeois and partly puritanical republic. It had renounced its bourgeois origins and elaborated and painfully rationalized its institutional, legal, metaphysical, and religious defenses...When the crisis came it chose to fight. It proved to be the death struggle of a society, which went down in ruins." Perceived insults to Southern collective honor included the enormous popularity of *Uncle Tom's Cabin* (1852) and the actions of abolitionist John Brown in trying to incite a slave rebellion in 1859.

While the South moved toward a Southern nationalism, leaders in the North were also becoming more nationally minded, and rejected any notion of splitting the Union. The Republican national electoral platform of 1860 warned that Republicans regarded disunion as treason and would not tolerate it: "We denounce those threats of disunion...as denying the vital principles of a free government, and as an avowal of contemplated treason, which it is the imperative duty of an indignant people sternly to rebuke and forever silence." The South ignored the warnings: Southerners did not realize how ardently the North would fight to hold the Union together.

➢ **Lincoln's Election**

The election of Lincoln in November 1860 was the final trigger for secession. Efforts at compromise, including the *Corwin Amendment* and the *Crittenden Compromise*, failed. Southern leaders feared that Lincoln would stop the expansion of slavery and put it on a course toward extinction. The slave states, which had already become a minority in the House of Representatives, were now facing a future as a perpetual minority in the Senate and Electoral College against an increasingly powerful North. Before Lincoln took office in March 1861, seven slave states had declared their secession and joined to form the Confederacy.

➢ **Beginning the War**

Lincoln's victory in the presidential election of 1860 triggered South Carolina's declaration of secession from the Union in December, and provisional Confederate States of America followed in February. A pre-war February Peace Conference of 1861 met in Washington, Lincoln sneaking into town to stay in the Conference's hotel its last three days. The attempt failed at resolving the crisis, but the remaining eight slave states rejected pleas to join the Confederacy following a two-to-one no-vote in Virginia's First Secessionist Convention on April 4, 1861.

➢ **The War**

The Civil War was a contest marked by the ferocity and frequency of battle. Over four years, 237 named battles were fought, and many more minor actions and skirmishes. In the scales of world military history, both sides fighting were characterized by their bitter intensity and high casualties. "The American Civil War was to prove one of the most ferocious wars ever fought". Without geographic objectives, the only target for each side was the enemy's soldier.

➢ **End of War**

Conquest of Virginia

At the beginning of 1864, Lincoln made Grant commander of all Union armies. Grant made his headquarters with the Army of the Potomac, and put Major General William Tecumseh

Sherman in command of most of the western armies. Grant understood the concept of total war and believed, along with Lincoln and Sherman, that only the utter defeat of Confederate forces and their economic base would end the war. This was total war not in terms of killing civilians but rather in terms of destroying homes, farms, and railroads. Grant devised a coordinated strategy that would strike at the entire Confederacy from multiple directions. Generals George Meade and Benjamin Butler were ordered to move against Lee near Richmond, General Franz Sigel (and later Philip Sheridan) were to attack the Shenandoah Valley, General Sherman was to capture Atlanta and march to the sea (the Atlantic Ocean), Generals George Crook and William W. Averell were to operate against railroad supply lines in West Virginia, and Major General Nathaniel P. Banks was to capture Mobile, Alabama.

Union forces in the East attempted to maneuver past Lee and fought several battles during that phase ("Grant's Overland Campaign") of the Eastern campaign. Grant's battles of attrition at the Wilderness, Spotsylvania, and Cold Harbor resulted in heavy Union losses, but forced Lee's Confederates to fall back repeatedly. An attempt to outflank Lee from the south failed under Butler, who was trapped inside the Bermuda Hundred river bend. Grant was tenacious and, despite astonishing losses (over 65,000 casualties in seven weeks), kept pressing Lee's Army of Northern Virginia back to Richmond. He pinned down the Confederate army in the Siege of Petersburg, where the two armies engaged in trench warfare for over nine months.

Grant finally found a **commander**, General Philip Sheridan, aggressive enough to prevail in the Valley Campaigns of 1864. Sheridan was initially repelled at the Battle of New Market by former U.S. Vice President and Confederate Gen. John C. Breckinridge. The Battle of New Market would prove to be the Confederacy's last major victory of the war. After redoubling his efforts, Sheridan defeated Major General Jubal A. Early in a series of battles, including a final decisive defeat at the Battle of Cedar Creek. Sheridan then proceeded to destroy the agricultural base of the Shenandoah Valley, a strategy similar to the tactics Sherman later employed in Georgia.

These dead are from Ewell's May 1864 attack at Spotsylvania, delaying Grant's advance on Richmond in the Wilderness

The Peacemakers on the River Queen, March 1865. Sherman, Grant, Lincoln, and Porter pictured discussing plans for the last weeks of the Civil War

Meanwhile, Sherman maneuvered from Chattanooga to Atlanta, defeating Confederate Generals Joseph E. Johnston and John Bell Hood along the way. The fall of Atlanta on September 2, 1864, guaranteed the reelection of Lincoln as president. Hood left the Atlanta area to swing around and **menace** Sherman's supply lines and invade Tennessee in the Franklin-Nashville Campaign. Union Major General John Schofield defeated Hood at the Battle of Franklin, and George H. Thomas dealt Hood a massive defeat at the Battle of Nashville, effectively destroying Hood's army.

Leaving Atlanta, and his base of supplies, Sherman's army marched with an unknown destination, laying waste to about 20% of the farms in Georgia in his "March to the Sea". He reached the Atlantic Ocean at Savannah, Georgia in December 1864. Sherman's army was followed by thousands of freed slaves; there were no major battles along the March. Sherman turned north through South Carolina and North Carolina to approach the Confederate Virginia lines from the south, increasing the pressure on Lee's army.

Lee's army, thinned by desertion and casualties, was now much smaller than Grant's. Union forces won a decisive victory at the Battle of Five Forks on April 1, forcing Lee to evacuate Petersburg and Richmond. The Confederate capital fell to the Union XXV Corps, composed of black troops. The remaining Confederate units fled west and after a defeat at Sayler's Creek, it became clear to Robert E. Lee that continued fighting against the United States was both tactically and logistically impossible.

➢ **150th Anniversary**

The year 2011 included the American Civil War's 150th anniversary. Many in the South attempted to incorporate both black history and white perspectives. A Harris Poll given in March 2011 suggested that Americans were still uniquely divided over the results and appropriate memorials to acknowledge the occasion. While traditionally American films of the Civil War feature "brother versus brother" themes film treatments of the war are evolving to include African American characters. Benard Simelton, president of the Alabama NAACP, said celebrating the Civil War is like celebrating the "Holocaust". In reference to slavery, Simelton said that black "rights were taken away" and that blacks "were treated as less than human beings". National Park historian Bob Sutton said that slavery was the "principal cause" of the war. Sutton also claimed that the issue of state rights was incorporated by the Confederacy as a justification for the War in order to get recognition from Britain. Sutton went on to mention that during the 100th **anniversary** of the Civil War white southerners focused on the genius of southern generals, rather than slavery. In Virginia during the fall of 2010, a conference took place that addressed the slavery issue. During November 2010, black Civil War **reenactors** from around the country participated in a **parade** at Harrisburg, Pennsylvania.

(length: 3,117 words)

Vocabulary

abolish	v. 废除	abolitionist	n. 废奴主义者

administration	n. 管理，行政	mobilization	n. 动员，调动
anniversary	n. 周年纪念日	parade	n./v. 游行
complementary	a. 补充的	propaganda	n. 宣传
confederate	n. 同盟者	reconstruction	n. 再建，复兴
counterargument	n. 抗辩	reenactor	n. 重演者
commander	n. 指挥官	revolt	n./v. 造反，起义
hostility	n. 战争，敌意	secession	n. 脱离，分离
initiate	n./v. 开始	sentiment	n. 感情，情绪
menace	n./v. 威胁，恐吓	slavery	n. 奴隶，奴隶制度

□ Passage 2 Knight

A **knight** is a person granted an honorary title of knighthood by a **monarch** or other political leader for service to the monarch or country, especially in a military capacity. Historically, in Europe, knighthood has been conferred upon mounted warriors. During the High Middle Ages, knighthood was considered a class of lower nobility. By the Late Middle Ages, the rank had become associated with the ideals of chivalry, a code of conduct for the perfect courtly Christian warrior. Since the Early Modern period, the title of knight is purely honorific, usually bestowed by a monarch, as in the British honours system, often for non-military service to the country.

Historically, the ideals of **chivalry** were popularized in medieval literature, especially the Matter of Britain and Matter of France, the former based on Geoffrey of Monmouth's *Historia Regum Britanniae* ("History of the Kings of Britain"), written in the 1130s. Sir Thomas Malory's *Le Morte d'Arthur* ("The Death of Arthur"), written in 1485, was important in defining the ideal of chivalry which is essential to the modern concept of the knight as an elite warrior sworn to uphold the values of faith, loyalty, courage, and honour. During the Renaissance, the genre of chivalric romance became popular in literature, growing ever more idealistic and eventually giving rise to a new form of realism in literature popularised by Miguel de Cervantes' *Don Quixote*. This novel explored the ideals of knighthood and their incongruity with the reality of Cervantes' world. In the late medieval period, new methods of warfare began to **render** classical knights in **armour** obsolete, but the titles remained in many nations.

Some orders of knighthood, such as the Knights Templar, have become the subject of legend; others have disappeared into obscurity. Today, a number of orders of knighthood continue to exist in several countries, such as the English Order of the Garter, the Swedish Royal Order of the Seraphim, and the Royal Norwegian Order of St. Olav. Each of these orders has its own criteria for eligibility, but knighthood is generally granted by a head of state to selected persons to recognise some meritorious achievement.

Knighthood in the Middle Ages was closely linked with horsemanship (and especially the joust) from its origins in the 12th century until its final flowering as a fashion among the high nobility in the Duchy of Burgundy in the 15th century. This linkage is reflected in the etymology of "chivalry", "cavalier" and related terms (see Etymology section below). The special prestige given to mounted warriors finds a parallel in the "furusiyya" in the Muslim world, and the Greek "hippeus" and the Roman "eques" of Classical Antiquity.

➢ Etymology

The word "knight", from Old English "cniht" (boy or servant), is a cognate of the German word "Knecht" (servant, bondsman). This meaning, of unknown origin, is common among West Germanic languages (origin: Old Frisian "kniucht", Dutch "knecht", Danish "knægt", Swedish "knekt", Norwegian "knekt", Middle High German "kneht", all meaning "boy, youth, lad", as well as German "Knecht" meaning "servant, bondsman, vassal"). Anglo-Saxon "cniht" had no particular connection to horsemanship, referring to any servant. A "rādcniht" (meaning "riding-servant") was a servant delivering messages or patrolling coastlines on horseback. Old English "cnihthād" (knighthood) had the meaning of adolescence (i.e. the period between childhood and manhood) by 1300.

A narrowing of the **generic** meaning "servant" to "military follower of a king or other superior" is visible by 1100. The specific military sense of a knight being a mounted warrior in the heavy cavalry emerges only in the Hundred Years' War. The verb "to knight" (i.e. to make someone a knight) appears around 1300, and from the same time, the word "knighthood" shifted from "adolescence" to "rank or dignity of a knight".

In this respect English differs from most other European languages, where the **equivalent** word emphasizes the status and prosperity of war horse ownership. Linguistically, the association of horse ownership with social status extends back at least as far as ancient Greece, where many aristocratic names incorporated the Greek word for "horse", like Hipparchus and Xanthippe; the character Pheidippides in Aristophanes' *Clouds* has his grandfather's name with "hipp" inserted to sound more aristocratic. Similarly, the Greek "ἱππεύς" (hippeus) is commonly translated "knight"; at least in its sense of the highest of the four Athenian social classes, those who could afford to maintain a warhorse in the state service.

An Equestrian (Latin, from eques "horseman", from equus "horse") was a member of the second highest social class in the Roman Republic and early Roman Empire. This class is often translated as "knight"; the medieval knight, however, was called "miles" in Latin, (which in classical Latin meant "soldier", normally infantry). Both Greek "hippos" and Latin "equus" are derived from the Proto-Indo-European word root "ekwo" meaning "horse".

A Norman knight slaying Harold Godwinson (Bayeux tapestry, ca. 1070). The rank of knight developed in the 12th century from the mounted warriors of the 10th and 11th centuries.

In the later Roman Empire the classical Latin word for horse, "equus" was replaced in common parlance by vulgar Latin "caballus", sometimes thought to derive from Gaulish "caballos". From "caballus" arose terms in the various Romance languages cognate to the (French-derived) English "cavalier": Old Italian cavaliere, Italian cavallo, Spanish caballero, French chevalier, Portuguese cavaleiro, Romanian cavaler. The Germanic languages feature terms cognate to the English "rider": German Ritter, and Dutch and Scandinavian ridder. These words are cognates derived from Germanic "rīdan" meaning "to ride", derived from the Proto-Indo-European root "reidh".

➢ Origins of Medieval Knighthood

In Ancient Rome there was a knightly class "Ordo Equestris" (order of mounted nobles) from which European knighthood may have been derived.

Tournament from the Codex Manesse, depicting the mêlée.

Knighthood as known in Europe was characterized by the combination of two elements, feudalism and service as a mounted warrior. Both arose under the reign of the Frankish emperor Charlemagne, from which the knighthood of the Middle Ages can be seen to have had its genesis.

Some **portions** of the armies of Germanic peoples who occupied Europe from the 3rd century CE, had always been mounted, and some armies, such as those of the Ostrogoths, comprised mainly cavalry. However it was the Franks who came to dominate Western and Central Europe after the fall of Rome, and they generally fielded armies composed of large masses of infantry, with an infantry elite, the comitatus, which often rode to battle on horseback rather than marching on foot. Riding to battle had two key advantages: it reduced fatigue, particularly when the elite soldiers wore armour (as was increasingly the case in the centuries after the fall of the Western Roman empire); and it gave the soldiers more mobility to react to the raids of the enemy, particularly the Muslim invasions which reached Europe in 711. So it was that the armies of the Frankish ruler and warlord Charles Martel, which defeated the Umayyad Arab invasion at the Battle of Tours in 732, were still largely **infantry** armies, the elites riding to battle but dismounting to fight, providing a hard core for the levy of the infantry warbands.

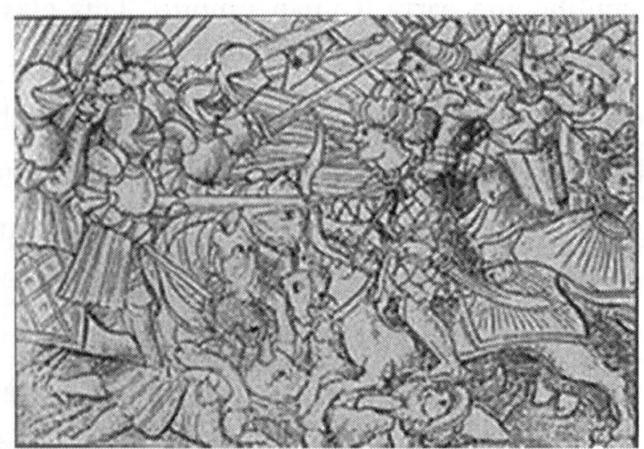

The battle between the Turks and Christian knights during the Ottoman wars in Europe

As the 8th century progressed into the Carolingian Age, the Franks were generally on the attack, and larger numbers of warriors took to their horses to ride with the Emperor in his wide-ranging campaigns of conquest. At about this time the Franks increasingly remained on horseback to fight on the battlefield as true cavalry rather than as mounted infantry, and would continue to do so for centuries thereafter. Although in some nations the knight returned to foot **combat** in the 14th century, the association of the knight with mounted combat with a spear, and later a lance, remained a strong one.

In the Early Medieval period any well-equipped horseman could be described as a "knight", or "miles" in Latin. In the course of the 12th century knighthood became a social rank with a distinction being made between "milites gregarii" (non-noble cavalrymen) and "milites nobiles" (true knights). As the term "knight" became increasingly confined to denoting a social rank the military role of fully armoured cavalryman gained a separate term, "man-at-arms". Although any Medieval knight going to war would automatically serve as a man-at-arms, not all men-at-arms were knights.

Coats of arms of Schäferhoff family in Germany

The first military orders of knighthood were the Knights Hospitaller founded at the First Crusade of 1099, followed by the Knights Templar in 1119. At the time of their foundation, these were intended as monastic orders, whose members would act as simple soldiers protecting pilgrims. It was only over the following century, with the successful conquest of the Holy Land and the rise of the crusader states, that these orders became powerful and prestigious.

The ideal of chivalry as the ethos of the Christian warrior, and the transmutation of the term "knight" from the meaning "servant, soldier", and of "chevalier" meaning "mounted soldier", to refer to a member of this ideal class, is significantly influenced by the Crusades, on one hand inspired by the military orders of monastic warriors, as seen retrospectively from the point of view of the beginning Late Middle Ages, and on the other hand influenced by Islamic (Saracen) ideals of furusiyya.

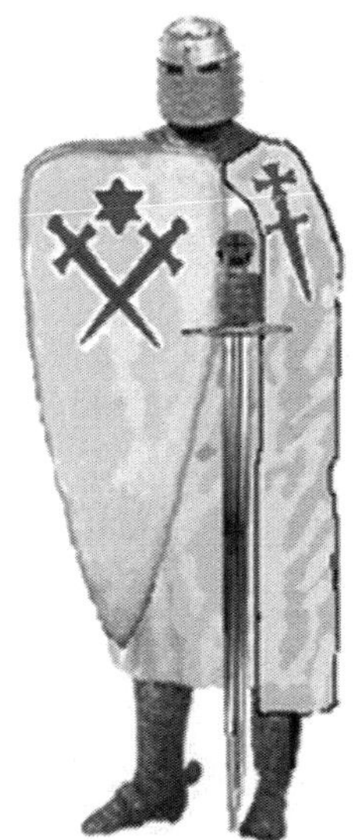

The knight of The Livonian Brothers of the Sword

Maximilian Ⅰ, Holy Roman Emperor (1459–1519) is often referred to as the last true knight. He was the last emperor to lead his troops onto the battlefield.

➢ Heraldry and Other Attributes

Knights are generally armigerous (bearing a coat of arms), and indeed they played an essential role in the development of heraldry. As heavier armour, including enlarged shields and enclosed helmets, developed in the Middle Ages, the need for marks of identification arose, and with coloured shields and surcoats, coat armory was born. Armorial rolls were created to record the knights of various regions or those who participated in various tournaments.

Additionally, knights adopted certain forms of regalia which became closely associated with the status of knighthood. At the Battle of Crécy (1346), Edward Ⅲ of England sent his son, Edward, the Black Prince, to lead the charge into battle and when pressed to send reinforcements, the king replied, "say to them that they suffer him this day to win his spurs". Clearly, by this time, spurs had already become emblematic of knighthood. The livery collar is also specifically associated with knighthood.

➢ **Types of Knighthood**

Military-monastic orders of knighthood

- Knights Hospitaller, founded during the First Crusade in 1099
- Order of Saint Lazarus established in about 1100
- Knights Templar, founded in 1118, and disbanded in 1307
- Teutonic Knights, established in about 1190, and ruled the Monastic State of the Teutonic Knights in Prussia until 1525

Other orders were established in the Iberian peninsula, under the influence of the orders in the Holy Land and the Crusader movement of the Reconquista:

- the Order of Aviz, established in Aviz in 1143
- the Order of Alcántara, established in Alcántara in 1156
- the Order of Calatrava, established in Calatrava in 1158
- the Order of Santiago, established in Santiago in 1164

➢ **Chivalric orders**

After the Crusades, the military orders became idealized and romanticized, resulting in the late medieval notion of chivalry, as reflected in the Arthurian romances of the time. The creation of chivalric orders was fashionable among the nobility in the 14th and 15th centuries, and this is still reflected in contemporary honours systems, including the term order itself. Examples of notable orders of chivalry are:

- the Order of Saint George, founded by Charles Ⅰ of Hungary in 1325
- the Order of the Most Holy Annunciation, founded by count Amadeus Ⅵ in 1346
- the Order of the Garter, founded by Edward Ⅲ of England around 1348
- the Order of the Dragon, founded by King Sigismund of Luxemburg in 1408
- the Order of the Golden Fleece, founded by Philip Ⅲ, Duke of Burgundy in 1430
- the Order of Saint Michael, founded by Louis Ⅺ of France in 1469
- the Order of the Thistle, founded by King James Ⅶ of Scotland (also known as James Ⅱ of England) in 1687
- the Order of the Elephant, which may have been first founded by Christian Ⅰ of Denmark, but was founded in its current form by King Christian Ⅴ in 1693
- the Order of the Bath, founded by George Ⅰ in 1725

➢ **Honorific orders of knighthood**

From roughly 1560, purely honorific orders were established, as a way to confer prestige and distinction, unrelated to military service and chivalry in the more narrow sense. Such orders were particularly popular in the 17th and 18th centuries, and knighthood continues to be conferred in various countries:

- The United Kingdom with British honours system and some Commonwealth of Nations countries
- Some European countries, such as The Netherlands

There are other monarchies and also republics that also follow this practice. Modern knighthoods are typically awarded in recognition for services rendered to society: services which are not necessarily martial in nature. The British musician Elton John, for example, is a Knight Bachelor, thus entitled to be called Sir Elton. The female equivalent is a "Dame".

In the British honor system, the knightly style of "Sir" is accompanied by the given name, and optionally the surname. So, Elton John may be called "Sir Elton" or "Sir Elton John", but never "Sir John". Similarly, actress Judi Dench DBE may be addressed as "Dame Judi" or "Dame Judi Dench", but never "Dame Dench".

Wives of knights, however, are entitled to the honorific "Lady" before their husband's surname. Thus Sir Paul McCartney's ex-wife was formally styled "Lady McCartney" (rather than "Lady Paul McCartney" or "Lady Heather McCartney"). The style "Dame Heather McCartney" could be used for the wife of a knight; however, this style is largely archaic and is only used in the most formal of documents, or where the wife is a Dame in her own right (such as Dame Norma Major, who gained her title six years before her husband Sir John Major was knighted). The husbands of Dames have no honorific, so Dame Norma's husband remained John Major until he received his own knighthood.

Since the reign of Edward Ⅶ a clerk in holy orders in the Church of England has not normally received the accolade on being appointed to a degree of knighthood. He receives the insignia of his honour and may place the appropriate letters after his name or title but he may not be called Sir and his wife may not be called Lady. This custom is not observed in Australia and New Zealand, where knighted Anglican clergymen routinely use the title "Sir". Ministers of other Christian Churches are entitled to receive the accolade. For example, His Eminence Sir Norman Cardinal Gilroy did receive the accolade on his appointment as Knight Commander of the Most Excellent Order of the British Empire in 1969. A knight who is subsequently ordained does not lose his title. A famous example of this situation was the Revd. Sir Derek Pattinson, who was ordained just a year after he was appointed Knight Bachelor, apparently somewhat to the consternation of officials at Buckingham Palace. A woman clerk in holy orders may be appointed a Dame in exactly the same way as any other woman since there are no military connotations attached to the honour. A clerk in holy orders who is a baronet is entitled to use the title Sir.

➢ **Hereditary Knighthoods**

In continental Europe different systems of hereditary knighthood have existed or do exist. "Ridder", Dutch for "knight", is a hereditary noble title in the Netherlands and Belgium. It is the lowest title within the nobility system and ranks below that of "Baron" but above "Jonkheer"

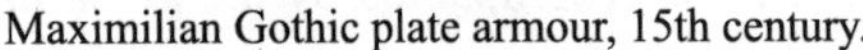

Maximilian Gothic plate armour, 15th century.

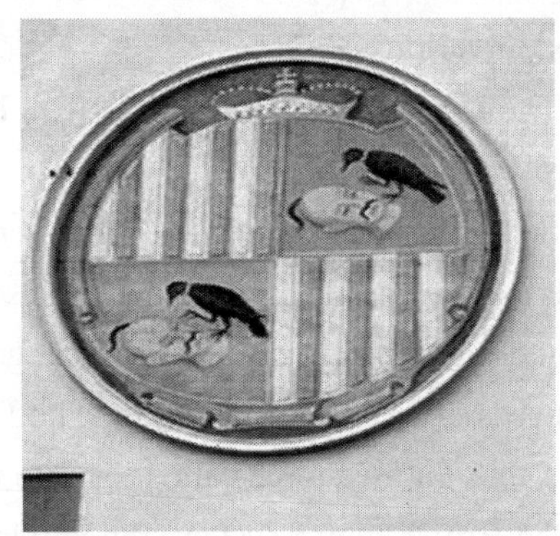

Coat of arms of the House of Schwarzenberg: a raven gnawing at Turkish heads.

(the latter is not a title, but a Dutch honorific to show that someone belongs to the untitled nobility). The collective term for its holders in a certain locality is the Ridderschap (e.g. Ridderschap van Holland, Ridderschap van Friesland, etc.). In the Netherlands and Belgium no female equivalent exists. Before 1814, the history of nobility is separate for each of the eleven provinces that make up the Kingdom of the Netherlands. In each of these, there were in the early Middle Ages a number of feudal lords who often were just as powerful, and sometimes more so than the rulers themselves. In old times, no other title existed but that of knight. In the Netherlands only 10 knightly families are still alive, a number which steadily decreases because in this country ennoblement or incorporation into the nobility is not possible anymore. Instead, Belgium, which still has a vibrant culture of ennoblement, does have 232 registered knightly families.

The German and Austrian equivalent of an hereditary knight is a "Ritter". This designation is used as a title of nobility in all German-speaking areas. Traditionally it denotes the second lowest rank within the nobility, standing above "Edler" and below "Freiherr". For its historical association with warfare and the landed gentry in the Middle Ages, it can be considered roughly equal to the titles of "Knight" or "Baronet".

France, Italy, and Poland also had the hereditary knighthood that existed within the nobility system.

(length: 3,277 words)

Vocabulary

chivalry	n. 骑士精神	knight	n. 骑士
combat	v. 与..战斗	monarch	n. 君主，帝王
equivalent	a. 等价的	peerage	n. 贵族
generic	a. 一般的，类的	portion	n. 部分
hereditary	a. 遗传的	render	v. 补偿
infantry	n. 步兵		

Section D Word Bank for This Unit

苏格兰	Scotland
威尔士	Wales
议会（英国国会）	Parliament
统一	unification
最初的	original
子孙	descendant
证实	confirm
给……荣誉	honor
永久的	permanent
殖民地	colony
大西洋	Atlantic Ocean
残余，剩余	remnant
救世主	the Saviour
印第安人	Indian
伽利略	Galileo
中世纪	Medieval Period
哥伦布	Christopher Columbus
商业革命	Commercial Revolution
殖民主义	colonialism
奴隶贸易	slave trade
文艺复兴	Renaissance
人文主义	humanism
莎士比亚	William Shakespeare
宗教改革	the Reformation
马丁·路德	Martin Luther
英国国王亨利八世	Henry Ⅷ
圈地运动	enclosure movement
都铎王朝	house of Tudor
斯图亚特王朝	house of Stuart
詹姆士一世	James Ⅰ
查理一世	Charles Ⅰ
英国国教	the Anglican Church
清教徒	puritan
克伦威尔	Oliver Cromwell
护国公	Lord Protector
查理二世	Charles Ⅱ
詹姆士二世	James Ⅱ
辉格党	Whig
托利党	Tory
光荣革命	Glorious Revolution
《权利法案》	Bill of Rights
君主立宪制	Constitutional Monarchy
波旁王朝	house of Bourbon
路易十四	Louis XIV
彼得大帝	Peter the Great
英国东印度公司	British East India Company
《航海条例》	Navigation Acts
七年战争	Seven Years' War
启蒙运动	enlightenment
路易十六	Louis XVI
三级会议	the Estate-General
国民议会	National Assembly
《独立宣言》	Declaration of Independence
亚伯拉罕·林肯	Abraham Lincoln
美国内战	the America Civil War

Chapter 3 Economy

美国是当今世界头号经济强国，对全球经济起着主导作用。同时，它也是世界的金融中心。纽约的华尔街，一条街的波动可以影响世界，足见美国经济在世界经济中所占的分量。高度发达的美国经济，使世界各地许多国家与美元挂钩，美国的证券市场行情也成了世界经济行情的晴雨表。

现代的英国经济繁荣，是西欧最大的资本主义经济体之一。19 世纪曾经的“日不落帝国”，虽在美国经济独领风骚、亚洲国家雄起的局势下，其在世界经济发展中的地位受到了强烈的冲击，但作为传统的经济工业强国，在世界经济发展的进程中仍然发挥着重要的作用。

2008 年华尔街金融危机以来，这些引擎全球经济的经济体，几乎是全体动力不足。美国被财政悬崖所累，欧洲也尚未走出危机泥潭。各国的经济缘何如此，目前的经济困难对社会的影响又有哪些，它们的未来又在哪里？希望通过以下的阅读材料能够窥一斑而见全豹。

Section A Intensive Reading

What the U.S. Debt Problem Means for the Global Economy

by Michael Schuman

Since the time of the Founding Fathers, U.S. leaders have believed in the concept of American **exceptionalism**, that the U.S. is a special country with a special mission. It is a notion that continues to this day. And when it comes to the threat its **deteriorating** national finances present to the world economy, the U.S. is truly exceptional. That danger was finally made clear by Standard & Poor's (S&P) on Monday, which changed the outlook on its U.S. **sovereign** rating to negative—in other words, the S&P is threatening to **downgrade** the U.S. from its traditional triple-A status. The implications of this move are incredibly far-reaching. No, it doesn't mean the U.S. is on the verge of a **debt crisis**. But it does mean the world can't act like an elephant isn't in the room. We've seen a debt crisis grip Europe and worries mount over the financial state of

Japan. Those problems are scary enough. But when it comes to terrifying debt-crisis **scenarios**, the U.S. stands in a universe all its own.

That's not because the U.S. debt burden is the biggest—Japan's government debt is more than twice as large, relative to its GDP—but because of the exceptional role the U.S. plays in the global economy. A debt crisis in Portugal could send ripples of uncertainty through world financial markets, and if a larger country like Spain fell into crisis, those ripples could prove mighty **destabilizing**. But U.S. debt runs the risk of crashing the entire operating system of the global economy. Here's what I mean:

Not only is the U.S. the world's largest economy—by far—but it also dominates the global monetary system. In many respects, the entire **architecture** of global finance is built upon the U.S. economy. Its **capital** markets are the most liquid. The dollar is the world's No. 1 **reserve currency** and the primary one used in foreign exchange transactions and trade. Countries like China and Japan have their national wealth stored to a great degree in U.S. debt. When investors get nervous, they rush to U.S. dollar-based assets, and especially U.S. debt. The perception has always been that the U.S. is the ultimate safe **haven**. Even as its financial condition sickens, that perception remains. Despite a dramatic increase in U.S. **deficits** and debt in recent years, the country has still been able to borrow at exceptionally low rates. In other words, the U.S. has benefited tremendously from its economic exceptionalism.

Now let's **speculate** on what would happen if that perception fundamentally changed. U.S. **Treasury securities** would be seen as riskier and would therefore become less attractive. **Interest rates** would rise in the U.S. as a result, not only making it harder for the government to finance budget deficits and debt, but also raising borrowing costs across the economy, and slowing investment and consumption. The U.S. dollar would weaken, **undermining** the value of currency reserves around the world and speeding us along to the day when the dollar is no longer the world's premier currency. All that would be destabilizing enough. It would likely mean slower growth in the world's largest economy, deteriorating living standards for Americans, and thus slower growth for the entire world economy.

But the bigger problem would be, what would take America's place? The U.S. is the standard by which risk is **assessed** in financial markets. If the U.S. isn't a safe haven, then what is? And what country's currency and capital markets are deep enough to accommodate the world's wealth if America's can't? Here's how Mohamed El-Erian, chief executive at PIMCO, put it on a blog post on the *Financial Times* website on Tuesday:

The world looks to America for a range of "global public goods" —including the reserve currency, the deepest and most liquid government debt markets, and the "risk free" standard. With no other country able and willing to step into this role, the result would be global efficiency losses and a higher risk of economic and financial **fragmentation**... The time has come for the US (and other advanced economies) to take better control of its **fiscal** destiny—for the sake of American society and for the well being of the global economy.

Even though America's exceptional role in the world economy makes its debt situation exceptionally dangerous, that role also apparently gives the U.S. exceptional protection as well. In theory, the S&P warning is a signal that the U.S. is not exceptional, that if it doesn't get its financial house in order, it will face downgrades just like those of Greece, Spain, and Japan. But the markets told us something very different. Treasurys weakened immediately after the announcement, a sign that investors were selling them, but then quickly recovered their strength. What's that, you say? Yes, rather than scaring investors away from U.S. debt, investors actually bought U.S. debt after the S&P warning. And the reaction from some major U.S. **bondholders** showed little concern about America's financial standing. "We continue to believe that U.S. Treasurys are an attractive product for us," Japanese Finance Minister Yoshihiko Noda told reporters.

Sound crazy? Not really. The world has a lot at stake in the continued stability of the American economy, and thus every **incentive** to keep U.S. debt from roiling the world economy. This gets us back to the exceptional position of the U.S. in world finance. With nothing to replace the U.S., the country is getting exceptional treatment from the global economy.

It seems to me that U.S. policymakers have been banking (perhaps subconsciously) on this very outcome—that the U.S. is simply too exceptional to face dangers other nations could never avoid. They've been acting this way. The U.S. is the only heavily indebted developed economy that doesn't have a credible plan to control deficits and debt. (Japan doesn't either, but because of the need to soften the blow from last month's devastating earthquake, we'll give Tokyo a pass here.) In other words, the U.S. is counting on being like AIG or GM and acting as if it is too big to fail.

Is that true? American exceptionalism will give Washington an exceptional opportunity to fix its financial mess without suffering the consequences of other debt-heavy nations. But what if the U.S. fails to grasp the opportunity? Can the U.S. and the world economy escape the **fallout**? Now that would be truly exceptional.

Vocabulary

architecture	n. 体系机构
assess	v. 估定，评定
at stake	phr. 在危险中；处于成败关头
bondholder	n. 债券持有人
capital	n. 资本，资金
debt crisis	phr. 债务危机
deficit	n. 赤字，生意亏损
destabilizing	a. 动摇的，动荡的，不稳定的
deteriorate	v. 变坏，退化，堕落
downgrade	v. 降低，贬低
exceptionalism	n. 例外论
fallout	n. 副作用或附带结果
fiscal	a. 财政的，国库的，国库岁入的
fragmentation	n. 分裂，破碎
haven	n. 港口，避难所
incentive	n. 刺激；诱因；动机
interest rate	phr. 利率
reserve currency	phr. 储备货币
scenario	n. 预料或期望的一系列事件的梗概或模式
sovereign	a. 至高无上的，君主的，完全的 n. 君主，统治
speculate	v. 推测，思索
Treasury securities	phr. 国库证券
undermine	v. 逐渐损坏；暗中破坏

Exercises

I. Comprehension

1. Recall

What is the situation of American economy now?

2. Understand

How would you explain "an elephant isn't in the room" in the first paragraph?

3. Analyze

Analyze what benefit America has received from its economic exceptionalism.

4. Evaluate

Prepare a case to present your view about the concept of American exceptionalism.

II. Further Study

1. Can you imagine what might happen when the U.S. is not the ultimate safe haven?
2. Do you think American debt problem is a good thing or bad thing for China?

Section B Extensive Reading

Why Economic Inequality Leads to Collapse

by Stewart Lansley

During the past 30 years, a growing share of the global economic pie has been taken by the world's wealthiest people. In the UK and the US, the share of national income going to the top 1% has doubled, setting workforces adrift from economic progress. Today, the world's 1,200 billionaires hold economic firepower that is equivalent to a third of the size of the American economy.

It is this concentration of income—at levels not seen since the 1920s—that is the real cause of the present crisis.

In the UK, the upward transfer of income from wage earners to business and the mega-wealthy amounts to the equivalent of 7% of the economy. UK wage-earners have around £100bn—roughly equivalent to the size of the nation's health budget—less in their pockets today than if the cake were shared as it was in the late 1970s.

In the US, the sum stands at £500bn. There a typical worker would be more than £3,000 better off if the distribution of output between wages and profits had been held at its 1979 level. In the UK, they would earn almost £2,000 more.

The effect of this **consolidation** of economic power is that the two most effective routes out of the crisis have been closed. First, **consumer demand**—the oxygen that makes economies work—has been **choked off**. Rich economies have lost billions of pounds of **spending power**. Secondly, the **slump** in demand might be less damaging if the winners from the process of upward **redistribution**—big business and the top 1%—were playing a more productive role in helping recovery. They are not.

Britain's richest 1,000 have accumulated fortunes that are collectively worth £250bn more than a decade ago. The biggest global corporations are also sitting on near-record levels of cash. In the UK, such corporate **surpluses** stand at over £60bn, around 5% of the size of the economy. This money could be used to **kickstart** growth. Yet it is mostly standing idle. The result is **paralysis**.

The economic **orthodoxy** of the past 30 years holds that a stiff dose of inequality brings more efficient and faster-growing economies. It was a theory that captured the New Labour leadership—as long as tackling poverty was made a priority, then the rich should be allowed to flourish.

So have the architects of market capitalism been proved right? The evidence says no. The wealth gap has soared, but without wider economic progress. Since 1980, UK growth and productivity rates have been a third lower and unemployment five times higher than in the postwar era of "regulated capitalism". The three post-1980 recessions has been deeper and longer than those of the 1950s and 1960s, **culminating** in the crisis of the last four years.

The main outcome of the post-1980 experiment has been an economy that is much more **polarized** and much more prone to crisis. History shows a clear link between inequality and instability. The two most damaging crises of the last century—the Great Depression of the 1930s and the Great Crash of 2008—were both **preceded** by sharp rises in inequality.

The factor linking excessive levels of inequality and economic crisis is to be found in the relationship between wages and productivity. For the two-and-a-half decades from 1945, wages and productivity moved broadly in line across richer nations, with the proceeds of rising prosperity evenly shared. This was also a period of sustained economic stability.

Then there have been two periods when wages have seriously lagged behind productivity—in the 1920s and the post-1980s. Both of them culminate in prolonged slumps. Between 1990 and 2007, real wages in the UK rose more slowly than productivity, and at a worsening rate. In the US, the decoupling started earlier and has led to an even larger gap.

The significance of a growing "wage-productivity gap" is that it upsets the natural mechanisms necessary to achieve economic balance. Purchasing power shrinks and consumer societies suddenly lack the capacity to consume.

In both the 1920s and the post-1980s, to prevent economies seizing up, the demand gap was filled by an explosion of private debt. But pumping in debt didn't prevent recession: it merely delayed it.

Concentrating the proceeds of growth in the hands of a small global financial elite not only brings mass **deflation**—it also leads to asset bubbles. In 1920s America, a rapid process of enrichment at the top merely fed years of **speculative** activity in property and the stock market.

In the build-up to 2008, rising corporate surpluses and **burgeoning** personal wealth led to a giant mountain of **footloose** global capital. The cash sums held by the world's rich (those with cash of more than $ 1m) doubled in the decade to 2008 to a massive $ 39 trillion.

Only a tiny proportion of this sum ended up in productive investment. In the decade to 2007, bank lending for property development and takeover activity surged while the share going to UK manufacturing shrank. While the contribution to the economy made by financial services more than doubled over this period, manufacturing fell by a quarter.

Far from creating new wealth, a **tsunami** of "hot money" raced around the world in search of faster and faster returns, creating bubbles—in property, commodities and business—lowering economic **resilience** and amplifying the risk of financial breakdown.

New Labour's leaders were right in arguing that the left needed to have a more coherent policy for wealth creation. That is the route to wider prosperity for all. But the central lesson of the last 30 years is that a widening income gap and a more productive economy do not go hand in hand.

An economic model that allows the richest members of society to accumulate a larger and larger share of the cake will eventually self-destruct. It is a lesson that is yet to be learned.

(length: 1,004 words)

Vocabulary

burgeon	v. 萌芽
choke off	v. 把……闷死，勒死，绞死
consolidation	n. 巩固，合并
consumer demand	phr. 消费需要,消费者需求
culminate	v. 达到顶点
deflation	n. 通货紧缩，物价低廉(尤指成本不降低时的反常情形)
footloose	a. 自由自在的，到处走动的
kickstart	v. 启动
orthodoxy	n. 正统
paralysis	n. 瘫痪，停滞，麻痹
polarized	a. 极化的；偏振的
precede	v. 领先（于），在……之前
redistribution	n. 财产重新分配，再分配
resilience	n. 适应力，弹性
slump	n. 消沉，衰退，（物价）暴跌
speculative	a. 投机的
spending power	phr. 消费力
surplus	n. 剩余，过剩，[会计]盈余
tsunami	n. 海啸

Exercises

I. Comprehension

1. Recall

What is the real cause of the present economic crisis?

2. Explain

What are the effects of the concentration of income?

3. Exemplify

Could you give an example to show the link between economic crisis and economic inequality?

4. Analyze

How is the Great Crash of 2008 similar to the Great Depression of the 1930s?

5. Imagine

What are the possible ways of solving the problem of excessive inequality?

II. Further Study

What do you think of the idea "a stiff dose of inequality brings more efficient and faster-growing economies"?

Section C Supplementary Reading

□ Passage 1 With the UK Economy Stuck in a Groove, What Prospects for 2013?

The sales have started early this year, which means the economy is struggling. Photograph: Stefan Rousseau/PA

On the Saturday before Christmas the shop windows told their own story. Up to 50% off at Hobbs. **Discounts** of 60% at LK Bennett. Similar reductions at French Connection and the Gap. The sales started early this year and that means the economy is struggling. Fearful of being left with large amounts of unsold stock, retailers are slashing prices to attract **hard-up** consumers.

It was the same a year ago. Hopes of recovery have been **dashed** in 2012, a year in which the UK has gone nowhere fast. Interest rates, gross domestic product and house prices are where they were in January. The economy is not collapsing but it is not growing either. For the past two years it has gone sideways, and the expectation at the Bank of England and the Treasury is that 2013 will be little better.

Historically, it is extremely unusual for the economy to be stuck in a **groove** like the needle on a vinyl record. Subsistence economies can have long periods of low or zero growth but modern western economies traditionally do not. There is a **cyclical** pattern in which periods of slow growth gain **momentum**, ending in a boom-bust phase. A recession, normally relatively brief, removes the excess and allows the cycle to begin again. For the past century, this process has been **lubricated** by government action: interest rates are raised to stifle mounting inflationary pressure in the boom then cut in order to get growth and employment rising again during the downturn. Tax and spending policy has tended to operate in the same counter-cyclical fashion.

The crisis of the past five years can be divided into two distinct phases. What happened in the first phase was entirely predictable: the financial collapse of 2008 and the economic **slump** of 2009 followed **inexorably** from the asset price bubbles of the mid-2000s. It was a big collapse because there was a big bubble.

Less easy to explain is the crab-like performance subsequently. The UK economy has not really **budged** since the autumn of 2010, something that has not happened since the Second World War and probably for a long time before that. Other western economies have broadly followed the same pattern. The US has grown a bit faster than the UK and the Eurozone is already in a mild double-dip recession, but there has been the same sense of economic **torpor**. A third year of the same would be distinctly weird.

Could it happen? Yes, of course it could. In some ways, not a lot has changed since before the crisis. Real income growth is still weak, but is no longer being **supplemented** by large **dollops** of borrowing. Banks are still recognisably the same creatures they were in 2007 but are sitting on vast quantities of **underperforming** assets. Macro-economic policy has been aggressive enough and persistent enough to prevent a fresh slump of the sort seen four years ago but no more than that.

Expectations are already so low that there is a chance that 2013 will surprise on the upside. The passage of time together with policy action could finally work over the coming months, particularly if the Americans come to a budget deal and the Eurozone gets to grips with its debt crisis. There is plenty of spare capacity in the global economy and that, in normal circumstances, would point to several years of above-trend growth.

Recent US data has looked relatively **perky**. Rising housing starts indicate that the long real-estate recession is over. Investment is picking up and jobs are being created. Barack Obama's second term will be easier than his first.

Similarly, the worst for the Eurozone may now be over. To be sure, the economic numbers are still **dire** and **austerity** is still hurting, but the financial markets were impressed by Mario Draghi's (President of the European Central Bank) insistence that the European Central Bank would do whatever it took to safeguard the future of the single currency. The next 12 months are not going to be easy, but historians could well look back to Draghi's speech in London in July 2012 as the moment the corner was turned.

What then do we look out for in 2013? For the UK, the short-term threats are a triple-dip recession and a credit downgrade. The rating agencies have the UK in their sights and it won't take much more bad news for the AAA status to be removed.

George Osborne (Chancellor of Exchequer) will not have an easy year and in the budget will face the dilemma of whether to tighten policy further in the face of fresh fiscal slippage despite weak growth. Some analysts, such as Vicky Redwood at Capital Economics, believe the UK has more spare capacity than the Office for Budget Responsibility is estimating and that the size of the structural deficit is therefore not as big as feared. That means that the plans for budgetary tightening are too tough and could be relaxed. This would be sensible but it is unlikely to happen.

So where is growth going to come from in 2013? Not from the government, which has pledged no **let-up** in the austerity programme. Not from the consumer, who is seeing rising prices reduce the value of near-worthless pay rises. Perhaps from exports if the skies clear over the Eurozone and the US does not hurtle over the fiscal cliff; perhaps from investment if brightening export prospects persuade companies to spend some of the cash balances they have accumulated in recent years.

Don't bank on it, though. On past form, Europe will find a way of snatching defeat from the jaws of victory and the UK will continue to remain highly risk-averse. The Bank of England's Funding for Lending Scheme may help to increase the flow of credit and reduce its cost but Threadneedle Street is fighting two powerful **headwinds**.

The first is the inability of first-time buyers to get a foot on the housing ladder due to the combination of high prices and the big deposits demanded by lenders. The second is that real incomes continue to be squeezed. Capital's victory over labour since the late 1970s has come at a price: workers lack the purchasing power to buy the goods and services they are producing, and they are no longer willing or able to borrow the money to do so. Hence the high street early bargains. There will be more, it is fair to assume, in 2013.

(length:1,094 words)

Vocabulary

austerity	n. 严峻，严厉
budge	v. 挪动，微微移动
cyclical	a. 轮转的，循环的
dash	v. 破坏，毁坏；猛掷，猛击
dire	a. 可怕的；灾难的
discount	n. 折扣
dollop	n. 块，团
groove	n. 沟，槽
hard-up	a. 缺钱的，手头紧的
headwind	n. 逆风
inexorably	ad. 无情地，冷酷地
let-up	n. 停止；放松，减弱
lubricate	v. 润滑；加润滑油
momentum	n. 冲力，势头
perky	a. 自信的，得意洋洋的
slump	n. 消沉，衰退，（物价）暴跌
supplement	v. 补充 n. 补充，附录，增刊
torpor	n. 迟钝，麻木，无精打采
underperforming	a. 表现不佳的，工作不如预期（或同行）的

□ Passage 2 Fiscal Cliff Reality Check: What's Really the Worst Thing That Could Happen?

Who's afraid of the big, bad fiscal cliff? The obvious answer to that question is the White House, the Business Roundtable and the Federal Reserve—and really, not many others outside the Beltway.

Economists including Dean Baker and Paul Krugman say that going over the cliff will not be so bad, given that we have weeks, if not months, to repair any economic damage.

The Business Roundtable, which represents the CEOs of major US companies, counters that the fiscal cliff will hurt the meager economic progress we have made in the past year—and in fact, has hurt it already—and should be avoided at all costs.

In the middle of the debate are numerous numbers, statistics, **benchmarks** and calculations that have been hoisted in front of the public eye as proof—**indubitable** proof—that the fiscal cliff is destroying the economy.

It turns out, however, that many of those damning numbers that prove the evil of the fiscal cliff are not, actually, so damning. Don't get us wrong: going over the fiscal cliff is not good, and there is strong **consensus** that damage is surely to come. There's also no good reason for Congress's theatrical refusal to end a fight that they themselves picked.

In the interest of playing devil's advocates—and just plain old reality-checking—we look at a few benchmarks that are supposed to prove that the fiscal cliff is the worst thing that has ever happened to America. Still, truth is one thing and **hysteria** is another. Here is some context that the 10 Americans paying attention to the fiscal cliff might find handy.

➢ **The stock market and corporate America are suffering because of the fiscal cliff**

The stock market, as measured by the S&P 500, is up 17% overall this year, according to Barclays. If that's painful, there are plenty of investors willing to take more of it.

There is also the complaint that the S&P has been flat since the election. Many have blamed that on the fears of the fiscal cliff. David Kotok, with Cumberland Advisors, doesn't buy it. He blames the flatness in the S&P on the drop in the value of Apple stock. Apple accounts for about 4.9% of the S&P 500 index. That was great when Apple stock was rocketing upwards to $700 a share in September, but now Apple has been steadily and steeply falling in value since, and now trades at $512 a share. Kotok believes Apple's fall is what's causing the dip in the S&P. He points other S&P indexes that have risen since the election, and aren't weighed down by Apple: the MidCap 400 Index, the S&P 600 SmallCap Index, and Guggenheim's Equal Weight 500.

Another reason the stock market is not suffering (yet) is the strong impression that the market now expects Washington to be **incompetent**, and it certainly doesn't expect any kind of answer to the fiscal cliff until the last possible minute, if that. As such, most fiscal cliff **theatrics** are being met with stock-market yawns. Peter Tchir, of TF Market Advisors, noted to his clients Wednesday: "Two weeks ago, news that the president was returning early to work on cliff deal would have sparked a 20-point move in the S&P 500. (Today) it didn't." The reason, in part? "Recent events have **eroded** what confidence was left in government, making any meaningful long term progress highly unlikely."

Corporate earnings have not been so hot, it's true. But that is unlikely to be a pure fiscal cliff issue; remember that the US is experiencing slow economic growth and not much demand. If you have to look to Washington, consider that for most of the year, a bitter election kept many companies on the sidelines, unsure of whether Obama or Romney would win.

Whatever uncertainty exists, it has not hurt the ability of companies to borrow money, which is important because would you lend money to anyone you suspect wouldn't be able to pay it back? You would not. Investors who buy bonds think exactly the same way: they only like to buy bonds when they're sure they're going to get paid back. It's significant that, even in the face of the fiscal cliff, investors are supporting US companies. Last week—in a slow week allegedly plagued by fiscal cliff fears—US companies sold $13bn of bonds and all are performing well, according to research by Jody Lurie of Janney Montgomery Scott. If investors were truly worried about the effect of the fiscal cliff on corporate earnings in the next few weeks, they would not be buying the bonds of big US companies.

Nor have shareholders suffered **unduly**. Barclays noted that companies in the S&P 500 paid shareholders big **dividends**; in fact, Barclays says, those S&P dividends are on pace for the highest year-over-year since the 1950s.

➢ **Holiday retail sales are suffering because of the fiscal cliff**

A damning Associated Press headline announced "US holiday retail sales growth weakest since 2008." That sure sounds **recessionary**. But a deeper dive into the story shows an **omnibus** of potential reasons: hurricane Sandy, the presidential election, the shootings in Newtown, and, of course, the fiscal cliff. There are a few problems with this **satchel** of excuses, not the least the idea that people stop shopping at times of distant school shootings. Most important, however, is this: when theories for an economic change are lined up like little soldiers, there is obvious **ambiguity** that the fiscal cliff is the most to blame.

In fact, the most likely reason for the drop in holiday retail sales is simply this: the Thanksgiving shopping week, including **Black Friday** and **Cyber Monday**, were huge. Black Friday sales were up both online and in retail stores, where millions more shoppers packed stores than they did in 2011; ComScore also said that Cyber Monday set a new record as the biggest online spending day in history, with consumers dropping $1.46bn on consumer goods. Consumers spent more than $1bn on both Black Friday and Cyber Monday.

Consumer experts know that when you have a big Black Friday and Cyber Monday, the rest of the holiday spending tends to be soft. Consumers, after all, don't have unlimited funds to keep spending for weeks and weeks on end. It's also likely that much of the holiday shopping haul—paid for with credit cards—will take a while for consumers to pay down. Currently, consumers are buying themselves financial breathing room by delaying their debt payments, according to the *Wall Street Journal*. The paper noted today that "US households spent 10.6% of their after-tax income on debt payments in the third quarter of the year, the lowest level since 1983." New holiday shopping bills are likely to pile on top of old debts, indicating that consumers probably won't spend much in any case for the next few months—fiscal cliff or not.

Also, let's be clear: a minority of Americans even understand what the fiscal cliff is, and according to Gallup, only around a third of Americans are watching the negotiations very closely.

➢ **The fiscal cliff has already subtly wrecked the economy**

This is one of the most **compelling** arguments against letting the US go over the fiscal cliff. It all hinges on "Because Ben Bernanke said so" —and indeed, the august chairman of the Federal Reserve did indeed say that not only is the fiscal cliff a big risk to the economy, but that we're already suffering from it.

But the economy, in fact, is not doing so badly. Inflation is under control. Gas prices—which have an enormous impact on household finances—are actually dropping. Unemployment seems to be improving, **albeit** at an **excruciatingly** slow pace. Manufacturing is solid, as is consumption and personal income. Housing is rebounding. Robert Johnson, an analyst with Morningstar, judged some of the economic data and concluded that not only is the fiscal cliff not hurting progress, but that the economic numbers "(look) almost a little too good to be true".

Sentiment measures—especially among small businesses—are not so hot. Still, if you remember how few Americans understand the fiscal cliff, you'll see why ignorance, in this case, has led to relative economic bliss.

Could we be growing faster? Perhaps. Still, there is no evidence that the economy has been backsliding; all the evidence so far indicates that the economy is getting back on its feet, no matter how incompetently Congress has handled this vote.

The only proper answer to the **allegation** that the fiscal cliff is "destroying" the economy is the baffled comment of Inigo Montoya, the **vengeful** Spaniard from *The Princess Bride*: "You keep using that word. I do not think it means what you think it means."

- **The fiscal cliff is the greatest looming threat to the US economy right now**

Unfortunately, the fiscal cliff is just one of the major economic disasters we're facing, and it's a distant, distant third. By consensus, the effect of the fiscal cliff on the economy will be slow and **agonizing**. But other crises are facing the US with more immediate impact.

The biggest economic crisis America is likely to face soon is the threat of a strike by **longshoremen**, which could shut down America's major ports. The last time that happened, it cost the US economy $1bn a day. A week ago, talks broke down between the International Longshoremen's Association (ILA) and the US Maritime Alliance Ltd. The ILA represents around 15,000 **dockworkers** and the Maritime Alliance represents the management at 14 of the biggest US ports, including Boston, New York, New Jersey, Philadelphia, Baltimore, Savannah, New Orleans, and Houston.

The longshoremen's contract **expires** on Friday, and a strike would begin on Saturday. The issue is so major that the National Retail Federation joined 100 other associations—including the Alliance of Automobile Manufacturers, American Apparel & Footwear Association, American Farm Bureau Federation, National Association of Manufacturers, National Retail Federation, Toy Industry Association and the US Chamber of Commerce—to send a letter to the president on Wednesday pleading for White House intervention.

A strike at those 14 ports would mean a widespread economic impact in the United States, since millions of jobs depend on what comes through the ports. Everything from agriculture to consumer goods could either be delayed or become more expensive as shippers look for different ways to get their goods into the US. The combined impact of a strike would be enormous; the University of Georgia has estimated that Georgia's ports alone account for nearly $40bn in the state economy. A port strike would also hit employment very hard, as jobs would be lost–perhaps temporarily, perhaps not—for not only dockworkers, but also potentially every kind of worker who depends on shipped goods for their jobs.

The second biggest issue facing the economy in coming days is that of the debt ceiling. It is poised to be **resurrected** as a horrible **sequel** in the economic spotlight—sort of like *Weekend at Bernie's 2*, in which two men use a corpse, revived by **voodoo**, to locate lost treasure; the plot involves magic, goats and sacrificial blood, which, in this case, could be a metaphor for the finances of taxpayers (the metaphors run deeper on further inspection, but would take us away from our primary mission).

In any case, savvy American readers will remember this pointless debt **tussle** from its first **incarnation** in the summer of 2011. Currently, the debt limit is set at $16.39tn; the Treasury has already borrowed $16.31tn; the Treasury estimates it will be less than 10 days before the US crashes into the debt ceiling again. The last time that happened, ratings firms issued the US its first-ever downgrade in its debt, which is akin to a consumer getting notched on his credit score. The effect the last time was minimal, because the US is still better at managing its money than, say, the Eurozone; it's **dubious**, however, whether the US can take strike two.

(length: 2,002 words)

Vocabulary

agonizing	a. 苦恼的，痛苦难忍的
albeit	conj. 虽然
allegation	n. 主张，断言，辩解
ambiguity	n. 含糊，不明确
benchmark	n. 基准，标准检查
Black Friday	phr. 黑色星期五；耶稣受难日
compelling	a. 强制的，强迫的，引人注目的
consensus	n. 一致同意
Cyber Monday	phr. 黑色星期五之后的星期一(在美国标志着感恩节至圣诞节之间网络购物旺季的开始)
dividend	n. 股息，红利
dockworker	n. 码头工人
dubious	a. 可疑的，不确定的
erode	v. 侵蚀，腐蚀，使变化；受腐蚀，逐渐消蚀掉
excruciatingly	ad. 极痛苦地；极其地
expire	v. 期满，终止
hysteria	n. 歇斯底里，不正常的兴奋，癔病
incarnation	n. 赋予肉体，具人形，化身
indubitable	a. 不容置疑的，确实的
longshoremen	n. 码头工人
omnibus	n. 公共汽车，公共马车，精选集
recessionary	a. （经济）衰退的，衰退期的
resurrect	v. 复兴
satchel	n. 书包，小背包
sequel	n. 结局，续篇
theatrics	n. 舞台效果，戏剧演出
tussle	n. 格斗，斗争，争斗
unduly	ad. 不适当地，过度地，不正当地
vengeful	a. 复仇心重的，（利于）报复的
voodoo	n. 伏都教（一种西非原始宗教），伏都教徒

Section D　Word Bank for This Unit

经济学家	economist
社会主义经济	socialist economy

资本主义经济	capitalist economy
集体经济	collective economy
计划经济	planned economy
自由经济	liberal economy
保护主义	protectionism
闭关自守	autarchy
经济平衡	economic balance
经济波动	economic fluctuation
经济衰退	economic depression
经济稳定	economic stability
控股公司	holding company
购买力	purchasing power, buying power
短缺	scarcity
停滞，萧条，不景气	stagnation
创办资本	initial capital
冻结资金	frozen capital
冻结资产	frozen assets
固定资产	fixed assets
不动产，房地产	real estate
流动资本	circulating capital, working capital
资金分配	allocation of funds
周转基金	contribution of funds, revolving fund
意外开支，准备金	contingency fund, reserve fund
缓冲基金，平准基金	buffer fund
偿债基金	sinking fund
汇率，兑换率	exchange rate
外汇	foreign exchange
浮动汇率	floating exchange rate
自由汇兑市场	free exchange rates
外汇兑换券	foreign exchange certificate
硬通货	hard currency
投机	speculation
通货紧缩	deflation
证券市场	securities business
股票市场	stock exchange
证券交易所	stock exchange corporation
报价，牌价	quotation
股份，股票	share
股票持有人，股东	shareholder, stockholder
股息，红利	dividend
股票经纪人	stock-jobber
证券公司	stock company, stock brokerage firm
有价证券	securities
普通股	share, common stock
优先股	preference stock
债券	bond, debenture
华尔街	Wall Street
短期贷款	short term loan
长期贷款	long term loan
中期贷款	medium term loan
债权人	lender, creditor
债务人，借方	debtor, borrower
利息	interest
利率	rate of interest
贴现，折扣	discount
年金	annuity
到期日，偿还日	maturity
摊销，摊还，分期偿付	amortization
偿还	redemption
保险	insurance
抵押	mortgage
拨款	allotment
补贴，补助金，津贴	allowance, grant, subsidy
成本，费用	cost
开支，支出	expenditure, outgoing
收入，收益	income
利润，收益	earnings
总收入，总收益	gross income, gross earnings
毛利，总利润，利益毛额	gross profit, gross benefit
纯收益，净收入，收益净额	net income
平均收入	average income
国民收入	national income
利润率，赢利率	profitability, profit earning capacity
产量收益，收益率	yield
增值，升值	increase in value, appreciation

Chapter 4
Diplomatic Relations and Strategies

地球上有60多亿人口，分布在200多个国家中。国家之间的外交关系是否良性发展决定着彼此之间能否和平相处。在外交实践中，外交政策与策略是主权国家的头等大事。外交策略的基本作用就是为外交实体规定其进行外交活动的行为准则，并据此提出外交实体的基本外交内容。

了解英美国家的外交政策与策略，能帮助我们更好地理解当今世界上的一些政治、经济、文化现象。大学生作为未来的国家栋梁，也可以从中学会思考问题、解决问题的方法。

本单元我们将引领大家了解美国总统奥巴马执政期间采取的外交立场和策略，知晓英美之间的外交关系。

Section A Intensive Reading

President Obama and the Middle East Challenge

by Jonathan Rynhold

Obama's Foreign Policy Outlook

One of the main themes of Obama's campaign was "change", including a rejection of George W. Bush's "ideological" approach to foreign policy, in favor of "**pragmatism**". Whereas Bush viewed the world in terms of good and evil and asked countries to choose sides, Obama speaks in terms of bridging divides. In contrast to Bush's unilateralism, Obama has emphasized the importance of American leadership acting multilaterally, in concert with **allies**. The Bush Doctrine called for the preventive use of force, while Obama has stressed diplomatic engagement, viewing the use of force as a last **resort**.

➢ **Iraq**

The key dividing line between Obama and Bush is the Iraq War, which Obama opposed. His **watchword** was pragmatism. He argued that while war was morally justified, Saddam was not an **imminent** threat, and war would be expensive and not achieve its political objectives. However, Obama also **explicitly** rejected the anti-imperialist, pacifist language of much of the anti-war movement. Obama advocates a staged withdrawal of US forces over a period of 18 months, at the end of which the US will retain a military force "over the horizon". **Simultaneously**, he plans to push a comprehensive regional and international diplomatic initiative, which includes Syria and Iran, designed to **broker** an end to civil war in Iraq.

➢ **The War on Terror**

Obama has argued that the US needs to refocus the war on terror by **reinforcing** the **commitment** in Afghanistan and being more **proactive** vis- à -vis Pakistan. He views Iraq as, at best, a distraction from **combating** al Qaeda.

➢ **Iran**

Obama recognizes that a nuclear Iran is a major threat to the **stability** of the Middle East and a global threat to the **non-proliferation regime**, which he has **championed**. He has not ruled out the use of force, and he promised both AIPAC and Israeli leaders that he will do everything in his power to prevent Iran from obtaining nuclear weapons. But his policy is, first and **foremost**, to vigorously pursue direct negotiations in which he will offer "big carrots and big sticks". In terms of carrots, there is talk of a grand bargain which will include the US providing the regime a security guarantee, the opening of normal relations, and economic cooperation. In terms of sticks, Obama has supported a serious ratcheting up of international sanctions, including banning the export of refined petroleum to Iran. One consequence of such a ban could be a naval **blockade** and ultimately military confrontation.

➢ **The Arab-Israeli Arena**

Obama differed from the norm for candidates in US elections. His rhetoric was certainly pro-Israel; but it was not uncritical. Overall it resembled the language used by many of Israel's

center-left friends in Europe, such as Tony Blair. Obama praised Israeli democracy, and emphasized his commitment to Israel's security and his support for continued aid to Israel as "one of America's most important allies". He also rejects negotiations with Hamas and Hizballah, unless they recognize Israel, abandon terrorism and accept previous agreements.

On the other hand, he came out clearly against settlements and what he termed the "Likud approach" to the peace process. Joe Biden also indicated a willingness to confront the pro-Israel lobby by declaring that AIPAC does not define the meaning of being pro-Israel. In the past, Obama was critical of President Clinton's closeness to Israel in the peace negotiations and referred to the Second Intifada in terms of a "cycle of violence". Obama has promised to make the peace process a "key diplomatic priority"; though he has rejected the idea of an **imposed** settlement. He views the conflict as a "constant sore" that affects US foreign policy. He argues that the US must work towards a settlement, not only for its own sake, but also because it will assist the war on terror and remove the excuse of Arab regimes for blocking the social, economic, political, and education reforms that are needed to deal with the underlying causes of instability and **extremism**.

➢ **The Importance of Foreign Policy Appointments**

Analyzing Obama's foreign policy program helps us get a sense of his thinking, but it is far from a blueprint for action. There is always a gap between campaign rhetoric and the real business of foreign policy. Obama's campaign promised to vigorously pursue peace between Israel and the Palestinians based on the two-state solution. But what does this mean in practice? One way of assessing this is by looking at the approach favored by those touted for senior foreign policy appointments. Broadly speaking there are three approaches to the Arab-Israeli conflict among Obama associates. First, there is the approach of Carter's former National Security Advisor, Zbigniew Brzezinski, former Clinton NSC official Rob Malley and Samantha Power. They are generally hostile to Israel and the pro-Israel lobby and favor the view that the US should seek to impose a settlement on Arab terms. This approach has been somewhat marginalized as Malley and Power had to resign from the campaign; though Republican senator Chuck Hagel has also been mentioned as a possible Secretary of State and his record on Israel is quite hostile.

A second approach is exemplified by Dan Kurtzer, the former US ambassador to Israel and Egypt, who believes that the US should vigorously pursue a comprehensive settlement based on the Clinton Parameters of 2000. Finally, there is the approach of Dennis Ross, who argues that given Hamas' control of Gaza and other factors, there is currently no prospect for a permanent settlement and consequently the US should focus on improving the situation on the ground through more modest measures such as security cooperation. Ross argues that at present the main priority is Iran.

These different approaches could all find expression in parts of the future Obama administration. In turn, this could lead to bureaucratic in-fighting and consequently policy incoherence, as has frequently occurred in the past.

➢ **Facing Reality—Difficult Choices**

Reality has a way of forcing a president to make hard choices, by **prioritizing** some polices over others. Obama's primary focus is bound to be on ensuring the recovery of the American economy. This might make him more **circumspect** about using force against Iran, fearing the economic fallout of a rise in oil prices. However, a focus on Iran is preferable, where time is of the essence. On paper it is possible to pursue a negotiated settlement vis- à -vis Iran, Iraq and the Arab-Israeli conflict simultaneously. In practice, hard choices will have to be made about what is the true priority. Here, it is important for Obama to realize that while containing and managing the Arab-Israeli conflict is a vital US interest, resolution of the conflict is a secondary concern. The US will probably need to engage in peace process diplomacy for a variety of reasons, but the prospects for implementing a workable Israeli-Palestinian final settlement are poor indeed. Moreover, the central strategic challenge **emanates** from Tehran, not Jerusalem or Ramallah. This is a message he is bound to hear not only from Israel but also, privately, from America's Arab allies. A nuclear Iran will **trigger** the nuclearization of the Middle East more broadly, which could allow radical actors access to these dangerous weapons. Given the past use of non-conventional weapons by Middle East actors and their **penchant** for using terrorist proxies to preserve deniability, there is no guarantee that **deterrence** will hold. If Obama does proceed with his stated policy, he will have to make a **stark** choice regarding the Russian role on Iran. Obama has taken a tough line against Russian policy in a number of important spheres; yet at the same time he seeks to work with Russia to convince Iran to stop developing nuclear weapons. It is highly unlikely that he can square the circle.

➢ **Carrots and Sticks**

On a more fundamental level there are bigger questions about Obama's strategy of multilateral engagement. Obama criticized Bush for pursuing a policy based mainly on sticks, but he could have equally criticized Clinton for focusing too much on carrots. Obama seeks to entice Iran and Syria to cooperate by offering them economic and political benefits based on inclusion in the global liberal economic system and an honorable place at the table in a multilateral, but still American-led, global order. In the past, as part of the carrot for peace, the Syrians and Palestinians were offered aid packages worth tens of billions of dollars by Clinton; yet they refused. At least part of the reason for this is that these regimes view economic liberalization and normalization as a threat and not as an opportunity. First, they see it as an **ideological** threat, as Ayatollah Khomeini once scoffed, "revolution is not about the price of watermelons". Second, they oppose it because peace, openness and reform threaten their grip

on power.

Paradoxically, the only way to make the carrot appetizing is to make the alternative unappealing. In other words, for Obama's diplomatic engagement to stand a chance of success, it must be backed by the credible threat of a large stick.

➢ The Implications for Israel

There is no doubt that McCain would have been the more comfortable option for Israel. If Netanyahu does form the next Israeli government, there could be difficult times ahead. This has happened previously, when Shamir and Bush Senior, as well as Clinton and Netanyahu, clashed in the 1990s. But this time Netanyahu's position would be weaker. In the past, Netanyahu was able to work with a Republican-led Congress to **thwart** a Democratic president hamstrung by political intrigue. This time Obama will have a Democratic-led Congress. In addition, the new dovish "J Street" lobby would support Obama against Netanyahu and would lessen the ability of AIPAC to challenge Obama. On the other hand, Netanyahu, if elected, may well adopt a relatively pragmatic position, and US attention may be focused elsewhere. More broadly, Obama's preferences regarding Iran and Iraq have serious implications for Israel. If the US were to leave Iraq unstable, with the perception being one of American weakness and failure, it will strengthen the resolve of all radical forces in the region that threaten Israel and its de facto allies in the Arab world, such as Jordan. Israel also fears that any US-Iranian grand bargain could come at its expense in terms of an arms control regime that could be **detrimental** to Israel or in terms of American policy on the Palestinian issue. Finally, Israel is concerned that the Iranians would simply use the dialogue to buy time, as they have done with the Europeans for years. Still, from Israel's perspective, a dialogue is not necessarily bad, if only because it is a prequel to building the international support required for a military strike. Even in the event that both the US and Israel decide not to strike Iran, it is unlikely that the US will abandon Israel. Rather, we can expect the US to be drawn into providing a form of extended deterrence to Israel and its Arab allies in the region.

➢ Conclusion

Aside from his policy preferences, Obama's foreign policy will be dependent on his managerial and decision-making abilities. He is smart and has run a superb campaign, but he lacks experience. The real tests are yet to come, and given the **volatility** of the Middle East, they will come thick and fast. In such situations, **ideologues** can fall back on a set of **assertions** that provide a clear guide for resolving ambiguity; pragmatists have to be more analytical and pay attention to shifting realities. The central challenge for Obama in the Middle East is neither democratization nor securing a comprehensive resolution to the Arab-Israeli conflict (though those are worthy long term objectives), but rather the maintenance of a stable pro-American balance of power in the region. First and foremost that means dealing with the Iranian nuclear issue.

(length: 1,970 words)

Vocabulary

ally	n. 联盟	impose	v. 强迫；勉强（某人做某事）
assertion	n. 声称；使用；主张；明确肯定	non-proliferation	n. 不扩散
blockade	n. 封锁；封锁部队；障碍物	penchant	n.（强烈的）倾向，爱好，嗜好
broker	v. 安排，协商	pragmatism	n. [哲]实用主义
Champion	v. 拥护，保卫	prioritize	v. 把……区分优先次序
circumspect	a. 谨慎小心的，周到的	proactive	a. 先发制人的，积极的
combat	v. 与……战斗	unilateralism	n. 单方，片面
Commitment	n. 承诺，保证；信奉	regime	n. 政治制度，政权，政体；方法
deterrence	n. 威慑，制止；制止物，制止因素	reinforce	v. 加固；使更结实；加强；充实
detrimental	a. 有害的；不利的 n. 有害的人（或物）	resort	n. 求助，凭借，诉诸
emanate	v. 发出，散发；放射；起源	simultaneously	ad. 同时地
explicitly	ad. 明白地，明确地	stability	n. 稳定
extremism	n. 极端主义；极端性；过激论	stark	a. 完全的；荒凉的；光秃秃的；僵硬的
foremost	ad. 首先，第一	thwart	v. 阻挠；使受挫折；挫败
ideological	a. 思想的；意识形态的	trigger	v.引发，触发
ideologue	n. 意识形态的拥护者，思想意识的盲目追从者	volatility	n. 挥发性；挥发度
imminent	a.（通常指不愉快的事）即将发生的；迫切的，危急的	watchword	n. 口令；暗语

Exercises

I. Comprehension

1. List

Can you briefly list Obama's diplomatic policy?

2. Integrate

Make a chart showing the similarity and difference between Obama's and Bush's diplomatic policies.

3. Hypothesize

Can you imagine what might happen if US adopt the "stick policy" towards Iran?

4. Judge

Do you think Obama's pro-Israel policy reasonable or not?

5. Evaluate

Is there a better solution to the prevention of nuclear weapons in the Middle East?

II. Further Study

Search online for Obama's campaign speech for the second term, and find out his words on diplomatic policies and strategies.

Section B Extensive Reading

UK and US Relationship

This passage is adapted from two articles, which to some extent give a picture of US and UK's relationship. One is the joint article *An Essential Relationship* UK's Prime Minister David Cameron and US President Barack Obama have written for *The Times* at the start of the US State Visit to the UK; the other is what Ambassador Nigel Sheinwald said in Fulton, Missouri while marking the 65th anniversary of Winston Churchill's seminal address at Westminster College.

UK and US: An Essential Relationship

Both of us came of age during the 1980s. Like so many others, we recall a **turbulent** decade that began with armies confronting each other across a divided Europe and ended with the Berlin Wall coming down.

The Cold War reached this conclusion because of the actions of many brave individuals and many strong nations, but we saw how the bond between our two countries—and our two leaders at the time—proved such a vital **catalyst** for change. It reminded us that when the United States and Britain stand together, our people and people around the world can become more secure and more **prosperous**.

And that is the key to our relationship. Yes, it is founded on a deep emotional connection, by sentiment and ties of people and culture. But the reason it **thrives**, the reason why this is such a natural partnership, is because it advances our common interests and shared values. It is a perfect **alignment** of what we both need and what we both believe. And the reason it remains strong is because it delivers time and again. Ours is not just a special relationship, it is an essential relationship—for us and for the world.

So as we meet today, facing immense economic, social and strategic challenges, it is natural that once again our two nations join together in common cause. Today the foundations of our partnership are rock solid. Our servicemen and women serve alongside one another, whether fighting in Helmand, protecting innocent people in Libya or combating piracy off the Horn of Africa. Every day our diplomats and security and intelligence agencies work together. We are working urgently to de-escalate tensions and prevent a return to war in Sudan's contested Abyei region. And we are unified in our support for a lasting peace between a secure Israel and a sovereign Palestine.

And we can honestly say that despite being two leaders from two different political traditions, we see eye to eye. We look at the world in a similar way, share the same concerns and see the same strategic possibilities. So we will build on the relationship between the UK and US, working closely together on areas of common interest to make it stronger still.

One area where we need to co-operate is on rebuilding our economies. In the past few years, the global economy has gone through a profound shock. And what's at stake now is whether new jobs and businesses take root in our countries or somewhere else. Now we are two different countries but our **destination** must be the same: strong and stable growth, reduced deficits and reform of our financial systems—so that they will never again be open to the abuses of the past.

Governments do not create jobs: bold people and innovative businesses do. We know that our nations are **self-reliant** and infused with the **entrepreneurial** spirit. We have proud traditions of out-innovating and out-building the rest of the world—and of doing it together. Today the US remains the largest investor in Britain, and Britain the largest investor in the US—each supporting around a million jobs in our countries. We want to encourage more of this exchange of capital, goods and ideas. So this week we will reaffirm our commitment to strong collaboration between our universities and research facilities.

We must also co-operate on ensuring our shared security. The death of Osama bin Laden marks the most significant blow against al-Qaeda since its inception—but it does not mark the end of the terror. Al-Qaeda and its **affiliates** will continue to pursue attacks against our countries so we must work together to protect our people from their poisonous ideology and the violence that flows from it. This means sharing information so we **trace, track** and **disrupt** terrorist plots—and bring those who plan them to justice. There can be no **impunity** and no refuge for those who wish to do us harm. And yes, this also means continuing our mission in Afghanistan, training the Afghan national army and police so they can provide security for their country, and our troops can come home.

But we also need to understand why people can become attracted to violent extremism in the first place. When young men and women feel that their rights are not respected, they can become more prone to the narrative of separateness and victimhood that al-Qaeda's ideology feeds off. This is just one reason why recent events in the Arab world and Middle East are so **momentous**. What we are seeing there is a groundswell of people demanding the basic rights, freedoms and dignities that we take for granted. We all share in their success or failure.

Progress in the region will be uneven and it is not our place to **dictate** the pace and scope of this change. But we will stand with those who want to bring light into dark, support those who seek freedom in place of **repression**, aid those laying the building blocks of democracy. We do so because democracy and respect for universal rights is a good for the people of the region, and also because it's a key part of the **antidote** to the instability and extremism that threatens our security. And we will not stand by as their aspirations get crushed in a **hail** of bombs, bullets and **mortar** fire. We are reluctant to use force but when our interests and values come together we know that we have a responsibility to act.

This is why we mobilized the international community to protect the Libyan people from Colonel Qadhafi's regime. We have degraded his war machine and prevented a **humanitarian catastrophe**. And we will continue to enforce the UN resolutions with our allies until they are completely complied with. Our actions in Libya are not, and will never be, a burden our countries carry alone. We will work with partners so they share the load and the costs and continue to support the legitimate and credible Transitional National Council and its efforts to prepare for an inclusive, democratic transition. Together we show the world that the principles of justice and freedom will be upheld by all.

Our efforts against al-Qaeda—and our mission in Libya—are critical to the type of world that we want to build. Bin Laden's ideology is one that has failed to take hold. Qadhafi's reign represents the region's past. We stand for something different. We see the prospect of democracy and universal rights taking hold in the Arab World, and it fills us with confidence and a renewed commitment to an alliance based not just on interests but on values. Yes, we are **mindful** of the risks and aware of the uncertainties. But we stand together, optimistic and confident that our two nations can achieve peace, prosperity and security in the years ahead.

➢ UK-US: An Alliance for the Future

The world has changed greatly since Churchill's famous speech in 1946—widely remembered for his reference to the "Iron Curtain" —but the Ambassador paid **tribute** to "certain constants" of international relations which Churchill would recognize and **embrace** today: ideas, values and alliances.

The rise of emerging powers is one such transformation of international relations that Churchill wouldn't recognize. But while it may be tempting to assume that the ideas Churchill **articulated** ended with the Cold War, the Ambassador argued that now more than ever we need to assume his passion for the values that unite the UK and US:

"We must be as energetic as Churchill was in making the case for shared rules and liberal principles. That does not mean expecting the emerging powers simply to **cleave** to our ways of doing things. That would be naive. But neither does it mean resiling from the idea that free and open markets, the rule of law, the respect of private property and indeed, representative governments are good for nations and good for the world."

In addition to **espousing** the ideas that bond the UK and US, Churchill also believed deeply in the values that the two countries share. Again, the global context has changed since Churchill's time. However, the Ambassador said the shared UK-US values of 1946 are still essential guides to forming a global outlook today:

"The most significant lesson we should draw from recent events in the Middle East is the importance of values. Protesters across the region are united in one thing—their aspiration for the rights and freedoms that we take for granted in the West, and their hope that we will help them to achieve them. These events have reinforced our conviction that those values are universal, and not limited by history, nation or **creed**."

And while the foundation of the UK-US alliance remains, the depth and range of British and American cooperation has **intensified** significantly since Churchill's time. From investment in each other's economies, to collaborating on research and fighting a new kind of enemy in Afghanistan, the Ambassador set out how the UK-US partnership has evolved to provide shared prosperity and security in the 21st century:

"We are each other's largest investors, with a million jobs in each country depending on that investment. Indeed UK investment here in the US is 570 times the level of China's."

"Between us, the US and the UK represent 50% of all citations in global science. We have won half of all the Nobel prizes ever awarded. We have between us all of the world's top ten universities."

"We are the top two troop contributors in Afghanistan, as we were in Iraq; and close allies in dealing with the threats of terrorism and **proliferation**, including in Iran."

The Ambassador closed by stressing that the roots of the UK-US relationship don't confine its relevance to Churchill's era. Instead, they prove that the alliance is ready to meet the demands of a changing world:

"Let us also not forget the strength of our ideas; of our values; and of our alliance. They are not the stuff of yesterday, or a **relic** of the past. They are the tools we have to meet the challenges of the future."

The speech concludes the Ambassador's five-day visit to Illinois and Missouri. Earlier in the week he addressed the Chicago Council on World Affairs and Washington University in St. Louis on the strength of the UK-US economic partnership.

(length: 1,858 words)

Vocabulary

affiliate	n. 附属企业；分支机构
alignment	n. 队列，排成直线；结盟
antidote	n. 解药，解毒剂；矫正方法
articulate	v. 清晰地发（音）；言语表达
catalyst	n. [化]触媒，催化剂；（比喻）触发因素
catastrophe	n. 大灾难；惨败
cleave	v. 劈开，剁开，割开

creed	n.（尤指宗教）信条，教义	momentous	a. 重大的；重要的
destination	n. 目的地	mortar	n. 迫击炮；砂浆
dictate	v. 口述；命令，指示；控制	proliferation	n. 增殖，分芽繁殖；再育；增生
disrupt	v. 使混乱；使分裂，使瓦解	prosperous	a. 繁荣的，兴旺的
embrace	v. 拥抱；包括；接受	relic	n. 遗物，遗迹；废墟；纪念物
entrepreneurial	a. 创业的，具有企业精神的	repression	n. 压抑；约束；抑制，镇压
espouse	v. 拥护；赞助；嫁娶	self-reliant	a. 依靠自己的，独立的
hail	n. 冰雹；一阵	thrive	v. 兴盛，兴隆；长得健壮
humanitarian	a. 人道主义的；博爱的；慈善的	trace	v. 跟踪，追踪；追溯，探索
impunity	n. 不受惩罚，无罪；不受损失	track	v. 跟踪；监看，监测；追踪
intensify	v. 增强，强化，加剧	tribute	n. 称赞，颂扬
mindful	a. 留心的，注意的；警觉的	turbulent	a. 骚乱的，混乱的；激流的

Exercises

I. Comprehension

1. Locate

Can you find out the key words that describe US and UK relationship in the two speeches?

2. Exemplify

Can you illustrate US and UK's cooperation in the political arena from the two speeches?

3. Make Inference

From Ambassador Nigel Sheinwald's speech, can you infer the role Churchill played in the 1940s?

4. Explain

In the joint article, the two leaders stated that "It reminded us that when the United States and Britain stand together, our people and people around the world can become more secure and more prosperous." Do you agree with them? Why?

5. Judge

In the joint article, the two leaders stated"we will continue to enforce the UN resolutions with our allies until they are completely complied with." Do you think it is a good thing for the rest of the world or a bad thing?

II. Further Study

Introduce a film on diplomatic relations to your classmates and present its merits and drawbacks.

Section C Supplementary Reading

☐ Passage 1 An Extract from "British Public Diplomacy in the 'Age of Schisms'"

There is a big contrast between the **cacophony** of debate in the United States on the political and diplomatic fall-out of Iraq for US grand strategy, and the relative lack of public and political debate about how the United Kingdom addresses changing **perceptions** of Britain and British foreign policy as a result of Iraq. This is surprising, as the consequences for the UK are arguably even greater than for the US. As the world's only superpower, the US can still **induce** or **pressurize** many countries into going along with its priorities (even if the costs are going up) by virtue of its raw power. The UK, by contrast, must rely much more on its ability to persuade others of the merits of its case and—perhaps even more important—its ability to be seen as a **trustworthy** and principled partner. In recent years British foreign policy has been based on three key **pillars**: the international rule of law, European engagement, and engaging the Americans in a progressive project for international community. Today we must face facts: the fall-out of the Iraq crisis leaves each of those pillars in a questionable state of repair. It has also had a corrosive effect on general, non-specific, trust in the UK in many parts of the world.

Since 1997, the British Government has worked hard to create a new atmosphere of trust with our European partners and the developing world. On the political side, Tony Blair set out a vision of the international community that draws on and **encapsulates** the values of the centre-left. His first term, refreshingly, replaced memories of Margaret Thatcher's foreign policy with an appeal to a vision of an international community. Beef wars with Europe gave way to support for the Europe; memories of support for **apartheid** were **banished** by inviting Mandela to address the House of Commons; and the ghost of inaction over Bosnia and Rwanda was laid to rest with swift humanitarian **interventions** in Kosovo and Sierra Leone. By and large, these gestures were welcomed and accepted by our partners (with **grudging** suspicion in some quarters, and enthusiasm in others).

On the cultural side, Tony Blair promised to transform Britain into "a young country" and set out his determination to renew our national identity, and to craft a sense of nationhood which reflected the reality of Britain at the end of the 20th century. The backdrop to this was a sense that British image abroad was often out-of-date and damaging to our political and economic goals. Research showed that the biggest problem for Britain was that we were **tarred** by out-of-date associations: seen as a country in decline, **stuffy**, traditional, white, racist and imperialist. The creation of Panel 2000, the work of the British Council and the rebranding of the British Tourist Authority (BTA) have all had an impact on the face of Britain. Although many people mocked what became known as "Cool Britannia", the polls show that this concerted set of activities has started to have an impact. Clearly, this kind of identity and image engineering can only work when it reflects substantial change in a society: this transformation did what such renewals do best—drawing attention in a focused and orderly way to a reality that was already coming, unsung, into existence.

In 2002, this work continued as the British Government launched a Public Diplomacy Strategy Board to co-ordinate the work that the government does in communicating and building relations with publics around the world—trying to bring together the activities of the FCO, the British Council, the British Tourist Authority and UK Trade and Investment. For the first time they have agreed a common public diplomacy strategy—with two themes, titled "dynamic tradition" and "principled and professional".

An article in the *Canadian National Post* in the summer of 2004 reflected well the international commentary: "Of course, the rebranding of all re-brandings is that of Cool Britannia in the mid-1990s." Britain (Trademark) is the case study that every politician under the age of 40 must know. The country's image of a nation of bad food, **stultified** class-ridden society, **stodgy** pasty people wasting away in council housing, and strikes, was firmly **entrenched** all over the world. Within a year, the new story of Britain was crafted and told: The New Britain was creative, multicultural and achingly hip, with a well-trained and highly motivated workforce...The marketing team **reconfigured** Britain as a hub, importing and exporting ideas, goods, services, people and cultures. It was non-conformist. Britons were silent revolutionaries who had created new forms of organization. The country had a long-established ethos of fair play and voluntary commitment. The 800-million pounds a year spent by the Foreign Office helped successfully sell the story abroad. And at home, Britain was "re-energized".

At the same time, much thought was going into the definition of cultural relations as a voice at least partially distinct from that of public diplomacy in its traditional sense. This thinking focused in particular on the trust deficit noted above, and stressed the advantages to the UK of organizations including, but not limited to, the British Council, which are able to win a particular kind of trust precisely by being **palpably** at arm's length from government. The Foreign Policy Centre described this as a **spectrum** of activity defined largely by its time-frame, with Cultural Relations work characterized by its long-term nature. But in many ways the more important **dichotomy** could be seen as between work that is visibly governmental and work that is visibly non-governmental. Seen in this light, Cultural Relations can deliver short-term as well as long-term impact, as long as its independence is constantly stressed and acted out.

The time has come to look again at how Britain is perceived in the world, and on how the hundreds of millions of pounds we spend on diplomacy and cultural relations can best be used. In many ways a new gulf has opened up between the professed aims of British foreign policy and the way they are perceived around the world. Whatever the rights and wrongs of the Iraqi campaign, it is impossible to deny that the events of the last two years have changed the way that Britain is seen. In broad terms, Britain's participation in the overthrow of Saddam and the occupation of Iraq have served to **reinvigorate** some of the **residual** doubts about Britain: is Britain really committed to Europe; or is it a Trojan Horse for American power (as De Gaulle argued)? Has Britain really put its own imperial past behind it, or does it still feel it has a right to invade and occupy developing countries? Is Britain really a multi-faith, multicultural country—or is it a Christian country that is launching new crusades against Islam?

➢ **The World After Iraq (War)**

Of course, Britain's changing image cannot be seen in a **vacuum**. These questions are being asked at a time when the world has been plunged into disorder. In many ways 2003 was the year that **crystallized** a series of global **schisms**—and Britain was right in the middle of many of them. During the Cold War, the world was shaped by a single schism—one that became the defining feature of geopolitics and **subordinated** the interpretation of all other schisms to its logic. Fifteen years after the end of the Cold War the old blocks that shaped the **contours** of the post-war world have started to **splinter** in violent and unpredictable ways. The West, above all, has started to fragment into Europe and America, "New" and "Old" Europe, and "Big" and "Small" Europe. At the same time, the Arab and Muslim worlds are in the grip of a series of bitter civil conflicts—pitting moderate against extremist Islamists; and régimes against civil society. As China, India and Brazil continue their rapid growth, they have led a new self-confident movement from the South to take on the North and have raised the prospect of a major global power transition, with all the potential fractions this entails.

Although many of the new divides have economic and political interests at their heart, the way they are expressed is often through culture, and owing to the lack of trust, it will often be impossible to address underlying economic and social differences before progress is made in the cultural sphere.

For argument's sake, this paper identifies six "cultural divides" under three broad heads:

(1) Political

Power-based order vs Rule-based order

Realpolitik vs Liberal Internationalism

(2) Religious

Traditionalism vs Liberalism

Faith-based vs **Secular** government

(3) Economic

Power vs Powerlessness

Pro-globalisation vs Anti-globalisation

These divisions neither fit into the old categories of the Cold Warnor do they fit into neat civilization boundaries. Instead they form a number of cross-cutting divisions that create new and surprising communities of interest. France and Turkey find themselves united in their commitment to secularism; whilst religion plays a very important part in public life in the US and the Middle East. It is important to realize that this is not an "Iraq" or "9/11" effect—many of these tensions have been building up for a long time, but were suppressed by the weight of the

Cold War bi-polarity.

What is more, these divisions do not seem just to be about diplomatic **wrangles**—but clashes between publics, where public opinion for the first time in many years is shaping and pressurizing foreign policy decisions. The last decade is full of examples of popular perceptions, rather than governments, setting the pace for international diplomacy. In Kosovo, a powerful military coalition risked defeat, not in the field, but in the media battleground for public support, as governments in Greece and Italy struggled to cope with **volatile** popular opinion. In Rwanda, ethnic conflict was mobilized through **inflammatory** radio broadcasts to civilians rather than by military command chains. Recent anti-globalization demonstrations have revealed a new diplomatic environment where state and nonstate actors compete for the public's attention. After the BSE (mad cow disease) crisis in Britain, the French government violated European Union law and continued to ban British beef, largely in response to public fears about safety. And the global competition for investment, trade, tourists, entrepreneurs, and highly skilled workers extends the influence of foreign publics beyond the political to the economic. But, above all, the sheer scale of popular mobilization over Iraq and the consequences of this have been greater than anything since Vietnam.

➤ A New Diplomatic Environment

Together these schisms seem to be pointing to the development of a new diplomatic environment. The last year has shown that achieving political change now means developing new coalitions by using a wide range of policy and communications tools to respond to a world where:

(1) The spread of democracy and—perhaps to an even greater extent—the **flexing** of extra-democratic populist pressure mean that governments are increasingly constrained by public opinion, which makes the **legitimacy** of policies increasingly important.

(2) The priority of multilateralism means that political action increasingly depends on mobilizing international coalitions, placing great importance on winning over public opinion in partner countries.

(3) The revolution in information and communications technology means that information travels more quickly, is more diffuse and is increasingly responsive to individual markets; we are also witnessing the new phenomenon of transnational public opinions operating and competing in a global space.

(4) Globalization means that governments are increasingly reliant on attracting international trade, investment, tourism and talent to drive their economies.

This new environment has two key characteristics. First, there is no longer a clear dividing line between domestic politics and foreign policy—because the political debates in one country affect the welfare of publics in other countries. Second, there is a dynamic relationship between who you are and what you do—where your identity forms an enabling or disabling environment which can be enhanced or damaged by particular actions or policy choices. That is why identity needs to be acknowledged—and cannot be separated from policy-making.

The term "public diplomacy" is often a **euphemism** for propaganda. But the proliferation of information in open societies (and, increasingly, in closed ones as well) makes it much more difficult for governments to control information. Attempts to distort the truth will eventually be exposed and therefore will create even greater **skepticism** of governments. Moreover, because most ideas that people absorb about a country are beyond the control of national governments—books, CDs, films, television programmes, or brands and consumer products with national connotations—governments can only have an impact at the margins by seeking to clear paths for the most positive messages to reach mass audiences while working directly to influence the opinions of **niche** audiences. We need though to be clear that the **efficacy** of these positive messages aimed at mass audiences, in contexts of popular hostility, is **dubious**, as US public diplomacy campaigns in the Middle East have tended to illustrate in the last two years.

If public diplomacy is to be aligned with the major challenges of the new century, a significant shift in thinking is required. At the "hard" end of the spectrum, governmental, message-orientated public diplomacy work needs the goals, target countries, campaigns and operating principles that have been shaping current public diplomacy initiatives to be reconsidered. In one major instance, this has already started to take place. The manifest difficulty of, and the pressing need for successful public diplomacy in the Middle East has led to a greater preparedness among some governments to **countenance** non-traditional approaches to campaigns in the region and to question the effectiveness of Cold War tools. Yet it is a mistake to believe that this is simply a regional **aberration** and that the usual methods can be deployed elsewhere. As we will illustrate, although the depths of hostility are not the same, gaps in worldview and significant public opinion challenges are also features of our relationships with key allies, major new powers and other parts of the developing world. The principles and practice of trust-building we set out need to be the rule for public diplomacy, not the exception.

In this paper, we set out five key lessons for British Public Diplomacy:

(1) Public diplomacy must be at the heart of our diplomatic strategy—not the 1990s variant of Cool Britannia but a strategy designed to show that Britain is a principled power that believes in international law, global development, and European unity. Public diplomacy today depends on reflecting truth, not fiction, so success will depend on reality. Public diplomacy in the future must focus as much on politics, and cultural divisions, as it has done on economics in the past.

(2) Public diplomacy requires much closer integration of public diplomacy and policy—consistency of action is the most important way of genuinely demonstrating commitment to ideals and ensuring that charges of **hypocrisy** cannot be levelled. This requires a **rigorous** assessment of the public diplomacy implications of certain policies at the earliest possible stage, as these are likely to have just as much impact on Britain's interests as the immediate consequences of the policy itself.

(3) British public diplomacy must focus much more strongly on traditional allies and industrialized countries and not just on threshold/developing nations. We need to be prepared to contemplate the transfer of resources from threshold nations to the developed world, where it is

appropriate, and a concerted attempt to work with other like-minded countries on shared outcomes.

(4) Governments are poor spokesmen. "Official public diplomacy work" must be paralleled by a continuous, concerted attempt to develop a parallel "people-to-people" conversation that works through NGOs, **diasporas**, political parties and other non-governmental avenues.

(5) There needs to be a revolution in the tone and character of British public diplomacy so that it focuses on trust and **mutuality**—rather than simply on message delivery.

(length: 2,630 words)

Vocabulary

aberration	n. 偏差，差错；脱离常规，越轨
apartheid	n. （南非曾经的）种族隔离制度
banish	v. 放逐，驱逐；消除，排除
cacophony	n. 刺耳的声音，不和谐的声音
contour	n. 外形，轮廓；等高线
countenance	n. 表情；面孔；赞同，支持
crystallize	v. （使）结晶；（使）成形，（使）明确
diaspora	n. 移民社群
dichotomy	n. 一分成二，对分
diffuse	v. 传播；四散 a. 四散的
dubious	a. 半信半疑的，犹豫不决的
efficacy	n. 功效；效力；生产率
encapsulate	v. 装入胶囊
entrench	v. 用壕沟围绕或保护……；牢固地确立……
euphemism	n. 委婉语；委婉说法
flexing	n. 挠曲，可挠性
grudging	a. 不情愿的，勉强的
hypocrisy	n. 伪善，虚伪
intervention	n. 介入，干涉
induce	v. 引诱；引起
inflammatory	a. 令人激动的；有煽动性的
legitimacy	n. 合法（性），正统（性）；合理
mutuality	n. 相互关系；相互依存
niche	n. 壁龛；（工作等）合适的位置
palpably	ad. 可触地；易觉察地
perception	n. 知觉；觉察（力）；观念
pillar	n. 柱；（组织、制度、信仰等的）核心
pressurize	v. 对……施加压力；给……增压
reconfigure	v. 重新装配，改装
reinvigorate	v. 使再振作，使复兴
residual	a. 残余的；残留的
rigorous	a. 严密的；缜密的
schism	n. 教会分立，分裂
secular	a. 现世的，俗界的
skepticism	n. 怀疑态度，怀疑论
spectrum	n. [物理学]谱，光谱；范围
splinter	v. （使）分裂
stodgy	a. 易饱的；滞涩的；古板的
stuffy	a. 闷热的；古板的，保守的；枯燥无味的
stultify	v. 使成为徒劳
subordinate	v. 使……居下位，使从属
tar	v. 以焦油或沥青覆盖或涂抹
trustworthy	a. 值得信赖的，可靠的
vacuum	n. 真空，空白
volatile	a. 易变的，不稳定的
wrangle	n. 争吵；吵架

□ Passage 2 Obama, Africa and Peace

➢ Reframing the Overall Approach to U.S. Relations with Africa

The Obama administration has an opportunity to fundamentally remake U.S. relations with Africa during its **tenure**, and a **cornerstone** of that effort needs to be a much greater emphasis on the most cost-effective element of our foreign policy tools: peacemaking. An investment in ending some of the world's deadliest, most destructive, and costliest wars would yield great results in those countries and the positive **repercussions** from such engagement would **rebound** across the continent.

As the first president of the United States with immediate African roots, President Obama not only has an important reservoir of goodwill on the continent, he also has the ability to move beyond the **tendentious** "North-South" debate between developed and less developed countries that has made more transformational policies difficult to attain. Efforts by the dying generation of Africa's strong men who believe they should rule for life, such as Zimbabwe's President Robert Mugabe, to portray President Obama as a former colonial master will have little resonance in Africa or elsewhere. President Obama will represent a fresh start, but the problems facing Africa and how best to address them will be no less acute. Equally important, an Obama administration can also leave behind the "for-us-or-against-us" strategies of the Bush administration that tended to ignore the worst behavior of "allies" while **demonizing** every action of those who were deemed "enemies." The Bush approach was in many ways a return to a Cold War **calculus** and approach to relations with the continent that did little to ameliorate the fundamental forces driving conflict on the continent or to improve the overall capacity of states to address such tensions. To be fair, the Bush administration did make a considerable investment in HIV/AIDS prevention in Africa through the President's Emergency Plan for AIDS relief, or PEPFAR and also deeply engaged in pursuit of an eventual peace deal between the Sudanese government and southern-based rebels. The Obama administration will need a much more nuanced approach, and it will need to work more closely with both governments and civil society on the continent to shape a shared agenda.

Given its thinly veiled hostility toward most forms of multilateral institution building, the Bush administration also placed limited emphasis on these issues in the context of Africa, despite a glaring need for Africa's regional institutions to improve their capability and effectiveness. The Bush administration's low regard for the United Nations in general also largely **precluded** the Security Council from playing an effective role in addressing Africa's multiple crises.

It is essential that the new administration invest significantly in peacemaking and take a smarter, more comprehensive approach to this peacemaking. However, it is vital that these investments in peacekeeping are accompanied by long-term investments in development, crisis prevention, and in shaping African regional institutions that are built around shared values. Too often, membership in African regional organizations has simply been a matter of geography—with democracies and autocracies lumped together. Yet, it is impossible to imagine effective regional institutions in Africa that lack a shared commitment to certain essential values, including democratic government, the responsibility to protect their own populations, and relatively open trade. Indeed, regional organizations in Europe and Latin America have only become more effective when certain membership criteria were added on top of geographic considerations.

The African Union in particular, has a wildly mixed record in this regard. As an organization, it has been far too willing to practice lowest common **denominator** policies, such as its relative tolerance of the Sudan regime's massive human rights abuses in Darfur. Similarly, both the African Union and the Southern African Development Community have struggled to come to terms with President Robert Mugabe's **ruinous** rule in Zimbabwe. Yet, the recent decision by the African Union to suspend Guinea's membership unless the military officers who conducted the coup in that country restore "constitutional rule" is exactly the kind of behavior a regional organization should be demanding. This also suggests that with the right kind of longterm support from the United States the **mantra** of "African solutions to African problems" could move beyond empty rhetoric. This will require two important developments:

• African regional institutions need to become increasingly responsive to the needs of African citizens and not just the **prerogatives** of African heads of state.

• The broader international community must recognize that war crimes, crimes against humanity, and **genocide** are not "African problems". They are international problems that demand international solutions.

Reshaping the overall approach to Africa will also demand that the Obama administration face some hard choices. Development resources are increasingly dominated by spending on HIV/AIDS. While responding to the HIV/AIDS **pandemic** is a crucial priority, if U.S. development assistance becomes **skewed** too far in this direction, it will become very difficult to make long-term investments in state building, the rule of law, basic education, and economic growth—the elements that are fundamental to changing Africa's course over the long haul.

The administration will also need to take a hard look at continued agricultural **subsidies** in the United States. These subsidies continue to **drain** federal funds at a time when there are **unprecedented** budget pressures, while simultaneously making it harder for many African states to compete in one of the few areas where they enjoy a comparative advantage. Cutting these subsidies would benefit Americans in three ways: they would pay fewer tax dollars to support unneeded subsidies; they would enjoy the fruits of greater competition as consumers; and, over time, they would need to invest fewer dollars in development and humanitarian relief as Africa has the chance to achieve greater prosperity. The same can be said for European agricultural subsidies. While it may sound strange to tie the issue of agricultural subsidies back to the questions of war and peace on the continent, it is essential to do so. For too long, U.S. efforts in development, economic development, trade, humanitarian relief, and diplomacy on the continent have been poorly connected threads, and all of these efforts have collectively suffered as a result.

➢ A Focus on Peacemaking

Sudan, Somalia, Congo, Chad, and northern Uganda are part of a region of east and central Africa that is **battered** by chronic conflict, with millions dead and even more displaced over the last couple decades. It is the deadliest zone of conflict in the world since World War II. Congo and Sudan alone account for nearly 8 million deaths due to the legacy of war in the past two decades.

As part of its fundamental rethink of Africa policy, the Obama administration will need to shift U.S. policy from simply managing the symptoms of Africa's biggest wars—in the form of billions of dollars in humanitarian aid and peace observation missions that are often unable to effectively protect civilians—to ending these conflicts. The existing model of conflict resolution in Africa has focused on one conflict at a time, treating Africa's wars as if they occur in isolation. Extreme examples of this include dealing with Sudan's north-south war while setting the issue of Darfur and eastern Sudan to the side; focusing on the situation in Somalia without effectively addressing the standoff between Ethiopia and Eritrea that fuels the conflict; and negotiating in northern Uganda without involving or sanctioning Sudan's ruling party, which has long supported the Lord's Resistance Army as a **proxy** force. Most of Africa's wars are complex and regional in nature, and they cannot be addressed by a **burcaucratic** process that encourages stove piping rather than coordination and synthesis.

The new administration needs to make an investment in competent, sustained conflict resolution, backed by focused **leverage** that transforms the logic of regional combatants from war to peace.

➢ **Enhancing U.S. Capacities for Peace**

The basic elements of an enhanced peacemaking strategy would include the following:

a) Diplomatic capacity: Additional diplomatic slots should be assigned and staffed in embassies throughout East and Central Africa with the primary emphasis of these positions on support for various peace processes in the region. Country teams in each embassy would work closely with Washington and with existing regional efforts to step up support for peace efforts. U.S. Diplomats would meet quarterly in the region to coordinate peacemaking strategies, strategize, and share information. Country and issue experts would be hired and shared regionally to support the ongoing and new peace processes with a focus on making them more effective. In general, the U.S. Embassies on the continent are not only grossly understaffed, but are badly lacking country and issue experts with specific peace-building experience.

b) Inter-agency task force: A senior official from the State Department or National Security Council should oversee and coordinate a Task Force that helps shape the diplomatic strategy in each of the conflicts of East and Central Africa: Sudan, Congo, Somalia, Chad, Ethiopia-Eritrea, Central African Republic, and the Lord's Resistance Army threat. The situation in Zimbabwe would also likely be included in this group. The Task Force can ensure the sharing of resources, personnel, and intelligence across the region to guarantee maximum coordination and provide strategic direction to multilateral efforts on each of the processes. Additional country and issue experts should be contracted to support the work of the Task Force and to purposefully think outside the box of existing approaches. Staff should also be placed in New York and Brussels to support enhanced diplomacy within the U.N. Security Council and European Union.

c) Special envoys: When appropriate, the president should appoint special envoys to add **gravitas** to peace efforts for specific conflicts. Envoys would work closely with the enhanced regional and D.C.-based capacities, and would be **deployed** when key messages need to be delivered or support for negotiations is required. Special envoys are by no means a magic bullet, and the effectiveness of many envoys in the past has been undercut by **simmering** tensions with existing bureaucratic structures and officials. This suggests that special envoys should only be deployed when they are sufficiently senior to command respect within the system and actually serve as a focal point for coordination and effective policymaking. The relationship between any such special envoy and the Task Force described above would need to be clearly articulated before such a person was deployed.

d) Washington meetings: When appropriate, the Obama administration should host ministerial or working-level meetings in Washington with key actors, including key diplomatic allies, to help jump-start stalled peace processes or launch new ones. The ability of the United States to bring warring parties to the negotiating table has been sadly underutilized in recent years.

e) Clear top-level leadership: Senior-level officials in the administration should run point for their departments and agencies to ensure maximal coordination and rapid response. Cabinet officials should clearly assign responsibility for leading on African conflict resolution issues to a senior official within his or her department or agency, thus minimizing confusion over responsibility. At times, these assigned officials could take a more direct role in support of negotiations if appropriate, and in close coordination with the Task Force described above.

（length: 1, 890 words）

Vocabulary

batter v. 连续猛击；捣碎，打烂

bureaucratic a. 官僚的，官僚作风的

calculus n. 结石；积石，牙垢；运算，演算

cornerstone n. 奠基石；基础；最重要部分

demonize v. 使成为魔鬼

denominator n. 分母；共同特性

deploy v.（尤指军事行动）使展开；施展；有效地利用

drain v. 使（精力、金钱等）耗尽
n. 排水；下水道

envoy n. 使节，外交官；全权公使

genocide n. 种族灭绝；灭种的罪行；斩尽杀绝

gravitas n. 庄严的举止，庄严

leverage n. 杠杆作用；优势，力量；影响力

mantra n. 颂歌，圣歌；咒语

pandemic n.（全国或全球性）流行病

preclude v. 阻止；排除；妨碍；使……行不通

prerogative n. 权利；特权；[英史]大主教法庭

proxy n. 代表权；代理人；委托书

rebound v. （使）弹回；（从诸如衰败或失望）中恢复过来

repercussion n. 弹回；后响；后果；反射

ruinous a. 耗资巨大的；无法承担的；破坏性的

simmer v. 炖；酝酿

skew v. 歪曲；曲解；使不公允

subsidy n. 补贴，津贴，补助金

tendentious a.（指演说、文章等）宣传性的；有偏见的

tenure n. 占有（职位、不动产等）；终身职位

unprecedented a. 前所未有的，史无前例的；空前的

Section D Word Bank for This Unit

弹性外交	elastic diplomacy
全方位外交	multi-faceted diplomacy
高层次、全方位的对话	high-level and all-directional dialogue
公认的国际关系原则	generally-accepted principles of international relations
国际关系的准则	norms governing international relations
国际惯例	international common practice
国家不分大小，应该一律平等	All countries, big or small, should be equal
捍卫国家主权、领土完整和民族尊严	safeguard national sovereignty, territorial integrity and national dignity
毫无根据的媒体报道	groundless media reports
和平共处五项原	the Five Principles of Peaceful Coexistence
多极化	multipolarity
霸权主义	hegemonism
强权政治	power politics
国家主权	national sovereignty
民族资源	national resources
边界谈判	boundary negotiation
不结盟国家	non-aligned countries
外交承认	diplomatic recognition
外交纷争	diplomatic dispute
外交攻势	diplomatic offensive
外交使团	diplomatic mission
外交政策的基石	cornerstone of a country's foreign policy
万国公法	Law of Nations
维持外交关系	maintain diplomatic relations
维护世界和平	safeguard world peace
武装冲突	armed conflict
西方国家利益	Western interests
外交部	Ministry of Foreign Affairs
礼宾司	Protocol Department
新闻司	Information Department
大使馆	embassy
公使馆	legation
总领事馆	consulate-general
领事馆	consulate
联络处	liaison office
外交家，外交官	diplomat
大使	ambassador
公报	communique
公告，通告	announcement
国书	letter of credence, credentials
互相承认	mutual recognition
建立外交关系	establishment of diplomatic relations
介绍书	letter of introduction
离任期间	during one's absence
声明	statement
外交惯例	diplomatic practice
外交豁免	diplomatic immunity
外交特权	diplomatic privilege
外交途径	diplomatic channel
委任书	letter of appointment
委任证书	certificate of appointment
召回公文	letter of recall
普通照会	verbal note
通知照会	circular note
正式照会	formal note
正常化	normalization
被任命为驻……大使	be appointed ambassador to
表示遗憾	to express regret
断绝外交关系	to sever diplomatic relations
返任	to resume charge of the office, to return to one's post
赴任	to proceed to take up one's post
递交国书	to present one's credentials
互派大使	to exchange ambassadors
恢复外交关系	to resume diplomatic relations
建立大使级外交关系	to establish diplomatic relations at ambassadorial level
建立领事关系	to establish consular relations
就任	to assume one's post
提出异议	to take exception to, to object to
外交关系升格	to upgrade diplomatic relations
向……提出交涉	to make representations to, to take up a (the) matter with
向……提出抗议	to lodge a protest with
征求……的同意	to request the consent of

中断外交关系	to suspend diplomatic relations
建设性战略伙伴关系	constructive strategic partnership
全面战略伙伴关系	overall strategic partnership
	rapprochement
高层协作	high-level cooperation
战略经济对话	Strategic and Economic Dialogue
建立邦交	establish diplomatic ties
相互信任	mutual trust
共同繁荣	common prosperity
友好访问	friendly visit, goodwill visit
非正式访问	informal visit
正式访问	official visit
私人访问	private visit
国事访问	state visit
国宴	state banquet
欢迎词	speech of welcome
欢迎宴会	welcoming banquet
鸡尾酒会	cocktail party
招待会	reception
祝酒词	toast
提议为……干杯	to propose a toast to
健康长寿	good health and a long life
盛情接待	cordial hospitality
双方	the two sides, the two parties
午宴	luncheon

贺电	message of greeting, message of congratulation
欣逢	on the happy occasion of
欣悉	on learning with great joy
致以衷心的祝贺和最好的愿望	to express one's sincere congratulations and best wishes
祝（某国）国家繁荣、人民幸福	to wish prosperity to a country and well-being to its people
唁电	message of condolence
深切哀悼	profound condolence
追悼会	memorial meeting
表示慰问	to convey one's sympathy
会见	to meet with
检阅仪仗队	to review the guard of honor
交换意见	to exchange views
接见	to receive
惊悉	to be shocked to learn of
认为	be of the opinion, to hold, to consider, to maintain
宴请……	to give a banquet in honor of
应邀	on invitation, upon invitation
应……邀请	at the invitation of
在……陪同下	in the company of, accompanied by

Chapter 5

Education

教育是立国之本，在任何一个国家都是如此。英美遵循公平的教育制度。特别是在 20 世纪 60 年代以后，发达国家更加注重教育从形式公平到实质公平，教育机会均等的内涵已由入学机会及接受共同教育机会均等，扩展为使处在社会经济不利地位的学生有弥补文化和教育资源不足的机会，以教育机会的平等，促进社会平等的实现。

此章节主要介绍英美两个国家有特色的教育方法和手段。这两个国家的教育制度既有相似之处也有不同之处。本章节将会就英国的高考形式的变化和美国的高考对孩子们的影响，以及英美的高校在课堂中所引用的独特的教学方式加以介绍。

Section A Intensive Reading

First Fall in GCSE Grades in Exam's History

There has been a fall in the **proportion** of GCSEs awarded an A*-C grade, for the first time since the exams were introduced 24 years ago. This year's results show 69.4% of entries earned grades A*-C, compared with 69.8% last year. There is also a fall in the proportion of pupils receiving the top A* and A grades, down to 22.4% from 23.2%. About 658,000 16-year-olds in England, Wales and Northern Ireland are receiving their results. A further 547,000 **candidates**, many of whom will have sat exams a year early or as adults, are also receiving their grades. The pass rate had steadily risen since the exams replaced O-levels and CSEs in 1988, when 42.5% of entries were awarded an A*-C grade. By 2010 69.1% were awarded these grades, prompting **accusations** of grade **inflation.**

➢ Grade boundaries

The proportion of entries awarded top grades had also risen every year.

In an attempt to address concerns of "**dumbing** down" and ensure results were comparable, England's exams regulator, Ofqual, told exam boards they would have to justify any results notably different to those of previous years. This year a number of new GCSE syllabuses, including English, mathematics and ICT, are being assessed for the first time. So extra measures are taken to ensure grades are comparable. The system known as "comparable outcomes" — which focuses on the proportion of students achieving each grade—sparked accusations that the exam boards were being asked to fix results. The Association of Teachers and Lecturers said there were concerns about the approach. An Ofqual spokeswoman said: "We don't 'fix' grades—but we do make sure that grades are right. We have developed our approach with the help of the best experts in the field, and we are open about what we do."

➢ Future changes to GCSEs

Modular GCSEs are being dropped in England, so that pupils starting GCSE courses this September will have to sit all their exams at the end of the course. GCSE exams sat in 2014 in English literature, geography, history and religious education will also be assessed for spelling, punctuation and grammar. Schools in Wales and Northern Ireland will continue to be able to opt for modular GCSEs. Changes that could see a return of O-level-style exams are planned for further down the line. She added: "Results do go up or down, for various reasons. They don't stay exactly the same each year, in each subject. But we have to be as sure as we can be that any movement is for a good reason, and that is what we do." Thursday's **statistics** show a decrease in the proportion of GCSEs awarded at least a C grade in the core subjects of English, maths and science. The fall is particularly pronounced in English. In English literature, 76.3% of exams were awarded A*-C, compared with 78.4% last year, and 23.2% earned at least an A, down from 25% in 2011.

In English language and combined English literature and language exams, results went down from 65.5% getting A*-C to 64.2%.

And head teachers representing dozens of schools say some students have been marked down by an entire grade in English compared with the results that teachers had predicted. But the Joint Council for **Qualifications,** which publishes the **annual** results, said they were happy with the grades awarded and the drop in A*-C English results was partly down to fewer candidates sitting the exam earlier, during the winter exam season.

➢ Gender gap

In science, which has been made tougher, there has been a 2.2 percentage point drop in the proportion of entries awarded an A*-C grade. Some 60.7% are achieving these good grades. There has also been a fall in A*-C results in maths, with 58.4% of entries getting at least a C grade, down from 58.8% in 2011. This year's results also show the gap between girls and boys stalled at the very top grades, with 18.9% of boys' entries achieving an A* and A, compared to 25.6% of girls' entries—a percentage gap of 6.7%, the same as in 2011. At grades A* to C, girls are outperforming boys, with 65.4% of boys' entries attaining that level, compared to 73.3% of girls' entries.

The decline in the number of pupils opting to take modern foreign languages slowed this year, with even a rise of 10% in the number of those sitting Spanish GCSE. The number of entries for French fell by 0.5%, compared to a 13.2% fall last year, and the entries for German fell by 5.5% compared to a 13.2% fall in 2011. There was also a rise of 13.7% in the uptake of other modern languages, including Arabic, Chinese, **Persian**, **Polish**, **Portuguese** and Italian, which all saw significant increases.

➢ Hard work

Schools minister Nick Gibb said: "Tens of thousands of young people are today reaping the rewards of their hard work over the last two years. It is right that we congratulate students on their results and thank the **inspirational** heads, teachers and support staff that have helped them succeed." Head of the Nasuwt teaching union Chris Keates said the government may seek to claim the dip in grades was the result of its "toughening up" exams, but that this was untrue. But she added that it would not be long before results were affected negatively by government spending cuts and its "elitist" reforms.

NUT general secretary Christine Blower said the raising of school GCSE targets to 40% of pupils getting five good GCSEs (including English and maths), combined with shifts in grade boundaries meant many schools would face "a double whammy".

She added: "If classified as 'failing', they (schools) will of course be more threatened with academy conversion." Pupils in Scotland, who take Scottish Standard Grade and Higher qualifications, rather than GCSEs and A-levels, received their results earlier in August.

(length: 976 words)

Vocabulary

accusation	n. 控告	Persian	n. 波斯语
annual	a. 年度的	Polish	n. 波兰语
candidate	n. 候选人	Portuguese	n. 葡萄牙语
dumbing	a. 沉默的	proportion	n. 比例
inflation	n. 通货膨胀	qualification	n. 资格
inspirational	a. 灵感的	statistics	n. 统计数据

Exercises

I. Comprehension

1. Recall

1) When was GCSE first introduced in UK?

2) How much did the results go down in English language and combined English literature and language exams?

2. Make inferences

What does the author mean by saying "dumbing down" in the second paragraph?

3. Analyze

What message is the author conveying through this passage?

4. Evaluate

1) If you have to take the GCSE, how will you do? Do you think you will like it?

2) What do you think is the difference between GCSE and Chinese College Entrance Examination?

II. Further Study

Can you give us an analysis of the Statistics of the Entrance Examination in 10 years and give a report about it in class?

Section B Extensive Reading

A Teenager Talks Back

by Graham Charles

Imagine the **average** American adult walking down the average city street and seeing several teenagers walk toward him. Brightly dressed, some are listening to **suggestive** music on **portable** stereos while others talk loudly about parties and **recreational** opportunities. As an **advocate** of peace and quiet, the God-fearing grown-up feels intense disappointment and fear on seeing the "Future of America" **personified**, and may even display a **contempt** almost bordering on **hatred**. From where does this **animosity** come? Why are adults attacking me, the American teenager?

As I see it, it begins with the **unflattering** images of **adolescents** in the media. Television and movies portray teens as an alien race with below-average intelligence and an insatiable appetite for sex, drugs and rock music. Newspaper and magazine articles document our hideous deficiencies in science, math and geography while pop-philosophy books about the generally poor state of students' minds are marketed to an all-too-hungry public by professors who spend more of their lives with Rousseau and Plato than with the people they write about. These books become best sellers, sucked in by adults-on-the-street who believe that young people constitute a separate species. This classification is only reinforced by our style of dress and by our music.

The line between the generations is drawn; teenagers are **subhuman**. Adults visualize us as drunk drivers, illiterate delinquents, punk rockers in leather, and then judge every young person they meet by that stereotype. They seem chilly when they deal with us; they keep their distance and segregate us by age. And we begin to dislike them for **withholding** the right to their friendship. Such skirmishes drive a wedge between us, solidifying the sides of the battle. I propose a truce.

First, adults must stop using studies designed to show how stupid we are. The statistics are **fascinating**, but they amount to little more than teen bashing. Too many articles today are halfhearted attempts to discover "why Johnny can't read", and barely **disguise** the perverse pleasures taken in seeing how stupid Johnny can be. To know what we do not know is only the staring point of an education, yet the most publicized findings detail how many students cannot locate the United States on a world map or say when Columbus landed in the New World. Unfortunately, the real problem of what teachers do or do not teach us is almost always **glossed** over.

Second, adults should avoid the trap baited by Allan Bloom, William Bennett and the other overlords of education who take statistics from misdirected studies and use Enlightenment philosophy to attack teenagers. As **intellectual** name-droppers, they blame kids for causing education's problems. They deprecate teenage lifestyles in their books and at their press conferences. We are ready targets: we sport easy-to-criticize clothes and haircuts; we do not vote, and we have relatively little purchasing power. Call us shallow, call us lazy, call us stupid, but adults know there is little chance of retaliation. Using teenagers as scapegoats is too easy.

Third, the **ceaseless** grading of students must be stopped. The various numbers that are attached to us are not much different from astrological forecasts: they seem about right, but they just don't fit the individual at all. SAT scores and grade-point averages are only rough indicators of our worthiness. But the need to get high numbers puts enormous pressure on us to achieve. "successful" students get measurably more respect than underachievers, as well as scholarship money and their first choice of college. Unfortunately, many work so hard to gain that illusory image of success that they remain ignorant about the qualities that are needed to be a successful human being.

The constant **categorizing** of students as successful or not only serves to strengthen the insidious process that treats teenagers as statistics, which, in turn, increases the pressure on them to distinguish themselves in some way. Eventually, the vicious cycle collapses, as do too many students.

Research should be devoted to improving education, not tearing students apart. Cut out these worthless surveys, as well as standardized tests administered to bolster both school and state rankings; they are only depleting school budgets. Use the money to improve schools in the inner-cities and to bring teachers' salaries up from the range of those who collect garbage.

I am not trying to blame all our problems on these heavily publicized studies or the philosophers who have had a field day interpreting the portents for the future. Solving the education crisis cannot be done in 1,000 words. But America's fascination with teen bashing hurts. We are belittled while we are being studied. And I am simply tired of being talked about as a percentage and not as a person. Aside from our parents and teachers, few adults even spend time with us.

To keep the truce, all adults must begin to talk to us. The infamous generation "gap" is caused less by grown-ups and teenagers not being able to talk to one another as by them not being willing to talk. Talk with a young person, not as one of "them", but as a person who just happens to be young. Accept our strange ways and dress; then perhaps we will accept yours. Only by coming together will we be able to begin resolving our educational shortcomings. By pulling apart, we have only **compounded** them.

(length: 897 words)

Vocabulary

adolescent	n. 青少年	gloss	v. 使光彩
advocate	n. 倡导者	hatred	n. 憎恨，敌意
animosity	n. 憎恨，敌意	intellectual	n. 知识分子
average	a. 普通的	personify	v. 拟人化
categorize	v. 分类	portable	a. 便携的
ceaseless	a. 不断的	recreational	a. 娱乐的，消遣的
compound	v. 组合，混合	subhuman	a. 类人的
contempt	n. 轻视，蔑视	suggestive	a. 暗示的
disguise	v. 假装	unflattering	a. 坦率的，不奉承的
fascinating	a. 迷人的，使着迷的	withhold	v. 克制

Exercises

I. Comprehension

1. Summarize

1) What is the main idea that the author tries to convey?

2) Why are adults attacking the American teenager according to the author?

2. Make Inferences

What does the author mean by saying "successful" students in paragraph 7?

3. Analyze

Who do you think wrote this passage

4. Evaluate

In your opinion, do you think the problems mentioned by the author exist in China? How to solve those problems?

II. Further Study

Write eight sentences using words from the columns below. Each sentence should include at least two words from two different columns. You may change the forms of the verbs but not of the nouns.

NOUN	VERB	MODIFIER
animosity	reinforce	insidious
delinquents	segregate	perverse

scapegoat	bolster	insatiable
skirmish	deprecate	hideous
retaliation	criticize	worthless
surveys	publicize	halfhearted

Example: The delinquents were segregated from the rest of the population.

1. ______________________________
2. ______________________________
3. ______________________________
4. ______________________________
5. ______________________________
6. ______________________________
7. ______________________________
8. ______________________________

Section C Supplementary Reading

□ Passage 1 Bittersweet Farewell of a Grown-Up Child

My parents have retired to Florida, and I am suffering an **empty nest syndrome**. They taught me the value of family, urged me to settle in town, **nurtured** the love of my children and then they left. I may be 31 years old and a liberated woman, but it still hurts. There are thousands of people like me, experiencing a kind of delayed separation anxiety. Our parents are leaving the old hometown and shaking our roots loose as they go.

In a **parody** of their **ancestors** who endured an arduous sea voyage in hopes of a better life, my well-heeled, lively parents tooled down I-95 in search of sunny days and four for bridge. They traded their snow shovels for golf clubs and left us behind to cope with real life.

Part of me is happy for them. Both in their 50's fit and independent, they have made a **gutsy** move. **Methodically**, they lightened their load, sold their house and my father's dental practice, and bought an apartment in Florida.

But somewhere inside, I'm uneasy. Certainly my own life, my husband's life and my children's lives are **diminished** by their absence. The daily calls or visits or just sightings of my mother's car parked in town were like touching down for a moment, a warm spot in each day. There were always noncritical ears to hear my side of an argument, a sensible voice to advise **compromise**. Mainly, the balance they provided on a daily basis is missing, the balance between past and present and the balance between my identity as a child and as a mother. That is all gone, because phone communication is brief and all the news is edited. The daily aches, fears and **squabbles** are deleted. Good news only, kids, it's Grandma calling.

I wonder about two active people retiring. What will they do for the next 30 or 40 years?

Can they really withdraw from the **tumult** of Northern life and embrace Southern ways? Or are they just exchanging one set of anxieties for another? Perhaps this is self-centered—I may be unwilling to scc my parents retire because it is another confirmation that I, too, am getting older.

There is anger in me as well. The child inside is holding her breath and turning blue; an unreasonable reaction, but let me explain.

We live in a lovely community where people don't grow up longing to find a better life for themselves. They long to be able to afford this one, right here.

My parents, sisters, and I lived in our house in Cedarhurst, L.I., for most of our lives. Not that we were overprotected, but I wouldn't sleep at a friend's house until I was 14. When it came time to go "away" to college, I only made it as far as New York University.

Of course, I married the boy I knew in high school, and we settled just down the road in Woodmere. Only my sister threatened our **geographic** unity. Always the independent one (she made it to Boston for college), she married and settled in Philadelphia.

I began making phone calls to her. "What if you both get a virus in the middle of the night?" I whispered, "What happens when you have a baby and Mom isn't there to help out?"

After three years, they moved just down the road to Hewlett. So there we were, all settled in, reveling in our togetherness, except Mom and Dad, apparently. They smiled lovingly at us all and announced their impending retirement.

I'm the first one to admit it was childlike, but I was angry. My father was always quoting Margaret Mead on the value of an extended family. Now he wanted to deprive his grandchildren of that experience.

Once the decision was made, my parents began shedding possessions as a dog shakes out fleas. For my husband and me, the house was part of our youth and romance. Memories mixed with the dust and plaster as pictures came down and **relics** were **hauled** up from the basement.

We all thought it would be fun to have a garage sale on the last weekend before they moved. Bits and pieces of ourselves, our old life was cold and traffic was slow. By afternoon, my father stood outside alone, handing our things to strangers.

Maybe part of the sadness was the air of finality. There were unmentioned but strongly felt parallels to the cleaning out and closing up that accompanies a death. My parents vacuumed up every trace of themselves, and they left town.

The woman in me shouts "**bravo**" for their daring and the new days before them. They didn't wait for widowhood or illness to force their retirement. They made a free choice.

But there is still the child in me, too, perhaps more **petulant** in this time of adjustment.

Several months ago, the night before my husband and I left for a vacation alone, I heard my 4-year-old daughter crying in bed. She didn't want us to go, she said. Patiently, logically, I explained that mothers and fathers need time away to themselves. She nodded her head, endured my explanation and asked, "But who will be my mother when you are gone?"

When we said goodbye to my parents, the child in me was asking the same question.

(length: 904 words)

Vocabulary

ancestor	n. 祖先	methodically	ad. 有方法地，系统地
bravo	int. 好极了	nurture	v. 培育
compromise	v. /n. 妥协，让步	parody	n. 拙劣的模仿者
confirmation	n. 证实	petulant	a. 暴躁的，任性的
diminish	v. 减少	relics	n. 遗迹，遗骸
empty nest	phr. 空巢	squabble	n. 争论，口角
geographic	a. 地理的	syndrome	n. 症状
gutsy	a. 勇敢的	tumult	n. 骚乱，吵闹
haul	v. 拖拽		

□ Passage 2 Inviting Parents in: Expanding Our Community Base to Support Writing

"I want you to try something," Cathy announces as she looks around at the 20 or so adults—parents, grandparents, aunts and uncles—gathered in the school library on a Tuesday evening last winter. "Think for a minute about something you have written lately. It could be something from work or school or something personal like a letter or a eulogy," She pauses. "Everybody got something in mind? OK, now I want you to visualize yourself writing that thing. Where were you? What were you doing as you to take three to four minutes to **freewrite** about the experience of writing that particular letter or report or whatever? Don't worry about spelling or complete sentences or perfect grammar. I just want you to use the writing to get out some ideas. No one will read what you've written, but we will ask you to talk about it afterwards."

And like magic (or so it seems), the adults start writing. They write about love letters they've created for work, difficult emails they've sent to relatives, eulogies they've written for loved ones, papers they've composed for their college or GED classes, and more. After a few minutes, we ask them to find a place to pause in their thoughts and begin sharing what they wrote about.

Hesitantly at first, the adults look at each other. Finally, one brave woman raises her hand and begins, "Well, I wrote about the time I wrote a grant proposal for work and it took forever. I had to keep writing and showing it to my boss and my team, and they kept offering feedback. It took a lot of work and I was so proud when we got the grant."

"Great," Cathy responds with a smile, "Thanks for sharing this. Anybody else have something? Maybe something that was different?"

Another parent responds, "I wrote about a text I wrote in the parking lot when I was waiting to pick up my daughter the other day. It was to a friend, but we'd had some problems, so I was really careful to get it just right."

"Another great example," Cathy goes on, "Anybody else?" And the adults continue to share, ready to talk as they hear the examples of others. As they share, we ask them to make some connections: "I notice that a lot of you are talking about writing on computers. Do all of you write on computers?" They think for a minute, and one parent finally says, "Well, it depends on what I'm writing."

"What do you mean?" Kim asks.

"If I'm writing something for work, it's always on computer. But if it's something more personal, like a letter to a friend or a letter of condolence, I use pen and paper." Others nod heads in agreement.

"That's really interesting. So, it depends on the audience and the genre or kind of writing? Well, what about revising? Remember how one parent just mentioned sharing her drafts of a grant proposal with co-orkers and her boss and that they gave feedback that helped her revise? What about in your writing? Do you revise? And how do you do it?"

And on it goes, the parents sharing their experiences with **drafting**, revising, prewriting; their understanding of genre and audience; their idiosyncratic approaches and what they have in common. Without even realizing it, these parents have captured the **essence** of writing through their own experiences and are now prepped to hear more about writing in schools and what they can do at home to help their children and teens with writing—the goal of this gathering.

➢ **Workshops for Parents (and Students)**

This **scenario** is one we have repeated dozens and dozens of times over the past five years in workshops we have designed as part of our National Writing Project site, the Eastern Michigan Writing Project. Known as the Family Literacy Initiative (FLI), the project began as a few workshops offered to parents of elementary students who wanted to know what they could do in the summer to keep their kids writing. Since that time the FLI has grown tremendously: in the past five years, we have offered 130 workshops, reaching more than 2,750 adults and students. We've grown from one-session workshops offered exclusively for parents to some for parents and children together to four-session workshops that lead to production of a parent-and-student written anthology. Most recently, we have partnered with the University Writing Center at Eastern Michigan University to create a new set of workshops that focus on teens, with a parent version titled "How to Help Prepare Your Teen for College Writing" and a parallel offering for teens called "Preparing for College Writing" .

At the heart of these workshops is our commitment to working with parents, inviting them into what can sometimes seem the closed community of schools, a place where they may not see themselves as having a role. Teachers, overwhelmed with the day-to-day obligations of creating meaningful learning environments for their students, too often don't have the energy to do more than offer parents small tidbits of information, perhaps through newsletters or **curriculum** nights. We want to suggest, though, that immersing parents in discussions of writing and offering them ways to help their own children and teens as writers can help send a message about the value of thoughtful writing instruction, a necessary message especially in the current climate.

➢ **Why Outreach to Parents Is So Important**

It's a truism that working with families and learning from them about their children gives us a kind of insider knowledge about our students' learning styles and backgrounds—an insider knowledge that is invaluable in understanding what makes students tick and what ways of teaching might work best. And as a predominately white middle-class teaching force meets an increasingly diverse and multicultural student population, we need these kinds of partnerships more than ever, so that we can approach the challenges of teaching with as much knowledge and understanding as possible.

But we want to argue that outreach to families has other purposes as well, especially as a means of helping families understand why we teach in the ways we do. Because the ways we teach writing are often quite different from the ways most of our students' parents learned to write, these parents are sometimes understandably confused about what literacy instruction is all about: both the terminology of writing instruction (process writing, minilessons, craft lessons) and the best ways they can help their children or teens with their writing. Especially in an age in which many in the community get their primary information about pedagogy from newspaper accounts and legislative mandates, we think it is incredibly important for us to reach out to parents and communities to help them understand the kinds of research-based practices we know work. Think of it in two ways: we want parents to be both informed, knowledgeable readers of educational reform and potential **advocates** for change.

➢ A Typical Workshop for Parents of Teens

Given the current fascination with the term college and career readiness, we find it no surprise that our newest workshops for parents of teens are gaining momentum. In the pages that follow, we introduce the standard format we've used for this workshop, but we also want to stress that we are constantly adapting the workshops. We tweak them based on the time we have, what we know about the parents and teens in that particular setting, and what we've seen that work well in certain contexts. There really isn't such a thing as a "typical workshop" for parents of teens, but to give a sense of what can happen, we describe our basic approach.

The goal in the workshop for parents of teens is threefold: ① to introduce them (in parent-friendly language) to some research-based understanding of writing instruction; ② to give them a sense of what college writing will be like (which is usually quite different from their own real or imagined experiences); ③ and to offer them some ideas of how they might support their teens in the years before college. As we do this workshop, often we have teens in the room next door having a parallel experience: first-year writing instructors from our university engage them in conversation about college writing, prompting them through fun writing activities that they might play with even after the **workshop** to help them become truly "college ready". Our goal has been that parents and teens might, in the car ride home, share what they've learned and continue the discussion about writing.

No matter what the context, we always begin with the prompt that introduces this article, inviting the parents to share their own writing experiences—a prompt that truly has worked almost magically in any setting we've been in. It begins the workshop with a shared experience and quickly establishes some shared language about writing. Then, drawing on what the parents have talked about, we introduce a handout about *Best Practices in Writing Instruction* The left side (adapted from Zemelman, Daniels, and Hydes's book *Best Practice: New Standards for Teaching and Learning in America's Schools*) summarizes for parents some research-based understandings of writing instruction that inform the ways teachers structure writing instruction in their classrooms. The right side is something we developed to adapt those understandings into parent-friendly implications: what we see as the first step in helping these adults think about what their role might be in helping their teens as writers—especially in helping them see their role as beyond "editor" of their kids' work.

For many parents, this one handout eases tension. Convinced prior to this evening that their role had to be that of ice-cold critic, limited to correcting spelling and **punctuation** for their teens, parents visibly heave a sigh of relief when they hear us talk of encouraging, supporting, lavishing praise, and asking heartfelt questions. This is something they can do!

Some parents, though, are still worried. For them, these ideas seem to be too much of a "feel-good" approach, research-based though they may be. ("But what will happen to my daughter in college if she can't remember the difference between *its* and *it's?*") And so we share with them some specifics about what college writing is really like, making distinctions among the typical kinds of writing their teens will experience in college [i.e., *writing to learn* (notes, journals, free writes), *writing to display* (essays, analyses, lab reports), *learning to write* (pieces and drafts that help students learn genres and conventions)], sharing some specific assignments gathered from various professors, and explaining how these multiple kinds of writing should be finished.

Encourage your adolescents to write—even if they struggle with the written word. In order to be successful and fluent writers, teens need to know they can write—even if their work doesn't look or sound perfect!

Help your teens use writing as a way to communicate their hopes, dreams, fears, and concerns. When your adolescents see writing as serving a real purpose, they will be more likely to try it.

Student writing should sound like student writing!

When teens believe that their writing is their own, they will become more likely to invest themselves in it.

Our teens, like all writers, have different ways of approaching writing tasks. Tune in to your adolescents' learning styles and needs as writers. Know that some writing is one draft and some other writing takes time and multiple drafts.

Talk with your adolescents about their ideas and encourage them to draw, freewrite, and make lists or webs in order to get started.

Listen to your teens' drafts and ask real questions about content. Heartfelt questions are the best way to encourage all writers to keep on writing.

If you notice errors in **conventions** in your adolescent's writing, pick just one area at a time to work on (such as punctuation, dialogue, or capitalization). You might also refer to real texts (books, newspapers, letters, magazines), to see how published authors tackle issues of punctuation, spelling, and more.

Help your teen find real audiences (family, friends, neighbors) to communicate with.

You can write just about anything at home: letters to family and friends, songs and plays to perform for the family, scripts for podcasts, blogs...The list is endless!

You job as a parent is to encourage and support the effort your teen makes in writing. Be lavish in praise and specific and limited in your suggestions for improvement.

Call for a variety of skills and thought processes. Becoming a successful college writer, we tell them, is certainly about the product their teens will create, but even more importantly, it's about the ways they'll approach the creation of that product—reminding them again of the issues they spoke of in the initial prompt.

Why this focus on the qualities of successful college writers, rather than on the nitty-gritty about specific ways to write? We, like many secondary and college teachers, have watched with great interest the current trend to define "college and career ready" students in ways that seem increasingly narrow and limiting. We are inspired by documents such as *Framework for Success in College Writing*, jointly written by the Council of Writing Program Administrators, NCTE, and the National Writing Project, a document that explains why a focus on "habits of mind", rather than **discrete** tasks or mastery over particular genres, is so important.

(length: 2,236 words)

Vocabulary

advocate	v. 提倡	fascination	n. 魅力，魔力
convention	n. 大会，惯例	freewrite	v. 自由写作
curriculum	n. 课程	punctuation	n. 标点符号
discrete	a. 离散的	scenario	n. 方案
drafting	n. 起草	workshop	n. 研讨会
essence	n. 本质，精华		

Section D Word Bank for This Unit

中学校长	principal	选修课	optional/selective course
小学校长	headmaster	文学	literature
小学校长（女）	headmistress	哲学	philosophy
登记，报到	register, enroll	社会学	sociology
开学典礼	opening ceremony	语言学	linguistics
学校介绍会	orientation meeting	心理学	psychology
报告	lecture	工程学	engineering
基础课	basic course	建筑学	architecture
专业课	specialized course	经济学	economics
必修课	required course	金融学	finance

会计学	accounting
银行学	banking
生物化学	biochemistry
幼儿园	kindergarten
幼儿园（美）	day-care center
托儿所	nursery school
初等教育	elementary education
中等教育	secondary education
高等教育	higher education
成人教育	adult education
免试入学制	open admission
小学（英/美）	primary/elementary school
中学	secondary school
男女生同校制度	coeducation
初中	junior high school
高中	senior high school
附中	attached middle school
技校	technical school
理工学院/科技大学	institute of technolgy
研究生院	graduate school
夜大，函大	open university
研究生	postgraduate
校友（男/女）	alumnus/alumna
本科	undergraduate
新生训练	orientation program
教学设施	teaching facilities
助学金	assistantship
奖学金	scholarship
礼堂	auditorium
学习年限	period of schooling
学分制	credit system
课程表	schedule, school timetable

自习	individual study
课外活动	after-school activity
社会调查	social investigation
义务劳动	voluntary labor
毕业评估	graduation appraisal
毕业典礼	graduation ceremony
毕业证书	diploma, graduation certificate
出勤率	attendance, participation
上课	attend a lecture
开除	expel sb from school
学费	tuition
杂费	miscellaneous expenses
讲义夹	lecture portfolio
一学期，半年	semester
毕业证	diploma
专科证书	associate diploma
学士	Bachelor
硕士	Master
（哲学）博士	Doctor of Philosophy
顾问	consultant
班主任，协调人	coordinator
副教授	associate professor
讲师	lecturer
导师	adviser, mentor
辅导老师	counselor
课程安排	course arrangement
申请表	application form
演讲	presentation
论文	paper, thesis, dissertation
表扬信	letter of recommendation
教授与学生面谈时间	office hour
研讨班	seminar

Chapter 6

Literature

文学是一个民族优秀思想文化的结晶，人类宝贵的精神财富。它反映了一个民族在社会、政治、经济、生活、习俗等许多方面的文化。英美文学作品当之无愧成了不可或缺的文化学习材料，为读者提供了一个了解英美文化传统、社会、经济发展和经济制度等背景知识的机会。

文学是语言大师经过加工提炼的语言作品，是我们学习与模仿的最好语言材料。它具有形象生动、凝练精美的特点。广泛阅读英美文学作品，体验原汁原味、经典精邃的文学语言，可以提高读者对语言的感受能力和对作品的鉴赏能力。

英美文学史上留下了一长串值得记忆的名字：杰弗雷·乔叟、威廉·莎士比亚、弗朗西斯·培根、约翰·弥尔顿、简· 奥斯汀、乔治·戈登·拜伦、约翰·济慈、查尔斯·狄更斯、托马斯·艾略特、托马斯·哈代、奥斯卡·王尔德、乔治·萧伯纳、詹姆斯·乔伊斯等；纳撒尼尔·霍桑、沃尔特·惠特曼、爱伦·坡、艾米莉·迪金森、马克·吐温、西奥多·德莱塞、弗朗西斯·司各特·菲茨杰拉德、欧内斯特·海明威、威廉·福克纳、约翰·斯坦贝克等。

他们的作品形式多样、色彩斑斓，其中不少是经久不衰的传世之作，达到了极高的艺术境界，也是世界文学宝库中令人瞩目的瑰宝。

Section A　Intensive Reading

Cat in the Rain

by Ernest Hemingway

There were only two Americans stopping at the hotel. They did not know any of the people they passed on the stairs on their way to and from their room. Their room was on the second floor facing the sea. It also faced the public garden and the war monument. There were big palms and green benches in the public garden. In the good weather there was always an artist with his **easel**. Artists liked the way the palms grew and the bright colors of the hotels facing the gardens and the sea. Italians came from a long way off to look up at the war monument. It was made of

bronze and **glistened** in the rain. It was raining. The rain dripped from the palm trees. Water stood in pools on the **gravel** paths. The sea broke in a long line in the rain and slipped back down the beach to come up and break again in a long line in the rain. The motor cars were gone from the square by the war monument. Across the square in the doorway of the cafe a waiter stood looking out at the empty square.

The American wife stood at the window looking out. Outside right under their window a cat was **crouched** under one of the dripping green tables. The cat was trying to make herself so **compact** that she would not be dripped on.

"I'm going down and get that kitty," the American wife said. "I'll do it," her husband offered from the bed.

"No, I'll get it. The poor kitty out trying to keep dry under a table."

The husband went on reading, lying **propped** up with the two pillows at the foot of the bed.

"Don't get wet," he said.

The wife went downstairs and the hotel owner stood up and bowed to her as she passed the office. His desk was at the far end of the office. He was an old man and very tall.

"Il piove," the wife said. She liked the hotel-keeper.

"Si, si, **Signora**, brutto tempo. It is very bad weather."

He stood behind his desk in the far end of the dim room. The wife liked him. She liked the deadly serious way he received any complaints. She liked his dignity. She liked the way he wanted to serve her. She liked the way he felt about being a hotel-keeper. She liked his old, heavy face and big hands.

Liking him she opened the door and looked out. It was raining harder. A man in a rubber cape was crossing the empty square to the cafe. The cat would be around to the right. Perhaps she could go along under the eaves. Behind her, it was the maid who looked after their room.

"You must not get wet," she smiled, speaking Italian. Of course, the hotel-keeper had sent her.

With the maid holding the umbrella over her, she walked along the gravel path until she was under their window. The table was there, washed bright green in the rain, but the cat was gone. She was suddenly disappointed. The maid looked up at her.

"Ha perduto qualque cosa, Signora?"

"There was a cat," said the American girl.

"A cat?"

"Si, il gatto."

"A cat?" the maid laughed. "A cat in the rain?"

"Yea," she said, "under the table." Then, "Oh, I wanted it so much. I wanted a kitty."

When she talked English the maid's face tightened. "Come, Signora," she said. "We must get back inside. You will be wet."

"I suppose so," said the American girl.

They went back along the gravel path and passed in the door. The maid stayed outside to close the umbrella.

As the American girl passed the office, the **padrone** bowed from his desk. Something felt very small and tight inside the girl. The padrone made her feel very small and at the same time really important. She had a momentary feeling of being of supreme importance. She went on up the stairs. She opened the door of the room. George was on the bed, reading.

"Did you get the cat?" he asked, putting the book down. "It was gone."

"Wonder where it went to," he said, resting his eyes from reading. She sat down on the bed.

"I wanted it so much," she said. "I don't know why I wanted it so much. I wanted that poor kitty. It isn't any fun to be a poor kitty out in the rain."

George was reading again.

She went over and sat in front of the mirror of the dressing table looking at herself with the handglass. She studied her **profile**, first one side and then the other. Then she studied the back of her head and her neck.

"Don't you think it would be a good idea if I let my hair grow out?" she asked, looking at her profile again. George looked up and saw the back of her neck clipped close like a boy's.

"I like it the way it is."

"I get so tired of it," she said. "I get so tired of looking like a boy."

George shifted his position in the bed. He hadn't looked away from her since she stared to speak.

"You look pretty darn nice," he said.

She laid the mirror down on the **dresser** and went over to the window and looked out. It was getting dark.

"I want to pull my hair back tight and smooth and make a big knot at the back that I can feel," she said. " I want to have a kitty to sit on my lap and **purr** when I stroke her."

"Yeah?" George said from the bed.

"And I want to eat at a table with my own silver and I want candles. And I want it to be spring and I want to brush my hair out in front of a mirror and I want a kitty and I want some new clothes."

"Oh, shut up and get something to read," George said. He was reading again.

His wife was looking out of the window. It was quite dark now and still raining in the palm trees.

"Anyway, I want a cat," she said, "I want a cat. I want a cat now. If I can't have long hair or any fun I can have a cat."

George was not listening. He was reading his book. His wife looked out of the window where the light had come on in the square.

Someone knocked at the door.

"Avanti," George said. He looked up from his book. In the doorway stood the maid. She held a big tortoise-shell cat pressed tight against her and swung down against her body.

"Excuse me," she said, "the padrone asked me to bring this for the Signora."

(length: 1,242 words)

Vocabulary

bronze	n. 青铜	gravel	n. 砂砾，砂砾层
crouch	v. 蜷缩，蹲伏	padrone	n.（意大利语）旅馆老板
compact	a. 紧凑的，不占空间的	profile	n. 侧面，外形，轮廓
dresser	n. 梳妆台	prop	v. 支撑，维持
easel	n. 画架，黑板架	purr	v. 咕噜咕噜叫，发出喉音
glisten	v. 闪光	Signora	n. 夫人；太太

Exercises

I. Comprehension

1. Recall

Where did the story happen?

2. Understand

Interpreting the symbolic meaning of the cat.

3. Analyze

Why did the wife want the cat?

4. Appreciate

What was the function of the "rain" in the story?

II. Further Study

1. How would you explain that the husband had a name while the wife was anonymous?

2. What were the differences between the husband and the hotel-keeper?

Section B Extensive Reading

The Last Leaf

by O.Henry

In a little district west of Washington Square the streets have run crazy and broken themselves into small strips called "places". These "places" make strange angles and curves. One Street crosses itself a time or two. An artist once discovered a valuable possibility in this street. Suppose a collector with a bill for paints, paper and **canvas** should, in **traversing** this route, suddenly meet himself coming back, without a cent having been paid on account!

So, to quaint old Greenwich Village the art people soon came **prowling**, hunting for north windows and eighteenth-century **gables** and Dutch **attics** and low rents. Then they imported some **pewter mugs** and a chafing dish or two from Sixth Avenue, and became a "colony".

At the top of a **squatty**, three-story brick Sue and Johnsy had their **studio**. "Johnsy" was familiar for Joanna. One was from Maine; the other from California. They had met at the table d'hote of an Eighth Street "Delmonico's", and found their tastes in art, **chicory** salad and **bishop sleeves** so **congenial** that the joint studio resulted.

That was in May. In November a cold, unseen stranger, whom the doctors called Pneumonia, stalked about the colony, touching one here and there with his icy fingers. Over on the east side this **ravager** strode boldly, smiting his victims by scores, but his feet trod slowly through the maze of the narrow and moss-grown "places".

Mr. Pneumonia was not what you would call a **chivalric** old gentleman. A mite of a little woman with blood thinned by California **zephyrs** was hardly fair game for the red-fisted, short-breathed old **duffer**. But Johnsy she smote; and she lay, scarcely moving, on her painted iron bedstead, looking through the small Dutch window-panes at the blank side of the next brick house.

One morning the busy doctor invited Sue into the hallway with a shaggy, grey eyebrow.

"She has one chance in—let us say, ten," he said, as he shook down the **mercury** in his clinical thermometer. "And that chance is for her to want to live. This way people have of lining-u on the side of the undertaker makes the entire **pharmacopoeia** look silly. Your little lady has made up her mind that she's not going to get well. Has she anything on her mind?"

"She—she wanted to paint the Bay of Naples some day." said Sue.

"Paint?—Bosh! Has she anything on her mind worth thinking twice—a man for instance?"

"A man?" said Sue, with a jew's-harp twang in her voice. "Is a man worth—but, no, doctor; there is nothing of the kind."

"Well, it is the weakness, then," said the doctor. "I will do all that science, so far as it may filter through my efforts, can accomplish. But whenever my patient begins to count the carriages in her funeral procession I subtract 50 per cent from the **curative** power of medicines. If you will get her to ask one question about the new winter styles in cloak sleeves I will promise you a one-in-five chance for her, instead of one in ten."

After the doctor had gone Sue went into the workroom and cried a Japanese **napkin** to a pulp. Then she **swaggered** into Johnsy's room with her drawing board, whistling **ragtime**.

Johnsy lay, scarcely making a ripple under the bedclothes, with her face toward the window. Sue stopped whistling, thinking she was asleep.

She arranged her board and began a pen-and-ink drawing to illustrate a magazine story. Young artists must pave their way to Art by drawing pictures for magazine stories that young authors write to pave their way to Literature.

As Sue was sketching a pair of elegant horseshow riding trousers and a **monocle** of the figure of the hero, an Idaho cowboy, she heard a low sound, several times repeated. She went quickly to the bedside.

Johnsy's eyes were open wide. She was looking out the window and counting—counting backward.

"Twelve," she said, and little later "eleven"; and then "ten," and "nine"; and then "eight" and "seven," almost together.

Sue look **solicitously** out of the window. What was there to count? There was only a bare, **dreary** yard to be seen, and the blank side of the brick house twenty feet away. An old, old **ivy vine**, **gnarled** and **decayed** at the roots, climbed half way up the brick wall. The cold breath of autumn had stricken its leaves from the vine until its **skeleton** branches clung, almost bare, to the crumbling bricks.

"What is it, dear?" asked Sue.

"Six," said Johnsy, in almost a whisper. "They're falling faster now. Three days ago there were almost a hundred. It made my head ache to count them. But now it's easy. There goes another one. There are only five left now."

"Five what, dear? Tell your Sudie."

"Leaves. On the ivy vine. When the last one falls I must go, too. I've known that for three days. Didn't the doctor tell you?"

"Oh, I never heard of such nonsense," complained Sue, with magnificent **scorn**. "What have old ivy leaves to do with your getting well? And you used to love that vine so, you naughty girl. Don't be a **goosey**. Why, the doctor told me this morning that your chances for getting well real soon were—let's see exactly what he said—he said the chances were ten to one! Why, that's almost as good a chance as we have in New York when we ride on the street cars or walk past a new building. Try to take some **broth** now, and let Sudie go back to her drawing, so she can sell the editor man with it, and buy port wine for her sick child, and pork chops for her greedy self."

"You needn't get any more wine," said Johnsy, keeping her eyes fixed out the window. "There goes another. No, I don't want any broth. That leaves just four. I want to see the last one fall before it gets dark. Then I'll go, too."

"Johnsy, dear," said Sue, bending over her, "will you promise me to keep your eyes closed, and not look out the window until I am done working? I must hand those drawings in by to-morrow. I need the light, or I would draw the shade down."

"Couldn't you draw in the other room?" asked Johnsy, coldly.

"I'd rather be here by you," said Sue. "Beside, I don't want you to keep looking at those silly ivy leaves."

"Tell me as soon as you have finished," said Johnsy, closing her eyes, and lying white and still as fallen statue, "because I want to see the last one fall. I'm tired of waiting. I'm tired of thinking. I want to turn loose my hold on everything, and go sailing down, down, just like one of those poor, tired leaves."

"Try to sleep," said Sue. "I must call Behrman up to be my model for the old hermit miner. I'll not be gone a minute. Don't try to move 'til I come back."

Old Behrman was a painter who lived on the ground floor beneath them. He was past sixty and had a Michael Angelo's Moses beard curling down from the head of a **satyr** along with the body of an **imp**. Behrman was a failure in art. Forty years he had **wielded** the brush without getting near enough to touch the hem of his Mistress's robe. He had been always about to paint a masterpiece, but had never yet begun it. For several years he had painted nothing except now and then a **daub** in the line of commerce or advertising. He earned a little by serving as a model to those young artists in the colony who could not pay the price of a professional. He drank gin to excess, and still talked of his coming masterpiece. For the rest he was a fierce little old man, who scoffed terribly at softness in any one, and who regarded himself as especial **mastiff**-in-waiting to protect the two young artists in the studio above.

Sue found Behrman smelling strongly of **juniper** berries in his dimly lighted **den** below. In one corner was a blank canvas on an easel that had been waiting there for twenty-five years to receive the first line of the masterpiece. She told him of Johnsy's fancy, and how she feared she would, indeed, light and fragile as a leaf herself, float away, when her slight hold upon the world grew weaker.

Old Behrman, with his red eyes plainly streaming, shouted his contempt and **derision** for such idiotic imaginings.

"Vass!" he cried. "Is dere people in de world mit der foolishness to die because leafs dey drop off from a confounded vine? I haf not heard of such a thing. No, I will not bose as a model for your fool hermit-dunderhead. Vy do you allow dot silly pusiness to come in der brain of her? Ach, dot poor leetle Miss Johnsy."

"She is very ill and weak," said Sue, "and the fever has left her mind **morbid** and full of strange fancies. Very well, Mr. Behrman, if you do not care to pose for me, you needn't. But I think you are a horrid old—old **flibbertigibbet**."

"You are just like a woman!" yelled Behrman. "Who said I will not bose? Go on. I come mit you. For half an hour I haf peen trying to say dot I am ready to bose. Gott! Dis is not any blace in which one so goot as Miss Johnsy shall lie sick. Some day I will paint a masterpiece, and we shall all go away. Gott! Yes."

Johnsy was sleeping when they went upstairs. Sue pulled the shade down to the window-sill, and motioned Behrman into the other room. In there they peered out the window fearfully at the ivy vine. Then they looked at each other for a moment without speaking. A **persistent**, cold rain was falling, mingled with snow. Behrman, in his old blue shirt, took his seat as the hermit miner on an upturned kettle for a rock.

When Sue awoke from an hour's sleep the next morning she found Johnsy with dull, wide-open eyes staring at the drawn green shade.

"Pull it up; I want to see," she ordered, in a whisper.

Wearily Sue obeyed.

But, lo! After the beating rain and fierce gusts of wind that had endured through the livelong night, there yet stood out against the brick wall one ivy leaf. It was the last one on the vine. Still dark green near its stem, with its **serrated** edges tinted with the yellow of **dissolution** and decay, it hung bravely from the branch some twenty feet above the ground.

"It is the last one," said Johnsy. "I thought it would surely fall during the night. I heard the wind. It will fall to-day, and I shall die at the same time."

"Dear, dear!" said Sue, leaning her worn face down to the pillow, "Think of me, if you won't think of yourself. What would I do?"

But Johnsy did not answer. The **lonesome** thing in the entire world is a soul when it is making ready to go on its mysterious, far journey. The fancy seemed to possess her more strongly as one by one the ties that bound her to friendship and to earth were loosed.

The day wore away, and even through the twilight they could see the lone ivy leaf clinging to its stem against the wall. And then, with the coming of the night the north wind was again loosed, while the rain still beat against the windows and pattered down from the low Dutch eaves.

When it was light enough Johnsy, the merciless, commanded that the shade be raised.

The ivy leaf was still there.

Johnsy lay for a long time looking at it. And then she called to Sue, who was stirring her chicken broth over the gas stove.

"I've been a bad girl, Sudie," said Johnsy. "Something has made that last leaf stay there to show me how wicked I was. It is a **sin** to want to die. You may bring a me a little broth now, and some milk with a little port in it, and—no; bring me a hand-mirror first, and then pack some pillows about me, and I will sit up and watch you cook."

And hour later she said:

"Sudie, some day I hope to paint the Bay of Naples."

The doctor came in the afternoon, and Sue had an excuse to go into the hallway as he left.

"Even chances," said the doctor, taking Sue's thin, shaking hand in his. "With good nursing you'll win." And now I must see another case I have downstairs. Behrman, his name is—some kind of an artist, I believe. Pneumonia, too. He is an old, weak man, and the attack is **acute**. There is no hope for him; but he goes to the hospital to-day to be made more comfortable."

The next day the doctor said to Sue: "She's out of danger. You won. Nutrition and care now —that's all."

And that afternoon Sue came to the bed where Johnsy lay, contentedly knitting a very blue and very useless woolen shoulder scarf, and put one arm around her, pillows and all.

"I have something to tell you, white mouse," she said. "Mr. Behrman died of **pneumonia** to-day in the hospital. He was ill only two days. The **janitor** found him the morning of the first day in his room downstairs helpless with pain. His shoes and clothing were wet through and icy cold. They couldn't imagine where he had been on such a dreadful night. And then they found a lantern, still lighted, and a ladder that had been dragged from its place, and some scattered brushes, and a **palette** with green and yellow colors mixed on it, and—look out the window, dear, at the last ivy leaf on the wall. Didn't you wonder why it never **fluttered** or moved when the wind blew? Ah, darling, it's Behrman's masterpiece—he painted it there the night that the last leaf fell."

(length: 2,379 words)

Vocabulary

acute	a. [医]急性的，剧烈的；敏锐的	monocle	n. 单片眼镜
attic	n. 阁楼，顶楼	morbid	a. 病的，病态的，恐怖的
bishop sleeves	phr. 主教袖；灯笼袖；紧口大袖	mug	n. 杯子(筒状饮杯，通常有把手)
broth	n. 肉汤	napkin	n. 餐巾，餐巾纸
canvas	n. 画布，油画	palette	n. 调色板，颜料
chicory	n. 菊苣	persistent	a. 持久的，持续的
chivalric	a. 有武士气概的，有武士风范的	pewter	n. 锡镴器皿，白镴（一种银灰色的锡合金）
congenial	a. 同类的，性格相似的，适意的	pharmacopoeia	n. 药典，处方书
curative	a. 医疗的，有疗效的	pneumonia	n. [医] 肺炎
daub	v. 涂抹，乱画	prowl	v. 巡游，潜行
decay	v. 腐朽，腐烂	pulp	n. 纸浆
den	n. 兽穴，洞穴，（舒适的）私室（作学习或办公用）	quaint	a. 古怪的，奇怪的
derision	n. 嘲笑	ravager	n. 毁坏者，掠夺者
dissolution	n. 分解，解散	ragtime	n. 拉格泰姆音乐(1890—1915 期间在美国流行的一种音乐)
dreary	a. 沉闷的；阴郁的	satyr	n. 好色之徒，性欲极强的男人
duffer	n. 笨蛋，不明道理的人	scorn	n. 轻蔑，嘲笑 v. 轻蔑，不屑做
flibbertigibbet	n. 饶舌的人，搬弄是非者	serrated	a. 锯齿状的，有锯齿的
flutter	v. 飘动，鼓翼；使焦急	sin	n. 罪，罪过
gable	n. 山形墙，三角墙，山墙	solicitously	ad. 热心地，热切地
gnarled	a. 饱经风霜的，粗糙的	squatty	a. 矮胖的
goosey	n. 呆子，笨蛋	studio	n. 画室，工作室
imp	n. 小鬼，小淘气，顽童	swagger	v. 昂首阔步，大摇大摆
ivy	n. [植]常春藤	traversen	v. 横过，穿过
janitor	n. 看门人，大楼管理员	vine	n. 蔓生植物（如甜瓜），藤，蔓
juniper	n. [植]刺柏属丛木或树木	wield	v. 挥
lonesome	a. 寂寞的	zephyr	n. 西风，和风，徐风
mastiff	n. [动]獒，大驯犬（大型猛犬之一种）		
mercury	n. 水银，汞		

Exercises

I. Comprehension

1. Recall

Where did the story happen? And how about the weather there?

2. Understand

Did the girl Johnsy die at the end of the story?

3. Explain

How would you explain that the leaf Mr. Behrman painted on the wall is his masterpiece?

4. Analyze

What kind of a person is Mr. Behrman?

5. Appreciate

Find out several sentences which can show O.Henry's humor.

II. Further Study

How would you appreciate O. Henry's ending?

Section C Supplementary Reading

□ Passage 1 Poems

➢ Poem 1

Sonnet XVIII

by William Shakespeare (1564-1616)

Shall I compare thee to a summer's day?
Thou art more lovely and more **temperate**.
Rough winds do shake the darling buds of May,
And often is his gold **complexion** dimmed;
And every fair from fair sometime declines,
By chance or nature's changing course untrimmed;
But thy eternal summer shall not fade,
Nor lose possession of that fair thou ow'st;
Nor shall death brag thou wander'st in his shade
When in eternal lines to time thou grow'st.
So long as men can breathe, or eyes can see,
So long lives this, and this gives life to thee.

➢ Poem 2

The Flea

by John Donne (1573-1631)

Mark but this flea, and mark in this,
How little that which thou deniest me is;
Me is sucked first, and now sucks thee,
And in this flea our two bloods mingled be;
Thou know'st that this cannot be said
A sin, or a shame, or loss of **maidenhead**,
Yet this enjoys before it **woo**,
And **pampered** swells with one blood made of two,
And this , alas, is more than we would do.

Oh stay, three lives in one flea spare,
Where we almost, nay more than married are.
This flea is you and I, and this
Our marriage bed and marriage temple is;
Though parents **grudge**, and you, we are met.
And **cloistered** in these living walls of jet.
Though use make you apt to kill me
Let not to that, self-murder added be,
And **sacrilege**, three sins in killing three.

Cruel and sudden, hast thou since
Purpled thy nail in blood of innocence?
Wherein could this flea guilty be,
Except in that drop which it sucked from thee?
Yet thou triumph'st and sy'st that thou
Find'st not thy self nor me the weaker now;
"Tis true; then learn how false fears be;
Just so much honor, when you yield'st to me.
Will waste, as this flea's death took life from thee.

➢ **Poem 3**

A Red, Red Rose

by Robert Burns (1759-1796)

O my luve is like a red, red rose,
That's newly sprung in June;
O my luve is like the melodie
That's sweetly played in tune.

As fair thou art, my bonie lass,
So deep in luve am I;
And I will luve thee still, my dear,
Till a' the seas gang dry.

Till a' the seas gang dry, my dear,
And the rocks melt wi' the sun;
And I will luve thee still, my dear,
While the sands o' life shall run.

And fare thee weel, my only luve,

And fare thee weel a while;
And I will come again, my luve,
Tho'it wre ten thousand mile!

➢ **Poem 4**

TO—

by Percy Bysshe Shelley （1792-1822）

One word is too often **profaned**
For me to profane it,
One feeling too falsely distain'd
For thee to **distain** it;
One hope is too like despair
For **prudence** to **smother**,
And pity from thee more dear
Than that from another.
I can not give what men call love:
But wilt thou accept not
The worship the heart lifts above
And the heavens reject not,
The desire of the moth for the star,
Of the nigth for the morrow,
The devotion to something afar
From the sphere of our sorrow.

➢ **Poem 5**

When You Are Old

by William Butler Yeats （1865-1939）

When you are old and grey and full of sleep,
And nodding by the fire, take down this book,
And slowly read, and dream of the soft look
Your eyes had once, and of their shadows deep;

How many loved your moments of glad grace,
And loved your beauty with love false or true,
But one man loved the **pilgrim** Soul in you,
And loved the sorrows of your changing face;

And bending down beside the glowing bars,
Murmur, a little sadly, how Love fled
And paced upon the mountains overhead,
And hid his face amid a crowd of stars.

➢ Poem 6

Wild Nights! Wild Nights!

by Emily Dickenson (1830-1886)

Wild Nights! Wild Nights!
Were I with thee,
Wild Nights should be
Our luxury!

Futile the winds
To a heart in port, —
Done with the compass,
Done with the chart!

Rowing in Eden!
Ah! the sea!
Might I but moor
To-night in Thee!

Vocabulary

cloister	v. 远离尘世，隐居	profaned	a. 亵渎的，粗俗的
complexion	n. 面色，肤色，外观	prudence	n. 谨慎，小心
distain	v. 使变色，弄脏，伤害名誉	sacrilege	n. 冒渎，亵渎圣物，悖理逆天的行为
grudge	v. 不给予；忌恨，怨恨	smother	v. 窒息，隐藏
maidenhead	n. 处女膜	temperate	a. 有节制的，适度的，温和的
pampered	a. 饮食过量的，饮食奢侈的	woo	v. 求爱，追求
pilgrim	n. 圣地朝拜者，朝圣		

□ Passage 2 "Tickets, Please!" (by D. H. Lawrence)

There is in the North a single-line system of **tramcars** which boldly leaves the county town and plunges off into the black, industrial countryside, up hill and down dale, through the long, ugly villages of workmen's houses, over canals and railways, past churches perched high and nobly over the smoke and shadows, through dark, grimy, cold little market-places, tilting away in a rush past cinemas and shops down to the hollow where the **collieries** are, then up again, past a little rural church under the ash-trees, on in a bolt to the **terminus**, the last little ugly place of industry, the cold little town that shivers on the edge of the wild, gloomy country beyond. There the blue and creamy coloured tramcar seems to pause and purr with curious satisfaction. But in a few minutes—the clock on the **turret** of the Co-operative Wholesale Society's shops gives the time—away it starts once more on the adventure. Again there are the reckless swoops downhill, bouncing the loops; again the chilly wait in the hill-top market-place: again the breathless slithering round the **precipitous** drop under the church: again the patient halts at the loops, waiting for the outcoming car: so on and on, for two long hours, till at last the city looms beyond, the fat **gasworks**, the narrow factories draw near, we are in the sordid streets of the great town, once more we sidle to a standstill at our terminus, abashed by the great crimson and cream-coloured city cars, but still jerky, jaunty, somewhat daredevil, pert as a blue-tit out of a black colliery garden.

To ride on these cars is always an adventure. The drivers are often men unfit for active service: **cripples** and **hunchbacks**. So they have the spirit of the devil in them. The ride becomes a **steeplechase**. Hurrah! We have leapt in a clean jump over the canal bridges—now for the four-lane corner! With a shriek and a trail of sparks we are clear again. To be sure a tram often leaps the rails—but what matter! It sits in a ditch till other trams come to haul it out. It is quite common for a car, packed with one solid mass of living people, to come to a dead halt in the midst of unbroken blackness, the heart of nowhere on a dark night, and for the driver and the girl-conductor to call: "All get off—car's on fire." Instead of rushing out in a panic, the passengers **stolidly** reply: "Get on—get on. We're not coming out. We're stopping where we are. Push on, George." So till flames actually appear.

The reason for this reluctance to dismount is that the nights are howlingly cold, black and windswept, and a car is a haven of refuge. From village to village the miners travel, for a change of cinema, of girl, of pub. The trams are desperately packed. Who is going to risk himself in the black gulf outside, to wait perhaps an hour for another tram, then to see the **forlorn** notice "**Depot** Only"—because there is something wrong; or to greet a unit of three bright cars all so tight with people that they sail past with a howl of **derision**? Trams that pass in the night!

This, the most dangerous tram-service in England, as the authorities themselves declare, with pride, is entirely conducted by girls, and driven by rash young men, or else by invalids who creep forward in terror. The girls are fearless young **hussies**. In their ugly blue uniforms, skirts up to their knees, shapeless old peaked caps on their heads, they have all the sang-froid of an old non-commissioned officer. With a tram packed with howling **colliers**, roaring hymns downstairs and a sort of **antiphony** of obscenities upstairs, the lasses are perfectly at their ease. They pounce on the youths who try to evade their ticket-machine. They push off the men at the end of their distance. They are not going to be done in the eye—not they. They fear nobody—and everybody fears them.

"Halloa, Annie!"

"Halloa, Ted!"

"Oh, mind my corn, Miss Stone! It's my belief you've got a heart of stone, for you've trod on it again."

"You should keep it in your pocket," replies Miss Stone, and she goes sturdily upstairs in her high boots.

"Tickets, please."

She is **peremptory**, **suspicious**, and ready to hit first. She can hold her own against ten thousand.

Therefore there is a certain wild romance aboard these cars—and in the sturdy bosom of Annie herself. The romantic time is in the morning, between ten o'clock and one, when things are rather slack: that is, except market-day and Saturday. Then Annie has time to look about her. Then she often hops off her car and into a shop where she has spied something, while her driver chats in the main road. There is very good feeling between the girls and the drivers. Are they not companions in **peril**, shipmates aboard this careering vessel of a tramcar, for ever rocking on the waves of a hilly land?

Then, also, in the easy hours the inspectors are most in evidence. For some reason, everybody employed in this tram-service is young: there are no grey heads. It would not do. Therefore the inspectors are of the right age, and one, the chief, is also good-looking. See him stand on a wet, gloomy morning in his long oilskin, his peaked cap well down over his eyes, waiting to board a car. His face is ruddy, his small brown moustache is weathered, he has a faint, **impudent** smile. Fairly tall and **agile**, even in his waterproof, he springs aboard a car and greets Annie.

"Halloa, Annie! Keeping the wet out?"

"Trying to."

There are only two people in the car. Inspecting is soon over. Then for a long and impudent chat on the footboard—a good, easy, twelve-mile chat.

The inspector's name is John Joseph Raynor: always called John Joseph. His face sets in **fury** when he is addressed, from a distance, with this abbreviation. There is considerable scandal about John Joseph in half-a-dozen villages. He **flirts** with the girl-conductors in the morning, and walks out with them in the dark night when they leave their tramcar at the depot. Of course, the girls quit the service frequently. Then he flirts and walks out with a newcomer: always providing she is sufficiently attractive, and that she will consent to walk. It is remarkable, however, that most of the girls are quite **comely**, they are all young, and this roving life aboard the car gives them a sailor's dash and recklessness. What matter how they behave when the ship is in port? Tomorrow they will be aboard again.

Annie, however, was something of a **tartar**, and her sharp tongue had kept John Joseph at arm's length for many months. Perhaps, therefore, she liked him all the more; for he always came up smiling, with impudence. She watched him **vanquish** one girl, then another. She could tell by the movement of his mouth and eyes, when he flirted with her in the morning, that he had been walking out with this lass, or the other the night before. She could sum him up pretty well.

In their subtle **antagonism**, they knew each other like old friends; they were as **shrewd** with one another almost as man and wife. But Annie had always kept him fully at arm's length. Besides, she had a boy of her own.

The Statutes fair, however, came in November, at Middleton. It happened that Annie had the Monday night off. It was a drizzling, ugly night, yet she dressed herself up and went to the fairground. She was alone, but she expected soon to find a pal of some sort.

The roundabouts were veering round and grinding out their music, the side-shows were making as much **commotion** as possible. In the coconut shies there were no coconuts, but artificial substitutes, which the lads declared were fastened into the irons. There was a sad decline in brilliance and luxury. None the less, the ground was muddy as ever, there was the same crush, the press of faces lighted up by the flares and the electric lights, the same smell of naphtha and fried potatoes and electricity.

Who should be the first to greet Miss Annie, on the show-ground, but John Joseph! He had a black overcoat buttoned up to his chin, and a tweed cap pulled down over his **brows**, his face between was ruddy and smiling and hardy as ever. She knew so well the way his mouth moved.

She was very glad to have a "boy". To be at the Statutes without a fellow was no fun. Instantly, like the **gallant** he was, he took her on the dragons, grim-toothed, round-about switchbacks. It was not nearly so exciting as a tramcar, actually. But then, to be seated in a shaking green dragon, uplifted above the sea of bubble faces, careering in a rickety fashion in the lower heavens, whilst John Joseph leaned over her, his cigarette in his mouth, was, after all, the right style. She was a plump, quick, alive little creature. So she was quite excited and happy.

John Joseph made her stay on for the next round. And therefore she could hardly for shame to **repulse** him when he put his arm round her and drew her a little nearer to him, in a very warm and **cuddly** manner. Besides, he was fairly **discreet**, he kept his movement as hidden as possible. She looked down, and saw that his red, clean hand was out of sight of the crowd. And they knew each other so well. So they warmed up to the fair.

After the dragons they went on the horses. John Joseph paid each time, she could but be **complaisant**. He, of course, sat astride on the outer horse—named "Black Bess"—and she sat sideways towards him, on the inner horse—named "Wildfire". But, of course, John Joseph was not going to sit discreetly on "Black Bess", holding the brass bar. Round they spun and heaved, in the light. And round he swung on his wooden steed, flinging one leg across her mount, and perilously tipping up and down, across the space, half-lying back, laughing at her. He was perfectly happy; she was afraid her hat was on one side, but she was excited.

He threw quoits on a table, and won her two large, pale-blue hatpins. And then, hearing the noise of the cinema, announcing another performance, they climbed the boards and went in.

Of course, during these performances, pitch darkness falls from time to time, when the machine goes wrong. Then there is a wild whooping, and a loud smacking of simulated kisses. In these moments John Joseph drew Annie towards him. After all, he had a wonderfully warm, cosy way of holding a girl with his arm, he seemed to make such a nice fit. And, after all, it was pleasant to be so held; so very comforting and cosy and nice. He leaned over her and she felt his breath on her hair. She knew he wanted to kiss her on the lips. And, after all, he was so warm and she fitted in to him so softly. After all, she wanted him to touch her lips.

But the light sprang up, she also started electrically, and put her hat straight. He left his arm lying nonchalant behind her. Well, it was fun, it was exciting to be at the Statutes with John

Joseph.

When the cinema was over they went for a walk across the dark, damp fields. He had all the arts of love-making. He was especially good at holding a girl, when he sat with her on a stile in the black, drizzling darkness. He seemed to be holding her in space, against his own warmth and gratification. And his kisses were soft and slow and searching.

So Annie walked out with John Joseph, though she kept her own boy dangling in the distance. Some of the tram-girls chose to be huffy. But there, you must take things as you find them, in this life.

There was no mistake about it, Annie liked John Joseph a good deal. She felt so pleasant and warm in herself, whenever he was near. And John Joseph really liked Annie, more than usual. The soft, melting way in which she could flow into a fellow, as if she melted into his very bones, was something rare and gratifying. He fully appreciated this.

But with a developing acquaintance there began a developing intimacy. Annie wanted to consider him a person, a man; she wanted to take an intelligent interest in him, and to have an intelligent response. She did not want a mere **nocturnal** presence—which was what he was so far. And she prided herself that he could not leave her.

Here she made a mistake. John Joseph intended to remain a nocturnal presence, he had no idea of becoming an all-round individual to her. When she started to take an intelligent interest in him and his life and his character, he **sheered** off. He hated intelligent interest. And he knew that the only way to stop it was to avoid it. The possessive female was aroused in Annie. So he left her.

It was no use saying she was not surprised. She was at first startled, thrown out of her count. For she had been so very sure of holding him. For a while she was staggered, and everything became uncertain to her. Then she wept with fury, indignation, desolation, and misery. Then she had a **spasm** of despair. And then, when he came, still impudently, on to her car, still familiar, but letting her see by the movement of his eyes that he had gone away to somebody else, for the time being, and was enjoying pastures new, then she determined to have her own back.

She had a very shrewd idea what girls John Joseph had taken out. She went to Nora Purdy. Nora was a tall, rather pale, but well-built girl, with beautiful yellow hair. She was somewhat secretive.

"Hey!" said Annie, **accosting** her; then, softly: "Who's John Joseph on with now?"

"I don't know," said Nora.

"Why tha does," said Annie, ironically lapsing into dialect. "Tha knows as well as I do."

"Well, I do, then," said Nora. "It isn't me, so don't bother."

"It's Cissy Meakin, isn't it?"

"It is for all I know."

"Hasn't he got a face on him!" said Annie. "I don't half like his cheek! I could knock him off the footboard when he comes round me!"

"He'll get dropped on one of these days," said Nora.

"Ay, he will when somebody makes up their mind to drop it on him. I should like to see him taken down a peg or two, shouldn't you?"

"I shouldn't mind," said Nora.

"You've got quite as much cause to as I have," said Annie. "But we'll drop on him one of these days, my girl. What! don't you want to?"

"I don't mind," said Nora.

But as a matter of fact Nora was much more **vindictive** than Annie.

One by one Annie went the round of the old flames. It so happened that Cissy Meakin left the tramway service in quite a short time. Her mother made her leave. Then John Joseph was on the qui vive. He cast his eyes over his old flock. And his eyes lighted on Annie. He thought she would be safe now. Besides, he liked her.

She arranged to walk home with him on Sunday night. It so happened that her car would be in the depot at half-past nine: the last car would come in at ten-fifteen. So John Joseph was to wait for her there.

At the depot the girls had a little waiting-room of their own. It was quite rough, but cosy, with a fire and an oven and a mirror and table and wooden chairs. The half-dozen girls who knew John Joseph only too well had arranged to take service this Sunday afternoon. So as the cars began to come in early, the girls dropped into the waiting-room. And instead of hurrying off home they sat round the fire and had a cup of tea.

John Joseph came on the car after Annie, at about a quarter to ten. He poked his head easily into the girls' waiting-room.

"Prayer meeting?" he asked.

"Ay," said Laura Sharp. "Ladies' effort."

"That's me!" said John Joseph. It was one of his favourite exclamations.

"Shut the door, boy," said Muriel Baggaley.

"On which side of me?" said John Joseph.

"Which tha likes," said Polly Birken.

He had come in and closed the door behind him. The girls moved in their circle to make a place for him near the fire. He took off his greatcoat and pushed back his hat.

"Who handles the teapot?" he said.

Nora silently poured him out a cup of tea.

"Want a bit o' my bread and dripping?" said Muriel Baggaley to him.

"Ay, all's welcome."

And he began to eat his piece of bread.

"There's no place like home, girls," he said.

They all looked at him as he uttered this piece of impudence. He seemed to be sunning himself in the presence of so many **damsels**.

"Especially if you're not afraid to go home in the dark," said Laura Sharp.

"Me? By myself I am!"

They sat till they heard the last tram come in. In a few minutes Emma Housely entered.

"Come on, my old duck!" cried Polly Birkin.

"It is perishing," said Emma, holding her fingers to the fire.

"But I'm afraid to go home in the dark," sang Laura Sharp, the tune having got into her mind.

"Who're you going with tonight, Mr Raynor?" asked Muriel Baggaley, coolly.

"Tonight?" said John Joseph. "Oh, I'm going home by myself tonight—all on my lonely-o."

"That's me!" said Nora Purdy, using his own ejaculation. The girls laughed shrilly.

"Me as well, Nora," said John Joseph.

"Don't know what you mean," said Laura.

"Yes, I'm toddling," said he, rising and reaching for his coat.

"Nay," said Polly. "We're all here waiting for you."

"We've got to be up in good time in the morning," he said, in the **benevolent** official manner. They all laughed.

"Nay," said Muriel. "Don't disappoint us all." "I'll take the lot, if you like," he responded, gallantly.

"That you won't, either," said Muriel. "Two's company; seven's too much of a good thing."

"Nay, take one," said Laura. "Fair and square, all above board, say which one."

"Ay!" cried Annie, speaking for the first time. "Choose, John Joseph—let's hear thee."

"Nay," he said. "I'm going home quiet tonight." He frowned at the use of his double name.

"Who says?" said Annie. "Tha's got to ta'e one."

"Nay, how can I take one?" he said, laughing uneasily. "I don't want to make enemies."

"You'd only make *one*," said Annie, grimly.

"The chosen *one*," said Laura. A laugh went up.

"Oh, ay! Who said girls!" exclaimed John Joseph, again turning as if to escape. "Well, good-night!"

"Nay, you've got to take one," said Muriel. "Turn your face to the wall, and say which one touches you. Go on—we shall only just touch your back—one of us. Go on—turn your face to the wall, and don't look, and say which one touches you."

They pushed him to a wall and stood him there with his face to it. Behind his back they all **grimaced**, tittering. He looked so comical.

"Go on!" he cried.

"You're looking—you're looking!" they shouted.

He turned his head away. And suddenly, with a movement like a swift cat, Annie went forward and fetched him a box on the side of the head that sent his cap flying. He started round.

But at Annie's signal they all flew at him, slapping him, pinching him, pulling his hair, though more in fun than in spite or anger. He, however, saw red. His blue eyes flamed with strange fear as well as fury, and he butted through the girls to the door. It was locked. He wrenched at it. Roused, alert, the girls stood round and looked at him. He faced them, at bay. At that moment they were rather horrifying to him, as they stood in their short uniforms. He became suddenly pale.

"Come on, John Joseph! Come on! Choose!" said Annie.

"What are you after? Open the door," he said.

"We sha'n't—not till you've chosen," said Muriel.

"Chosen what?" he said.

"Chosen the one you're to marry," she replied. The girls stood back in a silent, attentive group.

He hesitated a moment:

"Open the confounded door," he said, "and get back to your senses." He spoke with official authority.

"You've got to choose," cried the girls.

He hung a moment; then he went suddenly red, and his eyes flashed.

"Come on! Come on!" cried Annie.

He went forward, threatening. She had taken off her belt and, swinging it, she fetched him a sharp blow over the head with the buckle end. He rushed with lifted hand. But immediately the other girls flew at him, pulling him and pushing and beating him. Their blood was now up. He was their sport now. They were going to have their own back, out of him. Strange, wild creatures, they hung on him and rushed at him to bear him down. His tunic was torn right up the back. Nora had hold at the back of his collar, and was actually strangling him. Luckily the button-hole burst. He struggled in a wild frenzy of fury and terror, almost mad terror. His tunic was torn off his back as they dragged him, his shirt-sleeves were torn away, one arm was naked. The girls simply rushed at him, clenched their hands and pulled at him; or they rushed at him and pushed him, butted him with all their might.

At last he was down. They rushed him, kneeling on him. He had neither breath nor strength to move. His face was bleeding with a long scratch.

Annie knelt on him, the other girls knelt and hung on to him. Their faces were flushed, their hair wild, their eyes were all glittering strangely. He lay at last quite still, with face averted, as an animal lies when it is defeated and at the mercy of the **captor**.

Sometimes his eye glanced back at the wild faces of the girls. His breast rose heavily, his wrists were scratched and bleeding.

"Now then, my fellow!" gasped Annie at length.

"Now then—now—"

At the sound of her terrifying, cold triumph, he suddenly started to struggle as an animal might, but the girls threw themselves upon him with unnatural strength and power, forcing him down.

"Yes—now then!" gasped Annie at length. And there was a dead silence, in which the thud of heartbeating was to be heard. It was a **suspense** of pure silence in every soul.

"Now you know where you are," said Annie.

The sight of his white, bare arm maddened the girls. He lay in a kind of **trance** of fear and antagonism. They felt themselves filled with supernatural strength.

Suddenly Polly started to laugh—to giggle wildly—helplessly—and Emma and Muriel joined in. But Annie and Nora and Laura remained the same, tense, watchful, with gleaming eyes. He **winced** away from these eyes.

"Yes," said Annie, recovering her senses a little.

"Yes, you may well lie there! *You* know what you've done, don't you? You know what you've done."

He made no sound nor sign, but lay with bright, averted eyes and averted, bleeding face.

"You ought to be *killed*, that's what you ought," said Annie, tensely.

Polly was ceasing to laugh, and giving long-drawn oh-h-h's and sighs as she came to herself.

"He's got to choose," she said, vaguely.

"Yes, he has," said Laura, with vindictive decision.

"Do you hear—do you hear?" said Annie. And with a sharp movement, that made him wince, he turned his face to her.

"Do you hear?" she repeated, shaking him. But he was dumb. She fetched him a sharp slap on the face. He started and his eyes widened.

"Do you hear?" she repeated.

"What?" he said, **bewildered**, almost overcome.

"You've got to *choose*," she cried, as if it were some terrible **menace**.

"What?" he said, in fear.

"Choose which of us you'll have, do you hear, and stop your little games. We'll settle you."

There was a pause. Again he averted his face. He was cunning in his overthrow.

"All right then," he said. "I choose Annie."

"Three cheers for Annie!" cried Laura.

"Me!" cried Annie. Her face was very white, her eyes like coal. "Me—!"

Then she got up, pushing him away from her with a strange disgust.

"I wouldn't touch him," she said.

The other girls rose also. He remained lying on the floor.

"I don't want him—he can choose another," said Annie, with the same rather bitter disgust.

"Get up," said Polly, lifting his shoulder. "Get up."

He rose slowly, a strange, ragged, dazed creature. The girls eyed him from a distance, curiously, **furtively**, dangerously.

"Who wants him?" cried Laura, roughly.

"Nobody," they answered, with derision.

And they began to put themselves tidy, taking down their hair, and arranging it. Annie unlocked the door. John Joseph looked round for his things. He picked up the **tatters**, and did not quite know what to do with them. Then he found his cap, and put it on, and then his overcoat. He rolled his ragged tunic into a bundle. And he went silently out of the room, into the night.

The girls continued in silence to dress their hair and adjust their clothing, as if he had never existed.

(length: 4,332 words)

Vocabulary

accost	v. 对……说话，搭话	hunchback	n. 驼背
agile	a. 敏捷的，轻快的，灵活的	hussy	n. 野丫头，贱妇，轻佻或粗野的女子
antagonism	n. 对抗（状态），敌对	impudent	a. 放肆无礼的，厚颜无耻的
antiphony	n. 唱和，呼应	menace	n. 威胁，恐吓
benevolent	a. 慈善的，乐善好施的	nocturnal	a. 夜间的，夜曲的
bewilder	v. 使迷惑，使不知所措，使混乱	peremptory	a. 专横的，强制的
brow	n. 眉毛，额	peril	n. 危险
captor	n. 捕捉者，俘获者	precipitous	a. 陡峭的，险峻的
colliery	n. 煤矿	repulse	v. 拒绝，排斥
collier	n. 矿工，运煤船，煤船员	sheer	v. 避开，躲避
comely	a. 清秀的，标致的	shrewd	a. 精明的，狡猾的
commotion	n. 骚动，暴乱	spasm	n. （感情等）一阵发作，痉挛
complaisant	a. 彬彬有礼的，柔顺的	steeplechase	n. 障碍赛
cripple	n. 跛子	stolidly	ad. 迟钝地，神经麻木地
cuddly	a. 令人想拥抱的，喜爱抚的	suspense	n. 焦虑，忧虑，不安；悬念
damsel	n. 年轻女人，少女，处女	suspicious	a. （～ of）怀疑的，多疑的
depot	n. 车站	tartar	n. 凶悍的人，难对付的人
derision	n. 嘲笑	tatters	n. 破破烂烂的衣服
discreet	a. 小心的，慎重的	terminus	n. 终点，终点站
flirt	v. 调情，玩弄	tramcar	n. 有轨电车；矿车
forlorn	a. 被遗弃的，无望的	trance	n. 恍惚，出神
furtively	ad. 偷偷地，暗中地	turret	n. 小塔，塔楼，炮塔
fury	n. 狂怒，狂暴	vanquish	v. 征服，击败，克服
gallant	a. 英勇的，豪侠的，对妇女献殷勤的	vindictive	a. 报复性的，怀恨的
gasworks	n. 煤气厂	wince	v. 畏缩，退缩
grimace	v. 扮鬼脸，作苦相		

Section D Word Bank for This Unit

现代文学	contemporary literature	评论家	critic
古典文学	classical literature	作者	author
通俗文学	light literature	作家	writer
大众文学	popular literature	自由作家	freelancer
纯文学	pure literature	小说	fiction
讽刺文学	satire	通俗小说	popular novel
中国文学	Chinese literature	侦探小说	detective novel

历史小说	historical novel	传记	biography
爱情小说	love novel (= romance)	自传	autobiography
悬疑小说	mystery novel	回忆录	memoirs
推理小说	whodunit	名人录	who's who
冒险小说	adventure novel (= saga)	杂志	magazine
武侠小说	kung-fu novel	新闻杂志	news magazine
幽默小说	humorous novel	大众杂志	popular magazine
科幻小说	science fiction	评论杂志	review magazine
短篇小说	short story	文艺杂志	literary magazine
戏剧	drama	期刊	periodical, journal
短剧	short play	黄色书	dirty / foul book
喜剧	comedy	少年读物	juvenile book
悲剧	tragedy	廉价书	bargain / low-priced book
闹剧	farce	通俗读物	popular book
通俗剧	melodrama	有声书	audio book
诗歌	poem	百科全书	encyclopedia
诗集	poetry	精装书	hardbound book
散文诗	prose poem	平装书	paperback book
抒情诗	lyric	食谱	recipe
十四行诗	sonnet	手册	handbook
杂文	miscellany	纪念册	autograph book
短论	essay	地图	map
评论	review	笑话集	jest book
书评	book review	旅行手册	traveler's manual
故事书	storybook	神话	myth
传奇故事	legendary	游记	travels
民间故事	folklore	古书	classic
童话	fairy tale (= nursery story)	参考书	reference book
圣诞颂歌	carol	教科书	textbook
寓言	fable	畅销书	bestseller

Chapter 7

Royal Families and Presidential Life

我们听过王子和灰姑娘的故事，听过各种有关美丽可爱的公主的传说，古老的王室充满了神秘感……

英国是君主立宪制国家,它的国家元首和理论上的最高权力的拥有者仍然是一国君主。本章我们将引领大家了解英国的政治体制和皇室的作用。皇室作为凝聚国家力量的象征发挥作用，但并不具备实质性权力。国王是名义上的统治者，由世袭产生。首相是英国政府的最高领导人，通过民选产生，掌握最高行政权力。首相可就重大事项与国王磋商，但最终决定由议会和首相做出。

美国则是联邦制国家，政权组织形式为总统制，实行三权分立与制衡相结合的政治制度和两党制的政党制度。本章我们将领略美国成功连任的现任总统奥巴马演说的风采。

Section A　Intensive Reading

The Monarchy and the Constitution

Princess Elizabeth came to the throne on 6 February 1952 following the death of her father, George Ⅵ.

Her **coronation** took place in Westminster Abbey on 2 June 1953.

The British **monarchy** is the oldest and most fascinating monarchy on earth. It is almost impossible to consider British history without acknowledging the **centrality** of its monarchy, and it is almost impossible to imagine Britain without a monarchy.

In these articles we examine how the **sovereign** People, and the sovereign Queen, relate together within the sovereign Community of **the Realm**.

➢ **The British Constitution**

There are three areas of government—the **legislature**, that is the **law-making** power, the **executive**, that is the **law-enforcing** power, and the **judiciary**, which determines the law.

For centuries the monarch exercised **supreme** executive, **legislative** and **judicial** power in person.

The struggle between **Crown** and Parliament in the seventeenth century led in 1688-1689 to the establishment of a limited constitutional monarchy.

With the establishment of the **Party system** by the end of the nineteenth century, the monarch's direct role in politics became minimal.

Today, the two major roles of the Queen are as the Head of State and as a **National Icon**.

As Head of State the Queen does not owe her position to either **patronage** or a **vote**, and can more properly represent all the people in a way in which an elected President cannot.

As a National Icon, with a history stretching back centuries, the Queen is a distinct symbol of **national identity.** She represents Britain — the nation, its **constituent** parts, and the people—in a way in which a transitory politician can never do. In this role, she also provides a focused and **tangible** symbol of the **people's sovereignty.**

These are important roles, and in both of them she has political power—of a sort—but it is not the sort of power which by itself, could for example, take Britain out of the EU.

Under the present system, the legislature is Parliament, namely, **the House of Commons** and **the House of Lords**. The executive is the Queen, **the Prime Minister** and **the Cabinet.**

There is some connection between the three branches of government. For example, the Cabinet links the legislature with the executive, through its members. **The Lord Chancellor**, who is a Cabinet member, links the judiciary and the executive, and the **Lords of Appeal**—"the Law Lords"—sitting in the House of Lords, link the legislature and the judiciary.

"The Crown" is the symbol, and name, of the supreme governing authority. The Queen is the person of the Crown.

The governing functions of the Crown are exercised by ministers responsible to Parliament, in the name of the Queen. Hence the term, "**Her Majesty's Government**".

Bills go through the House of Commons, and the House of Lords and when they have been passed by both Houses, the Queen gives her "**Royal Assent**" to them.

"Can the Queen refuse to give her Royal Assent?"

The Queen is obliged to obey "the will of her Ministers" and if a bill has been passed by both the Commons and the Lords, then it will automatically receive the Royal Assent.

It is not realistic to imagine that the Queen can seriously refuse to give her assent to such bills.

Some **eurosceptics** lay hope in the unlikely possibility of the Queen refusing Royal Assent to pass a major bill which advances the designs of the EU. However, the only situation where it may be possible for the Queen to refuse assent, is if there were to be a major **constitutional crisis.**

For example, if a major EU treaty, with huge constitutional **implications** were to be rejected by the Lords—something which has never happened before—but the Government insisted on invoking the Parliament Act to **override** the Lords and push it through regardless, then the Queen could, conceivably, refuse assent.

Only in such a moment of constitutional crisis—where a sufficient number of the **electorates** understood what was happening, and where they were opposed to it, and where the Queen could be assured of the clear support of the majority of the population—could she intervene in her constitutional role as supreme **arbiter**, and refuse the Royal Assent.

Ultimately, however, it must be we, the people, who force our power up from below, so that one day the Queen will give her Royal Assent to "The Bill to Leave the EU".

"What is the point of **MPs** taking the **Oath of Allegiance**?"

Pledging allegiance to the Queen is not merely to pledge allegiance to Mrs. Windsor. It is to pledge allegiance to the national icon, and thereby pledge allegiance to the people of the nation which she represents.

Moreover, pledging allegiance to the Queen is pledging **loyalty** to her as the visible representative of the sovereign power which ultimately belongs to the people.

Some historians have spoken about the absolute **sovereignty** possessed by the "Queen-in-Parliament" and given the impression that Parliament, and not the people, is sovereign. They are wrong to give this impression.

Britain is a **democracy** and government rests, theoretically at least, on the will of the people—however unsatisfactorily it may be expressed within our present Party system, and our "representative" form of democracy. However, regardless of the type of **democratic system** which we have at the moment—or may have in the future—**vesting** sovereignty in the Queen does not deprive the people of it, but provides a focused and tangible symbol of the people's sovereignty.

Furthermore, by pledging allegiance to the Queen, a politician pledges allegiance to the collective nation and its entire people, and thereby makes a very inclusive statement. He or she rises, in theory at least, above the **factional** claims of the party, which may speak only for certain sections of the **community**, and which sometimes exclude, or are hostile, to others.

Those politicians who want to **bypass** the Queen and see the Oath of Allegiance replaced with a direct commitment to "the people" need to explain how this differs from what, effectively, is being done at the moment, and why their idea would necessarily represent a more progressive **moral order**.

"Why does **the *Act of Settlement*** forbid a **Catholic** monarch?"

The Act of Settlement of 1701 **decrees** that the monarch cannot be a **Roman Catholic**, and neither the Monarch nor the **heir** to the throne can marry a Roman Catholic.

This may seem **anachronistic**, in our **multi-religious** society today, but there is—whatever one may think of it—a reason.

At the Queen's coronation she is asked, "Will you solemnly promise and swear to govern the Peoples of the United Kingdom of Great Britain and Northern Ireland... and of your Possessions and the other **Territories** to any of them belonging or **pertaining**, according to their respective laws and customs?... Will you to your power cause Law and Justice, in Mercy, to be executed in all your judgements?... Will you to the utmost of your power maintain the Laws of God and the true profession of the **Gospel**? Will you to the utmost of your power maintain in the United Kingdom the **Protestant Reformed Religion** established by law?"

The Protestant doctrine is that the national monarch is supreme governor, next under God, of all **estates** in his or her realm.

At the **Pope**'s coronation it is said to him, "Receive the **Tiara** adorned with three crowns, and know that **thou art** Father of Kings and Princes, Ruler of the World, and **Vicar** on Earth of Jesus Christ."

The Roman Catholic doctrine is that the Pope has international **authority** over all national monarchs.

Thus, the Protestant and Catholic conceptions of monarchy are quite different.

A practising Catholic monarch would **submit** to the Pope as the highest **temporal** and **spiritual** authority in the land, and this would have religious, constitutional, political and social implications for the country—although the extent to which these would impact upon an increasingly **secular society**, is indeed arguable.

Protestants would advocate that the time to abolish the *Act of Settlement* is when the Pope abolishes his absolute claims.

However, don't expect a resolution tomorrow. This one could run and run!

(length: 1,394 words)

Vocabulary

anachronistic	a. 时代错误的
arbiter	n. 仲裁人
authority	n. 权威；当局
bill	n. 法案；账单
bypass	v. 绕开，忽视
Catholic	a. 天主教的
centrality	n. 集中性；中心
Communtity	n. 社区；社会团体
constituent	n. 选民
	a. 选举的
constitutional	a. 宪法的
constitutional crisis	phr. 宪政危机；宪法危机
constitutional monarchy	phr. 君主立宪制度
coronation	n. 加冕仪式
crown	n. 王冠
decree	v. 颁布，判决
democracy	n. 民主，民主政治
democratic system	phr. 民主制度
electorate	n. 选民，选区
estate	n. 庄园；地产
eurosceptics	n. 疑欧派
executive	n. 执法者
factional	a. 派系的，派别的
heir	n. 继承人
implication	n. 含义，暗示
judicial	a. 司法的，法庭的
judiciary	a. 司法的；法官的
	n. 司法部；法官

law-enforcing	a. 执法的	realm	n. 领域；范围；王国
law-making	a. 立法的	Roman Catholic doctrine	phr. 罗马天主教教义
legislative	a. 立法的	secular society	phr. 世俗社会
legislature	n. 立法机关	sovereign	n. 君主
loyalty	n. 忠诚，忠心	sovereignty	n. 主权，统治权
monarchy	n. 君主政体	spiritual	a. 精神的，心灵的
moral order	phr. 道德秩序	submit	v. 使服从；提交
multi-religious	a. 多宗教的	supreme	a. 最高的；至高的
national icon	phr. 国家的偶像	tangible	a. 有形的，具体的
national identity	phr. 国家认同；民族认同	temporal	a. 暂存的
override	v. 推翻	territory	n. 领土
party system	phr. 政党制度	thou art	（古英语）等于 you are
patronage	n. 赞助，资助	vesting	n. 既得利益；特别保护权
people's sovereignty	phr. 人民主权	vicar	n. 教区牧师
pertaining	a. 附属的	vote	v. 选举；投票
pledge allegiance to	phr. 对宣誓效忠		n. 投票
Protestant doctrine	phr. 新教教义		

Proper Names

Gospel	福音书	the Cabinet	内阁
Her Majesty	女王陛下	The Lord Chancellor	（英国上议院的）大法官
Lords of Appeal	英国上议院司法职能	Tiara	三重冕（Triregnum）是过去天主教教宗所戴的三层冠冕，由主教冠和三面王冠组成，后有两条垂带。在礼仪中教宗不会戴它，而是放在祭坛上。教宗只会在加冕典礼、向全世界发表“城市与世界”的祝辞、发表圣座隆重宣言，以及在出场、退场时戴上。
MPs (Members of Parliament)	英国下议院议员		
Oath of Allegiance	（对君主）效忠宣誓		
Pope	罗马教皇		
Prime Minister	首相		
Protestant Reformed Religion	新教的宗教改革运动		
Roman Catholic	罗马天主教		
Royal Assent	（国王对国会决议的）御准		
the Act of Settlement	王位继承法		

Exercises

I. Comprehension

1. Recall

Please make a list of legislature system in British government.

2. Illustrate

Can you illustrate what Royal Assent is?

3. Make Inferences

What are the major roles of the Queen in UK?

4. Analyze

Can you compare the Protestant doctrine and the Roman Catholic doctrine?

5. Evaluate

Do you think constitutional monarchy is a good or a bad thing?

II. Further Study

1. Do a research on Prime Ministers in British history and who do you think is the most important prime minister in UK. Then prepare a presentation about him/her in class.

2. Watch the movie *The Iron Lady* and write a report on it.

Section B Extensive Reading

Queen Elizabeth Ⅱ Biography

In 2012 Queen Elizabeth Ⅱ celebrates her **Diamond Jubilee**, having spent 60 years on the throne. This makes the Queen the second longest **reigning** British monarch, after her great-great-grandmother, Queen Victoria.

Her Majesty is the 38th in direct line of descent from Egbert (c. 775-839), King of Wessex from 802 and of England 827 to 839.

Christened Elizabeth Alexandra Mary Windsor, she is the elder daughter of King George Ⅵ (the Duke of York) and Elizabeth Bowes-Lyon.

Princess Elizabeth's early years were spent at 145 **Piccadilly**, the London house taken by her parents shortly after her birth, and at **White Lodge** in Richmond Park. She also spent time at the country homes of her **paternal** grandparents, King George Ⅴ and Queen Mary, and her mother's parents, the Earl and Countess of Strathmore.

In 1930, Princess Elizabeth gained a sister, with the birth of Princess Margaret Rose. The family of four was very close.

However her quiet family life was shattered in 1936, when her grandfather, **King George Ⅴ**, died. His eldest son came to the throne as **King Edward Ⅷ**, but, before the end of the year, the new king had decided to **relinquish** the throne in order to marry the woman he loved, the **divorcee** Wallis Simpson. With her father crowned king, Princess Elizabeth became next in line to the throne.

In 1942, Princess Elizabeth was appointed Colonel-in-Chief of the Grenadier Guards, and on her sixteenth birthday she carried out her first public engagement, when she inspected the **regiment**. Her official duties would now increase as she began to accompany the King and Queen on many of their tours around Britain.

On 6 February 1952, whilst visiting Kenya, Princess Elizabeth received the news of her father's death and her own **accession** to the throne. Her coronation took place in Westminster Abbey on 2 June 1953. She was 25.

Queen Elizabeth was still a Princess when she married Prince Philip of Greece and Denmark in November 1947. They have four children: Charles, Anne, Andrew and Edward. The couple also have eight grandchildren: Peter and Zara Phillips (born in 1977 and 1981); the Duke of Cambridge, Prince William and Prince Harry (born in 1982 and 1984); Princess Beatrice of York and Princess Eugenie of York (born in 1988 and 1990); and the Lady Louise Windsor and James, Viscount Severn (born in 2003 and 2007). The Queen and Prince Philip are now great grandparents to Savannah Phillips, born in December 2010.

Although the Royal House is named Windsor, it was **decreed** that the Queen's **decedents** should have the personal surname Mountbatten-Windsor.

After the Coronation, Elizabeth and Philip moved to Buckingham Palace. It is reported, however, that, as with many of her **predecessors**, she dislikes the Palace as a **residence** and considers Windsor Castle to be her home.

The Queen is the most widely-travelled head of state in history. From 1953 to 1954 she and Philip made a six-month, around the world tour, becoming the first monarch to **circumnavigate** the globe. She also became the first reigning monarch of Australia, New Zealand and Fiji to visit those nations.

As a **constitutional** monarch, Elizabeth does not express her personal political opinions publicly. She has maintained this discipline throughout her reign, doing little in public to reveal what they might be, and so her political views are not known. However, she is believed to hold centre, even slightly left of centre views. She was seen as closer to **Harold Wilson** than **Edward Heath** and was certainly closer to **Tony Blair** than **Margaret Thatcher**. She also enjoys especially close relations with Ireland, having expressed support for the **Good Friday Agreement** which eventually brought peace to Northern Ireland.

The Queen's personal relationships with a host of world leaders have been particularly warm and informal, developing friendships with **Nelson Mandela**, **Mary Robinson**, and **George W. Bush**—who was the first U.S. President in over 80 years to stay at Buckingham Palace.

Despite a **succession** of controversies surrounding the rest of the royal family, particularly throughout the 1980s and 1990s (including wide reporting of Prince Philip's **propensity** for **verbal gaffes**, and the **marital** difficulties of her children), Queen Elizabeth remains a remarkably uncontroversial and widely respected figure. However, this was tested in 1997, when she and other members of the Royal Family were perceived to be **unmoved** by the public outpouring of grief following the death of Diana, Princess of Wales.

The Golden Jubilee of 2002 marked the 50th anniversary of The Queen's Accession in

1952. However, it began with personal sadness for the Queen when her sister, Princess Margaret, died at the age of 71, following a **stroke**.

Elizabeth, the Queen Mother, died only a few weeks later. She was 101. The Queen attended her funeral at Westminster Abbey before a private **committal** at **St George's Chapel.** Windsor The Queen celebrated her 80th birthday on 21 April 2006, when she became the third-oldest reigning monarch in British and Commonwealth history. Despite being in excellent health she has started to hand over some public duties to her children, as well as to other members of the Royal Family.

However, her popularity among British people has remained extremely high, largely thanks to her dedication to **charitable** courses as patron of more than 600 charities and other organisations. Her reign is not without opposition from some quarters, but polls conducted in Britain in 2006 and 2007 revealed strong support for her.

In the 2006 **Ipsos MORI poll** conducted on behalf of the *Sun* newspaper, an overwhelming 72 per cent of **respondents** were in favour of **retaining** the monarchy and this may have been down to the country's undoubted respect and affection for Queen Elizabeth. An even greater percentage (85 per cent) were satisfied with the way the Queen carries out her role as monarch. When asked about if and when the Queen should retire, 64 per cent stated that she should "never retire".

Queen Elizabeth's popularity is not just restricted to the British Isles as more recently, **referendums** in **Tuvalu** in 2008 and **Saint Vincent** and **the Grenadines** in 2009 rejected proposals to abolish the monarchy.

During her Diamond Jubilee year the Queen and other members of the Royal Family will makes visits to England, Scotland, Wales and Ireland to mark Her Majesty's sixty years on the throne. The celebrations will centre around the long weekend beginning on 2 June, ending on a special **bank holiday** on 5 June. The festivities will include a concert at Buckingham Palace, and river **pageant** on the Thames, the Big Jubilee Lunch and a Service of Thanksgiving at St Paul's Cathedral.

Her Majesty will be 86 on her next birthday, an age at which most people would have been retired for many years. And although she and Prince Philip will be handing some of their responsibilities on to younger members of the Royal Family, 2012 is set to be packed full of visits and celebrations.

(length: 1,142 words)

Vocabulary

abolish	v. 废除	committal	n. 赞助；委托
accession	n. 就职	constitutional	a. 宪法的
charitable	a. 仁慈的，慷慨的	decedent	n. 已故者；死者
christen	v. 命名为	decree	n. 命令；颁布……为法令
circumnavigate	v. 环球航行	divorcee	n. 离婚者

marital	a. 婚姻的	residence	n. 住处；居住
pageant	n. 盛会，露天表演	respondent	n. 被上诉人
paternal	a. 父亲的，得自父亲的	retain	v. 保持；保留
predecessor	n. 前任；前辈	stroke	n. 中风
propensity	n. 嗜好；偏爱	succession	n. 继任；继承权
referendum	n. 公民投票权	unmoved	a. 无动于衷的；不动摇的
regiment	n. 军团	velinguish	v. 放弃；让出
reign	v. 统治；当政	verbal gaffes	phr. 失言

Proper Names

bank holiday	（英）银行假日	Margaret Thatcher	玛格丽特·撒切尔（英国保守党派人士）
Buckingham Palace	（英国皇宫）白金汉宫	Mary Robinson	玛丽·罗宾逊
Diamond Jubilee	伊丽莎白二世登基 60 周年"钻石庆典"	Nelson Mandela	纳尔逊·曼德拉（南非前总统）
Edward Heath	爱德华·希斯（1970—1974 年英国首相）	Saint Vincent	圣文森特岛（位于西印度群岛东南部）
George W. Bush	乔治·布什（即小布什）	St George's Chapel	圣乔治教堂
Golden Jubilee	50 周年纪念	Tony Blair	托尼·布莱尔（英国前首相）
Good Friday Agreement	受难日协议	Tuvalu	图瓦卢(西太平洋岛国，旧称"埃利斯群岛")
Harold Wilson	哈罗德·威尔逊（英国政治家）		
Ipsos MORI poll	莫里民意测验	the Grenadines	格林纳丁斯群岛（位于西印度洋）

Exercises

I. Comprehension

1. Recall

Who is the longest reigning British monarch?

2. Summarize

What is the passage mainly about?

3. Make Inferences

What political views does Queen Elizabeth Ⅱ hold?

4. Analyze

What kind of person is Queen Elizabeth Ⅱ? Cite evidence to support your answer.

5. Evaluate

Is it good for Britain to retain the monarchy? Cite evidence to support your answer.

II. Further Study

1. Do a research on Queen Victoria and her contribution to British history and prepare a presentation in class.

2. Choose from the following list of films to watch, and write down your reflections on British monarchy.

1) *The Lion In Winter* (《冬狮》)

2) *Brave Heart* (《勇敢的心》)
3) *A Knight's Tale* (《圣战骑士》)
4) *Henry V* (《亨利五世》)
5) *Richard III*(《理查三世》)
6) *The Black Adder* (《黑爵士》)
7) *The Tudors* (《都铎王朝》)
8) *Anne of the Thousand Days* (《安妮的千日》)
9) *Elizabeth* (《伊丽莎白》)
10) *Elizabeth: The Golden Age* (《伊丽莎白 2: 黄金年代》)
11) *Mary of Scotland* (《苏格兰女王玛丽》)
12) *To Kill a King* (《处死国王》)
13) *Victoria & Albert* (《维多利亚与艾伯特》)
14) *The Young Victoria* (《年轻的维多利亚》)
15) *The Lost Prince* (《失落的王子》)
16) *The Queen* (《女王》)
17) *The King's Speech* (《国王的演讲》)

Section C Supplementary Reading

□ Passage 1 The Wedding of Prince William and Catherine Middleton

The wedding of **Prince William** and **Catherine Middleton** took place on 29 April, 2011. It was a wonderful occasion shared by hundreds of personal guests, hundreds of thousands on the streets of London and billions of people all over the world via their TV sets or the Internet.

There was a really special feel about the whole day. It had all the **pomp** and ceremony one would expect from a Royal Wedding, but also, helped by advances in technology and perhaps the young couple's approach to being part of the monarchy, it was at the same time a truly intimate affair. It felt very much like one had been invited to a family wedding and the public had unprecedented access to catch all the special moments of the day, and there were so many of those special moments!

➢ **The day before the wedding**

From the eve of the wedding it was clear that both William and Catherine appreciated their public support and wished people to share in their happiness. Catherine Middleton paused outside the Goring Hotel where she spent her last night before her wedding, to wave at the waiting people and allow them to take photographs. Prince William went even further than that. Late on Thursday night, he and his brother Harry came out of Clarence House to talk to the people camped out on the pavement there.

"I hope I'm not too nervous tomorrow," Prince William said, before thanking the crowd. He even told them, "Make sure you wave at Charles and Camilla (his father and stepmother). "

Prince Harry joked that he would be camping out himself, because of the "fantastic" atmosphere. He said the brothers had come out to greet the crowds because they could actually hear them while they were inside.

➢ The journey to Westminster Abbey

The journey to Westminster Abbey was a modern one for Catherine Middleton, who was transported to the service with her father in a **burgundy Rolls Royce**, and for all but the principal guests, who arrived in Mercedes minibuses. Senior Royals took the more traditional carriages. Inside the Abbey, it wasn't quite audibe what the Royals were saying to each other but the cameras took us close enough to see Charles kiss his mother the Queen on the cheek and the Duke of Edinburgh to kiss his daughter-in-law Camilla on the cheek. We also got to see some good natured teasing between the brothers, no doubt attempting to keep William calm as he waited for Catherine to arrive.

Once the couple stood side by side at the **altar** it was impossible to miss the loving looks and the little giggles that passed between the betrothed couple. One didn't have to be expert in lip-reading to also **discern** that Prince William apparently told Catherine Middleton, "You look beautiful."

➢ Westminster Abbey decoration

The Abbey itself was decked out unusually as an English country garden which gave the wedding theme a really modern feel. Instead of **fussy floral** arrangements the **nave** was transformed into an avenue of maples which denote modesty and humility. The last two trees by the high altar were **hornbeams**, which signify faithfulness and eternal love. The wall of the altar had had its **tapestries** removed to reveal a beautiful **mosaic** and several Westminster Abbey treasures were brought out for the occasion.

➢ Wedding dress

The first real glimpse of Catherine's wedding dress was when she stepped out of the car at the Abbey. The style of the Sarah Burton wedding gown was simple **understated** elegance which suited Catherine's slender figure and small features beautifully. Burton is the creative director at the fashion house the late Alexander McQueen. Catherine's gown was fitted at the waist and hips, in ivory and white, with a low sweetheart neckline and **sheer** lace sleeves. It was decorated with hand-made **lace appliqué** flowers.

Catherine wore a simple long veil secured with a **halo** tiara which was borrowed from the Queen. It had been given to the then Princess Elizabeth as an 18th birthday present. The wedding dress **train** was 2.17 metres long. That is quite short compared to some other royal trains, but it suited the dress perfectly.

The small bouquet carried by Catherine, and the buttonholes worn by the men in the wedding party were all of white flowers. They included some Sweet William, as Catherine's **tribute** to her husband-to-be.

➢ **What the rest of the wedding party wore**

Prince William wore the dress uniform of a **Colonel** of the Irish Guards. Prince Harry wore the uniform of the Blues and Royals, the Household Cavalry.

There was the maid of honour, Philippa (Pippa) Middleton and four young bridesmaids. Two page boys wore **knickerbockers livery**.

➢ **Music**

The wedding music was a mix of new and deeply traditional. The hyms were: "Love Divine, All Love's Excelling", "Guide Me, O Thou Great Redeeemer" and the **patriotically stirring** "**Jerusalem**". A special song, "This is the Day", was composed by John Rutter for the occasion. "God Save the Queen" was also played at the wedding.

➢ **Vows**

The couple took the **wedding vows** on velvet kneelers. They both promised to "love, honour, comfort and keep" each other.

➢ **Wedding ring**

There was a little struggle to get the wedding ring on Catherine's finger, but then we saw that it was a plain band of Welsh gold, fashioned from a **nugget** given by the Queen to Prince William as a pre-wedding gift as has been traditional for recent Royal weddings. It was made by Royal jewellers, Wartski.

➢ **Titles**

After the ceremony, it was announced that Prince William and Princess Catherine would now also be called the **Duke** and **Duchess** of Cambridge and in Scotland, the **Earl** and **Countess of Strathearn**.

➢ **The wedding procession**

The wedded couple took a carriage ride back to Buckingham Palace. Emotional moment along the way came not only from their obvious love for each other but also Prince William's salutes to the **Cenotaph** and when passing the Household **Cavalry** guard.

➢ **The balcony kisses**

Crowds massed outside Buckingham Palace to wait for the bride and groom's appearance on the balcony. This provided one of the most truly special moments of the day, with not one but two kisses between the happy couple. The second at least seemed completely spontaneous and caused the crowd to gasp in delight and cheer wildly.

➢ **Leaving Buckingham Palace**

The couple then went inside to enjoy a standing buffet lunch. Afterwards, there was a wonderfully unexpected event. When William and Catherine emerged from Buckingham Palace to go to **Clarence House** for a larger, informal reception, Prince William was driving his bride in his father's 1969 Aston Martin, Charles' 21st birthday gift from his parents.

The **vintage** car has been restored to a green car, running on alcohol. Someone had decorated it for the Royal Wedding, with heart shaped balloons, ribbons and **streamers**. The attached number plate read "JUST WED". There was also an "L" plate on the back. The bride and bridegroom drove along, still in their wedding **outfits**, happily chatting to each other and waving to the crowd. Unusually for the Prince, they were alone in the car, although a **Royal Protection vehicle** followed them a little way behind.

With that, Prince William and Catherine, the Duke and Duchess of Cambridge went off to enjoy their party at Clarence House.

(length: 1,221 words)

Vocabulary

altar	n. 圣坛	halo	n. 光环，荣光
appliqué	a. 嵌花的；镶嵌的	hornbeam	n. 角树
balcony	n. 阳台	knickerbockers	n. 灯笼裤
burgundy	n. 酒红色	lace	n. 花边
cavalry	n. 骑兵	livery	n. 制服；侍从
cenotaph	n. 纪念碑；阵亡纪念	mosaic	n. 嵌花式图案；马赛克
colonel	n. 陆军上校	nave	n.（教堂的）中殿
countess	伯爵夫人；女伯爵	nugget	n. 珍品；珍闻
duchess	女公爵；公爵夫人	outfit	n. 一套衣服
discern	v. 识别，辨别	patriotically	ad. 爱国地
duke	公爵	pomp	n. 盛况，壮丽
earl	伯爵	sheer	a. 透明的；绝对的
floral	a. 花的；植物的	stirring	a. 激动人心的；活跃的
fussy	a. 爱挑剔的；易烦恼的	streamer	n. 燕尾服

tapestry	n. 挂毯	understate	v. 有意轻描淡写
train	n. 裙裾	vintage	a. 古老的，最佳的
tribute	n. 颂词；礼物		

Proper Names

Catherine Middleton	凯瑟琳 · 米德尔顿	Prince William	威廉王子
Clarence House	克拉伦斯宫（查尔斯王储的住处）	Rolls Royce	劳斯莱斯（世界顶级豪华轿车）
Jerusalem	耶路撒冷		

□ Passage 2 Obama's Re-election Victory Speech in Chicago

CHICAGO Nov 7, 2012 (Reuters)—U.S. President Barack Obama won **re-election** on Tuesday, defeating Republican challenger Mitt Romney.

Following are Obama's remarks early on Wednesday to thousands of supporters at a convention center in Chicago, the president's hometown.

Thank you. Thank you. Thank you so much.

Tonight, more than 200 years after a former **colony** won the right to determine its own destiny, the task of perfecting our union moves forward. It moves forward because of you. It moves forward because you **reaffirmed** the spirit that triumphs over war and depression. The spirit that has lifted this country from the depths of despair to the great heights of hope, the belief that while each of us will pursue our own individual dreams, we are an American family and we will rise and fall as one nation, and as one people.

Tonight in this election, you, the American people, reminded us that while our road has been hard, while our journey has been long, we have picked ourselves up, we have fought our way back, and we know in our hearts that for the United States of America, the best is yet to come. I want to thank every American who participated in this election. Whether you voted for the very first time or waited in line for a very long time; by the way we have to fix that. Whether you **pounded the pavement** or picked up the phone, whether you held an Obama sign or a Romney sign, you made your voice heard and you made a difference.

I just spoke with Governor Romney and I congratulated him and Paul Ryan on a hard-fought campaign. We may have battled fiercely, but it is only because we love this country deeply and we care so strongly about its future. From George to Lenore, to their son Mitt—the Romney family has chosen to give back to America through their public service and that is a legacy that we honor and applaud tonight.

In the weeks ahead I also look forward to sitting down with Governor Romney to talk about where we can work together to move this country forward. I want to thank my friend and partner of the last four years, America's "happy warrior" the best Vice President anybody could ever hope for, Joe Biden.

And I wouldn't be the man today without the woman who agreed to marry me 20 years ago; let me say this publicly—Michelle, I have never loved you more. I have never been prouder to watch the rest of America fall in love with you too as our nation's first lady. Sasha and Malia, before our very eyes you're growing up to become two strong, smart, beautiful young women just like your mom. And I am so proud of you guys; but I will say that for now one dog is probably enough.

To the best campaign team and volunteers in the history of politics, the best, the best ever. Some of you were new this time around and some of you have been at my side since the very beginning, but all of you are family. No matter what you do or where you go from here, you will carry the memory of the history we made together and you will have the lifelong appreciation of a grateful president.

Thank you for believing all the way, through every hill, through every valley. You lifted me up the whole way and I will always be grateful for everything that you have done and all the incredible work that you've put in. I know that political campaigns can sometimes seem small, even silly. And that provides plenty of fodder of the cynics who tell us that politics are nothing more than a contest of egos, or the domain of special interests. But if you ever get the chance to talk to folks who turned out at our rallies and crowded along a rope line in a high school gym, or saw folks working late at a campaign office in some tiny county far away from home, you'll discover something else.

You'll hear the determination in the voice of a young field organizer who's working his way through college and wants to make sure that every child has that same opportunity. You'll hear the pride in the voice of a volunteer who is going door to door because her brother was finally hired when the local auto plant added another shift. You'll hear the deep patriotism in the voice of a military spouse who's working the phones late at night to make sure that no one who fights for this country ever has to fight for a job, or a roof over their head when they come home.

That's why we do this; that's what politics can be; that's why elections matter. It's not small, it's big. It's important. Democracy in a nation of 300 million can be noisy and messy and complicated. We have our own opinions, each of us has deeply held beliefs. And when we go through tough times, when we make big decisions as a country, it necessarily stirs passions, it stirs up controversy. That won't change after tonight and it shouldn't. These arguments we have are a mark of our liberty, and we can never forget that as we speak, people in distant nations are risking their lives right now just for a chance to argue about the issues that matter—the chance to cast their ballots like we did today.

But despite all our differences, most of us share certain hopes for America's future. We want our kids to grow up in a country where they have access to the best schools and the best teachers—a country that lives up to its legacy as the global leader in technology and discovery and innovation. With all of the good jobs and new businesses that follow.

We want our children to live in an America that isn't burdened by debt, that isn't weakened up by inequality, that isn't threatened by the destructive power of a warming planet. We want to pass on a country that is safe, and respected, and admired around the world, a nation that is defended by the strongest military on earth and the best troops this world has ever known, but also a country that moves with confidence beyond this time of war to shape a peace that is built on the promise of freedom and dignity for every human being.

We believe in a generous America, in a compassionate America, in a tolerant America, open to the dreams of an immigrant's daughter who studies in our schools and pledges to our flag; to the young boy on the south side of Chicago who sees a life beyond the nearest street corner; to the furniture worker's child in North Carolina who wants to become a doctor or a scientist, an engineer or an entrepreneur, a diplomat or even a president. That's the future we hope for. That's the vision we share. That's where we need to go—forward. That's where we need to go.

Now, we will disagree, sometimes fiercely, about how to get there. As it has for more than two centuries, progress will come in fits and starts. It's not always a straight line. It's not always a smooth path. By itself, the recognition that we have common hopes and dreams won't end all the gridlock, resolve all our problems or substitute for the painstaking work of building consensus and making the difficult compromises needed to move this country forward. But that common bond is where we must begin.

Our economy is recovering. A decade of war is ending. A long campaign is now over. And whether I earned your vote or not, I have listened to you, I have learned from you, and you've made me a better president. And with your stories and your struggles, I return to the White House more determined and more inspired than ever about the work there is to do and the future that lies ahead.

Tonight you voted for action, not politics as usual. You elected us to focus on your jobs, not ours. And in the coming weeks and months, I am looking forward to reaching out and working with leaders of both parties to meet the challenges we can only solve together—reducing our deficit, reforming our tax code, fixing our immigration system, freeing ourselves from foreign oil. We've got more work to do.

But that doesn't mean your work is done. The role of citizen in our democracy does not end with your vote. America's never been about what can be done for us. It's about what can be done by us together through the hard and frustrating, but necessary work of self-government. That's the principle we were founded on.

This country has more wealth than any nation, but that's not what makes us rich. We have the most powerful military in history, but that's not what makes us strong. Our university, our culture are all the envy of the world, but that's not what keeps the world coming to our shores.

What makes America exceptional are the bonds that hold together the most diverse nation on earth, the belief that our destiny is shared—that this country only works when we accept certain obligations to one another and to future generations; the freedom which so many Americans have fought for and died for come with responsibilities as well as rights. And among those are love and charity and duty and patriotism. That's what makes America great.

I am hopeful tonight because I've seen the spirit at work in America. I've seen it in the family business whose owners would rather cut their own pay than lay off their neighbors, and in the workers who would rather cut back their hours than see a friend lose a job. I've seen it in the soldiers who **reenlist** after losing a limb and in those **SEALs** who charged up the stairs into darkness and danger because they knew there was a buddy behind them watching their back.

I've seen it on the shores of New Jersey and New York, where leaders from every party and level of government have swept aside their differences to help a community rebuild from the wreckage of a terrible storm. And I saw just the other day, in Mentor, Ohio, where a father told the story of his 8-year-old daughter, whose long battle with leukemia nearly cost their family everything had it not been for health care reform passing just a few months before the insurance company was about to stop paying for her care.

I had an opportunity to not just talk to the father, but meet this incredible daughter of his. And when he spoke to the crowd, listening to that father's story, every parent in that room had tears in their eyes, because we knew that little girl could be our own. And I know that every American wants her future to be just as bright. That's who we are. That's the country I'm so proud to lead as your president.

And tonight, despite all the hardship we've been through, despite all the frustrations of Washington, I've never been more hopeful about our future. I have never been more hopeful about America. And I ask you to sustain that hope. I'm not talking about blind optimism, the kind of hope that just ignores the enormity of the tasks ahead or the roadblocks that stand in our path. I'm not talking about the wishful idealism that allows us to just sit on the sidelines or shirk from a fight.

I have always believed that hope is that stubborn thing inside us that insists, despite all the evidence to the contrary, that something better awaits us so long as we have the courage to keep reaching, to keep working, to keep fighting.

America, I believe we can build on the progress we've made and continue to fight for new jobs and new opportunity and new security for the middle class. I believe we can keep the promise of our founders, the idea that if you're willing to work hard, it doesn't matter who you are or where you come from or what you look like or where you love. It doesn't matter whether you're black or white or Hispanic or Asian or Native American or young or old or rich or poor, able, disabled, gay or straight, you can make it here in America if you're willing to try.

I believe we can seize this future together because we are not as divided as our politics suggests. We're not as cynical as the pundits believe. We are greater than the sum of our individual ambitions, and we remain more than a collection of red states and blue states. We are and forever will be the United States of America.

And together with your help and God's grace we will continue our journey forward and remind the world just why it is that we live in the greatest nation on Earth.

Thank you, America. God bless you. God bless these United States.

(length: 2,237 words)

Vocabulary

colony	n. 殖民地	re-election	n. 再次竞选
pound the pavement	phr. 徘徊街头找工作	reenlist	v. 重新招募；延长兵役；再从军
reaffirm	v. 重申		

Proper Names

Barack Obama	巴拉克・奥巴马	SEALs	海豹部队
Mitt Romney	米特・罗姆尼		

Section D Word Bank for This Unit

公爵	Duke	金雀花王朝	House of Plantagenet
侯爵	Marquis	亨利三世	King Henry Ⅲ
伯爵	Earl (or Count)	"长脚王" 爱德华一世	King Edward Ⅰ Long Shank
子爵	Viscount	爱德华二世	King Edward Ⅱ
男爵	Baron (or Lord)	爱德华三世	King Edward Ⅲ
准男爵	Baronet	理查二世	King Richard Ⅱ
骑士	Knight	兰开斯特王朝	House of Lancaster
（美国）民主党	Democratic Party	亨利四世	King Henry Ⅳ
（英国）工党	Labor Party	亨利五世	King Henry Ⅴ
（英国）保守党	Conservative Party	亨利六世	King Henry Ⅵ
（英国）自由党	Liberal Party	约克王朝	House of York
（美国）共和党	Republic Party	爱德华四世	King Edward Ⅳ
诺曼王朝	House of Norman	爱德华五世	King Edward Ⅴ
"征服王"威廉一世	King William Ⅰ the Conqueror	理查三世	King Richard Ⅲ
"红毛王"威廉二世	King William Ⅱ Rufus	都铎王朝	House of Tudor
"儒雅王"亨利一世	King Henry Ⅰ Well-Educated, Beauclerc	亨利七世	King Henry Ⅶ
		爱德华六世	King Edward Ⅵ
（布洛瓦王朝）史蒂芬	King Stephen	简・格雷	Lady Jane Grey
安茹王朝	House of Anjor	"血腥玛丽"玛丽一世	Queen Mary Ⅰ the Bloody
"短斗篷王"亨利二世	King Henry Ⅱ Curtmantle	伊丽莎白一世	Queen Elizabeth Ⅰ
"狮心王" 理查一世	King Richard Ⅰ Coeur de Lion	斯图亚特王朝	House of Stuart
"无地王"约翰	King John Lackland	威廉三世和玛丽二世	King William Ⅲ and Queen

	Mary Ⅱ	萨克森-科堡-哥达王朝	House of Sachsen-Coburg-Gotha
安妮女王	Queen Ann	爱德华七世	King Edward Ⅶ
汉诺威王朝	House of Hannover	乔治五世	King George Ⅴ
乔治一世	King George Ⅰ	温莎王朝	The House of Windsor
乔治二世	King George Ⅱ	乔治五世	King George Ⅴ
乔治三世	King George Ⅲ	爱德华八世	King Edward Ⅷ
乔治四世	King George Ⅳ	乔治六世	King George Ⅵ
威廉四世	King William Ⅳ	伊丽莎白二世	Queen Elizabeth Ⅱ
维多利亚女王	Queen Victoria		

Chapter 8

Mass Media

英国传媒业发达，全国有 1200 多家报纸和超过 1 万家杂志，广播电视地面频道和卫星频道加起来超过 500 个。

对于英国人来说，看报是他们日常生活中不可缺少的一种消遣。英国有 10 份日报和 11 份星期天报可被称为全国性报纸，发行量占到全部报纸发行总量的 70%。全国性报纸又分成严肃大报（quality papers）和通俗小报（tabloid）两种，严肃大报以《泰晤士报》《卫报》为代表，通俗小报以《太阳报》为首。大报涉及国际国内重大新闻、经济信息、文化艺术方面的内容。小报虽然也会涉及国内外的一些重大新闻，但主要关注放在社会新闻上，因为内容的侧重点不同，所以各类报纸所拥有的读者层次也不尽相同。

Section A Intensive Reading

Newspapers in Britain

by Natalya Predtechenskaya

All newspapers in Britain, daily or Sunday ones, can broadly be divided into **the quality press** and **the popular press**. The quality newspapers are also known as "heavies" and they usually deal with home and overseas news, with detailed and extensive **coverage** of sports and cultural events. Besides, they also carry financial reports, travel news and book and film reviews.

The popular press or the "populars" are also known as **tabloids** as they are smaller in size being **half sheet** in format. Some people also call them the "**gutter press**" offering news for the people less interested in daily detailed news reports. They are characterised by large **headlines**, carry a lot of big photographs, and concentrate on the personal aspects of news, with reports of the recent **sensational** and **juicy** bits of events, not excluding the Royal family. The language of a tabloid is much more **colloquial**, if not specific, than that of quality newspapers.

Here is a possibly **witty** though true **classification** of English newspapers:

The Times is read by the people who run the country;

The Mirror is read by the people who think they run the country;

The Guardian is read by the people who think about running the country;

The Mail is read by wives of the people who run the country;

The Daily Telegraph is read by the people who think the country ought to be run as it used to be;

The Express is read by the people who think it is still run as it used to be;

The Sun is read by the people who don't care who runs the country as long as the naked girl at **page three** is attractive.

In Britain today there are four nationwide quality papers: *The Times*, *The Daily Telegraph*, *The Guardian* and *The Independent*. *The Daily Mail*, *The Daily Mirror*, *The Sun*, *The Daily Express* and *The Daily Star* are usually considered to be "populars".

THE TIMES

US nuclear overture to Russians

Eight die in helicopter crash

The Times founded in 1785, is read by the **minority** of people today. It has a rather small **circulation**, but its influence is greater than its circulation figures (100,000 copies a day). It is an **establishment newspaper**, read by lawyers, politicians, and businessmen, and by all those who work in the government **at large**. It is not an organ of the Conservative Party, but still is rather conservative in views it expresses, though it is reliable and **unbiased** and claims to be politically independent.

However, *The Times*, as many Englishmen stress themselves, always supports the government in power, the **bureaucracy**, because the bureaucracy in Britain, they say, does not change when the general elections take place. It is, thus, the newspaper for the upper **echelon** of the civil service.

The Daily Telegraph, founded in 1855, is a very conservative paper. However, it has a circulation twice as big as that of *The Times*, *The Guardian* or *The Independent*. It has a nickname—"The **Torygraph**" after the nickname "**Tory**" of the Conservative Party. This newspaper has rather a comprehensive news and sports coverage. Some say it has a more objective reporting of what is going on in the world than any other quality newspaper. It is **right of centre** and has always supported the Conservative Party.

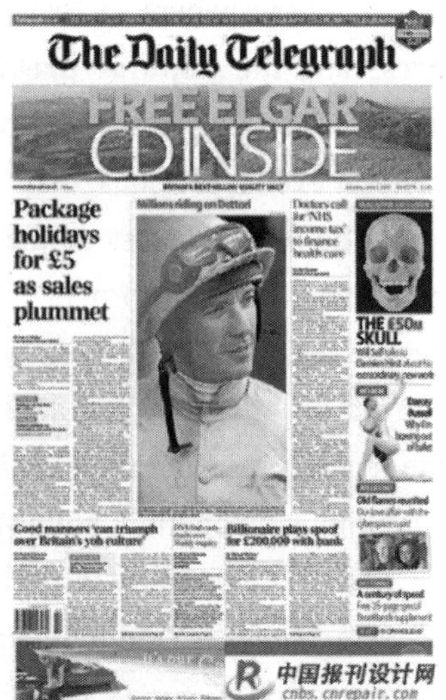
The Daily Telegraph

FREE ELGAR CD INSIDE

Package holidays for £5 as sales plummet

THE £50m SKULL

Good manners 'can triumph over Britain's yob culture'

Billionaire plays spoof for £200,000 with bank

It is notable that although newspapers are normally associated with a particular political viewpoint, either left or right, most of them have no formal or legal links with political parties.

The Guardian has a slightly bigger circulation than *The*

Times. It is a **liberal** newspaper, **noted** for its lively reporting and **campaigning** support for "worthy causes" such as education, medical reforms, the problems of aging people and **retirees**, protection of the environment, etc. It also claims to be politically independent, but it is **left of centre** and formally supports the Liberal Party of Britain. Some British people say that the reporting of *The Guardian* is **biased** and **trendy**, concentrating mostly on things like fashions, **homosexuals**, etc., but still it is enjoyed by its readers.

The Independent was founded in 1986 and has rapidly acquired a reputation for its excellent news coverage, intelligent reports, informal **commentaries**, and a good balanced sense of humour.

The Sun, founded in 1964, has a circulation of around four million and **outsells** all other "populars".

The Daily Mirror with a circulation of about three million, was founded in 1903 and has always traditionally supported the Labour Party. Both *The Daily Mail* and *The Daily Express* have circulations of about a million and a half, and were founded in 1900 and 1896 **respectively**. Of the above mentioned newspapers, *The Mail* is the most sophisticated of the others. The populars as a rule, however, express, though they are **mass circulation** papers, no news. There you will find **leading articles** about murders, games, **bingo** and **lotteries**. Because they are in constant competition with each other, and want to sell more copies than their competitors in an effort to increase the **readership** and circulation, they actually all have **nude** girls in **unconventional** poses on page three, and devote much room to advertising holidays, **vacation tours**, etc.

Actually all newspapers in Britain, both the quality and popular ones, have their sister Sunday issues. Thus, *The Sunday Times* **leads the field** in the Sunday qualities. It has a circulation of over a million and is known for its excellent reporting in eight separate sections: a main news section and others devoted to sports news review, business, the arts, job advertisements, fashion and travel as well as book reviews. It was founded in 1822 and is right of centre.

The Observer is the oldest Sunday paper. It was founded in 1791 and today has a circulation of around half a million and is politically **moderate** in views.

Founded in 1961 *The Sunday Telegraph* is more **right-wing** and its circulation has been steadily declining.

The **best-selling** Sunday popular newspaper is *The News of the World*. Its circulation is over five million, and it has a reputation for its detailed reports of crime and sex stories but also for its sports coverage.

The Sunday Mirror offers a lot of photographs and much gossip. Other Sunday mass papers resemble their daily **equivalents** in style, in coverage and colour.

In general, however, English people themselves, though slightly **sniffy** and **condescending** about their "populars", **underline** that the quality of newspapers in Great Britain of late is much better than 20 years ago. They argue that it is much lower if they take the example of *The Times* newspaper, which was taken over by **Rupert Murdoch** in the early eighties. He is the owner of **News International** and is among the people who have control over the press. Rupert Murdoch also owns *The Sun*, which is, as it has already been stressed, a very low quality newspaper. To increase readership into *The Times* he gradually increases a lot of techniques in it similar to those he introduced in *The Sun* paper.

Most people in Great Britain perceive the press in Great Britain as objective, since they claim that there is no **overt censorship**, no overt bias in reporting the news, and that there is a wide choice of newspapers apart from the national dailies.

There are a lot of different **regional** daily papers in Britain as well. One can mention the following ***The Scotsman*** and ***The Yorkshire Post***. There are also local weekly papers and many London and local papers delivered or distributed free and paid for entirely from advertising. Thus in Britain one can find newspapers of every political colour, from the far left to the far right. There are several socialist newspapers on sale each week, for example, ***Socialist Worker***, and many others. Most people are satisfied that there is a free and objective press. They say that the British press is also **investigative**, **uncovers scandals** in the governments, and if they are not satisfied with what they read in *The Times* and think it is not true, they have the opportunity to go and pick up another newspaper and compare **reportings**.

(length: 1,332 words)

Vocabulary

at large	phr. 大体上；一般地	campaign	v. 参加竞选；参加活动
best-selling	a. 最畅销的	censorship	n. 审查制度，审查机构
bias	v. 使产生偏见	circulation	n. 发行量；循环，流通
bingo	n. 宾戈游戏	classification	n. 分类；分级
bureaucracy	n. 官僚主义；官僚政治	colloquial	a. 口语的；通俗的

commentary n. 评论；说明
condescending a. 故意屈尊的；有优越感的
coverage n. 新闻报道；覆盖
echelon n. 阶层；梯队
equivalent n. 相等物
establishment newspaper phr. 官方报纸
gutter press phr. 黄色小报；低级趣味的小报
half sheet n. 半页
headline n. 头版头条新闻；大标题
homosexual n. 同性恋者
investigative a. 调查的；研究的
juicy a. 生动的；利润多的；多汁的
leading article phr. 头条新闻；主要文章；社论
lead the field phr. 处于领头地位
left of centre phr. 左派
liberal a. 自由主义的
lottery n. 彩票；抽奖
mass circulation phr. 大批量发行
moderate a. 温和的；适度的
v. 减轻；变缓和
minority n. 少数人；少数民族
noted a. 著名的；显著的
nude a. 裸体的；无装饰的
outsell v. 卖得比……多
overt a. 明显的；公然的
page three phr. 三版女郎（特指为英国通俗小报《太阳报》拍摄半裸照片的女模特）
respectively ad. 分别地；各自地
retiree n. 退休人员；退职者
readership n. 读者人数；读者总数
right-wing a. 右翼的；右派的
regional a. 地区的；区域的；局部的
reporting n. 报告；报道
right of centre phr. 右派
scandal n. 丑闻；流言蜚语
sensational a. 使人感动的；轰动的
sniffy a. 嗤之以鼻的；自命不凡的
tabloid n. 小报
the popular press phr. （英）小报；通俗报刊
the quality press phr. （英）大报
Tory phr. （英）保守党员；托利党
Torygraph phr. 《每日电讯报》的戏称
trendy a. 流行的；时髦的
unbiased a. 公正的；无偏见的
unconventional a. 非常规的；非传统的；不依惯例的
underline v. 强调；预告
uncover v. 揭开；揭露；发现
vacation tour phr. 度假旅游；假日旅行
witty a. 风趣的；诙谐的

Proper Names

News International 新闻国际公司（是默多克的新闻公司 News Corporation 在英国的子公司）
Rupert Murdoch 鲁珀特·默多克（美国著名的新闻和媒体经营者）
Socialist Worker （英）社会主义工人报
The Scotsman 苏格兰人报
The Yorkshire Post 约克郡邮报

Exercises

I. Comprehension

1. Recall

What can all newspapers in Britain be divided into?

2. Summarize

What is the passage mainly about?

3. Make Inferences

What kind of people read *The Times*?

4. Analyze

1) Can you compare the quality press and the popular press?

2) Why *The News of the World* is the best-selling Sunday popular newspaper?

5. Evaluate

What do you think of the popular press? Cite evidence to support your answer.

II. Further Study

1. Choose one British newspaper and find as much information as possible. Then prepare a presentation in class and talk about the newspaper you are interested in.

2. Choose one quality newspaper and one popular newspaper and discuss in what way they can attract readers.

3. Choose from the following list of newspapers to read, and write down your reflections on British newspapers.

1)《泰晤士报》(*The Times*)：1785 年由约翰•沃尔特在伦敦创刊，誉为“世界第一大报纸”(the First Newspaper in the World)。 www.thetimes.co.uk

2)《卫报》(*The Guardian*)：原名《曼彻斯特卫报》(*The Man-Chester Guardian*) , 1821 年创刊于曼彻斯特，后迁至伦敦，1959 年改称《卫报》。www.guardian.co.uk/

3)《金融时报》(*The Financial Times*)：1888 年于伦敦创刊，是英国金融资本的晴雨表。news.ft.com/home/rw

4)《每日电讯报》(*The Daily Telegraph*)：1855 年于伦敦创刊，该报以“时效性”而著称。www.dailytelegraph.co.uk

5)《观察家报》(*The Observer*)：1791 年创刊。www.observer.co.uk

6)《每日快报》(*The Daily Express*)：1900 年由比弗布鲁克爵士 (Lord Beaverbrook) 在伦敦创刊。www.express.co.uk/

7)《每日邮报》(*The Daily Mail*)：1896 年创刊，是一种知识性很强的通俗日报。www.dailymail.co.uk/

8)《镜报》(*The Mirror*)：1903 年创刊，1985 年以前名为《每日镜报》(*Daily Mirror*)。www.mirror.co.uk/

Section B　Extensive Reading

The Role and Influence of Mass Media

Mass media is communication—whether written, broadcast, or spoken—that reaches a large audience. This includes television, radio, advertising, movies, the Internet, newspapers, magazines, and so forth.

Mass media is a significant force in modern culture, particularly in America. **Sociologists** refer to this as a **mediated** culture where media reflects and creates the culture. Communities and individuals are **bombarded** constantly with messages from a **multitude** of sources including TV, **billboards**, and magazines, to name a few. These messages promote not only products, but moods, attitudes, and a sense of what is and is not important. Mass media makes possible the concept of **celebrity**: without the ability of movies, magazines, and news media to reach across thousands of miles, people could not become famous. In fact, only political and business leaders, as well as the few **notorious outlaws**, were famous in the past. Only in recent times have actors, singers, and other social **elites** become celebrities or "stars".

The current level of **media saturation** has not always existed. As recently as the 1960s and 1970s, television, for example, consisted of primarily three **networks**, public broadcasting, and a few local independent stations. These **channels** aimed their programming primarily at two-parent, middle-class families. Even so, some middle-class households did not even own a television. Today, one can find a television in the poorest of homes, and multiple TVs in most middle-class homes. Not only has **availability** increased, but programming is increasingly **diverse** with shows aimed to please all ages, incomes, backgrounds, and attitudes. This widespread availability and **exposure** makes television the primary focus of most mass-media discussions. More recently, the Internet has increased its role **exponentially** as more businesses and households "**sign on**". Although TV and the Internet have dominated the mass media, movies and magazines—particularly those lining the aisles at grocery checkout stands—also play a powerful role in culture, as do other forms of media.

What role does mass media play? Legislatures, **media executives**, local school officials, and sociologists have all debated this **controversial** question. While opinions vary as to the extent and type of influence the mass media **wields**, all sides agree that mass media is a permanent part of modern culture. Three main **sociological perspectives** on the role of media exist: the limited-effects theory, the class-dominant theory, and the culturalist theory.

- **Limited-effects theory**

The limited-effects theory argues that because people generally choose what to watch or read based on what they already believe, media exerts a **negligible** influence. This theory originated and was tested in the 1940s and 1950s. Studies that examined the ability of media to influence voting found that **well-informed** people relied more on personal experience, **prior knowledge**, and their own reasoning. However, media "experts" more likely **swayed** those who were less informed. Critics point to two problems with this perspective. First, they claim that limited-effects theory ignores the media's role in framing and limiting the discussion and debate of issues. How media frames the debate and what questions members of the media ask change the **outcome** of the discussion and the possible conclusions people may draw. Second, this theory came into existence when the availability and **dominance** of media was far less widespread.

- **Class-dominant theory**

The class-dominant theory argues that the media reflects and **projects** the view of a minority elite, which controls it. Those people who own and control the corporations that produce media comprise this elite. **Advocates** of this view concern themselves particularly with massive corporate **mergers** of media organizations, which limit competition and put big business at the **reins** of media—especially **news media**. Their concern is that when ownership is restricted, a few people then have the ability to **manipulate** what people can see or hear. For example, owners can easily avoid or silence stories that **expose unethical corporate** behavior or hold corporations responsible for their actions.

The issue of **sponsorship** adds to this problem. Advertising dollars fund most media. Networks aim programming at the largest possible audience because the broader the appeal, the greater the potential purchasing audience and the easier selling air time to advertisers becomes. Thus, news organizations may **shy away from** negative stories about corporations (especially **parent corporations**) that finance large advertising campaigns in their newspaper or on their stations. **Television networks** receiving millions of dollars in advertising from companies like **Nike** and other **textile** manufacturers were slow to run stories on their news shows about possible human-rights **violations** by these companies in foreign countries. Media watchers identify the same problem at the local level where city newspapers will not give new cars poor reviews or run stories on selling a home without an agent because the majority of their funding comes from **auto** and **real estate advertising**. This influence also extends to programming. In the 1990s a network cancelled a **short-run** drama with clear religious **sentiments**, Christy, because, although highly popular and beloved in rural America, the program did not rate well among young city **dwellers** that advertisers were targeting in ads.

Critics of this theory counter these arguments by saying that local control of news media largely lies beyond the reach of large corporate offices elsewhere, and that the quality of news depends upon good **journalists**. They **contend** that those less powerful and not in control of media have often received full media coverage and **subsequent** support. As examples they name numerous environmental causes, **the anti-nuclear movement**, **the anti-Vietnam movement**, and **the pro-Gulf War movement**.

While most people argue that a corporate elite controls media, a **variation** on this approach argues that a politically "liberal" elite controls media. They point to the fact that journalists, being more highly educated than the general population, hold more liberal political views, consider themselves "left of center", and are more likely to register as Democrats. They further point to examples from the media itself and the **statistical** reality that the media more often labels conservative **commentators** or politicians as "conservative" than liberals as "liberal".

Media language can be **revealing**, too. Media uses the terms "arch" or "ultra" conservative, but rarely or never the terms "arch" or "ultra" liberal. Those who argue that a political elite controls media also point out that the movements that have gained media attention—the environment, anti-nuclear, and anti-Vietnam—generally support liberal political issues. **Predominantly** conservative political issues have yet to gain **prominent** media attention, or have been opposed by the media. Advocates of this view point to **the Strategic Arms Initiative** of the 1980s **Reagan administration**. Media quickly characterized the defense program as "**Star**

Wars", linking it to an expensive fantasy. The public failed to support it, and the program did not get funding or **congressional** support.

➢ **Culturalist theory**

The **culturalist** theory, developed in the 1980s and 1990s, combines the other two theories and claims that people **interact** with media to create their own meanings out of the images and messages they receive. This theory sees audiences as playing an active rather than passive role **in relation to** mass media. One **strand** of research focuses on the audiences and how they interact with media; the other strand of research focuses on those who produce the media, particularly the news.

Theorists emphasize that audiences choose what to watch among a wide range of options, choose how much to watch, and may choose **the mute button** or the **VCR remote** over the programming selected by the network or **cable station**. Studies of mass media done by sociologists **parallel** text-reading and interpretation research completed by linguists (people who study language). Both groups of researchers find that when people approach material, whether written text or media images and messages, they interpret that material based on their own knowledge and experience. Thus, when researchers ask different groups to explain the meaning of a particular song or video, the groups produce widely **divergent** interpretations based on age, **gender**, race, **ethnicity**, and religious background. Therefore, culturalist theorists claim that, while a few elite in large corporations may **exert** significant control over what information media produces and distributes, personal perspective plays a more powerful role in how the audience members interpret those messages.

(length: 1,348 words)

Vocabulary

advocate	n. 提倡者；支持者
advertising	n. 广告业；广告
auto	n. 汽车；自动
availability	n. 有效性；可用性；实用性
billboard	n. 广告牌；布告板
bombard	v. 连珠炮似地提问；轰炸；炮击
cable station	phr. 有线电视台
celebrity	n. 名人；名声
channel	n. 频道；通道；海峡
commentator	n. 实况播音员；评论员
congressional	a. 国会的；议会的
contend	v. 主张；为……斗争
controversial	a. 有争议的；引起争论的
corporate	a. 法人的；共同的；公司的
culturalist	n. 文化主义
divergent	a. 分歧的；相异的；散开的
diverse	a. 多种多样的；不同的
dominance	n. 优势；支配；统治
dweller	n. 居民；居住者
elite	n. 社会名流；精英
ethnicity	n. 种族划分；种族
exert	v. 施以影响；运用；发挥
exponentially	ad. 迅速增长地；迅猛发展地
expose	v. 使曝光；揭发；揭露
exposure	n. 曝光；揭发；揭露
gender	n. 性别
in relation to	phr. 有关；关于；涉及
interact	v. 互相影响；互相作用
journalist	n. 记者；新闻工作者
manipulate	v. 操纵；控制
mediate	v. 调停；传达
media executive	phr. 媒介代表；媒介执行
media saturation	phr. 媒体饱和
merger	n. 合并；兼并；并购

mute button	phr. 静音按钮
multitude	n. 众多；多数；大量
negligible	a. 可忽略的；微不足道的
network	n. 广播网；网络
news media	phr. 新闻媒体
notorious	a. 臭名昭著的
outcome	n. 结果；结局
outlaw	n. 罪犯；歹徒
project	v. 呈现
parallel	v. 与……相似；与……相比；平行
parent corporation	phr. 控股公司；母公司
perspective	n. 观点
predominantly	ad. 主要地；显著地
prominent	a. 显著的；突出的；卓越的
prior knowledge	phr. 先验知识；已有知识
real estate	n. 房地产；不动产
rein	n. 统治；支配
remote	n. 远程遥控 a. 遥远的
revealing	a. 透露内情的；有启迪作用的
sign on	phr. 开始广播；签约雇用
shy away from	phr. 回避；躲避
sociological	a. 社会学的
sociologist	n. 社会学家
short-run	a. 短期的
sponsorship	n. 赞助；赞助式广告
statistical	a. 统计的；统计学的
strand	n. 串；线
subsequent	a. 随后的；后来的
sway	v. 使摇摆；影响；统治
television network	phr. 电视广播公司；电视发射台
textile	n. 纺织；纺织品
unethical	a. 不道德的；缺乏职业道德的
variation	n. 变化；变异
VCR	即 video cassette recorder，录像机
violation	n. 违反；违犯；侵犯
well-informed	a. 消息灵通的；见多识广的
wield	v. 使用；行使

Proper Names

Nike	耐克
Reagan administration	里根政府
Star Wars	星球大战
the anti-nuclear movement	反核运动
the anti-Vietnam movement	反越战运动
the pro-Gulf War movement	亲海湾战争
the Strategic Arms Initiative	战略防御计划（即“星球大战” 计划）

Exercises

I. Comprehension

1. Recall

What does mass media include?

2. Summarize

What role does mass media play from sociological perspectives?

3. Make Inferences

According to culturalist theorists, what plays a more important role in influencing people's interpretation of messages they receive?

4. Analyze

Who do you think the media can influence more, the well-informed people or less informed people? Please explain the reason?

5. Evaluate

What do you think of class-dominant theory? Cite evidence to support your answer.

II. Further Study

1. Choose one form of media and do a research on it. Then prepare a presentation in class and talk about the ways in which it has played an important role to convey information.
2. Choose from the following list of broadcasting companies and television stations to study, and write down the roles the mass media play.

1) 美国全国广播公司（National Broadcasting Company，简称 NBC）于 1926 年创办。www.nbc.com

2) 美国哥伦比亚广播公司（Columbia Broadcasting System，简称 CBS）于 1927 年创办。www.cbs.com

3) 美国广播公司（American Broadcasting Company, 简称 ABC）于 1943 年创办。www.abc.com

4) 美国之音（Voice of America，简称 VOA）于 1942 年创办。 www.voa.gov

5) 美联社（Associated Press，简称 AP）于 1848 年创办。 www.ap.org

6) 美国合众国际社（United Press International News Service，简称 UPI）于 1907 年创办。www.upi.com

7) 英国广播公司（British Broadcasting Corporation，简称 BBC）于 1922 年创办。www.bbc.com

8) 英国独立电视台（Independent Television，简称 ITV）于 1955 年创办。www.itv.com

Section C Supplementary Reading

□ Passage 1 Where Do We Get Our News?

According to a study released by the Pew Research Center for the People and the Press in July 2006, on an average day, 81 percent of Americans access news. Where are they getting it?

Overall audience trends:

The total number of Americans getting news on an average day is down almost 10 percent from 1994. Young Americans are the most likely to get no news at all, with 27 percent of people under 30 reporting they get no news on an average day. Of those who do get news, half go to multiple sources. On average, Americans spend 67 minutes of each day gathering news from various formats.

As points of comparison: on an average day, 63 percent of Americans watch non-news TV, 44 percent exercise or play a sport, 38 percent read a book, 24 percent read a magazine, 24 percent watch a movie at home, and 17 percent play video games.

A Closer Look

Television:

➢ **Evening News Broadcasts**

Television is Americans' favorite news source. But the popularity of the nightly network news has **plummeted** in the past decade. In 1993, 60 percent of Americans reported that they regularly watched the CBS, **ABC** or NBC evening news—today it's 28 percent. And only 9 percent of people under 30 **tune in to** the networks' nightly newscasts. Despite the highly-publicized **ratings** wars, the three big networks' news broadcasts were almost **tied** when Americans reported to Pew what they regularly watch: 15 percent watch NBC *Nightly News*, 14 percent watch ABC *World News Tonight*, and 13 percent watch the CBS *Evening News*. Five percent watch *The News Hour* with Jim Lehrer.

➢ **News Magazines**

As of November 2005, according to Nielsen Media Research, the networks' ***Primetime*** news magazines were attracting audiences ranging in size from 3.9 million for Nightline to 15 million for 60 Minutes. More recently, ***Dateline***'s "To Catch a Predator" **pedophile** stings have attracted audiences of 7 to 10 million. In its most recent season, by Nielsen's measures, FRONTLINE **premieres** have reached between 3 million and 11 million viewers.

➢ **Cable News**

CNN and **Fox News lead the pack** among the cable news networks: 23 percent regularly watch Fox and 22 percent regularly watch CNN, down from the early 1990s, when 35 percent of Americans are reported regularly watching CNN. **MSNBC** and **CNBC** each regularly attract 11 percent of the public.

➢ **Local News**

Local television news remains the most commonly watched TV news among Americans, but measuring trends across such a diverse category proves challenging. In general, local channels are experiencing a decline in **viewership** for their morning and early evening news broadcasts. The late-night local news, however, has seen on average a slight increase in ratings in recent years.

➢ **Newspapers**

In 1965, 71 percent of Americans reported reading a newspaper on an average day. As of 10 years ago, that number had fallen to 50 percent, and today it stands at 40 percent. The average circulation for a U.S. newspaper in 2005 was 37,492 for the weekday edition and 63,118 for the Sunday edition.

Among national newspapers, as of September 2006, the ***New York Times*** had an average daily circulation of just over 1 million and an average Sunday circulation of over 1.6 million. As of 2005, the ***Washington Post*** had a weekday circulation of just over 715,000 and a Sunday circulation of just under 1 million. the ***Los Angeles Times*** had a circulation in fall 2006 of roughly 900,000 on weekdays and 1.2 million on Sundays. ***USA Today*** and ***The Wall Street Journal*** both have weekday circulations over 2 million.

The *New York Times* and *USA Today* have the most popular newspaper web sites according to **the Pew Center** study. Five percent of people who get news online report using each of these sites. Local newspapers are struggling to attract readers to their web sites, with fewer than half of people who read newspapers online visiting local newspaper sites.

Radio:

Since 1998, the number of Americans getting news from the radio has dropped from 49 percent to 36 percent. One in five listen to **call-in** political or news programs—a group roughly equally split between Democrats and Republicans. Seventeen percent regularly listen to **NPR**; "**Morning Edition**", NPR's most popular program, has an average audience of 13 million people.

Satellite radio's audience is still comparatively very small, reaching roughly 10 million people compared to the 247 million people traditional radio reaches. **Internet radio stations** reach still fewer people, with **Arbitron**, the largest measurer of radio ratings, counting only 3.7 million listeners of the five largest online radio networks combined. Roughly 10 million people—6.6 percent of the population—have downloaded an **audio podcast**, a figure that includes news and non-news podcasts. NPR, which in August 2005 launched a podcast library that has now grown to nearly 400 titles, including over 50 news-related podcasts, reported that as of February 2007 it had delivered 80 million podcast downloads. In the future, these new alternatives will likely continue to grow and reshape how and where Americans listen to news.

Online:

The web is still primarily used in combination with other news sources. Only 4 percent of the population relies on the Internet alone for their news. When it comes to which sites Internet news **browsers** prefer, providing an exact ranking proves **tricky**. At this time, tools and methods for measuring web site traffic remain even less perfect than those for measuring radio and television audiences, and there's widespread debate about how to best count the visitors to various sites, making precise comparisons difficult. But the rough estimates provided by existing measurement techniques and the Pew survey results can still provide a useful sketch of the terrain.

MSNBC, **Yahoo!** and CNN are by far the most popular news sites among individuals who get their news online: 31 percent of Internet news users list MSNBC.com as one of the sites they use most often, 23 percent name Yahoo! and 23 percent name CNN.com. The next most popular sites include Google (preferred by 9 percent), FoxNews.com (8 percent), and **AOL.com** (8 percent). About three-quarters of people who get news online have used search engines like Google and Yahoo! to find specific stories, and 40 percent of users have emailed news stories to friends or colleagues.

Only 3 percent of Americans visit online news magazines—Slate.com says that translates to over 250,000 unique visitors each day. Salon.com measures 3.2 million unique visitors per month.

Only 4 percent of Americans regularly visit news blogs—but the percentage jumps to 10 percent in the 18-24 **age bracket. Rocketboom** founder Andrew Baron says his site attracts 300,000-350,000 people each day. Markos Moulistsas' **Daily Kos** gets just under 500,000 visits per day. Joshua Micah Marshall's three blogs—Talking Points Memo, TPMCafe and TPMmuckraker.com—together attract over 750,000 people each month. Power Line, the blog of John Hinderaker and Scott Johnson, averages just over 55,000 visits per day. **The Drudge Report**, which does not publish unique visitor statistics, averages over 10 million page views per day.

FRONTLINE's web site averages 80,000 daily visitors.

While the percentage of Americans getting news from all other media is falling, using the Internet to get news is on an **upward** trend. A recent study by the Pew Internet and American Life Project suggests that a main factor in that growth will be Americans' increasing adoption of **broadband Internet connections** that make surfing the web faster.

(length:1,242 words)

Vocabulary

age bracket phr. 年龄段；年龄组

audio a. 声音的，音频的

broadband Internet connection phr. 宽带网络连接

browser n. 浏览器，阅读器

call-in	a. 邀请听众打电话进来的 n. 电话交谈节目	primetime	n. 黄金时段
dateline	n. 国际日期变更线	rating	n. （电视节目的）收视率；评级；评分
Internet radio station	phr. 互联网广播电台	tie	v. 与……成平局；不分胜负
lead the pack	phr. 领先群雄	tricky	a. 棘手的；复杂的；狡猾的
pedophile	n. 恋童癖者	tune in to	phr. 收听，收看
plummet	v. 骤然落下；垂直落下	upward	a. 向上的
podcast	n. 播客	viewership	n. 电视观众的总称
premiere	n. 首映式		

Proper Names

ABC	美国广播公司	Morning Edition	晨报
AOL	即 America Online，美国在线公司	MSNBC	即 Microsoft and NBC，微软全国有线广播电视公司
Arbitron	即 Arbitron Radio Ratings and Media Research，美国的一家电视节目收看状况调查公司	NPR	即 National Public Radio，美国国家公共电台
CNBC	原本全名为"消费者新闻与商业频道"（Consumer News and Business Channel），美国全国广播公司财经频道	New York Times	纽约时报
		Rocketboom	网络视频博客的名称
		Satellite radio	卫星广播
		Scott Johnson	思考特·约翰逊
CNN	即 Cable News Network，美国有线电视新闻网	Talking Points Memo	谈话要点备忘录
		the Pew Center	皮尤研究中心
Daily Kos	每日科斯，以政治评论为主	The Wall Street Journal	华尔街日报
Drudge Report	德拉吉报道（美国新闻聚合网站）	USA Today	今日美国
Fox News	福克斯新闻频道	Washington Post	华盛顿邮报
Los Angeles Times	洛杉矶时报	Yahoo!	美国雅虎公司

□ Passage 2 Future of Mobile News

The era of **mobile digital technology** has crossed a new threshold.

Half of all U.S. adults now have a mobile connection to the web through either a **smartphone** or **tablet**, significantly more than a year ago, and this has major implications for how news will be consumed and paid for, according to a detailed new survey of news use on mobile **devices** by the Pew Research Center's Project for Excellence in Journalism (PEJ) in collaboration with **The Economist Group**.

At the center of the recent growth in mobile is the rapid embrace by Americans of the tablet computer. Nearly a quarter of U.S. adults, 22%, now own a tablet device—double the number from a year earlier. Another 3% of adults regularly use a tablet owned by someone else in their home. And nearly a quarter of those who don't have a tablet, 23%, plan to get one in the next six months. Even more U.S. adults (44%) have smartphones, according to the survey, up from 35% in May 2011.

News remains an important part of what people do on their mobile devices—64% of tablet owners and 62% of smartphone owners say they use the devices for news at least weekly, tying news statistically with other popular activities such as email and playing games on tablets and behind only email on smartphones (not including talking on the phone). This means fully a third of all U.S. adults now get news on a **mobile device** at least once a week.

Mobile users, moreover, are not just checking headlines on their devices, although nearly all use the devices for the latest new updates. Many also are reading longer news stories—73% of adults who consume news on their tablet read **in-depth** articles at least sometimes, including 19% who do so daily. Fully 61% of smartphone news consumers at least sometimes read longer stories, 11% regularly.

And for many people, mobile devices are adding how much news they consume. More than four in ten mobile news consumers say they are getting more news now and nearly a third say they are adding new sources.

These findings and others in this report build upon a comprehensive study conducted by PEJ and The Economist Group a year ago that provided an in-depth look at news consumption on tablets among **early adopters**. The new report, which is based on a survey of 9,513 U.S. adults conducted from June to August 2012 (including 4,638 mobile device owners), probes mobile news habits more deeply across the wider population of users, looks at smart phone use as well, and examines the financial implications of those habits for news.

The survey also finds that consumers have yet to embrace certain features that mobile devices offer. While mobile technology allows people to get news anywhere, and any time, most people get news on these devices when they are at home—and roughly half of mobile news users get news on their device just once a day. Similarly, the use of news **apps** on mobile devices, which many publishers hoped would be a way to charge for content, remains limited. Most people still use a **browser** for news on their tablet.

Perhaps most pressing for the industry, the survey shows continued resistance to paying for content on mobile devices. More mobile news users have print-only **subscriptions** than have digital ones. Just 24% of them are considering exchanging their **print** subscription for a digital one (though these tend to be younger subscribers, which suggests their numbers will grow).

When it comes to advertising, there are suggestions that ads seeking to deliver a message or reinforce a brand may have more potential than those tied to **e-commerce.**

Taken together, the data reveal that, even with a broadening population owning mobile devices that offer a range of activities, owners are still drawn heavily to news. What's more, there is a sizable cohort using mobile devices to broaden and strengthen their news experience, particularly male mobile news consumers who employ both apps and browsers, have a **wireless** data plan, get news multiple times throughout the day, and across a wide variety of platforms.

Among the detailed findings of the study:

The advent of the new lower-priced tablets in late 2011 brought in a new crop of tablet owners. Now, just over half, 52%, of tablet owners report owning an iPad, compared with 81% a year ago. Nearly half, 48%, now own an **Android-based** device; about half of them, 21%,

Kindle Fires. iPad owners, however, stand out from Android owners: they use their tablet more often in general and more often for news. **Android users** are more likely to use **social networks** and follow news that comes from friends and family.

Rather than replacing old technology, the introduction of new devices and formats is creating a new kind of **"multi-platform"** news consumer. More than half, 54%, of tablet news users, for instance, also get news on a smartphone; 77% get news on a desktop/laptop; 50% get news in print, and a quarter get news on all four platforms. Among smartphone news users, 47% still get news in print, while 75% get news on the laptop/desktop device and 28% get news on a tablet.

There is growing evidence that mobile devices are adding to how much news people get. As many as 43% say the news they get on their tablets is adding to their overall news consumption. And almost a third, 31%, said they get news from new sources on their tablet. The increases in news activity is the heaviest among those who use all four of the major text-based media for news-computers, smartphones, tablets and print. And when people are asked to recall time spent, the evidence suggests multi-device users spend as much time on each platform as other news users—not substituting one for another.

People who get news on both a smartphone and a tablet may carry added appeal for news organizations. These people tend to be more engaged news users than those who get news on just one device. They are more likely to read deeply (fully 82% sometimes or regularly read in-depth articles on their tablet compared with 62% of those who get news on just the tablet), to send or receive news through email or social networks and to read past issues of magazines. And, while the numbers are still small, dual-device mobile news users are also more likely than others to have paid for digital news content.

Similarly, those who get news throughout the day on their mobile devices are more engaged news consumers. People who get news on their devices multiple times per day, on either the smartphone or tablet, tend to turn to more sources, get news from new sources, read in-depth news articles, watch news videos, and send and receive news through email or social networks. Tablet news consumers who get news more than one time during the day are also twice as likely as those who get news once a day to have paid for news on their tablet (10% versus 4%).

Two distinct news audiences have emerged on tablets-new-found digital customers and customers who also remain loyal to the print product. Nearly a fifth of mobile news users, 19%, have paid for a digital news subscription of some kind in the last year, and a third of tablet news users with digital subscriptions have added new subscriptions since they acquired the device. But even more mobile news users, 31%, have print-only subscriptions, and three quarters of these have no plans to give them up. These print subscribers also prefer their app-based news to be more like a traditional reading experience rather than to have high-tech features. For the news organizations, this brings both the potential for new audiences as well as the challenge of accommodating the differing styles and approaches of these distinct audiences.

People notice ads on mobile devices and may be even more likely to click on them than they are to click on other digital ads. Half of mobile news users (49% of tablet news users and 50% of smartphone news users) sometimes or often notice ads when they are getting news on their mobile device. Following or acting on these ads is less common: roughly 15% click on ads when getting news on one of the mobile devices and about 7% actually buy something. These figures, however, outpace other digital click-through rates. A recent study by Ad Age finds click-through rates on browser-based display ads to be less than 1%.

There has been movement over the last year toward using the browser rather than apps for tablet news consumption. Fully 60% of tablet news users mainly use the browser to get news on their tablet, just 23% get news mostly through apps and 16% use both equally. In 2011, 40% got news mostly through a browser, 21% mostly through apps and 31% used both equally. But as was revealed in the 2011 survey, app news users—and those who use both apps and the browser equally—remain in many ways more engaged and deeper news users than those who mostly use their browser. The browser is preferred on the smartphone as well (61% get news mostly through a browser, 28% mostly through apps and 11% use both equally).

These mobile news users were also asked about their news habits on the conventional **laptop/desktop computer**. Their responses suggest that even as the population of tablet owners broadens, the idea that we have entered a **post-PC era** is overstated—at least when it comes to news. The desktop computer remains an enduring part of people's news consumption—perhaps because during weekdays it is a work tool. Despite all of the convenience of mobile, fully 41% of mobile users who still get news on the laptop and print prefer the conventional computer for doing so. Tablets rank second at 25%, followed by print. The smartphone ranked last. This is a shift from the very early adopters surveyed in 2011 who showed strong passion for their new devices, and it may speak to both the broadening population and a natural settling down as the "newness" factor wears off.

(length: 1,690 words)

Vocabulary

app	n. 应用程序；应用软件	multi-platform	n. 多平台
browser	n. 浏览器	post-PC era	phr. 后电脑时代
device	n. 设计；策略	print	n. 印刷业
early adopter	phr. 早期采用者	smartphone	n. 智能手机
e-commerce	n. 电子商务；电子交易	social networks	phr. 社交网络
in-depth	a. 彻底的；深入的	subscription	n. 订阅
laptop/desktop computer	phr. 笔记本电脑/台式电脑	tablet	n. 平板电脑
mobile device	n. 移动装置	wireless	a. 无线的

Proper Names

Android-based	基于安卓系统的	mobile digital technology	移动数字技术
Android user	安卓用户	The Economist Group	经济学家集团
Kindle	Kindle 品牌电子阅读器		

Section D Word Bank for This Unit

日报	daily
晨间版	morning edition
晚间版	evening edition
高级报纸	quality paper
大众报纸	popular paper
晚报	evening paper
官方报纸	government organ
商界报纸	trade paper
中文报纸	Chinese paper
英文报纸	English newspaper
本国文报纸	vernacular paper
日文报纸	Japanese paper
政治报纸	political news
新闻周刊	Newsweek
头版，第一版	the front page
晨版（日报的更早版）	bulldog edition
记事	article
标题	headline
头号大标题	banner headline
标题下署名行	byline
日期栏	dateline
头条新闻	big news
最新新闻	hot news
独家新闻	exclusive news
特讯	scoop
特写，花絮	feature
评论	criticism
社论	editorial
时评	review, comment
书评	book review
时事问题	topicality
社会新闻	city news
栏	column
读者投书栏	letters
一般消息栏	general news column
漫画	cartoon, comics
插图	cut
天气预报	weather forecast
新闻小说	serial story
讣闻	obituary notice
公告	public notice
广告	advertisement
分类广告	classified ad
大新闻	flash-news
号外	extra
运动栏	the sports page
文艺评论	literary criticism
周日特刊	Sunday features
记者采访地区	newsbeat
新闻管制	news blackout
禁止刊行	press ban
小报	tabloid
报社	newspaper office
发行人	publisher
总主笔	editor-in-chief
编辑，主笔	editor
新闻记者	newsman, newspaperman, journalist
初任记者	cub reporter
采访记者	reporter
随军记者	war correspondent, campaign badge
专栏记者	columnist
一流通讯员	star reporter
通讯员	correspondent
特派员	special correspondent
投稿人	contributor
新闻来源	news source
消息来源	informed sources
新闻战	newspaper campaign
自由撰稿人	free-lancer writer
记者席	press box
记者招待会	news conference, press conference
国际新闻协会	International Press Association
发行	distribution
发行量	circulation
报摊	newsstand, kiosk
报纸代售处	newspaper agency
报童	newsboy
报费	subscription (rate)

新闻用纸	newsprint
舰队街；英国伦敦新闻界	Fleet Street
杂志	magazine
期刊	periodical
过期杂志	back number
提前出版的	pre-dated
国际新闻	world news
国内新闻	home news
新闻社	news agency
编辑	editor
评论员	commentator
记者	reporter, correspondent, journalist
常驻记者	resident correspondent
特派记者	special correspondent
社论	editorial, leading article
特写	feature, feature article
标题	headline
通栏标题	banner headline
新闻报道	news report, news story, news coverage
连载	serial, to serialize
小说连载	serial story
编者按	editor's note
广告	advertisement, ad
新闻公报	press commnique
记者招待会	press conference
出版	publication
出版社	publishing house, press
发行者	publisher
初版	the first edition
再版	the second edition
第三版	the third edition
精装本	deluxe edition
平装本	paperback
袖珍本	pocket edition
普及版	popular edition
版权	copyright
排版	type-setting, composition
校对工作	proof-reading
校对（者）	proof-reader
编辑（工作）	editing
编辑（者）	editor
印刷	printing
印刷机	printing machine
排字工人	type-setter, compositor
对开本	folio
4 开本	quarto
8 开本	octavo
16 开本	16-mo
32 开本	32-mo
64 开本	64-mo
参考书	reference book
小册子，小书	booklet, pamphlet
期刊	periodical
周刊	weekly
半月刊	fortnightly
月刊	monthly
双月刊	bimonthly
季刊	quarterly
年刊	annual
年鉴	yearbook
（报纸）号外	extra issue
特刊	special issue
星期日报	Sunday newspaper
手册	manual, handbook
公文	document, paper
画报	pictorial magazine
纪念刊	memorial volume
选集	selected works, selections
全集	complete works
文集，文选	anthology
科学文献	scientific literature
索引	index
原版（书）	original edition
新版	new edition
修订版	revised edition
重印，翻印	reprint
廉价本	cheap edition, paperback
百科全书	encyclopedia
读本	reader
畅销书	best seller

Chapter 9

Customs and Etiquettes

要想学习一门语言及其所对应的文化，就要了解这一文化背景下的人们的生活习俗和礼仪，同时还要了解产生、使用这种语言的特定的社会文化背景；否则，就不能很好地掌握这门语言。了解外国文化背景知识不仅有助于学生提高阅读理解水平，培养学生跨文化交际的能力，也可以使学生在认识和了解西方社会文明的过程中，逐步提高个人的文化素质和修养。

本章着重从饮食和礼仪的角度来揭示英美两个国家的文化习俗。美国人在待人处事上表现得灵活随意，而几乎每个英国绅士都知道他们应该怎样做才不失绅士风度。该章节为那些准备出国深造的学生提供一个了解西方文化、礼仪、习俗的平台，帮助他们能够更快地适应异国的生活与学习环境。

Section A Intensive Reading

Fish and Chips

Fish and chips (sometimes written "fish 'n' chips") is a popular **take-away** food that originated in the United Kingdom in 1858 or 1863. It consists of deep-fried fish (traditionally **cod**, **haddock** or flounder) in batter or **breadcrumbs** with deep-fried chipped (slab-cut) potatoes.

Popular traditional associates the dish with the United Kingdom and Ireland; and fish and chips remains very popular in the UK and in areas **colonised** by British people in the 19th century, such as Australia, New Zealand, the United States and Canada. It has also been popular in the Faroe Islands since the time it was introduced during the British occupation of the Faroe Islands in World War II.

In the United Kingdom, fish and chips became a cheap food popular among the working classes with the rapid development of trawl fishing in the North Sea in the second half of the nineteenth century. In 1860, the first fish-and-chip shop was opened in London by Jewish proprietor Joseph Malin who married together "fish fried in the Jewish fashion" with chips.

Deep-fried "chips" (slices or pieces of potato) as a dish, may have first appeared in Britain in about the same period: the OED notes as its earliest usage of "chips" in this sense the mention in Dickens's *A Tale of Two Cities* (published in 1859)—"Husky chips of potatoes, fried with some **reluctant** drops of oil". (Note that Belgian tradition, as recorded in a manuscript of 1781, dates the frying of potatoes carved into the shape of fish back at least as far as 1680.)

The modern fish-and-chip shop ("chippy" or "chipper" in modern British slang) originated in the United Kingdom, although outlets selling fried food occurred commonly throughout Europe. According to one story, fried-potato shops spreading south from Scotland **merged** with fried-fish shops spreading from southern England. Early fish-and-chip shops had only very basic facilities. Usually these consisted **principally** of a large cauldron of cooking fat, heated by a coal fire. **Insanitary** by modern standards, such establishments also emitted a smell associated with frying, which led to the authorities classifying fish-and-chip supply as an "offensive trade", a stigma retained until the interwar period. The industry overcame this reputation because during World War II fish and chips remained one of the few foods in the United Kingdom not subject to rationing.

In the United Kingdom and Ireland, the fish Labelling Regulations 2003 enact directive 2065/2001/EC and generally means that "fish" must be sold with the particular species named; so "cod and chips" rather than "fish and chips" appears on menus. The Food Standards Agency guidance excludes **caterers** from this; but several local Trading Standards authorities and others do say it cannot be sold merely as "fish and chips".

Traditional frying uses beef dripping or lard; however, vegetable oils, such as peanut oil (used due to its relatively high smoke point) now predominate. A minority of vendors in the north of England and Scotland and the majority of vendors in Northern Ireland still use dripping or lard, as it imparts a different flavour to the dish, but it has the side-effect of making the fried chips unsuitable for vegetarians and for adherents of certain faiths. Lard continues to be in use in some other cases in the UK, especially in some living industrial history museums, such as the Black Country Living Museum.

In the UK, waste fat from fish and chips shops has become a useful source of biodiesel.

The British usually serve thicker slabs of potato than the French fries popularised by major multinational U.S. hamburger chains, resulting in a lower fat content per portion. In their homes or in non-chain restaurants, people in or from the U.S. may eat a thick type of chip, more similar to the British variant called "home fries" or "steak fries".

Cooking fat **penetrates** a relatively shallow depth into the potato during cooking, thus the surface area reflects the fat content proportionally. Thick chips have a smaller surface area per unit weight than French fries and thus absorb less oil per weight of potato. Chips also require a somewhat longer cooking time than fries.

Despite the differences in **terminology**, the combination of strips of potato flesh served hot with fish still has the name "fish and chips" in most U. S. restaurants which serve the dish, but a few U.S. restaurants will offer "crisps" instead of "fries" when a consumer orders "fish and chips".

(length: 732 words)

Vocabulary

breadcrumb	n. 面包碎屑	penetrate	v. 渗透
caterer	n. 备办酒席的人	principally	ad. 主要地，大部分地
cauldron	n. 大锅	reluctant	a. 不情愿的
colonized	a. 殖民的	stigma	n. 烙印
cod	n. 鳕鱼	take-away	n. 外卖
haddock	n. 黑线鳕鱼	terminology	n. 术语
insanitary	a. 不卫生的，有害健康的	trawl	n. 拖网
lard	n. 猪油	vendor	n. 供应商
merge	v. 合并，融合		

Exercises

I.Comprehension

1. Recall

Where was fish and chips popular in 19th century?

2. Summarize

What's the attitude of the author?

3. Make Inferences

What does the author mean by saying "In the UK, waste fat from fish and chips shops has become a useful source of biodiesel" in paragraph 8.

4. Evaluate

Is the fish and chips the same in the UK and the USA according to this passage?

II. Further Study

There are a variety of British food, choose one of them and give an introduction in class.

Section B Extensive Reading

American Food and Drink

An American housewife shopping for food for her family can find everything she needs in one large food store called a "supermarket". Inside the store, which may be as big as a city block, she serves herself, loading groceries from the shelves into a **pushcart**, which she pushes up and down the wide **aisles**. She pays for the food at a "checkout counter" or **cashier**. And within an hour she may be on her way home again with a week's supply of food loaded into her car. **Perishable** foods go into her refrigerator as soon as she is home, frozen foods into the freezer if she has one, or else into the freezing section of the refrigerator.

The supermarket has an amazing variety of foods to select from: fresh fruits and vegetables trucked in from distant growing areas, fish, dairy products, **staples** of flour, sugar, rice, a large bakery section, meats of all kinds, food for pets, candies, **spices**, **cereals**, canned soups and vegetables and fruits, row upon row of packaged dry cake "mixes", pancake "mixes", corn-bread and **pie-crust** "mixes" and long sections of packaged frozen foods with everything from frozen concentrated fruit juices to vegetables and potatoes and whole frozen dinners. Besides foods, the supermarket sells cleaning powders and soaps of all kinds, paper **napkins** and **towels**, and many other household items.

One thing that a shopper in such a supermarket finds is that there are no longer any seasons where food is concerned. Shoppers have gained the convenience of a year-round supply of fresh vegetables and fruits; they have lost the pleasure of finding the first asparagus or the first strawberries of the season. Besides a lack of seasons, people have also noticed a lack of seasoning. Because the packaged foods and the premixed foods are made to suit the greatest number of people, they are apt to be very lightly spiced, or bland.

Many foods are completely prepared. There are frozen pizza pies, canned or frozen stews, spaghetti and meat or macaroni-and-cheese dinners, precooked rice that needs only a quick steaming, powered potatoes to be heated with liquid, creamed chicken and noodles, Lobster Newberg. Frozen meals packaged in divided aluminum trays with one section for meat, one for potatoes, and one for vegetables are called "TV dinners" because a family can supposedly watch television while the dinners are cooking and then continue to watch as they eat their dinners right from the cooking trays.

From the packaged cake mixes a housewife can make dozens of varieties of cakes with no more efforts than it takes to light the oven and to add some liquid and possibly an egg or two to the already measured dry **ingredients** in the box. (Companies making these mixes found that housewives preferred adding their own eggs.) Actually, of course, it is usually cheaper and more to individual tastes to make one's own stews and dinners from the various ingredients, and many housewives greatly prefer to do their own measuring and mixing. There are also small **grocery** stores and speciality shops in which some people prefer to shop either all or part of the time.

In the supermarket there is almost nothing that isn't packaged or wrapped. Even bunches of carrots and heads of lettuce come in transparent plastic bags. Apples and potatoes often come in bags of measured amounts—five or ten pounds—labeled with the price. Meats are cut, wrapped, and labeled and stored in open refrigerated shelves, so that a shopper may pick up for example two one-pound packages of ground beef, a large plastic bag of chicken wings, several pounds of veal stew meat, and a large leg of lamb.

So many different kinds of cooking are to be found in America that it is hard to say any more what is typically American food. Waves of immigrants have brought their special ways of cooking to America through the years, so that many foreign dishes have become standard American fare at homes and restaurants—Italian spaghetti, Irish stew, French pastry, Japanese sukiyaki, Chinese chow mein, Russian beef stroganoff, Mexican tamales. Large cities have restaurants of nearly every nationality.

There are a number of foods, though, that were quite unknown to the rest of the world before America was discovered: potatoes, tomatoes, beans, clams, pumpkins, turkeys, maple syrup, and, of course, corn—that "sort of grain they call maize" —which was first recorded by Columbus. If it hadn't been for this corn and for the Indians' advice to the early Pilgrims on how to plant it and to fertilize it with fish heads, the early colonists might never have survived their first winter.

Different parts of the country have special crops: California and Florida oranges, Idaho potatoes, Louisiana yams, Southern water melon, Cape Cod blueberries. Many have special dishes: New England boiled dinner, Boston baked beans and brown bread, Pennsylvania shoofly pie, Southern beaten biscuits and Virginia hams, Louisiana gumbos, and Northwest baked salmon. You find all over the country typically American versions of corn bread, called by different names in different parts of the country.

There is an expression that something "is as American as apple pie", and indeed pie—apple or pumpkin or cherry—is a favorite American dessert, along with ice cream, which is eaten in great quantity and comes in a great variety of flavors. The hamburger and the hot dog are American favorites in food, along with sandwiches, and the milkshake (milk, ice-cream, flavorings) is a favorite drink to go with them. These can be bought almost anywhere, from restaurants to small stands at beaches and amusement parks, counters in drug-stores, or "drive-in" restaurants. Drive-ins are restaurants surrounded by parking lots, located just off a busy road. Families who are travelling or who want to eat a meal away from home can drive in, park, order, and eat, without ever leaving their cars.

Americans drink a great deal of milk, adults as well as children. They drink far more coffee than tea, and workers take time off in the middle of the morning or afternoon for a "coffee break".

Breakfast in America may be orange juice, toast and coffee, or juice and cold dry cereal with milk, or pancakes and syrup, but it has traditionally been a large meal, especially for farmers. A farm breakfast may include fruit, eggs, bacon or sausage or ham, toast, cereal, potatoes, and pie. Lunch in American is usually a small meal—a sandwich, salad, or soup. Men eat at restaurants near their work, at office or factory cafeterias, or carry their lunch to work with them. The big meal is in the evening, between 6 and 7, except on Sundays, when it is usually in the middle of the day.

(length: 1,124 words)

Vocabulary

aisle	n. 走廊	napkin	n. 餐巾
cashier	n. 出纳	perishable	a. 易腐的
cereal	n. 谷类	pie-crust	n. 面包皮
grocery	n. 杂货	pushcart	n. 手推车
ingredient	n. 组成部分，成分	staple	n. 主要商品

spice	n. 香料	towel	n. 毛巾

Exercises

I. Comprehension

1. Recall

Where does an American housewife pay for the goods she buys in a supermarket according to the passage?

2. Compare

Do you know the similarities and differences between American and Chinese lunch? Show us some examples.

3. Make Inferences

What does "something is as American as apple pie" mean in the 10th paragraph?

4. Analyze

Why lunch in American is usually a small meal?

II. Further Study

1. Write T for "true" in the blank before each statement that is true according to the passage. Write F for "false" if the statement is not true.

1)______An American housewife can buy everything her family needs in a large shop called a "supermarket".

2)______In the supermarket people select what they like to buy from the shelves and pay for what they buy at a "checker" or cashier.

3)______Besides foods, the supermarket sells cleaning powders and soaps of all kinds, clothes, furniture and some kinds of building material.

4)______Shoppers can buy some fresh vegetables and fruits in the supermarket only according to the seasons.

2. Content review: put the letter of the appropriate definition next to each word.

_____spaghetti	a. (of food) not hurting the stomach and without much taste
______cashier	b. an Italian food made of flour paste in long strings, usually sold in dry form for making soft again in boiling water
______bland	c. a person in charge of money receipts and payments in a bank, hotel, shop, etc.

Section C Supplementary Reading

□ Passage 1 Muffin

A **muffin** is a type of bread that is baked in small portions. Many forms are somewhat like small cakes or **cupcakes** in shape, although they usually are not as sweet as cupcakes and generally lack frosting. Savory varieties, such as cornbread muffins, also exist. They generally fit in the palm of an adult hand, and are intended to be consumed by an individual in a single sitting.

In Commonwealth countries muffin can also refer to a disk-shaped English muffin. As American-style muffins are also sold in Commonwealth countries, the term "muffin" can refer to either product, with the context usually making clear which is meant.

There are many varieties and flavors of muffins made with a specific **ingredient** such as blueberries, chocolate chips, cucumbers, **raspberry**, cinnamon, **pumpkin**, date, nut, lemon, banana, orange, peach, strawberry, **boysenberry,** almond, and carrot, baked into the muffin. Muffins are often eaten for breakfast; alternatively, they may be served for tea or at other meals.

Recipes for muffins, in their yeast-free "American" form, are common in 19th century American cookbooks. Recipes for yeast-based muffins, which were sometimes called "common muffins" or "wheat muffins" in 19th century American cookbooks, can be found in much older cookbooks.

A somewhat odd combination of circumstances in the 1970s and 1980s led to significant changes in what had been a rather simple, if not prosaic, food. The decline in home-baking, the health food movement, the rise of the specialty food shop, and the gourmet coffee trend all contributes to the creation of a new standard of muffin. Preservatives in muffin mixes led to the expectation that muffins did not have to go stale within hours of baking, but the resulting muffins were not a taste improvement over homemade. On the other hand, the baked muffin, even if from a mix, seemed almost healthy compared to the fat-laden alternatives of doughnuts and Danish pastry. "Healthy" muffin recipes using whole grains and such "natural" things as yogurt and various vegetables evolved rapidly. But for "healthy" muffins to have any shelf-life without artificial preservatives, the sugar and fat content needed to be increased, to the point where the "muffins" are almost indistinguishable from cupcakes. The rising market for gourmet snakes to accompany gourmet coffees resulted in fancier concoctions in greater bulk than the original, modestly sized corn muffin.

The marketing trend toward larger portion sizes also resulted in new muffin pan types for home-baking, not only for increased size. Since the area ratio of muffin top to muffin bottom changed considerably when the traditional small round exploded into a giant mushroom, consumers became more aware of the difference between the soft texture of tops, allowed to rise unfettered, and rougher, tougher bottoms restricted by the pans. There was a brief foray into pans that could produce "all-top" muffins, i.e., extremely shallow, large-diameter cups. The TV sitcom *Seinfeld* made reference to this in the "The Muffin Tops" episode in which the character Elaine Benes co-owns a bakery named "Top o' the Muffin to You!" that sold only the muffin tops. Along with the increasing size of muffins is a contrary trend of extremely small muffin. It is now very common to see muffin pans or premade muffins that are only one or two inches in diameter.

The English muffin, which predates the American muffin, is a type of light bread leavened with yeast. It is usually baked in a flat-sided disc-shaped tin, typically about 8 cm in diameter. Muffins are usually split in two, toasted and served with butter. Traditionally muffins were toasted in front of an open fire or stove, using a toasting fork. Muffins can also be eaten cold with a hot drink at coffee shops and diners, or split and filled similar to a sandwich (most famously the McDonalds chain's Egg McMuffin).

Muffins made from cornmeal are popular in the United States. Though corn muffins can simply be muffin shaped cornbread, corn muffins tend to be sweeter. Similar to the pan variety, corn muffins can be eaten with butter or as a side dish with stews or chili.

(length: 676 words)

Vocabulary

boysenberry	n. 杂交草莓	ingredient	n. 配料
bulk	n. 体积	muffin	n. 小松饼
cupcake	n. 纸杯蛋糕	pumpkin	n. 南瓜
gourmet	n. 美食家	raspberry	n. 覆盆子

□ Passage 2 Are the British Superstitious

Are the British **superstitious**? I think so. You often hear people say "Bless you" when someone **sneezes** or "touch wood" when they want to be lucky.

I found it quite interesting to learn the origins of these superstitions or beliefs as they are part of British culture.

These are what I found:

1. "Bless you." It is thought that when we sneeze, part of our soul is leaving our body during that quick yet uncontrollable moment, and the devil would seize that opportunity to steal our soul. If someone near you says "bless you" when you sneeze, you will be protected against the devil's will. This being the case you should always thank the person saying "bless you" as they are trying to protect you.

2. British people touch wood or knock on wood to prevent bad luck. Some believe that there is a little elf in the trees and the wood. So by touching wood or **furniture** you stop the devil listening to what you just said, so that you keep your good luck coming in. This could explain why the British tend to love wooden furniture.

3. British people love plants and flowers if you can find a clover with four leaves instead of the usual three, then you are thought to be very lucky as you has got something from God, something that can fend off bad luck.

4. Animals play an important part in British superstitions. For example, it is considered to be lucky to meet a black cat. You may notice that a lot of black cats are featured on many good luck greeting cards and birthday cards in this country. However, black cat means bad luck in North America such as the US and Canada.

5. According to some, one ancient British superstition holds that if a child rides on a bear's back it will be protected from whooping-cough. While in ancient times bears used to **roam**

Britain, now they are only kept in the zoos.

6. Another animal that has a superstitious colour is the **raven**. It has been long believed that if the ravens leave the London Tower then the crown of England will be lost, and the Empire will fall. So that tradition is still kept till this day at the Tower of London where the ravens are taken good care of but their wings slightly cut off.

7. Finally it's the numbers that are loved or hated. The number "7" is lucky whereas "13" is not, which I think is well-known **throughout** the world. I know that the Chinese love the number "8" but "4" is to be avoided as it sounds the same as the word "death". In Italy "13" and "17" are the unlucky numbers instead of "3" and "7", which are the lucky numbers.

I wonder what is the lucky number (or unlucky number) in your country and why.

(length: 491 words)

Vocabulary

ancient	a. 古代的	sneeze	n. 喷嚏
furniture	n. 家具		v. 打喷嚏
raven	n. 乌鸦	superstitious	a. 迷信的
roam	v. 漫步	throughout	ad. 全部
	n. 漫游		prep. 遍及

Section D Word Bank for This Unit

头盘及沙拉类	appetizers, starter and salad	蔬菜干豆汤	hearty lentil soup
腌熏三文鱼	smoked salmon	牛油梨冻汤	chilled avocado soup
恺撒沙拉	Caesar salad	西班牙番茄冻汤	gazpacho
鲜蘑鸡肝	Chicken liver terrine with morel	禽蛋类	poultry and eggs
奶酪瓤蟹盖	crab shells stuffed with cheese	红酒鹅肝	braised goose liver/foie gras in red wine
鲜果海鲜沙拉	seafood salad with fresh fruit		
主厨沙拉	chef's salad	奶酪火腿鸡排	chicken cordon bleu
金枪鱼沙拉	tuna salad	烧瓤春鸡卷	grilled stuffed chicken roll
尼斯沙拉	salad Nicoise	红酒烩鸡	braised chicken with red wine
汤类	soup	烤鸡胸酿奶酪蘑菇馅	baked chicken breast stuffed with mushroom and cheese
奶油蘑菇汤	cream of mushroom soup		
奶油胡萝卜汤	cream of carrot soup	炸培根鸡肉卷	deep-fried chicken and bacon roll
奶油芦笋汤	cream of asparagus soup	水波鸡胸配意式香醋汁	poached chicken breast with balsamic sauce
墨西哥辣味牛肉汤	Mexican chili beef soup		
番茄浓汤	tomato bisque soup	烤火鸡配红浆果沙司	roast turkey with cranberry sauce
海鲜周打汤	seafood chowder	烤瓤火鸡	roast stuffed turkey
法式洋葱汤	French onion soup	烧烤鸡腿	BBQ chicken leg
牛肉清汤	beef consommé	烤柠檬鸡腿配炸薯条	roasted lemon marinade chicken leg with French fries
匈牙利浓汤	Hungarian goulash		
香浓牛尾汤	oxtail soup	扒鸡胸	char-grilled chicken breast
意大利蔬菜汤	minestrone soup	咖喱鸡	chicken curry

火腿煎蛋	fried egg with ham
洛林乳蛋饼	quiche lorraine
熘糊蛋	scrambled egg
牛肉类	beef
红烩牛肉	beef stew
白烩小牛肉	fricasseed veal
牛里脊扒配黑胡椒酱	grilled beef tenderloin with black pepper sauce
扒肉眼牛排	grilled rib-eye steak
西冷牛排配红酒酱	roast sirloin steak with red wine sauce
T 骨牛扒	T-bone steak
烤牛肉	roast beef
青椒汁牛柳	beef tenderloin with green pepper-corn sauce
铁板西冷牛扒	sizzling sirloin steak
香煎奥斯卡小牛排	pan-fried veal steak Oscar in holl-andaise sauce
咖喱牛肉	curry beef
威灵顿牛柳	filet of beef Wellington
俄式牛柳丝	beef stroganoff
烩牛舌	braised ox tongue
红烩牛膝	osso buco
猪肉类	pork
烧烤排骨	BBQ spare ribs
烟熏蜜汁肋排	smoked spare ribs with honey
意大利米兰猪排	pork piccata
炸猪排	fried spire ribs
羊肉类	lamb
扒羊排	grilled lamb chops
扒新西兰羊排	grilled New Zealand lamb chops
烤羊排配奶酪和红酒汁	roast lamb chops in cheese and red (wine sauce)
鱼和海鲜类	fish and seafood
海鲜串	seafood kebabs
扒金枪鱼	grilled tuna filet
清蒸熏鱼	steamed smoked haddock
扒挪威三文鱼排	grilled Norwegian salmon filet
三文鱼扒配青柠黄油	grilled salmon with lime and butter
煎比目鱼	pan-fried flatfish
煎红加吉鱼排	grilled sea bream filet
黄油柠檬汁扒鱼柳	grilled fish filet in lemon and butter
扒大虾	grilled king prawns
蒜茸大虾	grilled king prawns with garlic, herb and butter
巴黎黄油烤龙虾	baked lobster with garlic and butter
奶酪汁龙虾	gratinated lobster in mornay sauce
香炸西班牙鱿鱼圈	deep-fried squid rings
荷兰汁青口贝	gratinated mussels with hollandaise sauce

Chapter 10

Leisure Life

在生活压力巨大的社会，人们要学会放松。通过对那些有成就的人的生活方式的研究，我们发现休闲对于加强时间管理、保证工作质量、把拖拉问题最小化是多么重要。对无忧休闲的坚定投入会让你重新充电，给你在生活中的各个方面都带来全新的动力、创造力和活力。

本章节精心挑选的文章将从以下几个方面就英美人的休闲生活做出鲜活介绍。其中有选自英国BBC节目中的一段广播，主要讲述的是两名主播关于大人学小孩这个行为现象的一段有趣的对话；也有美国人对漫画的欣赏；还有英国BBC节目总结出的欧美娱乐界2012年陨落的明星；另外，还有对英美经典音乐剧的介绍，以及对英美著名地标性建筑的介绍。希望同学们在学习英语的同时能够了解英美人的休闲娱乐生活。

Section A　Intensive Reading

Farewell in 2012

January saw the departure of one of America's **legendary** blues stars when Etta James, best known for her signature track *At Last*, died at the age of 73, prompting an outpouring of **tributes**. A generation of ***Blockbusters*** fans mourned the passing of jovial quizmaster Bob Holness, at the age of 83, while photojournalist Eve Arnold will be remembered for her striking **portraits** of figures such as Marilyn Monroe and Malcolm X and haunting documentation of "ordinary people" around the world.

Shock greeted the sudden death of pop sweetheart Whitney Houston at the age of 48, on the eve of the Grammy Awards in February. Her death was followed by another music icon later the same month, when Monkees star Davy Jones had a heart attack aged 66. A slew of British comics paid tribute to beloved funnyman Frank Carson, when he "set off for his final gig" aged 85. And the deaths of royal correspondent James Whitaker and war reporter Marie Colvin, the latter in **violent** circumstances in Syria, marked a huge loss to British journalism.

Supercalifragilisticexpialidocious was the **brainchild** of songwriter Robert B. Sherman, who died in March aged 86, after a lengthy career which saw him create some of Disney's best-loved tunes. Bluegrass legend Earl Scruggs, known for his unique three-fingered banjo playing style, also died peacefully in Nashville, aged 88. Film aficionados of the 1960s mourned the loss of Italian screenwriter Tonino Guerra, known for his work with Antonioni and Fellini, both legendary directors of the era. And there was an outpouring of **nostalgia** for *Catweazle* creator Richard Carpenter, who died aged 82.

April saw the passing of legendary American television presenter, Dick Clark, who died of a heart attack at the age of 82. The host of American Bandstand and the face of ABC's New Year's Eve celebrations, his production company is also synonymous with some of the best-loved US game shows. The same month saw fans and friends travel to Woodstock to bid farewell to The Band drummer and Bob Dylan buddy Levon Helm, who died at 71—while in Britain, guitar legends paid tribute to Bert Weedon, whose *Play In A Day* manual inspired a generation.

Two **giants** of popular music, Donna Summer and Robin Gibb, died within days of each other in May, at the ages of 63 and 62 respectively. Both had suffered from cancer. Their contribution to music, most particularly to the disco era of the 1970s, was hailed by musicians around the world. Also lamented by classical music fans was the great German baritone Dietrich Fischer-Dieskau, whose voice was once described as "a miracle". Author Maurice Sendak, beloved for his children's classic *Where The Wild Things Are*, died aged 83, with the promise of one more story—*My Brother's Book* is published posthumously in February 2013.

Renowned science fiction author Ray Bradbury, who died in June at the age of 91, had a "gift for storytelling" that influenced many in the arts world including film-maker Steven Spielberg and writers Stephen King and Joanne Harris. Screenwriter Nora Ephron was similarly lamented when she died later the same month, aged 71, from pneumonia. Hollywood's biggest stars turned out to pay tribute to the writer of *When Harry Met Sally*, who was branded a "latter-day, urbane Mark Twain". Emmy-winning actress Kathryn Joosten (far left of the picture below), fondly remembered by fans of *Desperate Housewives* and *The West Wing*, died after an 11-year battle with lung cancer, at the age of 72.

Eric Sykes, one of Britain's best-loved comedy actors and writers, died in July aged 89. A regular fixture on television in the 1960s and 1970s, alongside stars such as Hattie Jacques and Spike Milligan, he reinvented his career with a string of big screen cameos in the 1990s. Best-selling Irish author Maeve Binchy also died in July, after a short illness, aged 72. Tributes poured in from the world of politics and literature, with Jilly Cooper calling her "kind...funny and captivating". On the other side of the Atlantic, actor Ernest Borgnine died after a career which saw him win the best actor Oscar, for Marty, in 1955—and **inhabit** some of cinema's most memorable roles in *The Wild Bunch* and *The Poseidon Adventure*. He was 95.

Shock greeted the sudden death of film-maker Tony Scott, who jumped from a bridge in Los Angeles, aged 68. Why the *Top Gun* director took his own life remains unexplained. Also 68 was musician and composer Marvin Hamlisch, whose Oscar-winning *The Way We Were* was the love song for a generation of film fans. Author Nina Bawden died aged 87—her work was admired by adults and children alike and her semi-autobiographical *Carrie's War* became a staple of the school curriculum. The end of the month also saw the death of veteran British entertainer Max Bygraves, described as the "modest" yet "brilliant", who died in Australia aged 89.

A generation mourned the passing of animal lover and wildlife presenter Terry Nutkins, who died while being treated for leukaemia at the age of 66. September also saw the death of legendary crooner Andy Williams, at 84. The *Moon River* singer, whose TV show made him an international star in the 1950s, enjoyed a resurgence in popularity in the 1990s when his *Music To Watch Girls By* was used in a TV advert. And stars Tom Hanks and Jay Leno paid tribute to actor Michael Clarke Duncan following his death aged 54. The former bodyguard rose to prominence playing a death row inmate in the acclaimed film *The Green Mile*.

Bollywood's King of Romance, filmmaker Yash Chopra, died at the age of 80 after a career that spanned more than 40 years and saw him bring to the screen some of India's best-loved movies. Dutch actress Sylvia Kristel, who became famous around the world for her role as the promiscuous housewife in erotic French film *Emmanuelle*, died after suffering a stroke aged 60. The film was banned in Paris for six months after its release, but was later credited with bringing about a change in censorship laws.

Larry Hagman, who spent more than a decade playing TV villain JR Ewing in the hit US series *Dallas*, died at the age of 81 and was honoured with an outpouring of tributes from his former colleagues. Co-star Linda Gray, who joined him in a recent revamp of the series, called him "the Pied Piper of life". An altogether more British soap star, *Coronation Street's* Bill Tarmey, was similarly mourned when he died aged 71, with many cast members describing him as "a surrogate dad". *Dad's Army* actor Clive Dunn—also known as "Jonesy"—passed away at the ripe age of 90, having playing old men for most of his life, most famously on his chart-topping track *Grandad*. British actress Dinah Sheridan, best remembered for *The Railway Children*, also died at 92.

A trio of remarkable men passed away in early December: Sir Patrick Moore—astronomer, broadcaster and author—appeared on *The Sky At Night*, the TV show he made famous, less than a week before his death at the age of 89. Legendary sitar player Ravi Shankar, who was credited with bringing the musical sound and style of India to the West when he collaborated with The Beatles, died aged 92. And pioneering jazz pianist and composer Dave Brubeck whose **eponymous** quartet spawned the biggest-selling jazz single of all time, *Take Five*, died days before his 92nd birthday.

The Christmas period saw the loss of puppeteer Gerry Anderson, who shaped the childhoods of millions with his shows *Thunderbirds*, *Stingray* and *Captain Scarlett*. The 83-year-old died having suffered from Alzheimer's since 2010. His other creations included *UFO*, *Space*: *1999*, *Supercar* and *Fireball XL5*. American actor Charles Durning was twice Oscar-nominated and starred opposite Dustin Hoffman in *Tootsie*. The 89-year-old character actor, who also played memorable roles in *Dog Day Afternoon* and *The Sting*, died on Christmas Eve.

(length: 1,324 words)

Vocabulary

blockbuster	n. 了不起的人、事情	legendary	a. 传奇的
brainchild	n. 独创的观念	nostalgia	n. 怀旧
giant	n. 巨人	portrait	n. 肖像
farewell	n. 再见	tribute	n. 致敬
eponymous	a. 齐名的	violent	a. 暴力的
inhabit	v. 居住		

Exercises

I. Comprehension

1. Recall

How many famous stars passed away in 2012 according to this passage ?

2. Compare

What's the similarity and difference between Donna Summer and Robin Gibb?

3. Evaluate

What's your opinion on the movie *When Harry Met Sally*?

4. Explain

Why is Sylvia Kristel so famous?

II. Further Study

Many Asian famous stars passed away in 2012, can you write an article to name them and give a brief introduction to them?

Section B Extensive Reading

Comics: Tickle Your Fancy

You will find several comic strips or individual cartoons, drawn and written by some famous **cartoonists**.

➢ **The New Yorker**

The New Yorker is a weekly literary magazine that contains many cartoons on different subjects. The following cartoon is taken from the issue of April 24, 1989.

"Seems anybody can buy a gun these days."

➢ Doonesbury

Doonesbury is a daily **comic strip** that appears in hundreds of newspapers across the United States. It is drawn and written by Garry Trudeau, who began the strip in the 1970s, when he was a college student. This comic strip comments **extensively** on current political issues, as well as **contemporary** American society and culture.

➢ Peanuts

Peanuts is probably one of the most well-known comic strips in the world. It has been translated into many languages. Charles Schulz started the comic strip in 1950, and it is still very popular today.

➢ Calvin and Hobbes

Bill Watterson began drawing *Calvin and Hobbes* in the 1980s. It **depicts** a **mischievous** boy and his toy tiger. *Calvin and Hobbes* has become one of the most popular comic strips in the United States.

➢ Garfield

Garfield is a fat, lazy yellow cat and the famous star of a comic strip drawn and written by Jim Davis. In Garfield's comic strip home, he lives with his owner Jon and a dog, Odie. Garfield had been "**merchandised**" widely: that is, you can buy Garfield dishes, towels, clothing—just about anything you want.

(length: 379 words)

Vocabulary

cartoonist	n. 漫画家	extensively	ad. 广泛地
comic strip	n. 喜剧，连环画	merchandise	v. 推销
contemporary	a. 当代的	mischievous	a. 淘气的
depict	v. 描绘		

Exercises

I. Comprehension

1. Recall

1) What is happening in cartoon named *Seems anybody can buy a gun these days*?

2) How does Calvin's reply to Hobbes relate to what you know about American television viewing habits?

3) Why are the mice bringing Garfield a piece of pie in cartoon *Garfield*?

2. Explain

1) Explain the story told in the cartoon *Doonesbury*.

2) What do the mice mean by a "real" cat?

3. Evaluate

1) What do you think of the cartoon's author's commenting on in *Seems anybody can buy a gun these days*?

2) What do you think of the answers the girls gave to the exam question in *Peanuts*?

4. Create

How would you describe Calvin?

II. Further Study

There are many interesting comic strips in China, can you choose some of them and give a brief introduction in class?

Section C Supplementary Reading

□ Passage 1 Down with the kids

The following material is a script chosen from a BBC programme named "Authentic Real English". This programme uses dialogue as the main form, introducing the authentic English to English learners. The following passage is a script of the programme, which is composed of both Chinese and English.

Helen: 大家好。Welcome to ***Authentic*** *Real English* with me, Helen...

Rob: ...And me Rob. Hi there!

Helen: Rob, I like your **trainers**, very cool... and look at your designer jeans. Trendy! Rob 看起来挺时髦的，和以往大不一样啊！

Rob: So you like them then?

Helen: I do but... it's not really what someone at your age normally wears.

Rob: I see. But don't you think it makes me look cool and fashionable and... younger?

Why is Rob dressing like a teenager?

Helen: Erm...

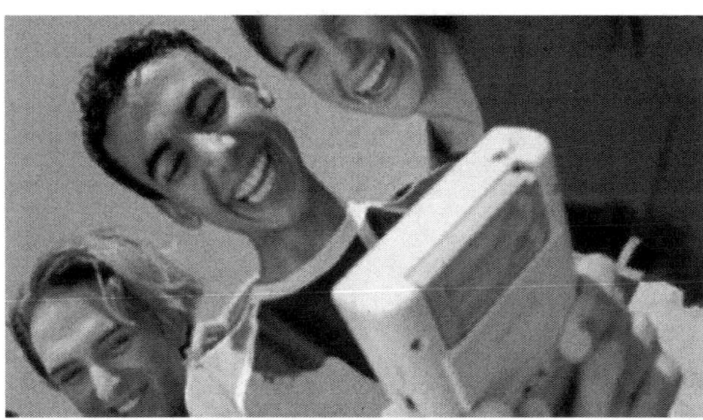

Rob: I'm just trying to get down with the kids.

Helen: The kids?! Rob 和孩子们出去一起玩？！ So you're down with the kids? Down where exactly?

Rob: Oh Helen, keep up! I'm not going anywhere. I mean I'm keeping in with the kids. I'm in tune with the younger generation—yeah!

Helen: 啊！你是说你要跟上你的孩子们或者是下一代的时尚步伐，不能脱节了。So Rob, to do this you have to dress like a teenager?

Rob: Not just that. I share the same interests as young people. I listen to their music on my mp3 player. Look...

Helen: Could you turn that down please! So you're acting young when really you aren't!

Well, you are certainly a big kid Rob!这个短语 **down with the kids** 的意思是大人学小孩。Let's hear some examples of people using this phrase.

- *My Dad's bought a new skateboard so that he can be down with the kids!*
- *I almost broke my neck snowboarding on holiday but hey, at least I'm down with the kids.*
- *She's dyed her hair red and pierced her nose just so she can be down with the kids!*

Helen: 大人跟着小孩儿学，这可有意思。So Rob, what else are you doing to be down with the kids?

Rob: Hey Helen, sort of, things like chillin' and being where it's at.

Helen: Rob, not all kids talk like that.

Rob: Oh right. Well, I've got some rollerblades so I can blade round the park. The only trouble is... I can't seem to get them on... Ouch, my back!

Helen: Are you OK? Rob 想玩滑旱冰，结果你看老骨头不行了吧，把腰给伤了。Do you need some help?

Rob: Thanks. I think I'll just put my **slippers** on—much more comfortable.

Helen: 别忘了，要想跟着小孩子们赶时髦，那还得花点儿工夫，没那么容易。我们下次节目再见。Bye bye!

Rob: Bye. Ouch, my back! Helen, could you just put that slipper on there? Thanks!

(length: 525 words)

Vocabulary

authentic	a. 真正的	slipper	n. 拖鞋
down with the kids	phr. 大人学小孩	trainers	n. 跑鞋
fashionable	a. 时髦的	teenager	n. 年轻人

□ Passage 2 Famous Landmark buildings in Britain and America

➢ St. Paul's Cathedral

St. Paul's Cathedral is an Anglican cathedral on Ludgate Hill, the highest point in the City of London, England, and is the seat of the Bishop of London. The present building dates from the 17th century and was designed by Sir Christopher Wren. It is generally **reckoned** to be London's fifth St. Paul's Cathedral, all having been built on the same site since 604 AD. The cathedral is one of London's most famous and most **recognisable** sights. At 365 feet (111m) high, it was the tallest building in London from 1710 to 1962, and its dome is also among the highest in the world.

Important services held at St. Paul's include the **funerals** of Lord Nelson, the Duke of Wellington and Sir Winston Churchill; Jubilee celebrations for Queen Victoria; peace series marking the end of the First and Second World Wars; the launch of the Festival of Britain and the thanksgiving services for both the Golden Jubilee and 80th Birthday of Her Majesty the Queen.

The Royal Family holds most of its important marriages, christenings and funerals at Westminster Abbey, but St. Paul's was used for the marriage of Charles, Prince of Wales and Lady Diana Spencer. The religious service for Queen Victoria's Diamond Jubilee was also celebrated there. St. Paul's Cathedral is still a busy working church, with hourly **prayer** and daily services.

The cathedral has a very substantial crypt, holding over 200 memorials, and serves as both the Order of the British Empire Chapel and the Treasury. The cathedral has very few treasures: many have been lost, and in 1810 a major **robbery** took almost all of the remaining precious artifacts. Christopher Wren was the first person to be interred, in 1723: on the wall above his tomb in the crypt is written, "Lector, si monumentum requires, circumspice" (Reader, if you seek his monument, look around you).

Most of the memorials commemorate the British military, including several lists of servicemen who died in action, the most recent being the Gulf War. There are special monuments to Lord Nelson in the south **transept** and to the Duke of Wellington in the north aisle; both are buried here. Also remembered are poets, painters, clergy and residents of the local parish. There are lists of the Bishops and cathedral Deans for the last thousand years.

The apse of the cathedral is home to the American Memorial Chapel. It honours American servicemen and women who died in World War II, and was dedicated in 1958. It was paid for entirely by donations from British people, and was designed, as a modern exercise in the Wren style, by Godfrey Allen and Stephen Dykes Bower. The roll of honour contains the names of more than 28,000 Americans who gave their lives while on their way to, or stationed in, the United Kingdom during the Second World War. It is front of the chapel's altar. The three chapel windows date from 1960; they feature themes of service and **sacrifice,** while the insignia around the edges represent the American states and the U.S. armed forces. The limewood paneling incorporates a rocked—a tribute to America's achievements in space.

The cathedral has been the site of many famous funerals, including those of Horatio Nelson, the Duke of Wellington, Sir Winston Churchill and George Mallory.

In 2009, St. Paul's Cathedral commissioned innternationally acclaimed artist Bill Viola to create two nare this bold for permanent display one with a theme of Mary, and one with a theme of Martyes. The project commenced production in mid 2009 with completion scheduled for early 2011. These two multi-screen video installations will be permanently located at the end of the Quire aisles, flanking the High Alter of the Cathedral and the American Memorial Chapel. Each work will employ an arrangement of multiple plasma screen panels configured in a manner similar to historic altarpieces.

In 2007, the World Monuments Fund and American Express awarded St. Paul's a grant as part of their Sustainable Tourism initiative. The project will open up rarely seen areas, relieve crowding in the nave—which suffers heavily from foot traffic and **fluctuations** in humidity—and fund a new Exploration Centre in the crypt. This centre will provide insight into a variety of topics relating to the cathedral, including architecture, history, science, music and, of course, religion. A lapidarium of recovered medieval stones and the room containing Wren's *Great Model* (currently only seen by appointment) will also be opened to the public.

➤ **Westminster Abbey**

The Collegiate Church of St. Peter at Westminster, which is almost always referred to popularly and informally as Westminster Abbey, is a large, mainly Gothic church, in Westminster, London, England, located just to the west of the Palace of Westminster. It is the traditional place of coronation and burial site for English, later British and later still (and currently) monarchs of the Commonwealth Realms. It briefly held the status of a **cathedral** from 1546-1556, and is a Royal Peculiar.

Westminster Abbey is governed by the Dean and Chapter of Westminster, as established by Royal Charter of Queen Elizabeth I in 1560, which created it as the Collegiate Church of St. Peter Westminster and a Royal Peculiar under the personal **jurisdiction** of the Sovereign. The members of the Chapter are the Dean and four residentiary Canons, assisted by the Receiver General and Chapter Clerk. One of the Canons is also Rector of St. Margaret's Church Westminster Abbey (who also holds the post of Chaplain to the Speaker of the House of Commons). In addition to the Dean and Canons there are at present two full time **minor canons**, one **precentor**, the other **succentor**. The office of Priest Vicar was created in the 1970s for those who assist the minor canons. Together with the Clergy and Receiver General and Chapter Clerk, various Lay Officers constitute the College, including the Organist and Master of the Choristers, the Registrar, the Auditor, the Legal Secretary, the Surveyor of the Fabric, the Head Master of the Choir School, the Keeper of the Muniments and the Clerk of the Words, as well as twelve Lay Vicars and ten of the **choristers** and the High Steward and High Bailiff. There are also forty Queen's Scholars who are pupils at Westminster School (the School has its own Governing Body). Those who are most directly concerned with liturgical and ceremonial matters are the two Minor Canons and the Organist and Master of the Choristers.

Henry Ⅲ rebuilt the Abbey in honour of the Royal Saint Edward the Confessor whose **relics** were placed in a shrine in the sanctuary and now lie in a burial vault beneath the 1268 Cosmati **mosaic pavement**, in front of the High Alter. Henry Ⅲ himself was interred nearby in a superb chest tomb with effigial monument, as were many of the Plantagenet kings of England, their wives and other relatives. Subsequently, most Kings and Queens of England were buried here, although Henry Ⅷ and Charles I are buried in St. George's Chapel at Windsor Castle, as are most monarchs and royals after George Ⅱ (Queen Victoria and some other members of the Royal Family are buried at Frogmore).

Aristocrats were buried inside chapels and monks and people associated with the Abbey were buried in the Cloisters and other areas. One of these was Geoffrey Chaucer, who was buried here as he had apartments in the Abbey where he was employed as master of the King's Works. Other poets were buried or **memorialised** around Chaucer in what became known as Poets' Corner. These include: William Blake, Robert Burns, Lord Byron, Samuel Taylor Coleridge, Charles Dickens, John Keats, the Bront Sisters, Rudyard Kipling, John Masefield, John Milton, Laurence

Olivier, Alexander Pope, Nicholas Rowe, Percy Bysshe Shelley, Jane Austen, Thomas Shadwell, Alfred Lord Tennyson, Dylan Thomas and William Wordsworth.

Abbey musicians such as Henry Purcell were also buried in their place of work. Subsequently, it became one of Britain's most significant honours to be buried or commemorated here. The practice spread from aristocrats and poets to generals, admirals, politicians, doctors and scientists such as Isaac Newton, buried on April 4, 1727 and Charles Darwin buried on April 19, 1882.

➢ **The Empire State Building**

The Empire State Building is a 102-story landmark Art Deco skyscraper in New York City at the intersection of Fifth Avenue and West 34th Street. Its name is derived from the nickname for the state of New York, The Empire State. It stood as the world's tallest building for more than 40 years, from its completion in 1931 until construction of the World Trade Center's North Tower was completed in 1972. Following the **destruction** of the World Trade Center in 2001, the Empire State Building once again became the tallest building in New York City and New York State.

9/11 Commission reported that the original plan for the September 11 attacks called for the **hijacking** of 10 planes, one of which was to be crashed into Empire State Building.

The Empire State building has been named by the American Society of Civil Engineers as one of the Seven Wonders of the Modern World. The building and its street floor interior are designated landmarks of the New York Cit Landmarks Preservation Commission, and confirmed by the New York City Board of Estimate. It was designated as a National Historic Landmark in 1986. In 2007, it was ranked No.1 on the List of America's Favorite Architecture according to the AIA. The building is owned and managed by W&H Properties.

In 1964, floodlights were added to **illuminate** the top of the building at night, in colors chosen to match seasonal and other events, such as St. Patrick's Day, Christmas, Independence Day or Bastille Day. After the 80th birthday and **subsequent** death of Frank Sinatra, for example, the building was bathed in blue light to represent the singer's nickname "O1' Blue Eyes". After the death of actress Fay Wray (King Kong) in late 2004, the building stood in complete darkness for 15 minutes.

The floodlights bathed the building in red, white and blue for several months after the destruction of the World Trade Center, then reverted to the standard schedule. On June 4, 2002, the Empire State Building donned **purple** and gold (the royal colours of Queen Elizabeth Ⅱ), in thanks for the United Kingdom playing the Star Spangled Banner during the Changing of the Guard at Buckingham Palace on September 12, 2001 (a show of support after the September 11 Attacks). This would also be shown after the Westminster Dog Show. Traditionally, in addition to the standard schedule, the building will be lit in the colors of New York's sports teams on the nights they have home games (orange, blue and white for the New York's Knicks, red, white and blue for the New York Rangers, and so on). The first weekend in June finds the building bathed in green light for the Belmont Stakes held in nearby Belmont Park. The building is illuminated in tennis-ball yellow during the U.S. Open tennis **tournament** in late August and early September.

It was twice lit in scarlet to support nearby Rutgers University: once for a football game against the University of Louisville on November 9, 2006 and again on April 3, 2007 when the women's basketball team played in the national championship game.

In 1995, the building was lit up in blue, red, green and yellow for the **release** of Microsoft's Windows 95 operating system, which was launched with a $300 million campaign.

The building has also been known to be illuminated in purple and white in honor of graduating students from New York University.

Every year in September, the building is lit in black, red and yellow, with the top lights off (for black) to celebrate the German-American Steuben Parade on Fifth Avenue.

Starting in 2008, the building along with New York City and many other cities around the world, participated in Earth Hour. The skyscraper's floodlights were turned off for exactly an hour to **conserve** energy.

In September, 2009, the building was lit for one night in orange colors, in celebration of the exploration of Manhattan Island by Henry Hudson 400 years earlier. The Dutch Prince Willem-Alexander and his wife Princess Maxima were present and turned on the lights from the lobby.

In 2009, the building was lit for one night in red and yellow, the colors of the Communist People's Republic of China, to celebrate the 60 years since its founding.

➤ **The Pentagon**

The Pentagon is headquarters of the United States Department of Defense, located in Arlington Country, Virginia. As a symbol of the U.S. military, "the Pentagon" is often used metonymically to refer to the Department of Defense rather than the building itself.

Designed by the American architect George Bergstrom (1876-1955), and built by Philadelphia, Pennsylvania, general contractor John McShain, the building was dedicated on January 15, 1943, after ground was broken for construction on September 11, 1941. General Brehon Somervell provided the major motive power behind the project; colonel Leslie Groves was responsible for overseeing the project for the Army.

The Pentagon is the world's largest office building by floor area, with about 6,500,000 sq ft (60,000 m²), of which 3,700,000 sq ft (344,000 m²) are used as offices. Approximately 23,000 military and civilian employees and about 3,000 non-defense support personnel work in the Pentagon. It has five sides, five floors above ground (plus two basement levels), and five ring **corridors** per floor with a total of 17.5 miles (28.2 km) of corridors. The Pentagon includes a five-acre (20,000 m²) central plaza, which is shaped like a **pentagon** and informally known as "ground zero", a nickname originating during the Cold War and based on the **presumption** that the Soviet Union would target one or more nuclear missiles at this central location in the outbreak of a nuclear war.

Since 1998, the Pentagon has been undergoing a major renovation, known as the Pentagon Renovation Program. This program, scheduled to be completed in 2010, involves the complete gutting and reconstruction of the entire building in phases to bring the building up to modern standards, removing **asbestos**, improving security and providing greater efficiency for Pentagon tenants. Recently, the process of sealing all of the building's windows began.

As originally built, most Pentagon office space consisted of open bays which spanned an entire ring. These offices used cross-ventilation from operable windows instead of air conditioning for cooling. Gradually, bays were subdivided into private offices with many using window air conditioning units. When renovations are completed, the new space will include a return to open office bays, with a new Universal Space Plan of standardized office furniture and **partitions** developed by Studios Architecture.

On September 11, 2001, exactly 60 years since the building's groundbreaking, hijacked American Airlines Flight 77 was crashed into the western side of the Pentagon, killing 189 people, including 64 people aboard the plane and 125 working in the building.

On March 4, 2010 at 6:40 p.m., two police officers working for the Pentagon Force Protection Agency were shot near an entrance to the Pentagon and fired back with their **pistols** at the suspect. The officers were slightly injured but were treated in a hospital and released. The suspect, identified as John Patrick Bedell (aged 36) died at the hospital. No clear motive was established.

The Pentagon has over 20 of its own fast food operations, including Subway, McDonald's, Dunking' Dounts, Pands Express, Starbucks and Sbarro, among others. A multibranded KFC, Pizza Hut and Taco Bell restaurant opened in 2003, when renovations to the food court were completed. Food services are managed by the Navy Exchange. The Center Courtyard Café reopened in Spring 2008, replacing the "Ground Zero Café" snack bar that was previously there. Before renovation, the Pentagon was built with double the number of bathrooms required, as it was built during **segregation**. Half the bathrooms were for blacks and the other half were for whites.

The Pentagon Athletic Center (PAC), a fitness center for military and civilian staff, opened in 2004 adjacent to the north side of the Pentagon, replacing the Pentagon Officers Athletic Club (POAC) which had operated for 55 years in a structure between Route 110 and the parade grounds. Each year, the Pentagon grounds are a major focus for hosting the Marine Corps Marathon and the Army Ten-Miler running events.

(length: 2,922 words)

Vocabulary

ablaze	n. 着火点	corridor	n. 走廊
aisle	n. 过道	destruction	n. 破坏
asbestos	n. 石棉	dismantle	n. 拆除
attic	n. 阁楼	fluctuation	n. 波动
cathedral	n. 大教堂	funeral	n. 葬礼
chorister	n. 唱诗班歌手	hijack	v. 劫持
colonnade	n. 廊柱	hue	n. 色彩
conserve	v. 保持	illuminate	v. 照亮

jurisdiction	n. 管辖权	presumption	n. 推测
mansion	n. 宅邸	purple	a. 紫色
memorialize	v. 纪念	reckon	v. 测算，估计
metonym	n. 换喻词	recognisable	a. 可辨识的
minor canon	phr. 低级牧师	release	n. 发布
mosaic	n. 马赛克	relic	n. 遗骸
namesake	n. 同名	robbery	n. 抢劫案
partition	n. 划分	sacrifice	n. 牺牲
pavement	n. 人行道	segregation	n. 种族隔离
pentagon	n. 五角形	succentor	n. 唱诗班副指挥
pistol	n. 手枪	subsequent	a. 随后的
prayer	n. 祈祷者	tournament	n. 锦标赛
precentor	n. 领唱人	transept	n. 教堂的十字形翼部
presidency	n. 总统任期		

Section D Word Bank for This Unit

爱好	hobby	喜剧	comedy
养宠物	keep pets	悲剧	tragedy
驯狗	tame dogs	恐怖片	horror movie
下象棋	play chess	情节	plot
打牌	play cards	有趣的，愉快的	entertaining
电脑游戏	computer game	热情的	enthusiastic
闲话	gossip	拍掌，鼓掌	clap
电视频道	TV channel	闲暇时间	leisure time
广播	broadcast	约会	date
现场直播	live broadcast	拜访某人	call on sb.
纪录片	documentary	好客的	hospital
商业广告	commercial advertisement	公用电话亭	telephone boot
电视剧场	TV theatre	长途电话	long-distance call
网球场	tennis court	挂上电话	hang up
足球比赛	football match	别挂电话	hold on
娱乐行业	entertainment industry	接线员	operator
暴力片	violence movie		

Chapter 11

Holidays and Festivals

节日是文化的缩影。对于西方国家节日的了解可以帮助我们更好地感受其历史文化积淀。透过复活节和圣诞节，我们可以看到西方人宗教信仰的影子；透过圣帕特里克节和愚人节，我们可以找到英美民族构成的渊源；透过感恩节、国旗日和一个个历史名人的诞辰，我们又会感受到英美历史的积淀……

你想更好地了解西方的节假日及风俗习惯吗？让我们一起来学习英国和美国的节假日文化。

Section A　Intensive Reading

Holidays and traditions in UK

➢ **How do the British celebrate Christmas?**

Christmas is Britain's most popular holiday and features traditions that date back hundreds of years. Many Christmas customs that **originated** in Britain have been **adopted** in the United States.

The first-ever Christmas card was posted in England in the 1840s, and the practice soon became an established part of the **build-up** to Christmas. Over a billion Christmas cards are now sent every year in the United Kingdom, many of them sold **in aid of charities**.

Christmas **decorations** in general have even earlier **origins**. **Holly, ivy** and **mistletoe** are associated with **rituals** going back beyond **the Dark Ages**. (The custom of kissing beneath a **sprig** of mistletoe is derived from an ancient **pagan** tradition.) The Christmas tree was introduced into the royal household by **Queen Charlotte,** wife of **King George Ⅲ**,

and **popularized** by **Prince Albert**, husband of **Queen Victoria**, in the 1840s.

Charles Dickens's short novel ***A Christmas Carol*** has **prompted** people the world over to associate Christmas with **Victorian England**. Originally published on 17 December 1843, the book was **rapturously** reviewed and became an instant success, the first 6,000 copies of its **initial** print-run being sold out by Christmas. **Theatrical**, television and movie **adaptations** of the book continue to be as popular in Britain as they are in the United States.

Every year since 1947, the City of **Oslo** in **Norway** has presented the City of **Westminster** with a large Christmas tree which stands in London's **Trafalgar Square in commemoration of Anglo-Norwegian** cooperation during the Second World War.

There is also a program of Christmas carols in Trafalgar Square each year.

Another Christmas tree, presented by the British Christmas Tree Growers Association, stands outside the Prime Minister's residence at **10 Downing Street**.

Pantomimes are popular among British children at Christmas time. These are song and dance **dramatizations** of well-known fairy tales that encourage audience participation.

Carols are often sung on Christmas Eve by groups of singers to their neighbors, and children hang a stocking on the **fireplace** or at the foot of their bed for Santa Claus (also called Father Christmas) to fill. Presents for the family are placed beneath the Christmas tree.

Christmas Day sees the opening of presents and many families attend Christmas services at church. Christmas dinner consists traditionally of a roast turkey, goose or chicken with **stuffing** and roast potatoes. This is followed by mince pies and Christmas pudding **flaming** with **brandy**, which might contain coins or **lucky charms** for children. (The pudding is usually prepared weeks **beforehand** and is **customarily stirred** by each member of the family as a wish is made.) Later in the day, a Christmas cake may be served—a rich baked fruit cake with **marzipan**, **icing** and sugar **frosting**.

The pulling of Christmas crackers often **accompanies** food on Christmas Day. Invented by a London baker in 1846, a cracker is a brightly coloured paper tube, twisted at both ends, which contains a party hat, riddle and toy or other **trinket**. When it is pulled by two people it **gives out** a **crack** as its contents are **dispersed**.

Another traditional feature of Christmas afternoon is the **Queen's Christmas Message** to the nation, broadcast on radio, television and the internet.

➢ **What do British people eat at Christmas?**

Christmas dinner is perhaps the largest meal of the year. Although we eat far less nowadays than the enormous **feasts** our **ancestors** indulged in, this **festive** holiday is not a time for watching the **waistline**.

The **centerpiece** of the British Christmas dinner, which is traditionally eaten in the early afternoon of Christmas Day, is roast turkey. Turkey was first brought to the UK from North America in the early part of the 16th century and before long it replaced the peacock and the goose as the "meat" for the main Christmas meal. **A wealth of trimmings** accompany the turkey—stuffing (made with breadcrumbs, sausage meat, **sage** and onion), bread sauce, sausages rolled in bacon, roast **chestnuts**, roast potatoes, and, of course, **brussels sprouts**, carrots and peas.

The main **course** is followed by Christmas pudding, brought to the table flaming in brandy. Made from dried fruit—raisins, **sultanas**, **currants**—**suet**, breadcrumbs, eggs, spices, milk and brandy, Christmas pudding must be **steamed** for several hours. Many cooks make their puddings months, if not a year, **in advance**. The pudding is traditionally served with **custard** (a **vanilla** flavored sauce made with milk and eggs) or brandy butter.

Then if you still have room, you could **squeeze** in a mince pie—a sweet, rich mixture of dried fruits and suet baked in a **pastry** case—or **a wedge of** fine Blue **Stilton** cheese.

➢ **What is Boxing Day?**

The day after Christmas Day, December 26, is known as **Boxing Day** in Britain. It was also known as the Feast of St. Stephen, when in **olden** days church **alms-boxes** were opened and the contents given to the poor. This custom turned into the giving of Christmas boxes, which were gifts of food, money or other items to household servants and then to public **tradesmen**, such as **postmen** and **dustmen** (garbage collectors).

In many parts of Britain these traditions **live on**, with gifts of food, clothing or money from local churches being given to the poor or **needy**, and many people still give small gifts to their favorite trades people.

Boxing Day is a public holiday in Britain. Banks and most shops are closed.

➢ **How does the United Kingdom celebrate the New Year?**

In Scotland, the New Year is called **Hogmanay**. It is marked by an evening of drinking and **merrymaking**, climaxing **at the stroke of midnight** when huge gatherings of people in Edinburgh and **Glasgow** greet the New Year by linking arms and singing ***Auld Lang Syne***.

Throughout Britain, the New Year is often launched with a party—either at home with family and friends or at a gathering in local pubs and clubs. **Festivities** begin on New Year's Eve and build up to midnight. The stroke of midnight is the cue for much cheering and the drinking of toasts.

Tradition has it that the first person over the **threshold** on New Year's Day will dictate the luck brought to the household in the coming year. This is known as First Footing. At midnight on

December 31, particularly in Scotland and Northern Ireland, 'first footers' step over the threshold bringing the New Year's luck. The first footer usually brings a piece of coal, a loaf of bread and a bottle of whisky. On entering he must place the fuel on the fire, put the loaf on the table and pour a glass of whisky for the head of the house, all normally without speaking or being spoken to until he wishes everyone "A Guid New Year tae Ane an' Aw" (A Good New Year to One and All). He must enter by the front door and leave by the back.

In Wales the back door is opened to **release** the Old Year at the first stroke of midnight. It is then locked up to "keep the luck in" and at the last stroke the New Year is **let in** at the front door.

London's New Year's Day Parade is the biggest parade of its kind in the world. The American-style **extravaganza** of 10,000 musicians, dancers, **acrobats**, clowns, **cheerleaders** and **floats, twirl**, march and drum their way from **Parliament Square**, via **Whitehall**, **Pall Mall**, **Lower Regent Street**, along Piccadilly before finishing in **Berkeley Square**.

The Parade starts at noon, just as Big Ben strikes, from Parliament Square, and arrives in Berkeley Street at 2:45 pm. Everyone is welcome to join in the **carnival** of music and New Year **merriment**!

(length: 1,284 words)

Vocabulary

accompany	v. 陪伴；伴随	customarily	ad. 通常；习惯上
acrobat	n. 杂技演员	decoration	n. 装饰；装饰品
adaptation	n. 改编；改写	disperse	v. 分散；使散开
adopt	v. 采取；采纳	dramatization	n. 编剧；改编成戏剧
alms	n. 捐献；施舍	dustman	n. 清洁工人
ancestor	n. 祖先	extravaganza	n. 铺张华丽的表演
at the stroke of midnight	phr. 午夜钟声	feast	n. 盛宴；款待
a wealth of	phr. 很多的	festive	a. 节日的；喜庆的；欢乐的
a wedge of	phr. 楔形的	festivity	n. 欢庆；庆典
beforehand	a. 提前的	fireplace	n. 壁炉
	ad. 事先；预先	flame	v. 泛红；焚烧
brandy	n. 白兰地酒	float	v. 摇摆；飘动
brussels sprout	phr. 球芽甘蓝		n. （复数）彩车
build-up	n. 组成	frosting	n. 霜状白糖
carnival	n. 狂欢节；嘉年华会	give out	phr. 发出（气味、热等）
centerpiece	a. 中心装饰品；桌面摆饰	holly	n. 冬青树
charity	n. 慈善	icing	n. 糖衣；酥皮
cheerleader	n. 拉拉队长	in aid of	phr. 用以援助
chestnut	n. 栗子	in commemoration of	phr. 纪念
crack	n. 破裂声；爆裂声	in advance	phr. 预先；提前
course	n. 一道菜	initial	a. 最初的
currant	n. 无核小葡萄干	ivy	n. 常春藤
custard	n. 蛋奶糊，蛋羹	let in	phr. 让……进来；嵌入

live on	phr. 靠……为生
lucky charm	phr. 幸运符；护身符
marzipan	n. 杏仁蛋白软糖
merriment	n. 欢喜；欢乐
merrymaking	a. 寻欢的；快乐的
mistletoe	n. 槲寄生
needy	a. 贫困的；贫穷的
olden	a. 古老的
origin	n. 起源
originate	v. 发源；发生
pagan	n. 异教徒 a. 异教的
pantomime	n. 哑剧 v. 演哑剧
pastry	n. 面点；点心
popularize	v. 普及；使通俗化
postman	n. 邮递员；邮差
prompt	v. 促进；激起
rapturously	ad. 兴高采烈地；狂喜地
release	v. 允许发表；发射
ritual	n. 仪式；典礼
sage	n. 圣人；贤人；鼠尾草（可用作调料） a. 明智的；贤明的
sprig	n. 小枝
squeeze	v. 挤；捏
steamed	a. 蒸熟的；熟的
Stilton	n. 斯第尔顿干酪/奶酪（世界三大蓝纹奶酪之一）
stir	v. 搅拌；激起
stuffing	n. 填料；填塞物
suet	n. 伴油；牛脂
sultana	n. 小葡萄干
theatrical	a. 戏剧的；剧场的
trimmings	n. 香肠原料肉
trinket	n. 小装饰品；不值钱的小玩意 v. 密谋
tradesman	n. 零售商
threshold	n. 门槛
twirl	v. （使）快速旋转；转动
vanilla	n. 香草
waistline	n. 腰围；腰身部分

Proper Names

King George Ⅲ	英国国王乔治三世
Dark Ages	黑暗时代
Queen Charlotte	夏洛特皇后
Prince Albert	阿尔伯特亲王
Queen Victoria	维多利亚女王
Charles Dickens	查尔斯·狄更斯
A Christmas Carol	圣诞颂歌
Victorian England	维多利亚时代的英国
Oslo	奥斯陆（挪威首都）
Norway	挪威
Westminster	威斯敏斯特(伦敦市的一个行政区）
Trafalgar Square	特拉法加广场
Anglo-Norwegian	盎格鲁-挪威
10 Downing Street	唐宁街 10 号
Queen's Christmas Message	英皇圣诞文告
Boxing Day	节礼节
Hogmanay	（苏格兰的）除夕
Auld Lang Syne	友谊地久天长（歌名）
Glasgow	格拉斯哥（英国城市名）
Parliament Square	议会广场
Whitehall	白厅（英国）
Pall Mall	蓓尔美尔街(伦敦一街名，以俱乐部多出名）
Lower Regent Street	摄政街
Berkeley Square	伯克利广场

Exercises

I. Comprehension

1. Recall

What is boxing day?

2. Summarize

How do the British celebrate Christmas?

3. Make Inferences

Do the people in Britain call the New Year Hogmanay?

4. Analyze

1) Can you compare the differences in New Year's celebration in Scotland and in England?

2) Are "first footers" important to Scottish people? Why?

5. Evaluate

What do you think of the Christmas celebration in UK? Cite evidence to support your answer.

II. Further Study

Choose British and American Christmas celebration to compare and report the differences to the class.

Section B Extensive Reading

Easter Celebrations in the UK

➢ **Easter in the UK**

In the UK Easter is one of the major Christian festivals of the year. It is full of customs, **folklore** and traditional food. However, Easter in Britain has its beginnings long before the arrival of Christianity. Many **theologians** believe Easter itself is named after the Anglo-Saxon goddess of the dawn and spring—**Eostre**.

In Britain Easter occurs at a different time each year. It is observed on the first Sunday after the first full moon following the first day of spring in the Northern Hemisphere. This means that the festival can occur on any Sunday between March 22 and April 25. Not only is Easter the end of the winter it is also the end of **Lent**, traditionally a time of **fasting** in the Christian calendar. It is therefore often a time of fun and celebration.

The Friday before Easter Sunday and the Monday after are a bank holiday in the UK. Over Easter schools in the UK close for two weeks, just enough time to digest all the chocolate.

➢ **Good Friday**

On the Friday before Easter, Christians **commemorate** the **crucifixion** of Jesus Christ. It is a day of mourning in church and special Good Friday services are held where Christians **meditate** on Jesus's suffering and death on the **cross**, and what this means for their faith.

Calling it "Good Friday" may seem a bit bizarre, but some people think that it was once called God's Friday or Holy Friday.

➢ **Symbols of Easter**

Many of the symbols and traditions of Easter are connected with **renewal**, birth, good luck and **fertility**.

➢ **The Cross**

Of course as it is a Christian festival one of the main symbols is a cross, often on a hill. When Jesus was **crucified**, the cross became a symbol of suffering. Then with the **resurrection**, Christians saw it as a symbol of victory over death. In A D 325, **Constantine** issued a **decree** at **the Council of Nicaea**, that the Cross would be the official symbol of Christianity.

➢ **Palms**

The week of Easter begins on **Palm Sunday**. Why *Palm* Sunday? In Roman times it was **customary** to welcome **royalty** by waving palm branches, a bit like a **ticker-tape parade**. So, when Jesus arrived in **Jerusalem** on what is now known as Palm Sunday, people welcomed him with palm branches **carpeting** the streets and waving them. Today, on Palm Sunday, Christians carry palm branches in parades, and make them into crosses and **garlands** to decorate the Church.

➢ **Easter Eggs**

Easter eggs are a very old tradition going to a time before Christianity. Eggs after all are a symbol of spring and new life.

Exchanging and eating Easter eggs is a popular custom in many countries. In the UK before they were replaced by chocolate Easter eggs, real eggs were used, in most cases, chicken eggs. The eggs were hard-boiled and dyed in various colors and patterns. The traditionally bright colours represented spring and light. Sadly, nowadays if you gave a child in Britain a hard-boiled egg on Easter Sunday, you would probably end up wearing it!

An older more traditional game is one in which real eggs are rolled against one another or down a hill. The owner of the egg that stayed **uncracked** the longest won. Even today in the north of England, for example as at **Preston** in **Lancashire**, they still carry out the custom of egg rolling. Hard boiled eggs are rolled down slopes to see whose egg goes furthest. In other places another game is played. You hold an egg in the palm of the hand and bang against your opponent's egg. The loser is the one whose egg breaks first.

Nowadays people give each other Easter eggs made of chocolate, usually hollow and filled with sweets. On TV you will see **adverts** for **Cadbury's** Creme Eggs, a very sweet **confectionery**. The **catchphrase** for the adverts is "How do you eat yours?" And Britain children hunt for (chocolate) Easter eggs hidden about the home or garden by **the Easter bunny**.

The Easter Bunny

Rabbits, due to their **fecund** nature, have always been a symbol of fertility. The Easter bunny (rabbit) however may actually be an Easter hare. The hare was **allegedly** a companion of the ancient Moon goddess and of Eostre.

Strangely the bunny as an Easter symbol seems to have its origins in Germany, where it was first mentioned in German writings in the 16th Century. The first edible Easter bunnies appeared in Germany during the early 1800s, they were made of pastry and sugar.

In the UK children believe that if they are good, the "Easter Bunny" will leave (chocolate) eggs for them.

Sadly hare hunting (hare coursing) used to be a common pastime at Easter. But this might please some of the more fundamentalist Christians, who consider the **fluffy** fellow to be **unchristian**.

Morris Dancing

Morris dancing is a traditional English form of **folk dance** which is also performed in other English-speaking countries such as the USA and Australia. The roots of Morris dancing seem to be very old, probably dating back to the Middle Ages.

In the dance men dress up in costumes with hats and ribbons and bells around their ankles. They dance through the streets and one man often carries an **inflated pigs bladder** on the end of a stick. He will run up to young women in the street and hit them over the head with the pigs bladder, this is supposed to be lucky!

Dressing Up For Easter

Easter was once a traditional day for getting married, that may be why people often dress up for Easter. Women would make and wear special Easter **bonnets**—decorated with flowers and **ribbons**. Even today in Battersea in London there is a special Easter Parade, where hand-made bonnets are shown off.

Hot Cross Buns

Hot cross buns, now eaten throughout the Easter season, were first baked in England to be served on Good Friday. These small, lightly sweet **yeast** buns contain **raisins** or currants and sometimes chopped candied fruit. Before baking, a cross is **slashed** in the top of the bun. After baking, a **confectioners**' sugar icing is used to fill the cross.

An old rhyme was often sung by children awaiting their sugary treat:

"Hot cross buns,
hot cross buns,
one a penny, two a penny,
hot cross buns.
If you do not like them,
give them to your sons,

one a penny, two a penny,
hot cross buns."

> **Simnel Cake**

A traditional way of breaking the **Lenten fast** is to eat some **simnel cake**. These are raised cakes, with a **crust** made of fine flour and water, coloured yellow with **saffron**, and filled with a very rich plum-cake, with plenty of candied lemon peel, and dried fruits.

An old **Shropshire** tale has it that long ago there lived an honest old couple, Simon and Nelly, and it was their custom to gather their children around them at Easter. Nelly had some **leftover unleavened dough** from Lent, and Simon reminded her there was some plum pudding still **left over** from Christmas. They could make some **treats** for the visiting family.

Nell put the leftovers together, and Sim insisted the cake should be boiled, while she was just as certain that it should be baked. They had a fight and **came to blows**, but **compromised** by doing both. They cooked the cake over a fire made from furniture broken in the **scuffle**, and some eggs, similarly broken, were used to **baste** it. The **delicacy** was named after this **cantankerous** couple.

(length: 1,261 words)

Vocabulary

advert	n. 广告	fasting	n. 禁食；斋戒
allegedly	ad. 据称；假设	fecund	a. 多产的；肥沃的
baste	n. 调味品；涂抹液	fertility	n. 多产；肥沃
bonnet	n. 软帽	folk dance	phr. 民间舞蹈
cantankerous	a. 脾气坏的；爱吵架的	folklore	n. 民间传说
carpet	n. 毛毯；地毯 v. 铺以地毯	fluffy	a. 蓬松的；松软的
		garland	n. 花环
catchphrase	n. 广告用语；名言	inflated pigs bladder	phr. 膨胀的猪膀胱
commemorate	v. 纪念	left over	phr. 剩余；留下
compromise	n. 让步；妥协	leftover	n. 吃剩的饭菜
cross	n. 十字架	meditate	v. 冥想；沉思
come to blows	phr. 开始互殴	pastry	n. 面粉糕饼
confectioner	n. 糖果商	renewal	n. 更新；复兴；恢复
confectionery	n. 糖果糕点；糖果店	raisin	n. 葡萄干；提子干
crucifixion	n. 被钉十字架；苦痛的考验；受难	resurrection	n. 复活；复兴
crucify	v. 将……钉在十字架上	ribbon	n. 带状物；丝带
crust	n. 外壳；面包皮	royalty	n. 皇室；王权
customary	a. 习惯的；惯例的	saffron	n. 藏红花
decree	n. 命令	scuffle	n. 混战；扭打
delicacy	n. 美味；佳肴	simnel cake	phr. 重油水果蛋糕
dough	n. 生面团	slash	v. 猛砍；严厉批评
fast	n. 禁食 v. 禁食	slope	n. 斜坡
		ticker-tape parade	phr. 抛彩带欢迎仪式

treat	n. 宴请；款待
uncracked	a. 未裂开的；无裂缝的
unchristian	a. 不信基督教的；粗野的
unleavened	a. 未经发酵的
yeast	n. 酵母；发酵粉

Proper Names

Cadbury	吉百利（巧克力公司及其产品名）
Constantine	君士坦丁
Easter bunny	复活节兔子
Eostre	厄俄斯特女神（通常象征平安和昌盛）
Hot cross buns	热十字面包
Jerusalem	耶路撒冷
Lancashire	兰开夏郡（英格兰西北部的郡）
Lent	（宗教）大斋节（指复活节前为期 40 天的斋戒及忏悔，以纪念耶稣在荒野禁食）
Lenten	四月斋的
Morris dancing	英格兰传统的化妆舞“莫里斯舞”
Palm Sunday	圣枝主日(即复活节前的星期日）
Preston	普勒斯顿（英国港市名字）
Shropshire	什罗浦郡（英格兰西部）
the Council of Nicaea	尼西亚会议(这过程就交给被拣选的少数人所组成的团体）

Exercises

I. Comprehension

1. Recall

What else is “Good Friday” called?

2. Summarize

What do British people do to celebrate the Easter?

3. Make Inferences

Do people practice fasting during Easter season?

4. Analyze

What does the Easter Bunny symbolize? Why?

5. Evaluate

What do you think of the colorful Easter eggs?

II. Further study

Choose the celebration of Easter in the UK and find as much information as possible. Then prepare a presentation in class and talk about the celebrations you have searched.

Section C Supplementary Reading

□ Passage 1 Other Special Days in UK

➤ Burns Night

Burns Night is the commemoration of the life and works of **Robert Burns**, Scotland’s most famous poet. It is celebrated with traditional suppers, which have been held annually on his birthday for more than 200 years.

Burns was born on 25 January 1759, in Alloway, Ayrshire in south-west Scotland. He is renowned worldwide as a great poet and songwriter. A keen social commentator, Burns wrote movingly about love, universal brotherhood and the human condition. He wrote from the heart and, to this day, his words are considered timeless.

The Burns Night supper ritual was started in 1796, a few years after his death, by his close friends as a tribute to his memory. The basic format for the evening still follows the same pattern whether it is held in formal dining rooms or the local pub. The ceremony begins when the designated "chairman" of the evening invites "the company" (guests) to receive the **haggis**—a traditional Scottish dish made of **minced offal** with suet, onions, **oatmeal** and **seasonings**.

Next comes the reciting of a prayer, *Selkirk Grace* (written by Burns):

"Some hae meat and canna eat,
And some wad eat that want it;
But we hae meat and we can eat,
And sae the Lord be thankit."

The company are then asked to stand to receive the haggis. A **piper** in full traditional Scottish dress and playing the **bagpipes** (a musical instrument featuring an air-filled bag fitted with pipes) leads the chef, carrying the haggis to the **top table**.

The bagpipes play an essential part in a traditional Burns supper, but contrary to popular belief, the bagpipes are not of Scottish origin. The first version of the instrument can be traced back to the **Middle East**, well over 2,000 years ago. Then, it was most likely a rather **crude** instrument comprised of **reeds** stuck into a goatskin bag. As civilisation spread throughout the Middle East and into **Mediterranean** lands, the people brought their music with them. Some of their instruments were adaptations of the early bagpipe.

As the ceremony continues, the chairman recites Burns' famous ***Address To A Haggis***. When he reaches the line "an' cut you up wi' ready slight", he **slices** open the haggis with a sharp knife. It is customary for the company to applaud the chairman and to stand and toast the haggis with a glass of whisky.

The traditional Burns supper menu consists of **cock-a-leekie soup** (or Scotch **broth**) and haggis with **"tatties** and **neeps"** (potatoes and rutabagas), **Tipsy Laird** (**sherry trifle**) followed by **oatcakes** and cheese, all washed down with liberal **tots** of the "water of life"—**Scotch whisky**.

One of the central features of the evening is when an invited guest is asked to give a short speech on Burns. Known as the Immortal Memory speech, it can be **light-hearted** or **literary** but the aim is to **outline** the greatness and relevance of the poet today. Various humorous speeches follow.

Once the speeches are complete the evening continues with songs and poems written by Burns. Favourites include *Tam O'Shanter*, *Address To The Unco Guid*, *To A Mouse,* and *Holy Willie's Prayer*.

The evening ends with the company standing, linking hands and singing one of Burns's most famous works, *Auld Lang Syne*.

It is not just in Scotland that the Burns supper tradition is maintained. On or around 25 January, the life and works of the poet are celebrated everywhere from Moscow to Manhattan, Newfoundland to New Zealand.

➢ Guy Fawkes Day

November 5 is celebrated in Britain to commemorate the failure of Guy Fawkes and other terrorist conspirators to blow up the Houses of Parliament in 1605. Public firework displays are organized with effigies of Fawkes burned on bonfires, and smaller parties take place in back gardens throughout the land. The 5th of November is also called "Firework Night", "Bonfire Night", or "Guy Fawkes Day". In the days leading up to it, children traditionally take their home-made effigies, or "Guys", out into the streets and ask passers-by for "a penny for the Guy", using the money to buy fireworks.

The conspiracy to blow up the Houses of Parliament on November 5, 1605, is known as the "Gunpowder Plot", and was discovered the night before the explosion was to occur. The origins of the plot remain unclear and the truth will probably never be known. Generations of historians accepted it was an attempt to re-establish the Catholic religion. In more recent times, others have suspected that the plot was the work of a group of agents-provocateurs, anxious to discredit the Jesuits and reinforce the ascendancy of the Protestant religion.

The plot centered around five conspirators, Robert Catesby, Thomas Winter, Thomas Percy, John Wright, and Guy (or Guido) Fawkes, later joined by Robert Keyes, who were determined to blow up of the House of Lords in 1605. The detonation was to take place on State Opening day, when the King, Lords, and Commons would all be present in the Lords Chamber.

There is no doubt that Fawkes, though remembered wrongly as the principal conspirator, was in fact a minor cog in the wheel. Born in 1570 in York, he was brought up as a Protestant. In 1593, he enlisted as a mercenary in the Spanish Army in the Netherlands—he became a Catholic shortly before that date. He was at the capture of Calais in 1595, where he apparently distinguished himself greatly. He may have been chosen for his skills when it was planned to tunnel under the House, and it was an advantage that, having been abroad for some time, he was not known in London.

The plot was discovered, in the official version, through an anonymous letter to Lord Monteagle, a Catholic, warning him not to attend the State Opening. Whether the letter was genuine or a forgery is uncertain. In any event, on November 4 an initial search was made of Parliament. The cellar was thoroughly searched at midnight and Fawkes was found with the gunpowder. He was then arrested.

All the conspirators (except Robert Winter) were killed or arrested by November 12 and taken to the Tower of London. They were probably subjected to extensive torture, which formed part of the punishment for treason at the time. Fawkes and the other conspirators who remained alive were tried for high treason and were convicted and sentenced to death. The executions included hanging, drawing and quartering. The heads and other portions of the conspirators' bodies were set up at various points around Westminster and London.

The Houses of Parliament are still searched by the Yeomen of the Guard just before the State Opening to ensure no latter-day Fawkes is concealed in the cellars, though this is retained as a picturesque custom rather than a serious anti-terrorist precaution (for which, of course, there are proper means).

➢ **Remembrance Day**

The Armistice that brought an end to the fighting of the First World War was signed on November 11,1918. Remembrance Day is commemorated annually in Britain on the Sunday nearest to November 11.

Two weeks before Remembrance Day paper poppies made by ex-service personnel begin to be sold by volunteers all over Britain. The red poppies represent the poppies that grew in the cornfields of Flanders where many thousands of soldiers lost their lives in the First World War. Wearing a poppy—the symbol of remembrance—remains a small yet significant gesture which helps British people to remember the price of freedom. It is a price which is still being paid, with more than 12,000 British servicemen and women killed or injured in active service since 1945, and 53% of the regular armed forces currently under the age of 30.

The funds raised by the Poppy Appeal represent half of the $83 million the Royal British Legion spends each year on the welfare of ex-service personnel and their families.

It was an American woman, Moina Michael, who thought of the idea of selling poppies to help care for disabled soldiers and their families. While working at the YMCA training headquarters at Columbia University in New York in 1918, she was inspired by the poem *In Flanders Fields* by Canadian Army doctor John McCrae. The poem's first verse is:

"In Flanders fields the poppies blow
Between the crosses, row on row,
That mark our place; and in the sky
The larks, still bravely singing, fly
Scarce heard amid the guns below."

Remembrance Day is commemorated by church services around the country and by a special ceremony at the Cenotaph (from the Greek, meaning an empty tomb) in London. At 11:00 a.m., a two-minute silence is observed at the Cenotaph and elsewhere in the country to honor those who lost their lives in the First and Second World Wars, as well as subsequent conflicts including the Falklands War and the war in Iraq.

The Cenotaph was first built as a temporary wood and plaster structure for use as a saluting base in Whitehall during the First World War Victory Parade. Public enthusiasm for this hurriedly prepared design by Edwin Lutyens, (later the architect of the British Embassy in Washington D.C.), prompted the government to re-erect the Cenotaph in a permanent form on the same site, as a national memorial to the war dead. The unveiling of the stone structure on November 11, 1920 was combined with a ceremony to mark the passing of the body of the Unknown Warrior for re-burial in Westminster Abbey. The first of the annual ceremonies of remembrance took place at the Cenotaph on the same date of the following year.

The Cenotaph Ceremony is a unique expression of national homage, attended by the Queen, the Prime Minister, and all the principal representatives of Parliament, the governments of the Commonwealth, the armed forces and the churches. The ceremony takes the form of a short "service of dedication" preceded by observation of the two-minute silence and official wreath laying.

For this purpose the Cenotaph is enclosed in a square formed by detachments from branches of the fighting services, by a contingent from civilian services vital in time of war and by a large body of ex-servicemen and women. The general public is invited to take part in the service, and the ceremony is broadcast on radio and television.

(length: 1,719 words)

Vocabulary

bagpipe	n. 风笛	outline	v. 概述
cock-a-leekie	n.（苏格兰烹饪）韭菜鸡汤	piper	n. 风笛手
crude	a. 天然的；未加工的	reed	n. 哨片；簧乐器
haggis	n.（苏格兰）肉馅羊肚；羊肉杂碎布丁	seasoning	n. 调味品；调料
laird	n. 领主；地主	sherry	n. 雪利酒（西班牙产的一种烈性白葡萄酒）
light-hearted	a. 轻松的；快活的	slice	v. 切片
literary	a. 文学的	soup broth	phr. 肉汤
minced	a. 切碎的；切成末的	tattie	n. 马铃薯
neep	n. 萝卜	tipsy	a. 喝醉的；歪曲的；不稳的
oatcake	n. 燕麦饼	top table	phr. 上座；首席
oatmeal	n. 燕麦粥；燕麦片	tot	n. 小玻璃杯
offal	n. 内脏	trifle	n. 蛋糕；少量

Proper Names

Address To A Haggis	羊肚脍颂	Robert Burns	罗伯特·彭斯（苏格兰诗人）
Mediterranean	地中海沿岸居民	Scotch whisky	苏格兰威士忌
Middle East	中东		

□ Passage 2 Thanksgiving

In 1621, the **Plymouth** colonists and **Wampanoag** Indians shared an autumn harvest feast that is acknowledged today as one of the first Thanksgiving celebrations in the colonies. For more than two centuries, days of thanksgiving were celebrated by individual colonies and states. It wasn't until 1863, in the midst of **the Civil War**, that President **Abraham Lincoln proclaimed** a national Thanksgiving Day to be held each November.

➢ Thanksgiving at Plymouth

In September 1620, a small ship called the Mayflower left Plymouth, England, carrying 102 passengers—an **assortment** of religious **separatists** seeking a new home where they could freely practice their faith and other individuals **lured** by the promise of prosperity and land ownership in the New World. After a **treacherous** and uncomfortable **crossing** that lasted 66 days, they dropped **anchor** near the tip of **Cape Cod**, far north of their intended destination at the mouth of **the Hudson River**. One month later, the Mayflower crossed **Massachusetts** Bay, where the **Pilgrims**, as they are now commonly known, began the work of establishing a village at Plymouth.

Throughout that first **brutal** winter, most of the colonists remained on board the ship, where they suffered from exposure, **scurvy** and **outbreaks** of contagious disease. Only half of the Mayflower's original passengers and crew lived to see their first New England spring. In March, the remaining settlers moved ashore, where they received an astonishing visit from an **Abenaki** Indian who greeted them in English. Several days later, he returned with another Native American, Squanto, a member of the Pawtuxet tribe who had been kidnapped by an English sea captain and sold into slavery before escaping to London and returning to his homeland on an **exploratory expedition**. Squanto taught the Pilgrims, **weakened** by **malnutrition** and illness, how to cultivate corn, **extract sap** from **maple** trees, catch fish in the rivers and avoid poisonous plants. He also helped the settlers **forge** an **alliance** with the Wampanoag, a local tribe, which would endure for more than 50 years and tragically remains one of the sole examples of harmony between European colonists and Native Americans.

In November 1621, after the Pilgrims' first corn harvest proved successful, Governor **William Bradford** organized a **celebratory** feast and invited a group of the **fledgling** colony's Native American allies, including the Wampanoag chief Massasoit. Now remembered as American's "first Thanksgiving"—although the Pilgrims themselves may not have used the term at the time—the festival lasted for three days. While no record exists of the historic **banquet**'s exact menu, the Pilgrim chronicler Edward Winslow wrote in his journal that Governor Bradford sent four men on a "**fowling**" mission in preparation for the event, and that the Wampanoag guests arrived bearing five deer. Historians have suggested that many of the dishes were likely prepared using traditional Native American spices and cooking methods. Because the Pilgrims had no oven and the Mayflower's sugar supply had **dwindled** by the fall of 1621, the meal did not feature pies, cakes or other desserts, which have become a **hallmark** of contemporary celebrations.

➢ Thanksgiving Becomes an Official Holiday

Pilgrims held their second Thanksgiving celebration in 1623 to mark the end of a long drought that had threatened the year's harvest and prompted Governor Bradford to call for a religious fast. Days of fasting and thanksgiving on an annual or occasional basis became common practice in other New England settlements as well. During the **American Revolution**, the **Continental Congress designated** one or more days of thanksgiving a year, and in 1789

George Washington issued the first Thanksgiving proclamation by the national government of the United States; in it, he **called upon** Americans to express their gratitude for the happy conclusion to the country's war of independence and the successful **ratification** of the U.S. Constitution. His successors **John Adams** and **James Madison** also designated days of thanks during their presidencies.

In 1817, New York became the first of several states to officially adopt an annual Thanksgiving holiday; each celebrated it on a different day, however, the American South remained largely unfamiliar with the tradition. In 1827, the noted magazine editor and **prolific** writer Sarah Josepha Hale—author, among countless other things, of the nursery rhyme *Mary Had a Little Lamb*—launched a campaign to establish Thanksgiving as a national holiday. For 36 years, she published numerous editorials and sent scores of letters to governors, senators, presidents and other politicians. Abraham Lincoln finally **heeded** her request in 1863, **at the height of** the Civil War, in a proclamation **entreating** all Americans to ask God to "commend to his tender care all those who have become widows, orphans, **mourners** or sufferers in the **lamentable** civil **strife**" and to "heal the wounds of the nation". He scheduled Thanksgiving for the final Thursday in November, and it was celebrated on that day every year until 1939, when **Franklin D. Roosevelt** moved the holiday up a week **the Great Depression** retail sales during the Great Depression. Roosevelt's plan, known **derisively** as Franksgiving, was met with passionate opposition, and in 1941 the president reluctantly signed a bill making Thanksgiving the fourth Thursday in November.

➢ **Thanksgiving Traditions**

In many American households, the Thanksgiving celebration has lost much of its original religious significance; instead, it now centers on cooking and sharing a **bountiful** meal with family and friends. Turkey, a Thanksgiving **staple** so **ubiquitous** it has become all but **synonymous** with the holiday, may or may not have been on offer when the Pilgrims hosted the **inaugural** feast in 1621. Today, however, nearly 90 percent of Americans eat the bird—whether roasted, baked or **deep-fried**—on Thanksgiving, according to the **National Turkey Federation**. Other traditional foods include stuffing, mashed potatoes, cranberry sauce and pumpkin pie. Volunteering is a common Thanksgiving Day activity, and communities often hold food drives and host free dinners for the less fortunate.

Parades have also become an integral part of the holiday in cities and towns across the United States. Presented by **Macy's** department store since 1924, New York City's Thanksgiving Day parade is the largest and most famous, attracting some 2 to 3 million **spectators** along its 2.5-mile route and drawing an enormous television audience. It typically features marching bands, performers, elaborate floats conveying various celebrities and giant balloons shaped like cartoon characters.

Beginning in the mid-20th century and perhaps even earlier, the president of the United States has "pardoned" one or two Thanksgiving turkeys each year, **sparing** the birds from **slaughter** and sending them to a farm for retirement. A number of U.S. governors also perform the annual turkey pardoning ritual.

- **Thanksgiving Controversies**

For some scholars, the jury is still out on whether the feast at Plymouth really constituted the first Thanksgiving in the United States. Indeed, historians have recorded other ceremonies of thanks among European settlers in North America that **predate** the Pilgrims' celebration. In 1565, for instance, the Spanish explorer Pedro Menéndez de Avilé invited members of the local Timucua tribe to a dinner in St. Augustine, Florida, after holding a mass to thank God for his crew's safe arrival. On December 4, 1619, when 38 British settlers reached a site known as Berkeley Hundred on the banks of **Virginia's James River**, they read a proclamation designating the date as "a day of thanksgiving to Almighty God".

Some Native Americans and others take issue with how the Thanksgiving story is presented to the American public, and especially to schoolchildren. In their view, the traditional narrative paints a **deceptively** sunny portrait of relations between the Pilgrims and the Wampanoag people, masking the long and bloody history of conflict between Native Americans and European settlers that resulted in the deaths of millions. Since 1970, **protesters** have gathered on the day designated as Thanksgiving at the top of Cole's Hill, which overlooks **Plymouth Rock**, to commemorate a "National Day of Mourning". Similar events are held in other parts of the country.

- **Thanksgiving's Ancient Origins**

Although the American concept of Thanksgiving developed in the colonies of **New England**, its roots can be traced back to the other side of the Atlantic. Both the Separatists who came over on the Mayflower and the **Puritans** who arrived soon after brought with them a tradition of **providential** holidays—days of fasting during difficult or **pivotal** moments and days of feasting and celebration to thank God in times of plenty.

As an annual celebration of the harvest and its **bounty**, moreover, Thanksgiving falls under a category of festivals that **spans** cultures, continents and millennia. In ancient times, the Egyptians, Greeks and Romans feasted and **paid tribute to** their gods after the fall harvest. Thanksgiving also **bears a resemblance to** the ancient Jewish harvest festival of **Sukkot**. Finally, historians have noted that Native Americans had a rich tradition of commemorating the fall harvest with feasting and merrymaking long before Europeans **set foot on** their shores.

(length: 1,468 words)

Vocabulary

alliance	n. 联盟；联合	bountiful	a. 丰富的
anchor	n. 锚	bounty	n. 慷慨
assortment	n. 各色具备之物	brutal	a. 残忍的
at the height of	phr. 在鼎盛时期	call upon	phr. 号召；摆放
banquet	n. 宴会	celebratory	a. 快乐的
bear a resemblance to	phr. 与……相似	crossing	n. 横渡

deceptively	ad. 迷惑地；骗人地	pilgrim	n. 朝圣者
deep-fried	a. 油炸	pivotal	n. 关键事务
derisively	ad. 嘲弄地；嘲笑地		a. 关键的
designate	v. 指定；特指	predate	v. 早于
dwindle	v. 缩小	proclaim	v. 宣告；声明
entreat	v. 恳求；乞求	prolific	a. （艺术家、作家等）多产的
expedition	n. 探险队	protester	n. 抗议者
exploratory	a. 考察的	providential	a. 幸运的
extract	v. 榨出；抽取	ratification	n. 批准；认可
fledgling	n. 刚会飞的幼鸟	sap	n. 树液
forge	v. 伪造	scurvy	n. 坏血病
fowling	n. 捕鸟；打鸟	separatist	n. 分离主义者
hallmark	n. 特点	slaughter	n. 屠杀
heed	v. 注意；留心	span	n. 跨越；跨度
inaugural	a. 就职演讲；开幕词	spectator	n. 观众
lamentable	a. 可悲的；令人惋惜的	staple	n. 主食
lure	v. 引诱	strife	n. 斗争；冲突
malnutrition	n. 营养失调	synonymous	a. 匿名的
maple	n. 枫树	treacherous	a. 危险的；叛逆的
mourner	n. 哀悼者；悲伤者	ubiquitous	a. 普遍存在的
outbreak	n. 爆发；发作	weaken	v. 减弱
pay tribute to	phr. 称赞		

Proper Names

Abenaki	阿布纳基人（北美印第安人）	Plymouth	普利茅斯
Abraham Lincoln	亚伯拉罕·林肯（第十六任美国总统）	Plymouth Rock	普利茅斯石（据说 1620 年移民美国的英格兰清教徒在此处登岸）
American Revolution	美国独立战争		
Cape Cod	科德角（美国地名）	Puritan	清教徒
Continental Congress	大陆会议	Sukkot	住棚节（又称收藏节，是犹太民族和犹太教的节日）
Franklin D. Roosevelt	富兰克林·D·罗斯福（美国前总统）	the Civil War	美国内战
James Madison	詹姆斯·麦迪逊（美国前总统）	the Great Depression	美国经济大萧条
John Adams	约翰·亚当斯（美国前总统）	the Hudson River	哈德逊河（位于纽约州东部）
Macy's	梅西百货	Virginia's James River	圣詹姆士河
Massachusetts	马萨诸塞州	Wampanoag	万帕诺亚格人
National Turkey Federation	全国火鸡协会	William Bradford	威廉·布拉德福德
New England	新英格兰		

Section D Word Bank for This Unit

薄煎饼日	Pancake Day	独立日	Independence Day

复活节	Easter/Easter Sunday
父亲节	Father's Day
复活节次日	Easter Monday
盖伊·福克斯日	Guy Fawkes'Day
感恩节	Thanksgiving Day
哥伦布日	Columbus Day
国庆日	National Day
华盛顿诞辰日	Washington's Birthday
节礼日	Boxing Day
劳动节	Labor Day/ May Day/May 1st
林肯诞辰日	Lincoln's Birthday
美国国旗纪念日	Flag Day
母亲节	Mother's Day
女王诞辰日	Queen's Birthday
女王法定诞辰日	Queen's Official Birthday
情人节	St. Valentine's Day
莎士比亚纪念日	Shakespeare's Day
神圣星期四	Maundy Thursday
圣大卫日	St David's Day
圣诞节	Christmas Day
圣诞节前夜	Christmas Eve
圣灵降临日	Pentecost（也称为 White Sunday）
圣母玛丽亚日	Lady's Day（又称 Annunciation Day）
圣帕特里克日	St Patrick's Day
圣乔治日	St George's Day
圣星期六	Holy Saturday（Easter 的前一天）
圣烛节	Groundhog Day
停战日	Armistice Day/Veterans Day
万圣节	Hallowmas，All Saints' Day
万圣节前夕	Halloween
五朔节	Beltane
五月节	May Day
新年	New Year's Day
耶稣升天节	Ascension Day（也称 Holy Thursday）
耶稣受难日	Good Friday
银行假日	Bank holiday
英联邦纪念日	Commonwealth Day
愚人节	April Fool's Day
元旦新年	New Year's Day
阵亡将士纪念日	Memorial Day
植树节	Arbor Day
仲夏夜	Midsummer's Day
祖父母节	Grandparents' Day

Chapter 12

Sports

生命在于运动。运动有助于保持健康，锻炼意志，头脑清醒；运动令人更加自信，热爱生活，提升品质，精神飒爽。乐于运动可以造就灿烂多彩的人生。

运动的形式多种多样。你知道吗，2012 年伦敦奥运会就有 26 个大项，300 个小项的运动比赛。很多运动，如跑步、游泳、球类运动已经成为我们日常生活不可或缺的部分。

足球运动是目前全球体育界最具影响力的单项体育运动，有世界第一运动的美称。英国的英格兰地区是现代足球的发源地，所以足球运动在英国相当普及。

你是否了解足球的发展史？你是否领略过足球的魅力？足球术语你又知道哪些呢？让我们一起顺着足球运动的轨迹，体会射门的喜悦，感怀惜败时的扼腕叹息。

Section A　Intensive Reading

History of Football

➢ **The Origins**

The **contemporary** history of the world's favourite game **spans** more than 100 years. It all began in 1863 in England, when rugby football and association football branched off on their different courses and the Football Association in England was formed—becoming the sport's first governing body.

Both codes **stemmed** from a common root and both have a long and intricately branched **ancestral** tree. A search down the centuries reveals at least half a dozen different games, varying to different degrees, and to which the historical development of football has been traced back. Whether this can be justified in some instances is **disputable**. Nevertheless, the fact remains that people have enjoyed kicking a ball about for thousands of years and there is absolutely no reason to consider it as an **aberration** of the more "natural" form of playing a ball with the hands.

On the contrary, apart from the need to employ the legs and feet in tough tussles for the ball, often without any laws for protection, it was recognized right at the outset that the art of controlling the ball with the feet was not easy and, as such, required no small measure of skill. The very earliest form of the game for which there is scientific evidence was an exercise from a military manual dating back to the second and third centuries BC in China.

This Han Dynasty forebear of football was called Tsu' Chu and it consisted of kicking a leather ball filled with feathers and hair through an opening, measuring only 30-40cm in width, into a small net fixed onto long bamboo canes. According to one variation of this exercise, the player was not permitted to aim at his target unimpeded, but had to use his feet, chest, back and shoulders while trying to withstand the attacks of his opponents. Use of the hands was not permitted.

Another form of the game, also originating from the Far East, was the Japanese Kemari, which began some 500-600 years later and is still played today. This is a sport lacking the competitive element of Tsu' Chu with no struggle for possession involved. Standing in a circle, the players had to pass the ball to each other, in a relatively small space, trying not to let it touch the ground.

The Greek "Episkyros"—of which few concrete details survive—was much livelier, as was the Roman "Harpastum". The latter was played out with a smaller ball by two teams on a **rectangular** field marked by **boundary** lines and a centre line. The objective was to get the ball over the opposition's boundary lines and as players passed it between themselves, **trickery** was the order of the day. The game remained popular for 700-800 years, but, although the Romans took it to Britain with them, the use of feet was so small as to scarcely be of consequence.

➢ **Britain, the home of Football**

For all the evidence of early ball sports played elsewhere in the world, the evolution of football as we know it today took place in Britain. The game that **flourished** in the British Isles from the 8th to the 19th centuries featured a considerable variety of local and regional versions, which were **subsequently** smoothed down and **smartened** up to create the modern-day sports of association football, rugby football and, in Ireland, Gaelic football.

Primitive football was more disorganized, more violent, more **spontaneous** and usually played by an indefinite number of players. Frequently, games took the form of a heated contest between whole villages—through streets and squares, across fields, **hedges**, fences and streams. Kicking was allowed, as in fact was almost everything else. Sometimes kicking the ball was out of the question due to the size and weight of the **sphere** being used—in such cases, kicking was instead limited to taking out opponents.

Curiously, it was not until nine years after the rules of football had been first established in 1863 that the size and weight of the ball were finally **standardized**. Up to then, agreement on this point was usually reached by the parties concerned when they were arranging the match, as was the case for a game between London and Sheffield in 1866. This encounter was also the first where the **duration** was prearranged for 90 minutes.

Shrovetide football, as it was called, belonged in the "mob football" category, where the number of players was unlimited and the rules were fairly **vague**. For instance, according to an ancient handbook, any means could be employed to get the ball to its target with the exception of murder and **manslaughter**.

One theory is that the game is Anglo-Saxon in origin. In both Kingston-on-Thames and Chester, local legend has it the game was played there for the first time with the severed head of a vanquished Danish prince. In Derby, it is said to have originated in the third century during the victory celebrations that followed a battle against the Romans. Yet there is **scant** evidence of the sport having been played at this time, either in Saxon areas or on the continent. Indeed prior to the Norman Conquest, the only trace found of any such ball game comes from a Celtic source.

Another theory regarding its origin is that when "mob football" was being played in the British Isles in the early centuries AD, a similar game was thriving in France, particularly in the northern regions of Normandy and Brittany. So it is possible that the Normans brought this form of the game to England with them.

Scholars have also suggested that besides the natural impulse to demonstrate strength and skill, in many cases pagan customs, especially fertility rites, provided a source of motivation for these early "footballers". The ball **symbolized** the sun, which had to be conquered in order to secure a **bountiful** harvest. The ball had to be **propelled** around, or across, a field so that the crops would flourish and the attacks of the opponents had to be **warded** off.

A similar significance was attached to contests between married men and bachelors that **prevailed** for centuries in some parts of England, and, likewise, to the game between married and unmarried women in the Scottish town of Inveresk at the end of the 17th century which, perhaps by design, was regularly won by the married women. Women's football is obviously not as new as some people think.

For all the conflicting views on the origins of the game, one thing is **incontestable**: football has flourished for over a thousand years in diverse **rudimentary** forms, in the very region which we describe as its home, Britain.

➢ **Opposition to the Game**

If early football generated tremendous enthusiasm among common folk in Britain, it also withstood repeated—and unsuccessful—**interventions** from the authorities who frowned on this often violent recreation.

As long ago as 1314 the Lord Mayor of London saw fit to issue a **proclamation forbidding** football within the city due to the chaos it usually caused. **Infringement** of this law meant **imprisonment**.

During the 100 Years' War between England and France from 1337 to 1453 the royal court was unfavorably disposed towards football. Kings Edward Ⅲ, Richard Ⅱ, Henry Ⅳ and Henry Ⅴ all made the game punishable by law because it prevented their subjects from practicing more useful military disciplines, particularly **archery**.

All the Scottish kings of the 15th century deemed it necessary to **censure** and even prohibit football. Particularly famous was the decree proclaimed by the parliament convened by James Ⅰ in 1424, which read: "That na man play at the Fute-ball." None of these efforts had much effect. The popularity of the game among the people and their obvious delight in the rough and **tumble** for the ball went far too deep to be uprooted.

The passion for football was particularly **exuberant** in Elizabethan times. An influence that may have played a part in intensifying the native popularity for the game came from Renaissance Italy, notably from Florence although Venice and other cities also produced their own brand of the sport known as Calcio. This was more organized than the English equivalent and was played by teams dressed in colored livery at important gala events held on certain holidays in Florence.

In England the game was still as rough and lacking in **refinement** as ever, but it did at this time find a prominent supporter who commended if for other reasons. This supporter was Richard Mulcaster, the great **pedagogue** and head of the famous London schools of Merchant Taylors and St. Paul's. He pointed out that the game, if requiring a little refinement, had a positive educational value as it promoted health and strength. His belief was that it would benefit from introducing a limited number of participants per team and, more importantly, a stricter referee.

Resentment of football up to this time had been focused on its capacity for public **disturbance**. For example, in Manchester in 1608, the game was banned because so many windows had been smashed. In the course of the 16th century a new type of attack was launched. With the spread of Puritanism, the cry went up against "frivolous" amusements, and sport happened to be classified as such, football in particular.

The main objection was that it supposedly constituted a violation of peace on the Sabbath. Similar attacks were made against the theatre, which strait-laced Puritans regarded as a source of idleness and **iniquity**. This laid the foundations for the entertainment ban on Sundays—and from then on football on that day was taboo.

This remained the case for some 300 years, until the ban was lifted once again, at first unofficially and ultimately with the formal consent of The Football Association, albeit on a rather small scale.

All told there was scarcely any progress at all in the development of football for hundreds of years. However, although the game was persistently forbidden for 500 years, it was never completely **suppressed**.

➢ **The Global Growth**

A change did not come about until the beginning of the 19th century when school football became the custom, particularly in the famous public schools. This was the turning point. In this new environment, it was possible to make innovations and refinements to the game.

The rules were still relatively free and easy, with no standard form of the game. Each school in fact developed its own adaptation and, at times, these varied considerably. The traditional aspects of the game remained but innovations depended for the most part on the playing ground available. If use had to be made of a paved school playground, surrounded by a brick wall, then there was simply not enough space for the old hurly-burly "mob football".

Circumstances such as these prompted schools like Charterhouse, Westminster, Eton and Harrow to favor a game more dependent on the players' dribbling **virtuosity** than the robust energy required in a scrum. On the other hand, schools such as Cheltenham and Rugby were more inclined towards the more rugged game in which the ball could be touched with the hands or even carried.

As the 19th century progressed, a new attitude developed towards football. The education authorities observed how well the sport served to encourage such fine qualities as loyalty, selflessness, cooperation, subordination and **deference** to the team spirit. Games became an integral part of the school curriculum and participation in football compulsory. Dr Thomas Arnold, the head of Rugby School, made further advances in this direction, when in 1846 in Rugby the first truly standardized rules for an organized game were laid down.

These were in any event quite rough enough: for example, they permitted kicking an opponent's legs below the knees, with the reserve that he should not be held still while his shins were being worked on. Handling the ball was also allowed—and had been ever since the historic occasion in 1823 when William Webb Ellis, to the amazement of his own team and his opponents, made a run with the ball tucked under his arm. Many schools followed suit and adopted the rules laid down in Rugby; others, such as Eton, Harrow and Winchester, rejected this form of football, and gave preference to kicking the ball. Charterhouse and Westminster were also against handling the ball. However, they did not isolate their style as some schools did—instead they formed a nucleus from which this style of game began to spread.

Finally, in 1863, developments reached a climax. At Cambridge University, where in 1848 attempts had already been made by former pupils from the various schools to find a common **denominator** for all the different adaptations of the game, a fresh initiative began to establish some uniform standards and rules that would be accepted by everyone.

It was at this point that the majority spoke out against such rough customs as tripping, shin-kicking and so on. As it happened, the majority also expressed disapproval at carrying the ball. It was this that caused the Rugby group to withdraw. They would probably have agreed to refrain from shin-kicking, which was in fact later banned in the Rugby regulations, but they were reluctant to relinquish carrying the ball.

This Cambridge action was an endeavor to sort out the utter confusion surrounding the rules. The decisive meeting, however, came on 26 October 1863, when eleven London clubs and schools sent their representatives to the Freemason's Tavern. These representatives were intent on clarifying the muddle by establishing a set of fundamental rules, acceptable to all parties, to govern the matches played among them. This meeting marked the birth of The Football Association. The eternal dispute concerning shin-kicking, tripping and carrying the ball was discussed thoroughly at this and consecutive meetings until eventually on 8 December the die-hard exponents of the Rugby style—led by Blackheath—took their final leave. A stage had been reached where the ideals were no longer **compatible**. On 8 December 1863, football and rugby finally split. Their separation became totally **irreconcilable** six years hence when a provision was included in the football rules forbidding any handling of the ball (not only carrying it).

From there progress was lightning-quick. Only eight years after its foundation, The Football Association already had 50 member clubs. The first football competition in the world, the FA Cup, was established in 1872. By 1888 the first league championship was under way.

International matches were being staged in Great Britain before football had hardly been heard of in Europe. The first was played in 1872 and was contested by England and Scotland. This sudden boom of organized football accompanied by staggering crowds of spectators brought with it certain problems with which other countries did not face until much later on.

Professionalism was one of them. The first moves in this direction came in 1879, when Darwin, a small Lancashire club, twice managed to draw against the supposedly invincible Old Estonians in the FA Cup, before the famous team of London amateurs finally scraped through to win at the third attempt. Two Darwin players, the Scots John Love and Fergus Suter, are reported as being the first players ever to receive **remuneration** for their football talent. This practice grew rapidly and the FA found itself obliged to legalize professionalism as early as 1885. This development predated the formation of any national association outside of Great Britain (namely, in the Netherlands and Denmark) by exactly four years.

After the English FA, the next oldest are the Scottish FA (1873), the FA of Wales (1875) and the Irish FA (1880). Strictly speaking, at the time of the first international match, England had no other partner association against which to play. When Scotland played England in Glasgow on 30 November 1872, the Scottish FA did not even exist—it was not founded for another three months. The team England played that day was actually the oldest Scottish club team, Queen's Park, but as today the Scottish side wore blue shirts and England white (albeit with shorts and socks in the colors of their public schools). Both teams employed what might today be considered rather attacking formations—Scotland (2-2-6), England (1-1-8)—but back then the game still retained many of the mob-football characteristics of kicking and rushing and, in tactics at least, probably more closely resembled modern-day rugby than football.

The spread of football outside of Great Britain, mainly due to the British influence abroad, started slowly, but it soon gathered momentum and rapidly reached all parts of the world.

The next countries to form football associations after the Netherlands and Denmark in 1889 were New Zealand (1891), Argentina (1893), Chile (1895), Switzerland, Belgium (1895), Italy (1898), Germany and Uruguay (both in 1900), Hungary (1901) and Finland (1907).

When FIFA was founded in Paris in May 1904 it had seven founder members: France, Belgium, Denmark, the Netherlands, Spain (represented by Madrid FC), Sweden and Switzerland. The German Football Federation cabled its intention to join on the same day.

This international football community grew steadily, although it sometimes met with obstacles and setbacks. In 1912, 21 national associations were already affiliated to the Fédération Internationale de Football Association (FIFA). By 1925, the number had increased to 36, while in 1930—the year of the first World Cup—it was 41.

Between 1937 and 1938, the modern-day Laws of the Game were set out by future FIFA President Stanley Rous. He took the original Laws, written in 1886 and subject subsequently to piecemeal alterations, and drafted them in a rational order. (They would be revised a second time in 1997.)

By the late 1930s there were 51 FIFA members; in 1950, after the **interval** caused by the Second World War, that number had reached 73. Over the next half-century, football's popularity continued to attract new devotees and at the end of the 2007 FIFA Congress, FIFA had 208 members in every part of the world.

(length: 3,000 words)

Vocabulary

aberration	n. 偏差
ancestral	a. 祖先的
archery	n. 剑术
boundary	n. 分界线
bountiful	a. 丰富的，充裕的
censure	v. 指责，谴责
compatible	a. 兼容的
contemporary	a. 当代的，现代的
deference	n. 顺从
denominator	n. 分母；共同特性
disputable	a. 可争辩的，可商榷的
disturbance	n. 打扰；骚乱
duration	n. 持续；持续期间
exuberant	a. 生气勃勃的
flourish	v. 挥舞；茂盛
forbid	v. 禁止
hedge	n. 树篱；保护手段
imprisonment	n. 关押；监禁
incontestable	a. 不可争辩的
infringement	n. 侵权；违背
iniquity	n. 邪恶；极不公正
interval	n. 间隔；幕间休息
intervention	n. 介入；干涉
irreconcilable	a. 不可调和的，不相容的
manslaughter	n. 杀人；过失杀人
momentum	n. 势头；动力；契机
pedagogue	n. 卖弄学问的教师
prevail	v. 流行；占优势
primitive	a. 原始的；落后的
proclamation	n. 宣布；公布
propel	v. 推进；驱动
Puritanism	n. 清教徒主义
rectangular	a. 矩形的；成直角的
refinement	n. 精炼；改良品
remuneration	n. 酬报；偿还
rudimentary	a. 基本的；未成熟的
scant	a. 不充分的，不足的
smarten	v. 打扮；使漂亮，使整洁
sphere	n. 范围
standardize	v. 使标准化
stem	v.（~ from）来自于
span	v. 跨越时间和空间
spontaneous	a. 自发的
subsequently	ad. 随后；接着
suppress	v. 镇压；压制
symbolize	v. 象征；用符号表示
trickery	n. 欺骗，哄骗
tumble	v. 摔倒，跌倒
vague	a. 模糊的
virtuosity	n. 精湛技艺
ward	v. 保卫；监护

Exercises

I. Comprehension

1. Recall

1) What kinds of games are regarded as the earlier form of football?

2) According to the author, why did people play football 1000 years ago?

2. Compare

Compare and find out the similarities and differences between Tsu' Chu, Kemari and Harpastum.

3. Explain

Can you explain why the rulers once prohibited football playing?

4. Evaluate

What's your opinion of the Rugby regulations?

5. Create

Can you think of a new way to present the history of football?

II. Further Study

Football has become an indispensable part of many people's lives. It brings happiness and misfortune as well. Watch the movie about football (see the list below) and tell your classmates what changes football brings to the hero in the movie.

1) *Fever Pitch* 《极度狂热》

2) *Bend It like Beckham* 《我爱贝克汉姆》

3) *Gracie* 《足球女将》

4) *Green Street Hooligans* 《足球流氓》

5) *Game of Their Lives* 《挑战王者》

Section B Extensive Reading

Top Five Popular Sports in America

Sports play an important role in American society. They enjoy tremendous **popularity** but more important they are vehicles for **transmitting** such values as justice, fair play, and teamwork. Sports have contributed to racial and social **integration** and over history have been a "social glue" **bonding** the country together.

Early Americans like Benjamin Franklin and President Thomas Jefferson stressed the need for exercise and fitness promoting for example running and swimming. In the 20th century, American presidents Theodore Roosevelt, Dwight D. Eisenhower and John F. Kennedy continued to encourage physical activity.

President Dwight D. Eisenhower founded the President's Council on Youth Fitness in 1956 to encourage America's youth to make fitness a **priority**. The Council later became the President's Council on Physical Fitness and Sports, including people of all ages and abilities and promoting fitness through sports and games. Today, the Council continues to play an important role in promoting fitness and healthy living in America.

The United States offers limitless opportunities to engage in sports—either as a participant or as a spectator. Team sports were a part of life in colonial North America. Native American peoples played a variety of ball games including some that may be viewed as earlier forms of **lacrosse**. The typical American sports of baseball, basketball ad football, however, arose from games that were brought to America by the first settlers that arrived from Europe in the 17th century. These games were re-fashioned and elaborated in the course of the 19th century and are now the most popular sports in the United States. Various social **rituals** have grown up around athletic contests. The local high school football or basketball game represents the biggest event of the week for residents in many communities across the United States. Fans of major universities and professional football teams often gather in parking lots outside stadiums to eat a "**tailgate**" picnic lunch before kickoff, and for parties in front of television sets in each other's homes during the professional championship game, the Super Bowl. Thousands of baseball fans flee the snow and ice of the North for a week or two each winter by making a **pilgrimage** to training camps in the South and Southwest to watch up close their favorite players prepare for the spring opening of the professional baseball season.

Individual competitions accompanied the growth of team sports. Shooting and fishing contests were part of the colonial experience, as were running, boxing, and horse racing. Golf and tennis emerged in the 1800s. Recent decades have given birth to a wide variety of challenging activities and contests such as sail boarding, mountain biking, and sport climbing, collectively referred to as "extreme sports".

➢ **Baseball**

The sport that evokes more **nostalgia** among Americans than any other is baseball. So many people play the game as children that it has become known as "the national pastime".

The exact origins of baseball are unknown, but most historians agree that it is based on the English game of rounders. It became quite popular in the early 19th century; many sources report the growing popularity of a game called "townball", "base", or "baseball". In 1845, Alexander

Cartwright **formalized** a list of rules by which all teams could play. Rules, scoring and record-keeping gave baseball **gravity**. As one sport historian noted, "Baseball without records is **inconceivable**." For most Americans, for example, it is common knowledge that Roger Maris' 61 home runs (balls that cannot be played because they have been hit out of the field) in 1961 broke Babe Ruth's record of 60 in 1927.

The first professional baseball league was established in 1871. By the start of the 20th century, most large cities in the eastern United States had a professional baseball team but baseball truly came of age in the 1920s, as Babe Ruth (1895-1948) playing for the New York Yankees became a national hero.

Over the decades, every team has had its great players. Jackie Robinson (1919-1972) played for the Brooklyn Dodgers. A gifted and courageous athlete, he was the first African-American player in the major leagues in 1947. Prior to Robinson, black players had been restricted to the Negro League.

Starting in the 1950s, baseball expanded its **geographical** range. Western cities lured teams to move from eastern cities or formed so-called expansion teams with players made available by established teams. From the start, major league baseball has been divided into the National League and the American League.

The major league baseball season lasts from April to October and includes the regular season, the playoffs, and the World Series. The most **victorious** team in each league is said to have won the "pennant"; the two pennant winners met after the end of the regular season and a series of playoff within league subdivisions in the World Series. The winner of this series becomes the major league world champion.

Until the 1970s, because of strict contracts, the owners of baseball teams virtually owned the players. Since then, the rules have changed so that players are free, within certain limits, to sell their services to any team. The results have been bidding wars; stars are paid millions of dollars a year. Disputes between the players' union and the owners have at times **halted** baseball for months at a time. Baseball is both a sport and a business. Many **disgruntled** fans sometimes view the business side as the dominant one.

Major League Baseball (MLB) is the highest level of professional baseball competition in North America including teams from the United States and Canada.

Today, baseball is played in the United States on the **amateur** level in Little League, high schools and universities and various community leagues.

Over the course of the 20th century, baseball spread to many nations and areas, notably many Latin American countries, including Cuba, the Dominican Republic, Nicaragua, Venezuela and Puerto Rico, but also Japan and Australia. Cuba's first professional league was formed in 1878, just shortly after the first American league was established. Baseball became popular in Japan after American soldiers introduced it during the occupation following World War II.

Baseball was a demonstration sport at the 1912, 1936, 1956, 1964, 1984 and 1988 Olympic Games. It became a medal sport in 1992. Cuba has won three of the four gold medals since then, with the U.S. claiming gold in 2000. Softball, a variation of baseball, was added in 1996. In 2005, the International Olympic Committee voted to **eliminate** baseball from the Olympics after 2008. The 2008 Beijing Olympics will probably be the last Games with baseball and softball for the **foreseeable** future.

Comparable to the soccer World Cup, the first annual World Baseball Classic took place in **venues** in the United States, Japan and Puerto Rico in March 2006. The purpose of the four-round **tournament**, which featured 15 teams from overseas plus a United States squad, is twofold—first to build worldwide exposure for the game, and second, to encourage **grassroots** development of the sport and athletes in both traditional and nontraditional baseball nations.

➢ **American Football**

American football began in the mid-late 1800s when players represented their college or university. The American football birthdate in the United States is commonly regarded as November 6, 1869, when teams from Rutgers and Princeton universities met in New Brunswick, New Jersey, for the first **intercollegiate** football game. American football is the most popular sport in America because it's exclusively played in America. American football's most famous tradition is the Super Bowl that started in 1935. The development of this nation-wide event brought Americans closer to the sport and arguably gave new meaning to the game. Today, the Super Bowl has the highest viewer ratings than any other television program in the country. There are many famous players and stadiums that have kept American football the most popular sport in America. Quarterback for the Indianapolis Colts Johnny Unitas, better known as Johnny "U", is one of the greatest quarterbacks to ever play the game. Walter Payton, a running back who played for the Chicago Bears is one of the greatest running backs to play the game. Lambeau Field, home to the Green Bay Packers, is the longest continually occupied NFL stadium that held its first game in 1957.

➢ **Basketball**

Basketball is a game that nearly 300 million people play worldwide today. In America, it is one of the most popular sports, but is also a very popular sport in other countries as well. Interestingly enough, America and Russia are two countries that hold basketball to a high level of popularity. Players from Russia and surrounding countries are playing in the NBA. It is a culturally diverse sport and opening up new doors for foreign athletes to **excel** in an American-based sport. Michael Jordan is probably the most recognized player in basketball. His athletic talent on the court along with his consumer appeal in advertising has **broadened** his image to fans across the world.

➢ **Hockey**

Hockey is not an American-based sport, but people in America understand that hockey is one of the most popular sports in America. The continent's first hockey league was supposedly launched in Kingston, Ontario, in 1885, and it included four teams. A sport richly influenced by Canadian athletes, the game of hockey has transcended into America and become a popular sport for teenagers and young adults that enjoy playing street hockey, a similar version to traditional hockey on ice.

➤ Golf

Golf is one of America's most popular sport for one reason alone—Tiger Woods. He has taken over the world of golf and also advertising. His face is seen everywhere in the media and is arguably the most recognized athlete in the world today. His phenomenal talent has inspired many African American's to play the game today. His statement to America is that it doesn't matter what color you are when it comes to playing a sport. He's a **quintessential** role model for young teenagers and a sporting **icon** for golfers in America. Because golf originated in Scotland, it's been played all around the world. But because Tiger Woods and other well-respected golfers are still playing and winning tournaments, golf will continue to be extensively covered in America's mainstream media.

(length: 1,694 words)

Vocabulary

amateur	a. 业余的
bond	v. 使结合
broaden	v. 使变宽；扩展
disgruntled	a. 不高兴的
eliminate	v. 淘汰；除掉
excel	v. 优于；擅长
formalize	v. 使正式，形式化
foreseeable	a. 可以预见的
geographical	a. 地理学的；地理的
grassroot	n. 草根
gravity	n. 重力；重要性
halt	v. 使停止，使中断
icon	n. 偶像；图标
inconceivable	a. 不能想象的，不可思议的
integration	n. 结合；混合
intercollegiate	a. 学院间的
lacrosse	n. 长曲棍球
nostalgia	n. 怀旧
pilgrimage	n. 朝圣之旅
popularity	n. 普及；流行
priority	n. 优先，优先权
quintessential	a. 典型的
ritual	n. 仪式；例行公事；老规矩
tailgate	v. 使紧密衔接
tournament	n. 锦标赛，联赛
transmit	v. 传送；传递
venue	n. 体育比赛场所
victorious	a. 胜利的

Exercises

I. Comprehension

1. Recall

1) What are the five most popular sports in America according to the author?

2) Was Golf a native sport in US?

2. Compare

Do you know the similarities and differences between Football and American Football? What are they?

3. Infer

From the last paragraph of the passage, can you infer the author's opinion about the relationship between sports and media?

4. Analyze

According to the author, what is the relationship between the government's promotion of sports and the popularity of certain sports?

5. Evaluate

Do you agree with the author's idea"Sports have contributed to racial and social integration and over history have been a 'social glue' bonding the country together"? Explain why.

II. Further Study

Choose one from the following films on baseball to watch, learn the sportsmanship and the other values refected in the film.

1) *Major League*《大联盟》

2) *A League of Their Own*《红粉联盟》

3) *Remember the Titans* 《冲锋陷阵》

Section C Supplementary Reading

□ Passage 1 Hooliganism

The "English Disease"

The term "hooligan" dates to 19th-century England. Originally a hooligan was a person who engaged in any kind of **rowdy**, possibly criminal, behavior. In the mid-1960s the contemporary concept of a distinctive "football hooligan" was born: a person bent on rowdy, possibly criminal, football-related behavior, most importantly, fighting.

Football hooliganism is found throughout the world. But historically it has been most **prominent** in the country where it emerged: the United Kingdom. The English seem to have exported their hooliganism to countries such as Holland, Germany, Italy, Hungary, and France, where some copy the **chants** and styles of English Hooligans. Other incidents involving hooligans have even occurred in countries in South America, Asia, and Africa. Hooliganism's **heyday** was between the mid-1960s and the mid-1980s. Because of its British prominence, during those decades it came to be called the "English Disease".

Football hooligans are almost **exclusively** male. Most are in their 20s and come from working-class backgrounds. According to a sample of more than 500 persons arrested for various football-related "disorders" in the mid-1970s, the average hooligan was 19 years old. More than 80 percent of hooligans were **manual** laborers or unemployed. And 36 percent of them had histories of previous **convictions**. In the 1980s the hooligan population became slightly older and more socioeconomically diverse. But the typical hooligan remains a young, working-class man.

Hooligans are distinct from "ordinary" football fans who might occasionally drink too much and find themselves in **altercations** with the fans of opposing teams. The former persons see conflict with likeminded rival fans as one of their primary ends. They attach as much, if not more, importance to participating in such conflict than participating in the enjoyment of the football matches that provide occasion for it. The latter do not.

Hooligans **derive** utility from fighting. Our claim that hooligans derive utility from fighting shouldn't be taken to mean that they derive no utility from officially recognized aspects of football, however. Many hooligans care about the football matches that **frame** hooliganism. But fighting is an equally, if not more, important part of the overall experience for **hardcore** hooligans. In the words of one hooligan, "being involved in football violence is the most incredibly exciting and enjoyable thing. To anyone who has not been a part of it, that will probably be an **astonishing** statement but nevertheless, it is the truth". Far from hoping to avoid conflict, hooligans seek it out. As one English football hooligan colorfully described it, "I go to a match for one reason only: the **aggro** (i.e., fighting)… I get so much pleasure when I'm having aggro that I nearly wet my pants… I go all over the country looking for it… every night during the week we go around town looking for trouble." Or, in the words of another hooligan, "We don't—we don't go—well, we do go with the intention of fighting, you know what I mean…(W)e look forward to it… It's great". For hooligans, fights surrounding football rivalries are a central part of the sport, or even a sport itself .

Hooligans are different from most other people in that they enjoy fighting. However, they're similar to most other people in that they don't enjoy being seriously injured. Hooligans aren't **masochists**. Hooligans are willing to subject themselves to a reasonably small **probability** of serious injury, which naturally attends any altercation. That probability is necessary to make hooligan fighting "real" and thus a source of excitement. But most hooligans are unwilling to subject themselves to a high probability of serious injury, which is simply masochism.

In football hooliganism's earliest days, hooligans organized in small, informal groups around **kinship**, friendship, and neighborhood ties. Subsequent football hooligans organized in more formal, rival groups called "firms" associated with rival football teams. Some prominent English hooligan firms include "The Red Army" (Manchester United), the "Head-hunters" (Chelsea), "The Gooners" (Aresnal), the "United Service Crew" (Leed), the "Bushwhackers" (Millwall), the "Blades Business Crew" (Sheffield United), and the "Inter City Firm" (West Ham United).

Hooligan firm sizes vary considerably. But they can be surprisingly large. At its height in the 1980s the "Inter City Firm" boasted 150 core members, with numbers **swelling** to 500 in larger **confrontations**.

Football matches and the activities that surround them, such as **patronizing** pubs and traveling to and from matches, provide a convenient focal point for persons interested in fighting one another. Team rivalries supply ready and willing opponents: hooligan fans of opposing teams. And large excited crowds make it less risky for hooligans to clash in public since they're less likely to be arrested for creating a disturbance. Indeed, to avoid legal trouble, rival hooligan firms sometimes prearrange meeting times and places to fight outside of football-related events.

Occasionally hooligan conflicts are extremely violent. Naturally these fights are the ones that receive attention from the media, which has done much to **exaggerate** the extent of hooligan violence. But many hooligan fights are **ritualistic** and non-violent . They involve verbal conflicts, such as **taunting**, name calling, and chasing. Even physically violent hooligan conflicts, which may involve **punching**, kicking, and weapons, rarely result in serious injuries.

This is puzzling. Hooligans are clearly capable of seriously injuring one another. Most are young men—**aggressive** persons in their physical **prime**. Equally important, hooliganism would seem to suffer from a severe selection problem. Hooliganism is an activity known for violent conflict. It threatens to attract **sadistic** persons—persons who enjoy seriously injuring others in violent conflicts. Thus we would expect hooliganism to suffer from uncontrolled conflict and generate **rampant** serious injuries. But it doesn't.

➢ Why is Hooliganism Linked to Football?

In many ways, football is seen as an appropriate venue for these sorts of aggressive rivalries, partly because of the working class roots and traditions of the game but also because of the culturally prescribed "territorial" and masculine values which are **intrinsic** to it. In England a football match is a kind of symbolic struggle between the representatives of **predominantly** working class male communities. **Terrace** fights go beyond this symbolic representation to a "real" struggle between young men who have strong masculine attachments to their own areas, teams and friends, and a considerable emotional investment in performing in a "manly" way when confrontations occur.

Often, the most celebrated football players for fans of this kind are those who have their own reputations for "hardness" and aggression on the field. A top English player was fined £ 20,000 by the FA a few years ago for his role in the production of a video about the game's "hard men". However, over the longer period, violence on the field is almost certainly decreasing, though more subtle forms of cheating ("diving"; deceiving the referee; pretending to be injured, etc.) may be on the increase in the modern period.

Incidents of violence, or poor refereeing on the field, can **trigger** hooligan disturbances but, once again, it is difficult to argue that such incidents are a deep cause of hooliganism. After all, some hooligan incidents occur hours before a match has even kicked off! Also, there are many more violent sports than football which have not had the same problems of hooliganism. Finally, the culture of the playing side of the game in England is certainly beginning to change following the arrival of so many foreign stars in the Premier League. Some of the **brute** force of the English game is, arguably, giving way to more deep thinking about the game and to more skillful and **strategic** play. Perhaps the heroes of the 1990s will be the McManamans, Juninhos and Zolas?

Unfortunately, some players and officials within the game hardly seem to help this situation with their "revelations" in newspapers about dressing-room "punch ups", their boasts about being "hard men" and their preparations for a "battle" against a rival team's "hit man". Recently, though he was severely provoked and perhaps racially abused, one famous player, Eric Cantona, even jumped into the crowd to attack a fan during a match. The Professional Footballers Association is concerned about the problem of player behaviour and press revelations and urges players not to damage the game's image in this way. It seems that **tabloid** newspapers are as interested in these sides of the game as they are in what happens on the pitch.

➢ **Is There Hooliganism at Other Sports?**

Yes, there is. It probably lacks some of the organizational aspects of hooliganism at football, but hooliganism at sports like boxing, rugby league and cricket provoke **periodic** panics about the behaviour of spectators. Recently, too, there have been fears expressed about standards of behaviour at major horse-race meetings, and disturbances involving spectators at bike-race meetings are also reported but they seldom seems to get the sort of newspaper **coverage** which hooliganism at football seem to attract. Nor are these problems as institutionalized and routinized as they seem to be at football.

It is important to point out, too, however that disorderly behaviour and **hostility** towards foreigners is not just found among football fans or among "working class" people; far from it. Problems caused by traveling rugby union clubs, for example, are fairly commonplace. Also an article in the *Daily Telegraph* described the English people on the Oxbridge Ski tour at a **resort** in France, as a **mob** of "ignorant, arrogant middle class yobs", who abused foreigners and soiled their bedrooms and **chalets**.

(length: 1,674 words)

Vocabulary

aggressive	a. 侵略的，爱打架的
aggro	n. 暴力行为
altercation	n. 争辩，争吵
astonishing	a. 使人吃惊的，惊人的
brute	a. 残忍的；动物的；无理性的
chalet	n.（屋顶陡斜的）木造农舍，小木屋
chant	n. 咏唱，咏唱的话语
confrontation	n. 对抗；面对；遭遇；对峙
conviction	n. 确信；判罪；定罪；证明有罪
coverage	n. 范围，规模；保险项目；〈美〉（新闻）报道
derive	v. 得到，导出；源于，来自
exaggerate	v.（使）扩大；（使）增加
exclusively	ad. 唯一地；专门地，特定地；专有地；排外地
frame	v. 设计；表达；使适合（某一特殊用途）
hardcore	n. 核心部分，中坚分子
heyday	n. 盛世，全盛期；壮年
hostility	n. 敌意，敌对状态
intrinsic	a. 固有的，内在的，本质的
kinship	n. 亲属关系
manual	a. 手的；手制的，手工的；体力的
masochist	n. 性受虐狂者，受虐狂者
mob	n. 暴徒；犯罪团伙，黑手党；民众，乌合之众；〈美俚〉匪帮，一群罪犯
patronize	v. 经常光顾；资助
periodic	a. 周期的；定期的；回归的；间歇的，时而发生的
predominantly	ad. 占主导地位地；显著地；占优势地
prime	n. 精华；初期；全盛时期；青年
probability	n. 可能性；概率；或然性
prominent	a. 突出的，杰出的；突起的；著名的
punch	v. 用拳猛击；打孔；冲压；冲切
rampant	a. 蔓延的；猖獗的；（植物）疯长的
resort	n. 娱乐场，度假胜地
ritualistic	a. 仪式的，固守仪式的；惯例的
rowdy	a. 吵闹的；粗暴的
sadistic	a. 虐待狂的
strategic	a. 战略（上）的；战略性的；至关重要的
swell	v. 增强；肿胀；（使）凸出
tabloid	n. 小报，通俗小报
taunt	v. 嘲讽；嘲弄；辱骂；奚落
terrace	n. 台阶，阳台；柱廊，门廊；斜坡上房屋间的街巷
trigger	v. 引发，触发；扣……的扳机

□ Passage 2 Nine Disgraced Sports Heroes

We love turning sports stars into heroes. Is it fair or rational to do so? Maybe, maybe not.

On the one hand, pro athletes are just people like you or me, the only difference being that they were born with **innate** abilities the rest of us don't have. Why do we expect them to serve as role models when you don't expect the average guy walking down the street to serve as a role model? On the other hand, we do have some expectations for the average guy walking down the street. For example, we expect that he won't be **spewing obscenities**, and that he will be wearing pants. And shouldn't people getting paid millions of dollars to play sports be considered kind of a **privileged**? And isn't it the fans who indirectly pay their salaries? And so don't we have the right to expect these guys to live up to certain standards?

Well, however you feel about the issue, the fact is we do turn sports figures into heroes and, inevitably, some of them let us down. In fact, just today we learned that the biggest sports hero of his generation—Lance Armstrong—will be officially **stripped** of greatest accomplishments. So you know what that means: it's the perfect time to take a look at the most disgraced sports heroes of all time.

Where does Lance fit in? You'll have to keep reading to find out. So lets' get started.

➢ **9. Hulk Hogan**

Some might wonder whether you can call Hulk Hogan a sports hero given that everything about his was fake—including his **persona** and, most importantly, his victories.

However, I say that it's precisely because everything about Hogan was fake that he was such a hero. The guy won his first WWF title by defeating the America-hating, terrorist-loving Iron Sheik. And pretty much every single match featured the **wholesome** Hulkster falling behind and coming to the **brink** of defeat before picking himself up, rallying, and winning. Isn't that basically the premise of every feel-good sports movie ever made? I mean, little kids (and naive adults) just ate that stuff up. So, yeah, he was a hero. And that's what made the recent sex tape scandal so incredibly **bizarre**—it soiled the fond childhood memories of millions of people.

➢ **8. Brett Favre**

Brett Favre was the **iconic**, **rugged**, All-American ironman quarterback playing for an iconic All-American, fan-owned **franchise**. I mean, the guy was a spokesman for Wrangler jeans, which I think they only sell at Walmart. So you know he was wholesome. He was so beloved, in fact, that when he admitted that he had addition to Vicodin back in 1996, no one condemned him. The guy was a quarterback who played every game! Of course he got addicted to painkillers! How could he not? Besides, he totally cried at the press conference, and that takes a real man.

But then, you know, Favre texted a picture of his **dong** to a sideline reporter while he was playing for the Jets. And that kind of sullied his reputation as a hard-working family man.

Funny how dong texts can do that.

➢ **7. Sammy Sosa & Mark McGwire**

Sammy Sosa and Mark McGwire revived America's interest in baseball back in 1998. Since the 1994 lockout that cancelled the World Series, the country had been kind of luke-warm toward the sport. But when these two guys engaged in an **epic** race to see who could be the first person to break Roger Maris's single-season home-run record—the most cherished record in American sports—and suddenly baseball was on the front page of every newspaper again. It was almost too good to be true.

And of course, it was. Turns out, they were both **juiced** out of their minds. It just took Barry Bonds to make us realize it. Then we all felt pretty dumb for being so naive and buying into the **hype** of the great home run race of 1998.

➢ **6. Pete Rose**

Pete Rose, also known as Charlie Hustle, was baseball's ultimate blue-collar hero. No one played harder than Rose, and no one wanted to win more than Rose. His determination was an **inspiration** to millions, and it led him to become baseball's all-time hits king on September 11, 1985, when he surpassed Ty Cobb by cracking his 4,192nd hit.

Yay! True American hero!

Then it was revealed that, while he was playing for and coaching the Reds, Rose bet on baseball games. Every day. And while he maintains that he never bet against his team, that doesn't really matter—you can't place a bet on a game in which you are taking part. It's just too dirty.

Hero status: **revoked**.

➢ **5. O.J. Simpson**

Orenthal James Simpson was one of the greatest running backs in the history of football, and that, combined with his good looks and charm, made him one of the most popular athletes in America. He then used his fame to become a successful actor, appearing in such films as *Roots*, *The Towering Inferno*, and, of course, the *Naked Gun* **trilogy**.

Then, according to a jury of his peers, he totally didn't stab his ex-wife to death outside her **condo** in Brentwood.

However, nobody else believed that. And O.J. went on to prove himself a **douche** in other ways—like when he wrote that book called *If I Did It* and made money off the murders.

➢ 4. Tiger Woods

Tiger Woods was as **squeaky** clean a sports champion as they come. He was clean-cut, polite, intelligent, **articulate, dedicated**, and he had a **gorgeous** Scandinavian bikini model for a wife. Then his wife found out he liked to get busy with **strippers** and porn stars and beat him over the head with a golf club. Then the press found out, and one classy lady after another came forward with evidence of a **fling** with Tiger. And that was pretty much the end of Tiger's good image.

But hey, at least he didn't cheat on the course.

➢ 3. Shoeless Joe Jackson

This is probably the only disgraced athlete on this list who really didn't do what he was accused of.

You all know about the infamous Black Sox Scandal, right? Basically, a group of Chicago White Sox players were bribed by some underworld types to throw the 1919 World Series. At the time, "Shoeless" Joe Jackson was thought to be one of these players, and he apparently was made to look bad in court proceedings. However, it turns out that the guy was probably illiterate, and thus was most likely misled into signing admissions and other untrue statements by the team's lawyer—who was out to make sure the ownership didn't look bad. On top of that, the other 7 players involved in the scandal always said that Jackson was never present at any of the meetings in which they planned how they'd tank the series. And, of course, there's the fact that Jackson had a Series-leading .375 BA and hit the Series' only home run.

Nevertheless, Jackson was banned for life from Major League Baseball. And a **fictional** new report from the time (yes, those were common) quoted a made-up kid as saying, "Say it ain't so, Joe", outside the courthouse.

➢ 2. Lance Armstrong

Lance was the greatest sports hero of his generation, a guy who beat **testicular** cancer and then won the Tour de France, one of the greatest sports events in the world, a record 7 times. Then he used his fame for good—inspiring others and raising money for cancer research at the same time with his Livestrong movement. And the thing that made his story so powerful was that he supposedly accomplished everything with nothing but hard work and determination. (Just take a look at his 2001 Nike commercial.)

But of course, it turns out that it was all a bunch of lies. Sure, we ignored the claims of PED use for years when they were coming from the French sporting press. But then the United States Anti-Doping Agency investigated Lance, and what they found, through the **testimony** of 11 of his teammates, was that he helped orchestrate "the most sophisticated, professionalized and successful doping program that sport has ever seen".

And now the International Cycling Union, the sport's governing body, has announced that they are stripping Armstrong of his Tour de France titles.

Yep, it's pretty depressing.

➢ 1. Joe Paterno

Speaking of depressing, how about the case of Joe Paterno? He was only the winningest and most respected D-I college football coach ever, having led Penn State to two National Championships and 37 bowl appearances.

But of course, you know what's happened. Last November, former assistant coach Jerry Sandusky was arrested for child abuse, and an investigation revealed that Paterno had, at minimum, not taken sufficient actions to alert authorities or, at maximum, actively tried to cover up the abuse. Either way, it's pretty **despicable**, and as a result the 85-year-old CFB legend was fired.

If you ask me, that's the biggest fall from grace in the history of sports.

(length: 1,590 words)

Vocabulary

articulate	a. 发音清晰的；善于表达的
bizarre	a. 离奇的；奇特的（指态度，容貌，款式等）
brink	n.（悬崖峭壁的）边沿；（危险的）边沿；边缘
condo	n. 各户有独立产权的公寓（大楼）
dedicated	a. 专注的，投入的；献身的
despicable	a. 可鄙的，卑鄙的
dong	n. 盾（越南的货币单位）；（俚语）阴茎，此处指不雅照
douche	n. 灌注法，灌水法，灌水器
epic	a. 史诗般的；宏大的，壮丽的
fictional	a. 虚构的；小说的
fling	n. 一时的行乐
franchise	n. 选举权；参政权；特许权；经销权
gorgeous	a. 华丽的，艳丽的；极好的；光彩夺目的
hype	n. 天花乱坠的广告宣传
iconic	a. 符号的；图标的；图符的；偶像的
innate	a. 天生的；特有的，固有的；内在的，直觉的
inspiration	n. 灵感；鼓舞人心的人或事；启发灵感的人（或事物）
juice	v. 挤出汁来，使有活力
obscenity	n. 淫秽；猥亵；下流
privilege	v. 给予……特权，特免
persona	n. 人物角色；伪装的外表

revoke	v. 撤销，取消；废除	testicular	a. 双丸状的（如两个并列的块茎）
rugged	a. 崎岖的；凹凸不平的	testimony	n.（法庭上证人的）证词；证明，证据；表示，表明
spew	v. 呕吐；（使某事物）喷出；涌出	trilogy	n.（小说、戏剧、音乐等的）三部曲
squeaky	a. 吱吱响的，发轧声的	wholesome	a. 有益健康的；健全的；合乎卫生的
strip	v. 剥光；表演脱衣舞；剥除		
stripper	n. 脱衣舞表演者，脱衣舞女		

Section D Word Bank for This Unit

Football Terms

足球场	field, pitch	拉拉队	cheer team
足球运动员	football player	观众的喊声	yell
教练	coach	记者	journalist
主教练	head coach	拾球童	ball picker
裁判	referee	球迷	crowd, fans
巡边员	lineman	开幕式	opening ceremony
队长	captain, leader	分组	grouping
替补	substitute, reserve	八分之一决赛	eighth-final
守门员	goalkeeper, goaltender	四分之一决赛	quarterfinal
后卫	back	半决赛	semi-final
左后卫	left back	决赛	final match
右后卫	right back	预赛	preliminary match
中卫	centre forward, centre	药品检验	doping test
前卫	half back	抽签	draw, sortition
左前卫	left half back	平局	draw
右前卫	right half back	一边倒的比赛	one-side game
前锋	forward	联赛	league
中锋	half back	第一轮	first round
左内锋	inside left forward, inside left	循环赛	round-robin
右内锋	inside right forward, inside right	淘汰赛	elimination match, kick-out
左边锋	outside left forward, outside left	加时赛	extra time
右边锋	outside right forward, outside right	伤停补时	injury time
边线	touchline, sideline	比赛日程	schedule
球门线	goal line	中场休息	half time
（点球）罚球点	penalty area	红牌（表示判罚出场）	red card
禁区（罚球区）	goal area	黄牌（表示警告）	yellow card
球门框	crossbar, bar	对不公平裁判的抗议	protest
球鞋	boot	球票卖完	sellout
球衣	jersey	球场骚乱	riot
比赛条例	competition regulations	记分牌	indicator, score board
取消比赛资格	disqualification	禁赛命令	match ban
运动员的道德，风格	sportsmanship	排名	ranking

全攻全守足球战术	total football
拉开的足球战术	open football
积极的抢射战术	shoot-on-sight tactics
拖延战术	time wasting tactics
巴西阵式，4-2-4 阵式	Brazilian formation
四后卫制	four backs system
4-3-3 阵式	four-three-three formation
4-2-4 阵式	four-two-four formation
中场	midfield
开球	kick-off
倒钩球	bicycle kick, overhead kick
平胸球	chest-high ball
角球	corner ball, corner
球门球	goal kick
地面球	ground ball, grounder
手触球	hand ball
头球	header
点球	penalty kick
罚点球	spot kick
罚任意球	free kick
掷界外球	throw-in
控制球	ball handling
正面抢截	block tackle
身体阻挡	body check
合理冲撞	fair charge
传球	to pass the ball
接球	to take a pass
球传到位	spot pass
脚底停球	to trap
截球	to intercept
带球过人	to break through, to beat
胸部挡球	chesting
盯人防守	close-marking defense
短传	close pass, short pass
连续传球	consecutive passes
假动作	deceptive movement
鱼跃顶球	diving header
跳起顶球	flying header
定位球	place kick
盘球，控球，运球	dribbling
边线传球	flank pass
交叉传球	scissor pass
凌空传球	volley pass
三角传球	triangular pass
滚地传球	rolling pass, ground pass
射门	to shoot
贴地射门	grazing shot
近射	close-range shot
远射	long drive
未射中	mishit
踢出界	kick-out
乌龙球	own goal
帽子戏法	hat-trick
进球荒	goal drought
越位	offside
摆脱	to break loose
控球中场	to control the midfield
破坏防守	to disorganize the defence
筑人墙	to set a wall
掌握进攻节奏	to set the pace
击退一次攻势	to ward off an assault
破坏一次攻势	to break up an attack
控球技术	ball playing skill
突破	to break through
扑救	to save
用身体保护球	shielding
技术犯规	technical foul
犯规	to foul
罚下场	sending-off

Main Items in Olympic Games

射箭	Archery
田径	Athletics
篮球	Basketball
羽毛球	Badminton
拳击	Boxing
皮划艇激流/静流	Canoe Slalom/Sprint
公路/小轮车/山地/场地自行车	Cycling Road/BMX/ Mountain/Track
跳水	Diving
马场马术/三项赛/场地障碍赛	Equestrian Dressage/ Eventing/Jumping
击剑	Fencing
足球	Football
韵律体操/艺术体操/蹦床	Gymnastics Rhythmic/

	Artistic/Trampoline	花样游泳	Synchronised Swimming
手球	Handball	乒乓球	Table Tennis
曲棍球	Hockey	跆拳道	Taekwondo
柔道	Judo	网球	Tennis
五项全能（现代五项）	Modern Pentathlon	铁人三项	Triathlon
划船（赛艇）	Rowing	排球	Volleyball
帆船	Sailing	水球	Water Polo
射击	Shooting	举重	Weightlifting
游泳	Swimming	摔跤	Wrestling

Chapter 13

Celebrities

英美历史涌现了一批又一批颇有建树的名人们。从影响世界观念的弗朗西斯・培根、托马斯・亨利・赫胥黎、伯兰特・罗素等思想名人，到改变世界格局的乔治・华盛顿、温斯顿・丘吉尔、玛格丽特・撒切尔、富兰克林・罗斯福等政坛名人，到杰克・韦尔奇、比尔・盖茨、史蒂夫・乔布斯等商业名人，再到值得世人敬仰的艾萨克・牛顿、托马斯・爱迪生、阿尔伯特・爱因斯坦、斯蒂芬・霍金等科学名人，以及曾活跃在社会其他各领域的卡尔・刘易斯、迈克尔・乔丹、大卫・贝克汉姆等体坛名人，以及威廉・莎士比亚、查尔斯・狄更斯、沃尔特・惠特曼、欧内斯特・海明威等文学名人，他们才华横溢，终身勤勉，为后人留下了浓墨重彩、永不泯灭的文明华章。

我们在享受着这些精神财富的同时，也渴望与他们更近距离的了解。时光的长河虽然无法跨越，但我们可以追忆历史，探寻他们生命的足迹……

Section A　Intensive Reading

A Man of Greatness: Winston Churchill

by Professor Kraus

One of the glorious **triumvirate** of World War II and founder of the strong Anglo-American friendship that is still apparent today, Winston Churchill has long been one of the world's **preeminent** leadership role models. Churchill was a strong leader who took a leading part in laying the foundations of the welfare state in Britain, prepared British troops for World War I, and eventually emerged as one of the world's greatest leaders in World War II. Becoming Prime Minister on the very day that Hitler invaded France in 1940, he **braced** the British people to continue fighting and eventually led British people to victory.

Churchill possessed many great qualities of a leader, but these qualities shined the brightest during war time. According to Joseph Nye, "Followers are more likely to **attribute** charisma to leaders when they feel a strong need for change, often in the context of a personal, organization, or social crisis." Therefore, many people argued that Churchill would have been a minor figure in the history books if Hitler had not invaded France in May 1940. By leading his country through the Second World War, Churchill used his vision, confidence, communication, and contextual intelligence to **empower** and elevate his people in order to fight against Hitler. Possessing both strong soft and hard power skills, and his contextual intelligence, Churchill became the man who fitted the moment. The main pillars of his leadership: vision and communication skill, organizational and **Machiavellian** Political skills, coupled with his contextual intelligence, all played an essential role in shaping his leadership in World War II.

Winston Churchill was indeed a man of greatness. According to Best, Churchill was a courageous and imaginative man who also had a powerful and **fertile** intellect. In addition to all of Churchill's great leadership qualities, Best also attempts to make his faults and weakness into his unique qualities that made him the unique great leader. Although his **egotism** irritated those around him, yet his vast egotism was "inseparable from **originality**, the energy, the willpower and the courage both physical and moral that made him unique". A great leader often attributes his success to dramatic **episodes** in the histories of nations and people. Those episodes almost always consist of armed struggle, **sacrifice** and heroism. However, according to Best, Churchill's unique inner element of his individual thoughts and actions **defies** explanation in terms of social context. His love for his country and his way of thinking were glorious, but due to the changing political landscape in Britain and the world, a man like Churchill would unlikely appear in the human history again.

Churchill's ability to **proclaim** effective vision and his strategic **foresight** not only helped him lead his country during the time of war, but also during the time of peace. After the Munich Agreement in 1938, Churchill was the most prominent of the few leaders of British who refused to believe this policy of **appeasement**. While others chose to appease Hitler, Churchill was worried about the seriousness of German **rearmament** and the profound aggressiveness of Germany's **dictator**. He had feared German military **resurgence** from the earliest moment since the formulation of the **Treaty of Versailles** in 1919. It turned out that Churchill has been right all along. In addition, Churchill's broad strategic vision of Anglo-American co-operation was critical which not only enabled Britain to survive, but also ultimately led to **triumph**. The continuing correspondence through letters and telegrams with President Roosevelt helped develop a lasting friendship between them long before American joined the war. Thus when Churchill became Prime Minister there was no need for **preliminary skirmishing** before starting the negotiations which led to Lend-Lease, military staff talks and Churchill's first meeting with Roosevelt after Germany had invaded Russia. So by the time of the attack on Pearl Harbor a close personal relationship had been well established between the two leaders.

This important and influential **alliance** and friendship between the two enabled a smooth working relationship within which differences could be discussed without **rancor**. His strategic vision served him well even after the war. While very few British people and Americans wanted to believe that their Russian wartime ally was going to become a peacetime **menace**, Churchill perceived early that this was very likely to happen.

Vision, ability to communicate and inspire, organizational and political skills were main pillars of Churchill's leadership, but his contextual knowledge combined both his soft and hard power into a smart power strategy and made him the Savior of his nation. According to Nye, "an effective leader must have contextual intelligence in order to develop smart strategies." The extensive experiences that Churchill had **accumulated** were central to his leadership style. Winston Churchill entered the Royal Military College of Sandhurst, and graduated with honors in December of 1894. He saw military action in Cuba, India, Egypt, Sudan, the front lines of World War I, and commanded the 6th Battalion of the Royal Scots Fusiliers. Churchill was elected to Parliament at the age of twenty five and began his career as a statesman in the **House of Commons**. He went on to serve as First Lord of the Admiralty, Minister of Munitions, Chancellor of the **Exchequer**, ultimately Prime Minister. Churchill constantly sought for the most updated information. In order to gain the first impression and better understanding of the situation, Churchill made many **hazardous** journeys to America, Moscow, battle fronts of North Africa, Italy, Normandy and into Germany as well as various Middle Eastern destinations. He was also able to influence and **inspire** people by being next to them. In addition, he wanted any matter, no matter how complicated or how small, summed up on a single sheet of quarto paper, in order to allow him to possess all the information needed for well-informed decision-making. Based on the most accurate information, Churchill was able to provide the most effective and efficient leadership.

The British public did not see Churchill as a **charismatic** leader in 1939, but a year later, his vision, confidence, and communications skills made him charismatic in the eyes of the British people given the anxieties they felt after the fall of France and the Dunkirk evacuation. Although someone else would have been on the seat of Prime Minister if Churchill had not providentially been there at the right time, it is unlikely that any one of other "possible" could have filled the position so successfully. Many leaders possess both soft and hard power like Churchill did, but it was the right combination of both, coupled with the right contextual intelligence that made Churchill the right leader for the job. He possessed everything what Joseph Nye would called effective leadership style, and his ability to understand context so that his hard and soft power can be successfully combined into a smart power strategy that effectively led his people through the war and successfully established the postwar landscape. He was a transformational leader who was able to induce his followers to **transcend** their self interest for the sake of the higher purposes of the nation and the world.

(length: 1,201 words)

Vocabulary

accumulate	v. 积聚，堆积	charismatic	a. 超凡魅力的
alliance	n. 联盟，联合	defy	v. 公然反抗，藐视，挑衅
appeasement	n. 缓和，平息，绥靖政策	dictator	n. 独裁者
attribute	v. (~ to) 归结于	egotism	n. 自我中心，自尊自大

empower	v. 授权于，使能够	preeminent	a. 卓越的
episode	n. 插曲，有趣的事件	preliminary	a. 预备的，初步的
Exchequer	n. 财政部	proclaim	v. 显示，显露；宣布，声明
fertile	a. 肥沃的，丰富的	rancor	n. 深仇，怨恨
foresight	n. 远见，深谋远虑	rearmament	n. 重整军备，改良装备
hazardous	a. 危险的，冒险的	resurgence	n. 复活，复苏
House of Commons	n. （英国议会）下议院	sacrifice	n./v. 牺牲，献身
induce	v. 劝诱，促使	skirmish	n. 小冲突
inspire	v. 鼓舞，激发；使产生灵感	transcend	v. 超越，胜过
Machiavellian	a. 马基雅弗利的，权谋术的	Treaty of Versailles	n. 凡尔赛条约
menace	n. 威胁，危险物	triumph	n. 胜利，成功
originality	n. 创意，新奇，开创性	triumvirate	n. 三人执政，三头政治

Exercises

I. Comprehension

1. Recall

Make a list of qualities that Churchill possessed to be a great leader.

2. Understand

How would you explain the importance of these qualities?

3. Apply

If you are the monitor of your class, what qualities do you think you need to develop to be an excellent one?

4. Analyze

If Hitler had not invaded France in May 1940, would Churchill have been such an important figure in the history books?

5. Evaluate

In your opinion, has the author given a whole picture of the qualities which has made Churchill so great?

II. Further Study

1. Choose several great leaders in the world and summarize their common great qualities. Prepare a presentation in class.
2. What can you learn from Winston Churchill?

Section B Extensive Reading

Jack Welch

Bold, competitive, and controversial are all traits that describe Jack Welch, one of the world's most powerful business leaders. Welch was born on November 19, 1935 into a middle class family in Peabody, Massachusetts, the only child of a train conductor/union leader and a strong-willed mother, Grace. Welch's father worked **grueling** hours to support his family, often leaving the house at 5:30 a.m. and not getting home until 7:30 p.m. Grace and the boy used to wait for the elder Welch at the train station. Welch recalls that the talks he had with his mother at the station served as his early education.

Welch's competitive fires can be traced back to his teenage years playing **hockey**, basketball, and baseball. In high school, Welch was co-captain of the golf team, lettered in hockey, and served as treasurer of the senior class. The five-foot-eight-inch Welch was known as a **feisty** competitor whose will to win was limitless. Welch's mother also **instilled** in him a fierce will to achieve through long discussions and games of **blackjack** and **gin rummy**. "I had a **pal** in my mom," Welch told John A. Byrne of *Business Week*. "We had a great relationship. It was a powerful, unique, wonderful, **reinforcing** experience."

Welch combined popularity and intelligence with a quick wit. He was the class **jokester**. With his mother encouraging him, Welch studied chemical engineering at the University of Massachusetts, becoming the first person in his family to go to college. Several professors acted as Welch's **mentors** and persuaded him to attend graduate school. He then went on to earn a doctorate from the University of Illinois in 1960. When he got the degree, his mother was so proud that she called the *Salem* newspaper to report that "Dr. Welch" received his Ph.D.

➢ **Joined General Electric**

After graduate school, Welch joined General Electric (GE) as a junior engineer in Pittsfield, Massachusetts. Frustrated by the company's **bureaucracy**, Welch quit a year later. He saw little room for advancement at GE. His boss, Reuben Gutoff, recognized Welch's talent, and talked him into staying. Gutoff even promised Welch that he would provide him a more entrepreneurial work environment, although supported with all the resources of a corporate giant.

As Welch climbed the corporate ladder, he was convinced that even a huge corporation like GE could remain **nimble**. By 1967, Welch was among the rising young stars in the GE Plastics division. He kept the small company mentality close to heart and would later lead the charge to erase the big company **malaise** that could **stifle** ideas and action. In his early years, he helped GE Plastics explode from a $28 million after-thought into a billion dollar business.

➢ **The "Neutron Jack" Years**

Welch moved through several different divisions as he progressed. Eventually, at age 42, he moved to the corporate headquarters in Fairfield, Connecticut, when he was named one of three vice-chairmen. After a fierce competition for the top spot, Welch was named chairman in 1981, the youngest CEO ever appointed at GE. "I think I'm the happiest man in America today," Welch told Thomas C. Hayes of *The New York Times*, "and I'm certainly the most fortunate."

Welch attracted **controversy** almost immediately. He was much different than his **predecessor**, the British gentleman Reginald H. Jones. Welch was **brash** and told managers that if they did not move quickly enough, he would "**kick ass**". The new leader was **obsessed** with turning GE into a flexible, lean business that ranked first or second in every industry in which it did business.

An early spotlight was thrust on Welch when GE purchased RCA, the parent company of NBC, in late 1985 for $6.3 billion in cash. At the time, it was the largest corporate acquisition in history and brought RCA back into the family. GE had founded RCA in 1919, but had to sell the **subsidiary** in 1933 because of antitrust threats. After the initial **euphoria** surrounding the deal wore off, Welch realized that NBC was losing $150 million a year, despite dominating prime time television and news ratings. Welch set high financial goals for NBC and turned the business around by cutting costs and replacing unhappy network executives. By 1997, after more than a decade of Welch's **cajoling**, NBC became the undisputed leader of network television. GE transformed NBC into a profitable company that still provided high quality.

Welch and GE were successful economically across the board. However, during his first seven years as CEO, Welch cast off more than 100,000 workers, nearly 25 percent of GE's workforce. The mass **layoffs** earned Welch the **derogatory** nickname "Neutron Jack". Critics equated his name with corporate **greed**, **arrogance**, and **contempt** for workers. GE sold off many of its traditional businesses, such as housewares and televisions, and moved into high-tech manufacturing, broadcasting, and investment banking. Welch was willing to take risks and change the company's **ingrained** corporate culture to fit his strategic vision.

Welch's supporters countered by noting GE's amazing return on equity. In Welch's first six years, GE's total return to **shareholders** reached 273 percent. Welch told Russell Mitchell of *Business Week* that he wanted GE "to become the most competitive business enterprise in the world".

➢ **World's Greatest CEO**

Despite picking up other monikers, such as "Trader Jack", based on his love of acquisitions, Welch transformed his image as GE's fortunes improved. Soon, he was becoming widely regarded as the best CEO in the world. The company had always been heavily watched by business analysts for the latest management trends, but under Welch's **tenure**, GE came to define successful business management.

Part of Welch's improving image was his emphasis on GE's Management Development Institute corporate training program. The center at Croton-on-Hudson (Crotonville), known within GE as "The Pit", was a **showcase** for Welch. The company spent $500 million a year on education and training at Crotonville. He appeared at the center more than 250 times over 17 years and worked with 15,000 GE managers and executives. "The students see all of Jack here," wrote Byrne of *Business Week*. "The management theorist, strategic thinker, business teacher, and corporate icon who made it to the top despite his working class background."

In recent years, Welch has turned his attention to "people" issues and has worked to create informality at the company. This push has allowed communications to open across layers and **fostered** a sense of entrepreneurship at the world's largest corporation. Throughout the year, Welch met with managers across several levels of leadership. As Byrne wrote, the meetings also allowed Welch "to make his **formidable** presence and opinions known to all".

When Welch needed information, he often slipped into factories and plants unexpectedly. A Welch trademark has been the handwritten notes he dashes off to employees. Welch wrote them out and then faxed them all over the company. Welch saw this extra effort as another way of breaking through the bureaucracy that initially hindered his progress at GE. "The idea flow from the human spirit is absolutely unlimited," Welch told Byrne. "All you have to do is to tap into that well. I don't like to use the word efficiency. It's creativity. It's a belief that every person counts."

Since taking over in 1981, Welch has used the company's economic diversity as a tool to move into other industries with fast-growing profits. He has reshaped GE with more than 500 acquisitions worth $53.2 billion. Welch was also instrumental in the mid-to-late 1980s movement among American companies to get leaner, tougher, and globally competitive. GE's non-U.S. sales grew to 45 percent in 1994, up from 22 percent in 1986. *Forbes* writer James R. Norman wrote, "Nearly every one of its (GE's) major products has become a growth business with the stepped-up development overseas."

(length: 1,290 words)

Vocabulary

arrogance	n. 傲慢态度，自大
blackjack	n. 二十一点（一种纸牌游戏）
brash	a. 仓促的，无礼的，性急的，傲慢的
bureaucracy	n. 官僚，官僚作风，官僚机构
cajole	v. 以甜言蜜语哄骗，勾引
contempt	n. 轻视，轻蔑，不尊敬
controversy	n. 争论，争议
derogatory	a. 贬损的
euphoria	n. 精神欢快，兴高采烈
feisty	a. 精力充沛的，活跃的
formidable	a. 令人敬畏的，不可思议的，可怕的
foster	v. 养育，抚育，培养
gin rummy	n. 拉米牌戏的一种形式
greed	n. 贪欲，贪婪
grueling	a. 折磨的，使精疲力竭的
hockey	n. 曲棍球
ingrained	a. 彻底的，根深蒂固的
instill	v. 慢慢地灌输
jokester	n. 喜欢开玩笑者
kick ass	v. 踢屁股；狠揍
layoff	n. 临时解雇，操作停止
malaise	n. 不舒服，身体不适
mentor	n. 良师益友，导师，指导者
moniker	n. 名字，绰号
nimble	a. 敏捷的，灵敏的
obsess	v. 迷住，使困扰
pal	n. <口>好朋友，伙伴
predecessor	n. 前辈，前任
reinforce	v. 加强，增援
shareholder	n. 股东
showcase	n. 陈列橱，显示优点的东西
stifle	v. 使窒息，抑制
subsidiary	n. 子公司，辅助物
tenure	n. （官职等的）保有，任期；（土地）使用期限

Exercises

I. Comprehension

1. Recall

Who persuaded Jack Welch to stay in GE when he wanted to quit the job as the junior engineer?

2. Exemplify

Can you illustrate why Jack Welch attracted controversy as the youngest CEO ever appointed at GE?

3. Make inferences

What does the sentence "The students see all of Jack here" mean in the last but three paragraph?

4. Analyze

What measures had Jack Welch taken to make GE so successful? And what qualities in him can be shown in doing so?

5. Evaluate

Do you think being competitive is a good or a bad thing?

II. Further Study

1. Write about your feelings after reading this passage.
2. Search on the internet for more information about Jack Welch and do a presentation about the controversies on him.

Section C Supplementary Reading

□ Passage 1 Biography of Thomas Edison

Thomas Alva Edison was born on February 11, 1847 in Milan, Ohio; the seventh and last child of Samuel and Nancy Edison. When Edison was seven his family moved to Port Huron, Michigan. Edison lived here until he struck out on his own at the age of sixteen. Edison had very little formal education as a child, attending school only for a few months. He was taught reading, writing, and **arithmetic** by his mother, but was always a very curious child and taught himself much by reading on his own. This belief in self-improvement remained throughout his life.

➤ Work as a Telegrapher

Edison began working at an early age, as most boys did at the time. At thirteen he took a job as a newsboy, selling newspapers and candy on the local railroad that ran through Port Huron to Detroit. He seems to have spent much of his free time reading scientific and technical books, and also had the opportunity at this time to learn how to operate a **telegraph**. By the time he was sixteen, Edison was **proficient** enough to work as a **telegrapher** full time.

➢ First Patent

The development of the telegraph was the first step in the communication revolution, and the telegraph industry expanded rapidly in the second half of the 19th century. This rapid growth gave Edison and others like him a chance to travel, see the country, and gain experience. Edison worked in a number of cities throughout the United States before arriving in Boston in 1868. Here Edison began to change his profession from telegrapher to inventor. He received his first **patent** on an electric vote recorder, a device intended for use by elected bodies such as **Congress** to speed the voting process. This invention was a commercial failure. Edison **resolved** that in the future he would only invent things that he was certain the public would want.

➢ Marriage to Mary Stilwell

Edison moved to New York City in 1869. He continued to work on inventions related to the telegraph, and developed his first successful invention, an improved stock ticker called the "Universal Stock Printer". For this and some related inventions Edison was paid $40,000. This gave Edison the money he needed to set up his first small laboratory and manufacturing facility in Newark, New Jersey in 1871. During the next five years, Edison worked in Newark inventing and manufacturing devices that greatly improved the speed and efficiency of the telegraph. He also found to time to get married to Mary Stilwell and start a family.

➢ Move to Menlo Park

In 1876 Edison sold all his Newark manufacturing concerns and moved his family and staff of assistants to the small village of Menlo Park, twenty-five miles southwest of New York City. Edison established a new facility containing all the equipment necessary to work on any invention. This research and development laboratory was the first of its kind anywhere; the model for later, modern facilities such as Bell Laboratories, this is sometimes considered to be Edison's greatest invention. Here Edison began to change the world.

The first great invention developed by Edison in Menlo Park was the tin foil **phonograph**. The first machine that could record and reproduce sound created a **sensation** and brought Edison international fame. Edison toured the country with the tin foil phonograph, and was invited to the White House to demonstrate it to President Rutherford B. Hayes in April 1878.

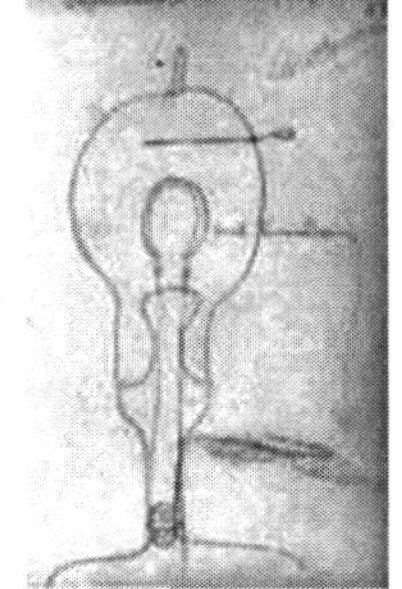

Edison next undertook his greatest challenge, the development of a practical **incandescent**, electric light. The idea of electric lighting was not new, and a number of people had worked on, and even developed forms of electric lighting. But up to that time, nothing had been developed that was remotely practical for home use. Edison's eventual achievement was inventing not just an incandescent electric light, but also an electric lighting system that contained all the elements necessary to make the incandescent light practical, safe, and economical.

➢ Thomas Edison Founds an Industry Based on Electricity

After one and a half years of work, success was achieved when an incandescent lamp with a

filament of **carbonized** sewing thread burned for thirteen and a half hours. The first public demonstration of the Edison's incandescent lighting system was in December 1879, when the Menlo Park laboratory complex was electrically lighted. Edison spent the next several years creating the electric industry. In September 1882, the first commercial power station, located on Pearl Street in lower Manhattan, went into operation providing light and power to customers in a one-square-mile area; the electric age had begun.

➢ **Fame & Wealth**

The success of his electric light brought Edison to new heights of fame and wealth, as electricity spread around the world. Edison's various electric companies continued to grow until in 1889 they were brought together to form Edison General Electric. Despite the use of Edison in the company title however, Edison never controlled this company. The tremendous amount of capital needed to develop the incandescent lighting industry had **necessitated** the involvement of investment bankers such as J.P. Morgan. When Edison General Electric merged with its leading competitor Thompson-Houston in 1892, Edison was dropped from the name, and the company became simply General Electric.

➢ **Marriage to Mina Miller**

This period of success was **marred** by the death of Edison's wife Mary in 1884. Edison's involvement in the business end of the electric industry had caused Edison to spend less time in Menlo Park. After Mary's death, Edison was there even less, living instead in New York City with his three children. A year later, while vacationing at a friends house in New England, Edison met Mina Miller and fell in love. The couple was married in February 1886 and moved to West Orange, New Jersey where Edison had purchased an estate, Glenmont, for his bride. Thomas Edison lived here with Mina until his death.

➢ **New Laboratory & Factories**

When Edison moved to West Orange, he was doing experimental work in **makeshift** facilities in his electric lamp factory in nearby Harrison, New Jersey. A few months after his marriage, however, Edison decided to build a new laboratory in West Orange itself, less than a mile from his home. Edison possessed both the resources and experience by this time to build, "the best equipped and largest laboratory **extant** and the facilities superior to any other for rapid and cheap development of an invention". The new laboratory complex consisting of five buildings opened in November 1887.

A three-story main laboratory building contained a power plant, machine shops, stock rooms, experimental rooms and a large library. Four smaller one-story buildings built perpendicular to the main building contained a physics lab, chemistry lab, **metallurgy** lab, pattern shop, and chemical storage. The large size of the laboratory not only allowed Edison to work on any sort of project, but also allowed him to work on as many as ten or twenty projects at once. Facilities were added to the laboratory or modified to meet Edison's changing needs as he continued to work in this complex until his death in 1931. Over the years, factories to manufacture Edison inventions were built around the laboratory. The entire laboratory and factory complex eventually covered more than twenty acres and employed 10,000 people at its peak during World War One (1914-1918).

After opening the new laboratory, Edison began to work on the phonograph again, having set the project aside to develop the electric light in the late 1870s. By the 1890s, Edison began to manufacture phonographs for both home, and business use. Like the electric light, Edison developed everything needed to have a phonograph work, including records to play, equipment to record the records, and equipment to manufacture the records and the machines. In the process of making the phonograph practical, Edison created the recording industry. The development and improvement of the phonograph was an ongoing project, continuing almost until Edison's death.

➢ **The Movies**

While working on the phonograph, Edison began working on a device that, "does for the eye what the phonograph does for the ear", this was to become **motion pictures**. Edison first demonstrated motion pictures in 1891, and began commercial production of "movies" two years later in a peculiar looking structure, built on the laboratory grounds, known as the Black Maria.

Like the electric light and phonograph before it, Edison developed a complete system, developing everything needed to both film and show motion pictures. Edison's initial work in motion pictures was pioneering and original. However, many people became interested in this third new industry Edison created, and worked to further improve on Edison's early motion picture work. There were therefore many contributors to the swift development of motion pictures beyond the early work of Edison. By the late 1890s, a thriving new industry was firmly established, and by 1918 the industry had become so competitive that Edison got out of the movie business all together.

➢ **Even a Genius Can Have a Bad Day**

The success of the phonograph and motion pictures in the 1890s helped **offset** the greatest failure of Edison's career. Throughout the decade Edison worked in his laboratory and in the old iron mines of northwestern New Jersey to develop methods of mining iron **ore** to feed the **insatiable** demand of the Pennsylvania steel mills. To finance this work, Edison sold all his stock in General Electric. Despite ten years of work and millions of dollars spent on research and development, Edison was never able to make the process commercially practical, and lost all the money he had invested. This would have meant financial ruin had not had Edison continue to develop the phonograph and motion pictures at the same time. As it was, Edison entered the new century still financially secure and ready to take on another challenge.

➢ **A Profitable Product**

Edison's new challenge was to develop a better storage battery for use in electric vehicles. Edison very much enjoyed automobiles and owned a number of different types during his life, powered by gasoline, electricity, and steam. Edison thought that electric **propulsion** was clearly the best method of powering cars, but realized that conventional lead-acid storage batteries were inadequate for the job. Edison began to develop an **alkaline** battery in 1899. It proved to be Edison's most difficult project, taking ten years to develop a practical alkaline battery. By the time Edison introduced his new alkaline battery, the gasoline powered car had so improved that electric vehicles were becoming increasingly less common, being used mainly as delivery vehicles in cities. However, the Edison alkaline battery proved useful for lighting railway cars and signals, **maritime buoys**, and miners lamps. Unlike iron ore mining, the heavy investment Edison made over ten years was repaid handsomely, and the storage battery eventually became Edison's most profitable product. Further, Edison's work paved the way for the modern alkaline battery.

By 1911, Thomas Edison had built a vast industrial operation in West Orange. Numerous factories had been built through the years around the original laboratory, and the staff of the entire complex had grown into the thousands. To better manage operations, Edison brought all the companies he had started to make his inventions together into one corporation, Thomas A. Edison Incorporated, with Edison as president and chairman.

➢ Aging Gracefully

Edison was sixty-four by this time and his role with his company and in life began to change. Edison left more of the daily operations of both the laboratory and the factories to others. The laboratory itself did less original experimental work and instead worked more on **refining** existing Edison products such as the phonograph. Although Edison continued to file for and receive patents for new inventions, the days of developing new products that changed lives and created industries were behind him.

In the 1915, Edison was asked to head the Naval Consulting Board. With the United States inching closer towards the involvement in World War One, the Naval Consulting Board was an attempt to organize the talents of the leading scientists and inventors in the United States for the benefit of the American armed forces. Edison favored preparedness, and accepted the appointment. The Board did not make a notable contribution to the final allied victory, but did serve as a precedent for future successful cooperation between scientists, inventors and the United States military. During the war, at the age of seventy, Edison spent several months on Long Island Sound in a borrowed navy vessel experimenting on techniques for **detecting submarines**.

➢ Honoring a Lifetime of Achievement

Edison's role in life began to change from inventor and **industrialist** to cultural **icon**, a symbol of American **ingenuity**, and a real life Horatio Alger story. In 1928, in recognition of a lifetime of achievement, the United States Congress voted Edison a special Medal of Honor. In 1929 the nation celebrated the golden **jubilee** of the incandescent light. The celebration **culminated** at a banquet honoring Edison given by Henry Ford at Greenfield Village, Ford's new American history museum, which included a complete restoration of the Menlo Park Laboratory. **Attendees** included President Herbert Hoover and many of the leading American scientists and inventors.

The last experimental work of Edison's life was done at the request of Edison's good friends Henry Ford, and Harvey Firestone in the late 1920s. They asked Edison to find an alternative source of rubber for use in automobile tires. The natural rubber used for tires up to that time came from the rubber tree, which does not grow in the United States. Crude rubber had to be imported and was becoming increasingly expensive. With his **customary** energy and thoroughness, Edison tested thousands of different plants to find a suitable **substitute**, eventually finding a type of **goldenrod** weed that could produce enough rubber to be **feasible**. Edison was still working on this at the time of his death.

➢ A Great Man Dies

During the last two years of his life Edison was in increasingly poor health. Edison spent more time away from the laboratory, working instead at Glenmont. Trips to the family vacation home in Fort Myers, Florida became longer. Edison was past eighty and suffering from a number of **ailments**. In August 1931 Edison **collapsed** at Glenmont. Essentially house bound from that point, Edison steadily declined until at 3:21 am on October 18, 1931 the great man died.

(length: 2,385 words)

Vocabulary

ailment	n. 疾病（尤指微恙）	makeshift	n. 将就，凑合，权宜之计
alkaline	a. [化]碱的，碱性的	mar	v. 弄坏，损害……的健全或完整
arithmetic	n. 算术，算法	maritime	a. 海上的，海事的，海运的
attendee	n. 出席者，参加者，在场者	metallurgy	n. 冶金，冶金术
buoy	n. 浮标，浮筒，救生圈	motion pictures	phr. 电影
carbonize	v. 使成碳，碳化	necessitate	v. 成为必要，迫使
collapse	v. 病倒；倒塌，崩溃	offset	v. 弥补，抵消
Congress	n. （美国）国会，议会	ore	n. 矿石，含有金属的岩石
culminate	v. 达到顶点，达到高潮	patent	n. 专利权，专利品
customary	a. 习惯的，惯例的	phonograph	n. 留声机，电唱机
detect	v. 侦查，探测	proficient	a. 熟练的，精通的
extant	a. 现存的，未毁的	propulsion	n. 推进，推进力
feasible	a. 切实可行的	refine	v. 精炼，精制，使文雅高尚
filament	n. 细丝，灯丝	resolve	v. 决心，决定；解决
goldenrod	n. [植]秋麒麟草属植物	sensation	n. 轰动，骚动
icon	n. 肖像，偶像	submarine	n. 潜水艇，潜艇
incandescent	a. 遇热发光的，白炽的		a. 水下的，海底的
industrialist	n. 工业家，实业家	substitute	n. 代用品，代替者，替代品
ingenuity	n. 独创性，精巧，灵活性	telegraph	n. 电报机，电报
insatiable	a. 不知足的，贪求无厌的	telegrapher	n. 报务员，电报员
(golden) jubilee	n. 50 周年纪念		

□ Passage 2 Biography of Margaret Thatcher

Margaret Thatcher's political career has been one of the most remarkable of modern times. Born in October 1925 at Grantham, a small market town in eastern England, she rose to become the first (and for two decades the only) woman to lead a major Western ***democracy****. She won three* ***successive*** *General Elections and served as British Prime Minister for more than eleven years (1979-1990), a record* ***unmatched*** *in the twentieth century.*

During her term of office she **reshaped** almost every aspect of British politics, **reviving** the economy, reforming outdated **institutions**, and **reinvigorating** the nation's foreign policy. She challenged and did much to **overturn** the psychology of decline which had become rooted in Britain since the Second World War, pursuing national recovery with striking energy and determination.

In the process, Margaret Thatcher became one of the founders, with Ronald Reagan, of a school of **conservative conviction** politics, which has had a powerful and **enduring** impact on politics in Britain and the United States and earned her a higher international **profile** than any British politician since Winston Churchill.

By successfully shifting British economic and foreign policy to the right, her government helped to encourage wider international trends which broadened and deepened during the 1980s and 1990s, as the end of the Cold War, the spread of democracy, and the growth of free markets strengthened political and economic freedom in every continent.

Margaret Thatcher became one of the world's most influential and respected political leaders, as well as one of the most **controversial**, **dynamic**, and **plain-spoken**, a reference point for friends and enemies alike.

Margaret Thatcher at a friend's house, summer 1935.

➢ 1925-1947: Grantham & Oxford

Margaret Thatcher's home and early life in Grantham played a large part in forming her political convictions. Her parents, Alfred and Beatrice Roberts, were **Methodists**. The social life of the family was lived largely within the close community of the local **congregation**, bounded by strong traditions of self-help, charitable work, and personal truthfulness.

The Roberts family ran a grocery business, bringing up their two daughters in a flat over the shop. Margaret Roberts attended a local state school and from there won a place at Oxford, where she studied chemistry at Somerville College (1943-1947). Her tutor was Dorothy Hodgkin, a pioneer of X-ray **crystallography** who won a Nobel Prize in 1964. Her outlook was profoundly influenced by her scientific training.

But chemistry took second place to politics in Margaret Thatcher's future plans. Conservative politics had always been a feature of her home life: her father was a local

councilor in Grantham and talked through with her the issues of the day. She was elected president of the student Conservative Association at Oxford and met many **prominent** politicians, making herself known to the leadership of her party at the time of its **devastating** defeat by Labour at the General Election of 1945.

➢ **1950-1951: Candidate for Dartford**

In her mid-twenties she ran as the Conservative **candidate** for the strong Labour seat of Dartford at the General Elections of 1950 and 1951, winning national publicity as the youngest woman candidate in the country.

Margaret Thatcher in her mid-twenties.

She lost both times, but cut the Labour majority sharply and hugely enjoyed the experience of campaigning. Aspects of her mature political style were formed in Dartford, a largely working class **constituency** which suffered as much as any from post-war **rationing** and shortages, as well as the rising level of taxation and state regulation. Unlike many Conservatives at that time, she had little difficulty getting a **hearing** from any audience and she spoke easily, with force and confidence, on issues that mattered to the voters.

➢ **1951-1970: Family & Career**

It was in Dartford too that she met her husband, Denis Thatcher, a local businessman who ran his family's firm before becoming an **executive** in the oil industry. They married in 1951. Twins—Mark and Carol—were born to the couple in 1953.

In the 1950s Margaret Thatcher trained as a lawyer, specialising in taxation. She was elected to Parliament in 1959 as Member of Parliament (MP) for Finchley, a north London constituency, which she continued to represent until she was made a member of the House of Lords (as Baroness Thatcher) in 1992. Within two years, she was given junior office in the administration of Harold Macmillan and during 1964-1970 (when the Conservatives were again in Opposition), established her place among the senior figures of the party, serving continuously as a shadow minister. When the Conservatives returned to office in 1970, under the **premiership** of Edward Heath, she achieved **cabinet** rank as Education Secretary.

➢ **1970-1974: Education Minister**

Margaret Thatcher had a rough ride as Education Minister. The early 1970s saw student **radicalism** at its height and British politics at its least civil. Protesters disrupted her speeches, the opposition **press vilified** her, and education policy itself seemed set immovably in a **leftwards** course, which she and many Conservatives found uncomfortable. But she mastered the job and was **toughened** by the experience.

The Heath Government itself took a beating from events during its tenure (1970-1974) and disappointed many. Elected on promises of economic revival through taming the trade unions and introducing more free market policies, it executed a series of policy **reverses**—nicknamed

Margaret Thatcher & Edward Heath: October 1970.

the "U turns"—to become one of the most **interventionist** governments in British history, negotiating with the unions to introduce detailed control of wages, prices, and **dividends**. Defeated at a General Election in February 1974, the Heath Government left a **legacy** of **inflation** and industrial **strife**.

➢ **1975: Elected Conservative Leader**

Many Conservatives were ready for a new approach after the Heath Government and when the Party lost a second General Election in October 1974, Margaret Thatcher ran against Heath for the leadership. To general surprise (her own included), in February 1975 she defeated him on the first **ballot** and won the contest **outright** on the second, though challenged by half a dozen senior colleagues. She became the first woman ever to lead a Western political party and to serve as Leader of the Opposition in the House of Commons.

Cradling the calf: 1979 General Election campaign.

➢ **1975-1979: Leader of the Opposition**

The Labour Government of 1974-1979 was one of the most crisis-prone in British history, leading the country to a state of virtual **bankruptcy** in 1976 when a **collapse** in the value of the currency on the foreign exchanges forced the government to negotiate credit from the International Monetary Fund (IMF). The IMF **imposed** tight **expenditure** controls on the government as a condition of the loan, which, **ironically**, improved Labour's public **standing**. By summer 1978, it even looked possible that it might win re-election.

But over the winter of 1978/1979, Labour's luck ran out. Trade union pay demands led to an **epidemic** of strikes and showed that the government had little influence over its **allies** in the labour movement. Public opinion swung against Labour and the Conservatives won a Parliamentary majority of 43 at the General Election of May 1979. The following day, Margaret Thatcher became **Prime Minister** of the United Kingdom.

➢ **1979-1983: Prime Minister-First Term**

The new government **pledged** to check and reverse Britain's economic **decline**. In the short-term, painful measures were required. Although direct taxes were cut, to restore **incentives**, the **budget** had to be balanced, and so indirect taxes were increased. The economy was already entering a **recession**, but inflation was rising and interest rates had to be raised to control it. By the end of Margaret Thatcher's first term, unemployment in Britain was more than three million and it began to fall only in 1986. A large section of Britain's inefficient **manufacturing** industry closed down. No one had **predicted** how severe the **downturn** would be.

But vital long-term gains were made. Inflation was checked and the government created the expectation that it would do whatever was necessary to keep it low. The budget of spring 1981, increasing taxes at the lowest point of the recession, offended conventional **Keynesian** economic thinking, but it made possible a cut in interest rates and **demonstrated** this newly found determination. Economic recovery started in the same quarter and eight years of growth followed.

Political support flowed from this achievement, but the re-election of the government was only made certain by an unpredicted event: the Falklands War. The Argentine Junta's invasion of the islands in April 1982 was met by Margaret Thatcher in the firmest way and with a sure touch. Although she worked with the US administration in pursuing the possibility of a diplomatic solution, a British military Task Force was **dispatched** to retake the islands. When diplomacy failed, military action was quickly successful and the Falklands were back under British control by June 1982.

The electorate was impressed. Few British or European leaders would have fought for the islands. By doing so, Margaret Thatcher laid the foundation for a much more vigorous and independent British foreign policy during the rest of the 1980s. When the General Election came in June 1983, the government was re-elected with its Parliamentary majority more than **trebled** (144 seats).

➢ **1983-1987: Prime Minister-Second Term**

The second term opened with almost as many difficulties as the first. The government found itself challenged by the miners' union, which fought a year-long strike in 1984-1985 under militant leadership. The labour movement as a whole put up bitter resistance to the government's trade union reforms, which began with **legislation** in 1980 and 1982 and continued after the General Election.

Margaret Thatcher & Ronald Reagan at Camp David, 22 December 1984.

The miners' strike was one of the most violent and long lasting in British history. The outcome was uncertain, but after many turns in the road, the union was defeated. This proved a crucial develop- ment, because it ensured that the Thatcher reforms would endure. In the years that followed, the Labour Opposition quietly accepted the popularity and success of the trade union legislation and pledged not to reverse its key components.

In October 1984, when the strike was still underway, the Irish Republican Army (IRA) attempted to murder Margaret Thatcher and many of her cabinet by bombing her hotel in Brighton during the Conservative Party annual conference. Although she survived unhurt, some of her closest colleagues were among the injured and dead and the room next to hers was severely damaged. No twentieth-century British Prime Minister ever came closer to **assassination**.

British policy in Northern Ireland had been a standing source of conflict for every Prime Minister since 1969, but Margaret Thatcher aroused the IRA's special hatred for her refusal to meet their political demands, notably during the 1980-1981 prison hunger strikes.

Her policy throughout was implacably **hostile** to terrorism, republican or loyalist, although she matched that stance by negotiating the Anglo-Irish Agreement of 1985 with the Republic of Ireland. The Agreement was an attempt to improve security cooperation between Britain and Ireland and to give some recognition to the political outlook of Catholics in Northern Ireland, an initiative which won warm endorsement from the Reagan administration and the US Congress.

The economy continued to improve during the 1983-1987 Parliament and the policy of economic liberalisation was extended. The government began to pursue a policy of selling state assets, which in total had amounted to more than 20 per cent of the economy when the Conservatives came to power in 1979. The British privatisations of the 1980s were the first of their kind and proved influential across the world.

Where possible, sale of state assets took place through offering shares to the public, with generous terms for small investors. The Thatcher Governments presided over a great increase in the number of people saving through the stock market. They also encouraged people to buy their own homes and to make private **pension** provision, policies which over time have greatly increased the personal wealth of the British population.

The left wing of the Conservative Party had always been uneasy with its chief. In January 1986, enduring divisions between left and right in the Thatcher Cabinet were publicly exposed by the sudden resignation of the Defence Minister, Michael Heseltine, in a dispute over the business troubles of the British helicopter manufacturer, Westland. The fallout from the "Westland Affair" challenged Margaret Thatcher's leadership as never before. She survived the crisis, but its effects were significant. She was subjected to heavy criticism within her own party for the decision to allow US warplanes to fly from British bases to attack targets in Libya (April 1986).There was talk of the government and of its leader being "tired", of having gone on too long.

Her response was characteristic: at the Conservative Party's annual conference in October 1986, her speech foreshadowed a mass of reforms for a third Thatcher Government. With the economy now very strong, prospects were good for an election and the government was returned with a Parliamentary majority of 101 in June 1987.

➢ 1987-1990: Prime Minister-Third Term

The legislative platform of the third-term Thatcher Government was among the most ambitious ever put forward by a British administration. There were measures to reform the education system (1988), introducing a national curriculum for the first time. There was a new tax system for local government (1989), the Community Charge, or "poll tax" as it was dubbed by opponents. And there was legislation to separate purchasers and providers within the National Health Service (1990), opening up the service to a measure of competition for the first time and increasing the scope for effective management.

Margaret Thatcher & Gorbachev at RAF Brize Norton, 7 December 1987.

All three measures were deeply controversial. The Community Charge, in particular, became a serious political problem, as local councils took advantage of the introduction of a new system to increase tax rates, blaming the increase on the Thatcher Government. (The system was abandoned by Margaret Thatcher's successor, John Major, in 1991.) By contrast, the education and health reforms proved enduring. Successive governments built on the achievement and in some respects extended their scope.

The economy boomed in 1987-1988, but also began to overheat. Interest rates had to be doubled during 1988. A division within the government over management of the currency emerged into the open, Margaret Thatcher strongly opposing the policy urged by her Chancellor of the Exchequer and others, of pegging the pound sterling to the Deutschmark through the European Exchange Rate Mechanism (ERM). In the process, her relations with her Chancellor of the Exchequer, Nigel Lawson, were fatally damaged, and he **resigned** in October 1989.

Behind this dispute there was profound disagreement within the government over policy towards the European Community itself. The Prime Minister found herself increasingly at odds with her Foreign Secretary, Sir Geoffrey Howe, on all questions touching European integration. Her speech at Bruges in September 1988 began the process by which the Conservative Party — at one time largely "pro-European"—became predominantly "Euro-sceptic".

Paradoxically, all this took place against a backdrop of international events profoundly helpful to the Conservative cause. Margaret Thatcher played her part in the last phase of the Cold War, both in the strengthening of the Western alliance against the Soviets in the early 1980s and in the successful unwinding of the conflict later in the decade.

The Soviets had **dubbed** her the "Iron Lady"—a tag she relished—for the tough line she took against them in speeches shortly after becoming Conservative leader in 1975. During the 1980s she offered strong support to the defence policies of the Reagan administration.

But when Mikhail Gorbachev emerged as a potential leader of the Soviet Union, she invited him to Britain in December 1984 and pronounced him a man she could do business with. She did not soften her criticisms of the Soviet system, making use of new opportunities to broadcast to television audiences in the east to put the case against Communism. Nevertheless, she played a constructive part in the **diplomacy** that smoothed the break-up of the Soviet Empire and of the Soviet Union itself in the years 1989-1991.

By late 1990, the Cold War was over and free markets and institutions **vindicated**. But that event **triggered** the next stage in European **integration**, as France revived the project of a single European currency, hoping to check the power of a reunited Germany. As a result, divisions over European policy within the British Government were deepened by the end of the Cold War and now became acute.

On November 1, 1990 Sir Geoffrey Howe resigned over Europe and in a bitter resignation speech **precipitated** a challenge to Margaret Thatcher's leadership of her party by Michael Heseltine. In the ballot that followed, she won a majority of the vote. Yet under party rules the margin was insufficient, and a second ballot was required. Receiving the news at a conference in Paris, she immediately announced her intention to fight on.

But a political earthquake occurred the next day on her return to London, when many colleagues in her cabinet—unsympathetic to her on Europe and doubting that she could win a fourth General Election—abruptly deserted her leadership and left her no choice but to **withdraw**. She resigned as Prime Minister on November 28, 1990. John Major **succeeded** her and served in the post until the landslide election of Tony Blair's Labour Government in May 1997.

➢ **Conclusion**

After 1990 Lady Thatcher (as she became) remained a potent political figure. She wrote two best-selling volumes of memoirs—*The Downing Street Years* (1993) and *The Path to Power* (1995)—while continuing for a full decade to tour the world as a lecturer. A book of reflections on international politics—Statecraft—was published in 2002. During the period she made some important interventions in domestic British politics, notably over Bosnia and the Maastricht Treaty.

In March 2002, following several small strokes, she announced an end to her career in public speaking.

Denis Thatcher, her husband of more than fifty years, died in June 2003, receiving warm tributes from all sides.

Margaret Thatcher remains an intensely controversial figure in Britain. Critics claim that her economic policies were divisive socially, that she was harsh or "uncaring" in her politics, and hostile to the institutions of the British welfare state. Defenders point to a transformation in Britain's economic performance over the course of the Thatcher Governments and those of her successors as Prime Minister. Trade union reforms, privatisation, **deregulation**, a strong anti-inflationary stance, and control of tax and spending have created better economic prospects for Britain than seemed possible when she became Prime Minister in 1979.

Critics and supporters alike recognise the Thatcher premiership as a period of fundamental importance in British history. Margaret Thatcher **accumulated** huge prestige over the course of the 1980s and often **compelled** the respect even of her bitterest critics. Indeed, her effect on the terms of political debate has been profound. Whether they were converted to "Thatcherism", or merely forced by the electorate to pay it lip service, the Labour Party leadership was transformed by her period of office and the "New Labour" politics of Tony Blair and Gordon Brown would not have existed without her. Her legacy remains the core of modern British politics: the world economic crisis since 2008 has revived many of the arguments of the 1980s, keeping her name at the centre of political debate in Britain.

(length: 3,223 words)

Vocabulary

accumulate	v. 积聚，堆积
ally	n. 同盟国，支持者
assassination	n. 暗杀
ballot	n. 选举票，投票，票数
bankruptcy	n. 破产
budget	n. 预算
cabinet	n. 内阁
candidate	n. 候选人，投考者
collapse	n. 倒塌，崩溃
compel	v. 强迫，迫使
congregation	n. 集合，集会；[宗]圣会
conservative	a. 保守的，守旧的
constituency	n. （选区的）选民，支持者
controversial	a. 争论的，有争议的
conviction	n. 深信，信念；定罪，宣告有罪
councilor	n. 议员，评议员
crystallography	n. 结晶学
decline	v. 下倾，下垂；拒绝，衰落
democracy	n. 民主政治
demonstrate	v. 示范，证明，论证；示威
deregulation	n. 违反规定，反常
devastating	a. 破坏性的，全然的
diplomacy	n. 外交
dispatch	v./n. 派遣
dividend	n. 股息，红利
downturn	n. 低迷时期，衰退
dub	v. [电影]配音；授予称号
dynamic	a. 有活力的，生气勃勃的
enduring	a. 持久的，不朽的
epidemic	n. 时疫，（风尚等的）流行
executive	n. 执行者，管理人员
expenditure	n. 支出，花费
hearing	n. 听证会，听取意见
hostile	a. 敌对的，敌方的
impose	v. 征税，强加，以……欺骗；利用，施影响
incentive	n. 刺激；诱因；动机
inflation	n. 通货膨胀，（物价）暴涨
institution	n. 公共机构，制度
integration	n. 综合，结合
interventionist	n. 干涉主义者
ironically	ad. 说反话地，讽刺地
Keynesian	a. 凯恩斯理论的
leftwards	ad. 左方地，左侧地
legacy	n. 遗赠（物），遗产
legislation	n. 立法，法律的制定（或通过）
manufacturing	n. 制造业
Methodist	n. 卫理公会派教徒
outright	ad.直率地，全部地
overturn	n. 倾覆，推翻
parliament	n. 国会，议会
pension	n. 养老金，退休金
plain-spoken	a. 坦率的，说话直截了当的
pledge	v. 保证，使发誓
precipitate	v. 猛抛，使陷入
predict	v. 预知，预言，预报
premiership	n. 总理、首相之职位与任期
press	n. 新闻界，新闻舆论
prime minister	n. 总理，首相
profile	n. 外形，轮廓
prominent	a. 卓越的，著名的
radicalism	n. 激进主义

rationing	n.（食物等的）配给	succeed	v. 继……之后，继任
reshape	v. 改造，采用新方针	successive	a. 继承的，连续的
revive	v.（使）苏醒，（使）复活	toughen	v.（使）变坚韧，（使）变坚强
recession	n.（工商业）衰退，不景气	treble	v. 成三倍，使增加两倍
reinvigorate	v. 使再振作，使复兴	trigger	v. 引发，引起，触发
resign	v. 辞去，辞职	unmatched	a. 无比的，无匹敌的
reverse	n. 相反，倒退	vilify	v. 诽谤，辱骂，贬低，轻视
standing	n. 身份，名望，地位	vindicate	v. 维护；证明……正确
strife	n. 斗争，冲突，竞争	withdraw	v. 收回，撤销；缩回，退出

Section D Word Bank for This Unit

乐观的	optimistic	有表现力的，富于表情的	expressive
活泼的，主动的	active	守信的，忠诚的	faithful
外向的	out-going	直率的，真诚的	frank
独立的	independent	宽宏大量的	generous
适应性强的	adaptable	有教养的，优雅的	genteel
有进取心的，好斗的	aggressive	温和的，文雅的	gentle
有雄心壮志的	ambitious	幽默的	humorous
和蔼可亲的	amiable	公正的	impartial
友好的	amicable	勤奋的	industrious
善于分析的	analytical	有独创性的	ingenious
有理解力的	apprehensive	目的明确的	motivated
有志气的，有抱负的	aspiring	理解力强的，有才智的	intelligent
大胆的，有冒险精神的	audacious	有学问的	learned
有能力的，有才能的	capable	条理分明的	logical
仔细的	careful	有方法的	methodical
正直的	candid	谦虚的	modest
能胜任的	competent	客观的	objective
建设性的	constructive	一丝不苟的，精确的	precise
有合作精神的	cooperative	守时的	punctual
富创造力的	creative	实事求是的	realistic
有奉献精神的	dedicated	负责的	responsible
可靠的	dependable	明白事理的	sensible
老练的，有策略的	diplomatic	扎实的，坚定不移的	steady
守纪律的	disciplined	系统的	systematic
尽职的	dutiful	意志坚定的，有目的的	purposeful
受过良好教育的	well-educated	性情温和的	sweet-tempered
有效率的	efficient	温和的，自我克制的	temperate
精力充沛的	energetic	孜孜不倦的	tireless

Chapter 14

Social Problems

美国是世界级的经济、科技和军事超级大国。美国的人均收入在世界上居于前列。英国作为世界上另一个重要的贸易实体、经济强国以及金融中心，是世界第六大经济体，也是全球最富裕、经济最发达和生活水准最高的国家之一。

英美两国的物质生活十分丰富，但人们的生活幸福指数是否很高呢？实际上在繁荣背后的另一种景象是社会的种种问题：贫富悬殊、失业率居高不下、种族歧视、毒品泛滥、犯罪低龄化等。在这些世界上最富有的国家里，在任何一个城市人们都能见到衣衫褴褛的流浪汉在街头行乞；近年来美国的校园枪击事件频频发生……

本章揭开英美社会问题的面纱，引领大家与英美的专家学者一起去思索社会问题的根源，寻找解决问题的办法吧。

Section A　Intensive Reading

Social Issues in the United States

by Geeta Dhavale

No doubt United States is a powerful country today in the world. It has made its mark in the history by building a strong economy that every other nation **envies** and **idolizes** too. But, all that **glitters** is not gold. America too has some serious social issues that need to be dealt with to maintain the position of power, **prestige**, and set a true example of ideal society in the world.

Unequal Distribution of Wealth: **Privatization** is increasing in America which provides opportunities only to those who can afford. The efforts of socialists, to distribute wealth equally are also been opposed by the ruling government. Due to this, rich people are becoming richer and poor becoming poorer.

Poverty: Yes, it is shocking but true. Around 13%-17% American population live below the federal poverty line. The US government does not have an absolute definition for poverty but it describes the same phenomenon as relative poverty, that is, how income relates to median income. The number of people living under poverty line is increasing at an **alarming** rate.

Unequal Educational Funding: The US government provides **compulsory** education for first 12 years. This education system is controlled by state government and a very little portion of control is held by local government, which determines the funding and school system of each **municipality**. Large number of childbearing families from **affluent** communities seem to be funded heavily compared to less affluent and fewer childbearing families. The problem of "school dropouts" is also increasing due to poor school condition and services.

Crime and Incarceration: Due to increased unequal opportunities, the crime rate is also increasing in the United States. Prison population in America is growing every day. Most of the prisoners are drug offenders who use or sell recreational drugs. **Incarceration** of criminals for long sentences has led to three strikes laws and ultimately to incarceration for life after three felonies.

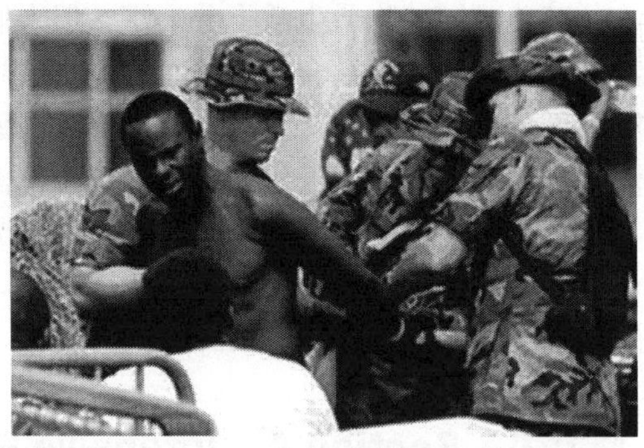

Health Issues: The United States does not provide health care to all. It does not have a socialized medicine or public health care system. Only employed people get health insurance as employee benefit but unemployed, part-time, self employed workers have to pay for their own insurance which is very expensive. Some studies have shown that medical bills are one of the major causes of declaring **bankruptcy** in the United States.

Increasing Cost of Living: With growing **inflation**, the cost of living in the United States is also increasing significantly. But the minimum wage is not increasing in the same fashion and so, many people find it difficult to fulfill their daily basic requirements. The working population make more money and again spend more on living which hardly leaves anything behind for savings. America has the lowest saving rate compared to any other developed nation.

Apart from these, there are many social issues in the United States that need immediate attention. Given below is the list of social issues in America:

•**Affirmative** Action

•**Ageism**

•HIV/AIDS

•Alcohol Abuse

•Airline Problems

•Anti Muslim **Discrimination** and Violence

•Automobile and Highway Safety

•Capital Punishment

•Child Abuse and Sexual **Molestation**
•Child Labor
•Church State Separation
•Civil Rights Movements
•Corporate Crime
•**Consumerism**
•Criminal Justice and Rights
•Defense and Security Issues
•Divorce and Child Support
•Domestic Violence
•Disability Rights
•Eating Disorders
•**Euthanasia**
•Environmental Issues, Wildlife, and **Extinct** Species
•Food Safety and Drug Safety
•Mafia Wars
•Gambling
•Global Warming
•**Homosexuality**—Gay and Lesbian Rights
•Public Health Care Reform
•Homelessness
•Housing Costs
•Human **Trafficking**
•Illegal Immigration
•Identity Theft
•Copyright and **Intellectual** Property Rights
•Juvenile Crime Justice
•Juvenile Reform
•Journalistic Reform
•Media **Bias**
•Media, Sex, and Violence
•Mental Illness
•Money **Laundering**
•Natural Disaster and Disaster Relief
•Nuclear Energy, Power, and Waste
•**Obesity**
•Organ and Tissue Transplant
•Organized Crime
•Psychological Health

•**Plagiarism**
•**Pornography**
•Prostitution
•Racism
•Recycling and Water Conservation
•**Reproductive** Rights and Technology
•Scientific Research Ethics
•Sex Education
•Sexual **Harassment**
•Single Parenting
•Stem Cell Research
•**Suicide**
•Terrorism
•Toxic Waste
•Traffic **Congestion**
•Unemployment
•Voting Issues
•Waste Management
•Nuclear Weapons and Mass destruction
•Women's Rights

The above list of social issues in the United States is not exclusive as there are many other specific socio-economic and cultural problems that America is faced with. An American governments needs to come up with stringent policies to solve the aforementioned issues. These issues require planning on both, micro and macro level to get resolved soon.

(length: 722 words)

Vocabulary

alarming	a. 使人害怕的，扰乱人心的；使人惊慌的；危言耸听的
affluent	a. 富裕的，富足的；流畅，滔滔不绝的
affirmative	a. 肯定的；赞成的，同意的；积极的，乐观的
ageism	n. 对老年人的歧视
bankruptcy	n. 破产，倒闭；彻底失败；（勇气）完全丧失
bias	n. 偏见 v. 使倾向于；使有偏见
compulsory	a. 必须做的，强制性的；义务的；必修的
congestion	n. 拥挤，堵车；阻塞；充血；（人口）过剩，稠密
consumerism	n. 消费主义；保护消费者利益主义
discrimination	n. 歧视；辨别，区别；辨别力；不公平的待遇
envy	n./v. 嫉妒，妒忌；羡慕
euthanasia	n. 安乐死
extinct	a. 灭绝的；绝种的；消逝的
glitter	v. 闪烁，闪耀 n. 灿烂的光辉；闪烁
harassment	n. 骚扰，扰乱
homosexuality	n. 同性恋关系
incarceration	n. 监禁，禁闭；钳闭
idolize	v. 将（某人）当做偶像崇拜
inflation	n. 通货膨胀

intellectual	a. 智力的；有才智的 n. 知识分子；脑力劳动者
laundering	n. 洗涤（衣等）；洗（钱）
molestation	n. 骚扰，干扰，调戏；折磨
municipality	n. 自治市；市政当局
obesity	n. 肥胖，过胖；肥胖症
plagiarism	n. 剽窃，抄袭；剽窃物，抄袭物
pornography	n. 色情文学；色情描写
prestige	n. 威信，威望，声望，声誉
privatization	n. 私有化
reproductive	a. 生殖的；再生产的；复制的
suicide	n. 自杀；自杀者；自杀行为
trafficking	n. 非法交易

Exercises

I. Comprehension

1. Recall

How many American people live below the poverty line according to the author?

2. Summarize

What is the main idea that the author tries to convey under the subtitle "Unequal Educational Funding"?

3. Make Inferences

What does the author mean by saying "all that glitters is not gold" in the first paragraph?

4. Analyze

What theme, or message, is the author conveying through this passage? Cite evidence to support your answer.

5. Evaluate

In your opinion, has the author given a whole picture of American social problems? Cite specific examples to support your opinion.

II. Further Study

1. Choose one from the list of American social problems in the text and do a research on it, prepare a presentation in class.
2. Choose from the following list of films to watch, and find out the social problems it tries to reflect. Write down your reflections on the problems.

1) *John Q* 《追在眉睫》
2) *Crash*《撞车》
3) *17 Again*《重返 17 岁》
4) *Fighting Club*《搏击俱乐部》
5) *Training Day*《训练日》
6) *Out Of Time* 《限时追捕》
7) *No Country For Old Man* 《老无所依》
8) *Erin Brockovich*《永不妥协》
9) *The Curious Case Of Benjamin Button*《本杰明 · 巴顿奇事》
10) *Home of the Brave*《星条旗永不落》

Section B Extensive Reading

Excerpt of How Life Gets Better While People Feel Worse

by Gregg Easterbrook

The Progress Paradox

Gregg Easterbrook

Standards of living keep rising, with the typical house now more than twice as large as a generation ago; middle-class income keeps rising. Although more slowly than income at the very top; more Americans graduate from college every year; **longevity** keeps rising; almost all forms of disease, including most cancers, are in decline; crime has dropped **spectacularly**; pollution, except for greenhouse gases, is in long-term decline; discrimination is down **substantially**. Yet despite all these positive indicators, the percentage of Americans who describe themselves as "happy" has not increased since the early 1950s, while incidence of **depression** keeps rising—and was doing so long before the morning of September 11, 2001.

This is the progress **paradox**: life gets better while people feel worse. Many explanations suggest themselves. One is the depressing effect of excess **materialism**, which I call "the **revenge** of the credit card". Another is fear that western society will break down, which might be called "**collapse** anxiety". A third is the uneasy feeling that accompanies actually getting what you dreamed of. Today, tens of millions of Americans have things their parents or grandparents could only dream of—nice houses, college educations. Although that is obviously good, Americans are finding that merely possessing the good life does not ensure happiness. This may tell us there is a "revolution of satisfied expectations"—that general **prosperity** brings with it an empty feeling.

Here is another possible explanation of the progress paradox: that along with getting better at manufacturing cell phones. DVD players and SUVs, society gets even better at manufacturing stress.

Stress is hardly a new phenomenon. To have been a pioneer **prairie** farmer in the 1800s, **cracking** hard soil with a hard plow: to have been a seamstress working 14-hour days for **starvation** wages in a sweatshop in the 1800s; these and many other past life circumstances were surely stressful. But the contemporary increase in stress is not in your mind; researchers believe Americans suffer from ever-higher levels of nervous tension. Higher stress, in turn, may be **offsetting** our appreciation of a better life.

Consider, first, that nature designed us to experience stress. "Stress is inevitable and not necessarily bad", says Bruse McEven, a researcher at Rockefeller University in New York and a leading authority on the biology of a stress. In reaction to noise, sudden movements and perceived dangers, an area of the brain called the **amygdale** secretes a **hormone** called **cortisol** that engenders stress. Stress hormones heighten the awareness of surroundings, while slightly improving vision and hearing.

Researchers believe the stress response **revolved** in **mammals** because stress **decreases** the odds of being caught and eaten by something. Today, the stress response is no less important as an **evolutionary** "adaptation" than it was in the era of **saber-toothed** tigers. Drive at 75 mph with other vehicles only a car-length away. And you'd better have heightened awareness of sudden small movements.

Stress is also a coping mechanism for the demands of life. At the workplace or at school, the stress response helps people be on guard regarding problems, and helps them work harder. Studies show that successful or high-income individuals tend to have more cortisol **pumping** their systems. (Whether the pressure of their positions cause the stress or the stress-response helps them attain their positions is not known.)

However researchers also shows that those who enjoy career success and exhibit stress **symptoms** are twice as likely as the population at large to describe themselves as "very unhappy". That the stressed-out are likely to be unhappy is a warning sign because stress, measured either by emotional state or by cortisol levels, is rising in American society. One reason is that the media get ever better at presenting us with information to worry about.

The 1800s prairie farmer would have **fretted** a great deal about the weather and the arrival of the Wells Fargo wagon. But he would have known hardly anything about crimes in distant cities or angry **chanting** mobs in other nations. Today everyone gets minute-by-minute readouts of killings, natural disasters and social unrest the world over. Even as most things get better for most people, there are even more entries on the list of worries, **activating** more stress.

The contemporary lifestyle also fosters stress. Americans now spend an average if almost an hour per day in the car, and being stuck in the traffic is stressful compared with walking, which can be relaxing and pleasant. Ever-decreasing physical **exertion** coupled with ever more calories means that today, the typical American is overweight. Stress and weight are related, as overweight people have a higher proportion of cortisol in their bodies than the lean.

The national decline in sleep is another factor in rising stress. Cortisol proportion stops during sleep; one of the fundamental reasons mammals sleep may be to give their bodies a break from stress hormones. Researchers believe 10 hours of sleep nightly was the norm for most of human history. By a generation ago, the US average had fallen to eight hours per night; the average is now seven hours and still falling.

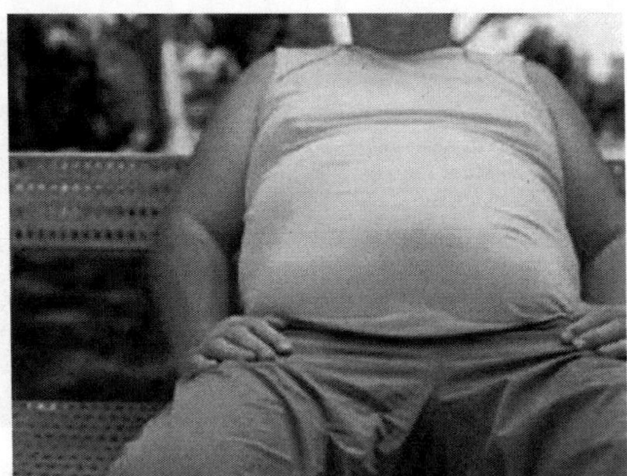

We don't sleep well, either, owing to bad habits such as eating or watching TV just before bed. Those who watch TV until lights-out often experience interrupted sleep, researchers say, whereas our ancestors, who read or knitted before bed, slept more soundly.

What can we do to reduce stress? First are short-term lifestyle changed. Cut calories; engage in 30 minutes of physical activity daily; turn off the television at least an hour before bedtime.

Long-term goals should be more ambitious. Society needs to find ways to make society less of a rat race; to render the economy less **tumultuous** and ease job anxiety; to slow the **hectic** pace of existence so that we can step back and appreciate our own lives. If living standards and stress continue rising in sync, we will endlessly be better off but not happier.

(length: 1,010 words)

Vocabulary

activate	v. 使活动，启动，触发；使开始作用
amygdale	n. 杏仁孔
chant	v. 吟诵，咏唱
cortisol	n. 皮质（甾）醇，氢化可的松
collapse	n./v. 倒塌；崩溃
crack	v. 破裂，打开；（使）开裂
decrease	v. 减少，减小
depression	n. 萎靡不振，沮丧
exertion	n. 努力；费力；（能力、权力等的）运用；行使
evolutionary	a. 进化的
fret	v. 磨损，腐蚀；焦急；（使）烦恼 n. 烦恼；腐蚀处
hectic	a. 繁忙的；兴奋的，狂热的；发烧的
hormone	n. 荷尔蒙；激素
longevity	n. 长寿；寿命；长期供职
mammal	n. 哺乳动物
materialism	n. 唯物主义；唯物论；实利主义，物质主义
offset	v. 抵消；补偿；形成分支，长出分枝
paradox	n. 反论，悖论；似是而非的论点；自相矛盾的人或事
prairie	n.（尤指北美的）大草原，大牧场；草原地带
prosperity	n. 繁荣；兴旺，昌盛；成功
pump	v. 用抽水机汲水；给……打气

revenge	n. 报仇，报复	substantially	ad. 本质上；大体上；充分地；相当多地
revolve	v.（使）旋转；反复考虑；（使）循环	symptom	n. 症状；征兆
saber-toothed	a. 有军刀形的，上犬齿的	tumultuous	a. 骚乱的；吵闹的；狂暴的；激烈的
spectacularly	ad. 壮观地，令人吃惊地		
starvation	n. 挨饿；饥饿；饿死；绝食		

Exercises

I. Comprehension

1. Recall

1) What evidence does the author provide to explain his statement in paragraph 3 that "life gets better while people feel worse"?

2) What facts do they explain that stress is not a new phenomenon?

3) What examples does the author provide to explain that stress is a coping mechanism?

2. Summarize

What strategy does the author use to introduce the thesis?

3. Make Inferences

According to the author, higher stress may be offsetting our appreciation of a better life. What does he mean?

4. Analyze

Throughout the essay, the author compares American life today to that of a prairie farmer in the 1800s. What purpose does this comparison serve?

5. Evaluate

1) The author says that for most people, there are "ever more entries on the list of worries, activating more stress". Do you agree with this statement?

2) Do you think the author's use of the term "progress paradox" (paragraphs 3-4) is ffective? Explain your answer.

3) How can we slow the pace of life and increase our appreciation of our circumstances? What suggestions do you have?

II. Further Study

1. Talk with your classmates about the stress in college life, present your discovery in class.
2. Write down your reflections on how to manage stress in college life.

Section C Supplementary Reading

□ Passage 1 Why Homeless People Don't Use Shelters

As someone who has worked in homeless shelters I am very aware that the vast majority of homeless shelter workers are good people who are doing their best. I am glad that homeless shelters exist to help people without homes. However, it would be an **injustice** to pretend that homeless shelters in America are **plentiful** enough or that all of those shelters that exist are safe enough, or free from downsides.

➢ **Fear of Contracting Parasites from Homeless Shelters**

No matter how clean a homeless shelter is kept, the danger of getting **parasites** by using it is still very high. Homeless people carry a lot of parasites, likely because they tend to sleep in lots of different places. So if you sleep every night in a different bed that a long string of other homeless people have slept in, eventually you are bound to get head lice, pubic lice or scabies. It's hard as **heck** to get rid of parasites when you are homeless.

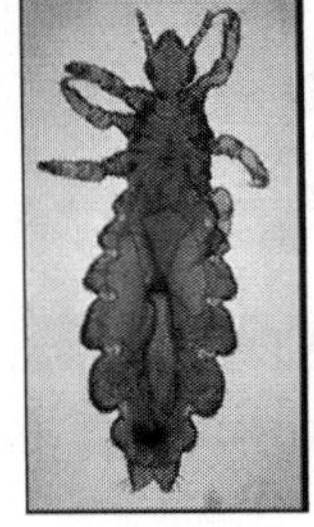

Bedbugs are another biting parasite that can easily **infest** a homeless person's bedroll even if it doesn't get opened in the homeless shelter. Homeless people don't want to infest the homes of people who give them a place to stay for the night or to bring bedbugs to work with them. Homeless shelter volunteers and employees also need to take **precautions** to avoid bringing bedbugs home with them.

The parasites commonly present in homeless shelters were my second most important reason for avoiding them. I'm **itching** right now just thinking about it.

➢ **Danger of Rape or Assault in or Near Homeless Shelters**

Homeless shelters and the areas around them are often hunting grounds for human **predators**. Some of the craftier ones get jobs at homeless shelters while others just watch for individuals departing the shelters. It's not just rapists, either. Predators in search of "excitement" will track a lone person leaving a shelter so they can beat him or **harass** him for fun.

Also, though there are usually **attendants** of some kind on watch almost none of them are trained to deal with violent behavior making homeless shelter users **vulnerable** to other shelter users who are predators.

For me, this was the number one reason to avoid homeless shelters. Once you get raped or **assaulted** in a homeless shelter or because you were trailed after leaving one you just don't want to try it again no matter how hot or cold or rainy or otherwise unpleasant it is outside.

Criminals are well aware that police take seldom complaints from homeless people seriously. Many people avoid shelters because pretending to not be homeless (which means avoiding homeless shelters, missions, and soup kitchens) is one of the most effective ways to avoid such predators.

➢ **Fear of Contracting Disease from Homeless Shelters**

One reason it's hard to fall asleep in a homeless shelter is the almost endless coughing. There's always at least one person in a homeless shelter with a cough. Many of those with

chronic coughs have chronic illnesses, **transmissible** diseases. **Tuberculosis** is frighteningly common among homeless people. When you may have to sleep out in the elements on any given night (there's no guarantee you'll get into a shelter every night) even the flu can be a dangerous disease to contract.

Keep in mind that many homeless people are homeless due to ill health and you'll see why homeless shelters full of sick people pose an even greater risk to them.

I honestly hadn't thought about this until I volunteered in a shelter and it was strongly recommended that I get a tuberculosis **vaccination** and a flu shot.

➢ Lack of Handicapped Accommodations in Homeless Shelters

I was shocked and sickened to see a man turned away from a homeless shelter because he was in a wheelchair. Another person and I offered to pull his chair up the stairs and help him inside the shelter if he needed it. They told us it had to do with insurance concerns and said that they were sorry but, no, he couldn't use the shelter. That was the first time I saw a handicapped person turned away from a homeless shelter but sadly, it was not the last.

Many homeless shelters are in old buildings re-purposed to fit a bunch of beds. Sometimes their beds are located above the first floor and they have no elevators. Some shelters don't have **railings** in the restrooms or ramps into the rooms or buildings either. While it is not the fault of those who run the homeless shelters some shelters are unable to accommodate people in wheelchairs.

Regardless of what the *Americans with Disabilities Act* says, some shelters turn away people in wheelchairs or with other mobility limitations such as the need to use a **walker** or **crutches** to get around. While sometimes they will offer a hotel **voucher** to the disabled person that doesn't always happen.

➢ Drug Addictions

Yes, some people avoid homeless shelters because of drug addictions—their own or those of other people.

Since many homeless shelters have signs insisting they are drug free zones, some drug users will avoid them. However, many drug users and dealers do not, making some homeless shelters hot spots of drug activity.

People frightened by drug related activity may come to avoid shelters because of this, fearing for their safety or their children's safety. Still others are themselves trying to get off drugs and being around other users makes it very difficult for them to do so, so they avoid homeless shelters while trying to kick their drug or alcohol habit.

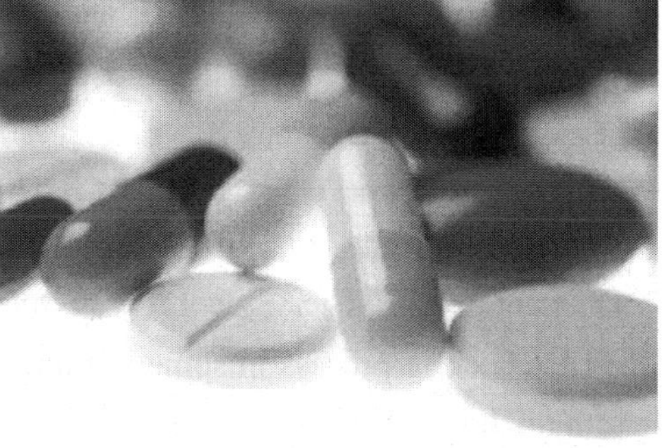

A homeless shelter is no shelter from drugs.

➢ **Separation of Family Members in Homeless Shelters**

Giving up family for shelter. This is a biggie and it's pretty horrible when you think about it. Most homeless shelters separate families.

Women can bring their pre-teen children into most women's shelters but teenage male children (as young as 13) may be required to goto a men's shelter which they may not even get into. Can you imagine a mother leaving her young teenage son to sleep alone on the street without her protection while she sleeps in a homeless shelter? Most don't, so the whole family sleeps in their car or outside.

Men and women usually cannot be in the same homeless shelter so husbands and wives are separated, knowing their spouse might not get a bed in a different shelter. These people are often elderly or disabled and depend on each other for safety and care. So again, most of them will **forgo** the use of homeless shelters so they can take care of each other.

Also, children cannot stay in the vast majority of men's homeless shelters. This leaves homeless single fathers in a very difficult spot. This seems not only heartbreaking but criminal.

➢ **Homeless Shelter Staff Assumptions about Drug Use and Criminality**

If you are homeless, you are guilty even if you are innocent. While it was not often said aloud, some shelter employees and volunteers regard all homeless people as drug addicts and criminals.

When you are homeless, many people will **automatically** treat you as a criminal and a drug user. This is another barrier to employment for homeless people.

Many people are unable to comprehend that a person without a home may just be someone down on his or her luck without any wrongdoing on his or her part.

While I'm sure they mean well, many shelters and shelter employees or volunteers take it upon themselves to cure homeless people of their sometimes non-existent addictions and criminal ways. Some shelters put a lot of pressure on people who use them to attend alcohol and drug abuse counseling even if they are not alcohol or drug abusers.

I remember the **smirks** and questioning looks when I insisted I had no drug or alcohol abuse issues. One shelter employee actually asked me, "Well, then, why are you so skinny?"

Forced participation in substance abuse counseling even for non-abusers takes time away from job searches and current employment which the average homeless person cannot afford, causing most employed homeless people and those actively seeking employment to avoid homeless shelters that require it.

➢ **An Invasive and Disrespectful Check in Process**

This answer has gotten me a lot of **flack**. Even though it played only a minor part in my decision not to use shelters, I feel it is an important part.

The check in process in some but not all homeless shelters is sometimes **humiliating** and **dehumanizing**.

I was asked questions such as "Do you have any sexual partners you could stay with?" as well as other questions about my sex life on more than one occasion. One shelter worker even suggested that I find a boyfriend to stay with; basically she was suggesting I exchange sexual favors for a place to sleep. Keep in mind that I, like most women homeless more than a few weeks, had already been the victim of sexual assault. I felt violated.

(length: 1,501 words)

Vocabulary

attendant	n. 服务人员，侍者；随从；伴随物
automatically	ad. 自动地；无意识地；不自觉地；机械地
assault	v. 袭击；强暴；发起攻击；动武
assumption	n. 假定，假设；承担；想当然
chronic	a. 慢性的；长期的；习惯性的
crutch	n. 拐杖，支持物
dehumanize	v. 使失去人性，使非人化
flack	n. 高射炮； 抨击
forgo	v. 没有也行，放弃
harass	v. 扰乱，骚扰；反复袭击
heck	int.& n. 真见鬼（hell 的委婉说法）
humiliating	a. 丢脸的；羞辱性的；
infest	v. 大批出没，成群出现；在……上寄生
injustice	n. 不公平；非正义
invasive	a. 侵略性的，侵害的；攻击性的
itch	v. 发痒
parasite	n. 寄生物，寄生虫
plentiful	a. 丰富的；富产的；丰饶的；充沛的
precaution	n. 预防，警惕；预防措施
predator	n. 以掠夺为生的人；食肉动物
railing	n. 栏杆
smirk	n. 傻笑，得意的笑；假笑
transmissible	a. 可传送的，可遗传的
tuberculosis	n. 肺结核；[医]结核病；痨；痨病
walker	n. 助步车
vaccination	n. [医]种痘，接种；牛痘疤
voucher	n. 凭证，收据
vulnerable	a.（地方）易受攻击的；易受伤的

□ Passage 2 British Riots

The following three sections explain the causes of British riots from different perspectives.

➢ British riots expose ugly social problems

It is, perhaps, **indicative** of our country's long-held **stereotypes** regarding the British that the news of bloody riots in London, Birmingham and other cities around Great Britain **garnered** relatively little attention here in the United States. People, after all, are **predisposed** as a matter of course to see only those things that confirm their **misconceptions**, and these riots exposed an ugly **underbelly** of British society that looks nothing like the **prim** and proper English **denizens** of American **lore**.

The situation in England (the riots have thus far spared Scotland and Wales) is indeed **grim**. People have been shot and killed, scores of buildings and vehicles have been torched, and many shops have been

looted by rioters as the violence spreads throughout the island. The crisis has also been a test of leadership for Prime Minister David Cameron, coming just a few weeks after a phone-hacking scandal with an English tabloid.

Like a forest fire, every riot has two causes: one **proximal** and one **ultimate**. The match that started this current **conflagration** was the shooting of alleged gangster Mark Duggan by London police on August 4. This particular **blaze** would never have gained such **momentum**, though, were it not for some underlying **tinder** of discontent that predisposed such a significant segment of the population to **wanton** violence.

But why would the citizens of one of the world's wealthiest countries bear such a **grudge** against their society? Answering this is crucial if we want to know how likely it is that such an event could happen here.

In response to this question, several theories have been proposed. The first explanation, popular with the left, is that riots are the result of urban poverty and despair brought on by **persistent** inequality and the lack of realistic job opportunities. Undoubtedly, riots are more likely to crop up in places where there are poor, unemployed and desperate people living in **squalor**. This theory is somewhat unsatisfying because criminals tend to be unable to hold down steady jobs and, as such, one would expect to find more of them in poorer areas. To some degree, then, this theory confuses correlation and causation.

A more popular theory—one that has been advanced by David Cameron himself—is that these riots represented "criminality, pure and simple". For Cameron, the underlying cause of the violence was the breakdown of society—namely, according to *The Economist*, "welfare dependency, broken homes and moral **nihilism**".

The distinction between these two interpretations is **subtle** but crucial. The first theory calls for more government intervention to clean up the urban decay on the grounds that it causes these riots. By contrast, the second suggests that government has actually been causing the problem by allowing society to **relinquish** its **obligations** to its fellow citizens. Herein lies the **dilemma**. To rephrase the famous quote by Ronald Reagan: "Is government the solution to our problems, or is government itself the problem? "

The best way to answer this question might be by making a comparison. The United States is not lacking in urban poverty, and neither are European countries like France or Britain. Yet, in recent years, this country has not seen the sort of urban unrest being witnessed in the poor districts of London now or the banlieues of France in 2005.

The difference between our country and European ones is that in Britain and France, the welfare state creates **perverse incentives** for the poor with disastrous results. As Stanford professor of economics Michael Boskin writes, "the size of the welfare state — and the **erosion** of incentives to work, save and invest, owing to high taxes and **bloated** transfer payments — is a major **impediment** to faster income growth."

Granted, there is a time and a place for welfare, especially during periods of **sluggish** economic growth like the present. But this violence, at its core, reminds us that, in the long-term, the government can never spend enough to do away with every social problem. We as citizens have a responsibility on an individual level to care for those in society that need our help. We cannot let government do the heavy lifting for us.

It is also unreasonable to expect that the older generations of adults will be able to solve these problems. Rioters are, by and large, dissatisfied youth who don't see much of a future for themselves in the present society. The only people who can help them are those who also experienced the particular stresses of their generation, and yet, through persistence and good fortune, managed to overcome those problems. Frankly, the people best equipped to this task are young college graduates, as many of us here at the University of Washington will soon be.

Ultimately, it will fall on our generation to **ameliorate** the struggles of the poor and **downtrodden**. It will take teachers, doctors, social workers and many others. But we must remember that the work we will do is primarily our responsibility and not the task of the government.

➢ **UK tackled social problems after riots**

Police officers lead a man away following a **raid** on a property in Pimlico, London, August 12, 2011.

Britain needs to **tackle** deep-seated social problems following riots and looting in English cities this week, the center-right government said, and a US street crime expert who has brought in, said arrests alone would not solve the problem.

"There are communities that have just been left behind by the rest of the country. There are communities that are cut-off from the economic life-blood of the rest of the country, " Finance Minister George Osborne said.

Prime Minister David Cameron, criticized by some in his Conservative party as being too liberal on crime and punishment, has taken a hard line on rioting in statements this week after returning from his summer holiday and recalling parliament.

He has also come under attack for **austerity** measures his government is introducing to tackle a huge debt burden.

Osborne said the government intends to press on with deep cuts to police numbers. The Conservative mayor of London, Boris Johnson, has said the riots weakened the case for those cuts.

The riots broke out a week ago after a demonstration against the police shooting of a suspect.

Cameron has said political and economic **grievances** had little to do with days of looting and violence in which five people were killed, calling it "criminality pure and simple" and saying gang violence lay at its heart.

He **enlisted** US street crime expert William Bratton on Friday to advise the government on handling it.

Bratton, credited with curbing street crime as police chief in New York, Los Angeles and Boston, told Reuters on Friday he would offer advice based on his experience tackling gangs.

"You can't arrest your way out of the problem," he said on US broadcaster ABC on Saturday. "Arrest is certainly appropriate for the most violent, the **incorrigible**, but so much of it can be addressed in other ways and it's not just a police issue, it is in fact a societal issue."

Cities were largely quiet yesterday and today. British police flooded the streets again on last night to ensure weekend drinking does not reignite the rioting that shocked Britons and **sullied** the country's image a year before it hosts the Olympic Games.

More than 1,200 people have been arrested in connection with violence disorder and looting and hundreds have been charged.

Osborne said lessons needed to be learned but throwing money at the problem was not the answer. "There are very deep-seated social problem which we need to tackle," he told BBC radio.

The scale and **ferocity** of the rioting, not only in inner-city areas but also in some middle-class suburbs, has generated a debate with starkly different views, with many people saying the police should have been tougher.

The ex-leader of one of London's most feared street gangs said they were not the **brainchild** of gang leaders but, in many cases, the result of a build-up of frustration among young people growing up on grim housing estates with little hope.

➢ **The theory of everything**

British academics Richard Wilkinson and Kate Pickett argue that almost every social problem, from crime to obesity, stems from one root cause: inequality.

Another day, another headline: today obesity, tomorrow teenage pregnancy, the day after crime figures. Social problems operate a revolving-door policy these days. As soon as one goes away, another turns up. For the most part, these problems are regarded as entirely separate from each other. Obesity is a health issue, crime a policing issue and so on. So the government launches new initiatives here, there and everywhere, builds new hospitals, puts more money into the police and prisons. And there's little real hope of improvement.

Until now, maybe. Quietly spoken, late middle-aged and quintessentially English, Richard Wilkinson is the last person you would expect to come up with a sweeping theory of everything. Yet that's precisely what this retired professor from Nottingham Medical School, in collaboration with his partner, Kate Pickett, a lecturer at the University of York, has done.

The opening sentence of their new book, *The Spirit Level*, cautions, "People usually exaggerate the importance of their own work and we worry about claiming too much"—yet by the time you reach the end you wonder how they could have claimed any more. After all, they argue that almost every social problem common in developed societie—reduced life **expectancy**, child **mortality**, drugs, crime, homicide rates, mental illness and obesity—has a single root cause: inequality.

And, they say, it's not just the deprived underclass that loses out in an unequal society: everyone does, even the better off. Because it's not absolute levels of poverty that create the social problems, but the differentials in income between rich and poor. Just as someone from the lowest-earning 20% of a more equal society is more likely to live longer than their counterpart from a less equal society, so too someone from the highest-earning 20% has a longer life expectancy than their alter ego in a less equal society.

Take these random headline statistics. The US is wealthier and spends more on health care than any other country, yet a baby born in Greece, where average income levels are about half that of the US, has a lower risk of infant mortality and longer life expectancy than an American baby. Obesity is twice as common in the UK as the more equal societies of Sweden and Norway, and six times more common in the US than in Japan. Teenage birth rates are six times higher in the UK than in more equal societies; mental illness is three times as common in the US as in Japan; murder rates are three times higher in more unequal countries. The examples are almost endless.

Inequality, it seems, is an equal-opportunity disease, something that has a direct impact on everyone. But doesn't that mean equality is no longer a matter of morality or **altruism** for the better off, but naked self-interest? There's a brief **hiatus** before Pickett says, "I'm not sure that's quite the message we're trying to get across." Then there's another brief pause, before Wilkinson adds, "But it is still true."

Pickett is more alert to the political implications of their findings, while Wilkinson is more happy to follow an argument to its conclusion, however uncomfortable that may be. You can understand Pickett's concern. If self-interest and greed create inequality, then you don't necessarily want to give the impression that the solution lies in more of the same. On the other hand, there's a pleasing irony to the idea that the well-off may have mistaken their self-interest for so long, and it's not often that bleeding-heart liberals get to combine their morality and self-interest. So, as Wilkinson points out, we should make the most of it.

They insist The Spirit Level is a collaborative effort, but some collaborations are more equal than others. While Pickett, in her early 40s, is a comparative newcomer, having completed her PhD in 1999, Wilkinson has been working on the social determinants of public health with varying levels of success and frustration for years. The spark for The Spirit Level came five years ago when extensive data first became available from the World Bank, and he realized that the phenomenon he had observed within his field—that health was driven by relative difference rather than absolute material standards—applied in other areas of social policy.

"It became clear," Wilkinson says, "that countries such as the US, the UK and Portugal, where the top 20% earn seven, eight or nine times more than the lowest 20%, scored noticeably higher on all social problems at every level of society than in countries such as Sweden and Japan, where the differential is only two or three times higher at the top."

The statistics came from the World Bank's list of 50 richest countries, but Wilkinson suggests their conclusions apply more broadly. To ensure their findings weren't explainable by cultural differences, they analyzed the data from all 50 US states and found the same pattern. In states where income differentials were greatest, so were the social problems and lack of **cohesion**.

Two things immediately became clear to Wilkinson. "While I'd always assumed that an equal society must score better on social cohesion," he says, "I'd always imagined you could only observe a noticeable effect in some kind of **utopia**. I never expected to find such clear differences between existing market economies."

There are **anomalies**. Suicide and smoking levels are both higher in more equal societies. "Violence tends to be directed towards other people or yourself," Wilkinson says, "and it is our guess that in societies with a higher sense of community responsibility, people tend to blame themselves rather than other people when things go wrong. Smoking is a little different: all countries seem to follow a similar **trajectory**. It starts among upper-class men, then moves to upper-class women and then down the social ladder; quitting smoking seems to follow a similar pattern."

Even so, the correlation between inequality and social problems remains startling. And it is the differential rather than any notional baseline of poverty that's critical. The US has its own benchmarked poverty line, with some 13% of the population falling below it: yet of those who come into this category, 80% have air-conditioning, 33% have a dishwasher and 50% have two or more cars, which is not quite what some other countries might call poverty.

In Britain, the Labour government, despite its protestations to the contrary, has only maintained inequality at the level at which it inherited it. "They've taken some positive action at the bottom income levels for pensioners and young families," says Pickett. "But the damage has all been done at the other end. Peter Mandelson said early in the Labour administration, 'We are intensely relaxed about people getting filthy rich,' and he's been as good as his word."

What is it about unequal societies that causes the damage? Wilkinson believes the answer lies in the psycho-social areas of hierarchy and status. The greater the differential between the haves and have-nots, the greater importance everyone places on the material aspects of consumption; what brand of car you drive carries far more meaning in a more hierarchical society than in a flatter one. It's the knock-on effects of this status anxiety that finds socially **corrosive** expression in crime, ill-health and mistrust.

Wilkinson draws on some **eclectic** illustrations. When monkeys are kept in a hierarchical environment, those at the bottom self-medicate with more cocaine; a caste gap opens in the performance of Hindu children when they have to announce their caste before exams; the stress hormone, cortisol, rises most when people face the evaluation of others; and so on. The result is always the same: fear of falling foul of the wealth gap gets under everyone's skin by making them anxious about their status.

For a while, Wilkinson and Pickett wondered if the correlations were too good to be true. The links were so strong, they almost couldn't believe no one had spotted them before, so they asked colleagues to come up with any other explanations. They looked at the **religiosity** of a society, multiculturalism, and anything they could think of. They even looked at the possibility they had got it the wrong way round and it was the social problems that were causing the inequality. But nothing else stood up to statistical analysis.

Wilkinson openly admits The Spirit Level is his swan-song. He feels that as an academic he has fulfilled his side of the bargain by identifying the problem; it's up to activists and politicians to work out the solutions. Pickett doesn't see things quite that way, and is largely the driving force behind the creation of the Equality Trust website to campaign for change. "There must be a possibility of change," she says. "Everything stacks up. Reducing inequality fits in with the environmental agenda; it benefits the developing world, as more equal societies give more in overseas aid; and most significantly, everyone is fed up with the corporate greed and bonus culture that have caused the current financial crisis, so if ever a government had the electorate's goodwill to act, it's now."

Wilkinson is fairly **blunt** about where government should start. "It has got to limit pay at the top end," he says. "It's the rich that got us into this mess and the rich who should get us out of it." Whether Labour has the nerve to upset those whom it has most **assiduously** courted is another matter. But he can always dream, and in the meantime he is off home to watch TV.

"I've become gripped by *Paris Hilton's Best Friend*," he laughs. "It's the perfect example of a **dysfunctional**, hierarchical society."

(length: 3,008 words)

Vocabulary

altruism	n. 利他主义，无私
ameliorate	v. （使）改善，改进
anomaly	n. 异常，反常，不规则异常现象
assiduously	ad. 勤勉地，恳切地
austerity	n. 严厉；严酷；简朴，朴素；节衣缩食，艰苦朴素
blaze	n. 火焰，烈火；光辉，闪耀
bloated	a. 发胀的；水肿的；傲慢的
blunt	a. 率直的，直言不讳的；钝的
brainchild	n. 某人的发明或主意
cohesion	n. 粘连，黏合；团结；凝聚力
conflagration	n. 大火（灾）
corrosive	a. 腐蚀性的；侵蚀性的；有害的
dilemma	n. 左右为难
denizen	n. 居民，住户
downtrodden	a. 被践踏的；受压迫的
dysfunctional	a. 功能失调的
eclectic	a. （人）兼收并蓄的；（方法、思想等）折中的
enlist	v.（使）入伍，（使）参军；获得（帮助或支持）
erosion	n. 腐蚀，侵蚀；磨损
expectancy	n. 期待；期望
ferocity	n. 凶猛,残暴
garner	v. 收集并（通常）贮藏（某物），获得
grievance	n. 委屈，苦衷，不满，怨恨
grim	a. 严酷的，无情的；讨厌的，糟糕的
grudge	n. 不满，怨恨，妒忌

hiatus n. 裂隙；缺漏；间断
impediment n. 妨碍某事物进展的人或物
incentive n. 刺激；诱因，动机
incorrigible a. 无法矫正的，屡教不改的
indicative a. 表明；标示；陈述的，直陈的，指示的
loot v. 抢劫，掠夺
lore n. 学问和传统；（专门的）知识
misconception n. 误解，错误想法，错误印象
momentum n. 动力，冲力，势头；[物]动量
mortality n. 必死性；大量死亡；死亡率
nihilism n. 虚无主义；极端怀疑论
obligation n. 义务；责任
persistent a. 持续的；不断的
predispose v. 使倾向于做；使易于患（病）
perverse a. 任性的，固执的；错误的，荒谬的
prim n. 循规蹈矩；整洁
proximal a. 最接近的
raid n. 突然袭击；劫掠，劫夺；突然查抄（搜捕）
religiosity n. 笃信宗教，虔诚
relinquish v. 交出，让给；放弃
sluggish a. 行动迟缓的，不机警的，无精打采的
squalor n. 污秽，肮脏，邋遢
stereotype n. 老套，模式化的见解
subtle a. 微妙的；难以捉摸的；细微的
sully v. 玷污，破坏名声
tackle v. 解决；应付
tinder n. 引火物；易燃物；导火线
trajectory n. [物]弹道，轨迹；轨道
ultimate a. 最后的，最终的
underbelly n. 下腹部的，物体的下方，易受攻击的地带
utopia n. 乌托邦（理想中美好的社会）
wanton a. 蛮横的，放肆的，无节制的，不受约束的

Section D Word Bank for This Unit

酗酒	alcohol abuse
老龄化	ageism
艾滋病	HIV/AIDS
童工	child labor
消费主义	consumerism
家庭暴力	domestic violence
残疾人权利	disability rights
因过度节食而导致的进食障碍	eating disorders
安乐死	euthanasia
濒危物种	extinct species
食品和药品安全	food safety and drug safety
赌博	gambling
全球变暖	global warming
同性恋	homosexuality
无家可归	homelessness
住房成本	housing cost
非法移民	illegal immigration
知识产权	intellectual property right
青少年犯罪	juvenile crime
媒体偏见	media bias
器官和组织移植	organ and tissue transplant

Appendix
References

Chapter 1　Traveling in Britain and America

Section A: http://www.uk.filo.pl/uk.htm

Section B: http://www.uk.filo.pl/uk_who_are_the_british.htm

Section C

Passage 1: http://www.english-online.at/geography/london/geography-of-london.htm

Passage 2: http://www.hoteltravel.com/usa/guides/sightseeing.htm

Chapter 2　History

Section A: http://www.bbc.co.uk/history/battle_of_britain

Section B: *China Daily.* Saturday, July 21, 2012

Section C

Passage 1: Wikipedia, the free encyclopedia

Passage 2: http://en.wikipedia.org/wiki/Knight

Chapter 3　Economy

Section A :

Section B: The Guardian Feb.5, 2012

Section C

Passage 1: The Guardian December 23rd 2012

Passage 2: http://www.guardian.co.uk/world/fiscal-cliff-blog/2012/dec/26/fiscal-cliff-reality-check

Chapter 4　Diplomatic Relations and Strategies

Section A: http://www.biu.ac.il/SOC/besa/perspectives50.html

Section B: website of UK foreign and commonwealth office

Section C

Passage 1: British Foreign Policy Centre

Passage 2: www. Enoughproject.org

Chapter 5　Education

Section A: http://www.bbc.co.uk/news/education-19349444

Section B: *Newsweek*, October 24, 1988

Section C

Passage 1: *New York Times*, March 22, 1979

Passage 2: *English Journal* 101.4 (2012): 29-36

Chapter 6 Literature

Section A :http://www.douban.com/note/634519661

Section B:The selected short stories of O·Henry,世界图书出版公司 2004.8

Section C

Passage 2: http://www.pseudopodium.org/repress/shorts/D_H_Lawrence-Tickets_Please.html

Chapter 7 Royal Families and Presidential Life

Section A: http://www.sovereignty.org.uk/features/articles/moncst.html

Section B: http://www.thebiographychannel.co.uk/biographies/queen-elizabeth-II.html

Section C

Passage 1: http://britishroyalfamily.com/the-wedding-of-prince-william-and-catherine-middleton/

Passage 2: http://cn.reuters.com/article/companyNewsEng/idCNL1E8M766020121107

Chapter 8 Mass Media

Section A: http://eng.1september.ru/2002/08/1.htm

Section B: http://www.cliffsnotes.com/study_guide/The-Role-and-Influence-of-Mass-Media.topicArticleId-26957,articleId-26946.html

Section C

Passage 1: http://www.pbs.org/wgbh/pages/frontline/newswar/part3/stats.html

Passage 2: http://www.journalism.org/analysis_report/future_mobile_news

Chapter 9 Customs and Etiquettes

Section A: 崔喜哲. 2011. 《每天读点英美文化》

Section B: 崔喜哲. 2011. 《每天读点英美文化》

Section C

Passage 1: 崔喜哲. 2011. 《每天读点英美文化》

Passage 2: Source:http://blog.qq.com/qzone/622000306/1314376620.htm

Chapter 10 Leisure Life

Section A: 30 December 2012 Last updated at 15:24 GMT
http://www.bbc.co.uk/news/entertainment-arts-20630753

Section B: 汪士彬. 1998. 《英语快速阅读》

Section C

Passage 1: http://www.bbc.co.uk/ukchina/simp/elt/english_now/2012/08/120807_ are_165_down_with_the_kids.shtml

Passage 2: 崔喜哲. 2011. 《每天读点英美文化》

Chapter 11 Holidays and Festivals

Section A: http://ukinusa.fco.gov.uk/en/about-us/faqs/holidays-traditions/xmas

Section B: http://www.learnenglish.de/culture/easter.htm

Section C

Passage 1: http://ukinusa.fco.gov.uk/en/about-us/faqs/holidays-traditions/xmas

Passage 2: http://www.history.com/topics/thanksgiving

Chapter 12 Sports

Section A: http://www.fifa.com/classicfootball/history/game/historygame4.html

Section B: http://www.uwtledger.com/2.13122/top-five-popular-sports-in-america-1.1701995

Section C

Passage 1: www. furd.org

Passage 2: http://www.totalprosports.com/2012/10/22/9-disgraced-sports-heroes/# 3

Chapter 13 Celebrities

Section A: http://wenku.baidu.com/view/4a47a1649b6648d7c1c7469d.html

Section B: http://biography.yourdictionary.com/jack-welch

Section C

Passage 1: http://www.margaretthatcher.org/essential/biography.asp

Passage 2: http://blog.sina.com.cn/s/blog_51383aa70100914d.html

Chapter 14 Social Problems

Section A: http://www.buzzle.com/articles/social-issues-in-the-united-states.html

Section B: google scholar

Section C

Passage 1: http://inventors.about.com/od/estartinventors/a/Edison_Bio.htm

Passage 2: http://dailyuw.com/archive/2011/08/16/opinion/british-riots-expose-ugly-social-problems;
http://www.buenosairesherald.com/article/75803/uk-to-tackle-social-problems-after-riots;
http://www.guardian.co.uk/society/2009/mar/12/equality-british-society